TEXT AND CONTEXT
Frank Coulson, Series Editor

ANTIQUARIAN VOICES

THE ROMAN ACADEMY AND THE COMMENTARY TRADITION ON OVID'S *FASTI*

Angela Fritsen

THE OHIO STATE UNIVERSITY PRESS
COLUMBUS

Copyright © 2015 by The Ohio State University.
All rights reserved.

Library of Congress Cataloging-in-Publication Data
Fritsen, Angela, author.
 Antiquarian voices : the Roman Academy and the commentary tradition on Ovid's Fasti / Angela Fritsen.
    pages cm — (Text and context)
 Includes bibliographical references and index.
 ISBN 978-0-8142-1284-4 (cloth : alk. paper)
 1. Ovid, 43 BC–17 AD or 18 AD Fasti. 2. Didactic poetry, Latin—History and criticism. I. Title. II. Series: Text and context (Columbus, Ohio)
 PA6519.F9F75 2015
 871'.01—dc23
                    2015008656

Cover design by AuthorSupport.com
Text design by Juliet Williams
Type set in Adobe Garamond Pro
Printed by Thomson-Shore, Inc.

Cover image: Calendar of Romulus. *P. Ovidii Nasonis Fastorum Libri diligenti emendatione typis impresse aptissimisque figuris ornate commentatoribus Antonio Constantio Fanensi Paulo Marso Piscinate viris clarissimis additis* (Toscolano: Alexander Paganinus, 1527), fol. A1r. *52L–479, Houghton Library, Harvard University.

∞ The paper used in this publication meets the minimum requirements of the American National Standard for Information Sciences—Permanence of Paper for Printed Library Materials. ANSI Z39.48–1992.

9 8 7 6 5 4 3 2 1

CONTENTS

List of Illustrations — vii
Abbreviations — viii
Acknowledgments — ix
Preface — xi

ONE · Reading Ovid's *Fasti* — 1
   The Author and His Work — 1
   Aetas Ovidiana — 7
   The Fate of Ovid's Severed Book — 23

TWO · Fifteenth-Century Revival — 29
   Time and Place — 29
   Teaching Particulars — 45
   The Dedication of the *Fasti* — 50

THREE · Commentary and Professional Identity — 63
   An Invitation to Comment — 63
   Aggravations of Print — 73
   Primacy and Print — 87
   Authorship — 95

FOUR · Antiquarianism I: The Roman Academy, the *Fasti,* and a New Historicism — 101
   Ovid as Guide to the City — 101

Context: The Roman Academy — 106
The Earlier Generation of Antiquarians — 116
The *Fasti* and First-Hand Observation in Rome — 128
Travel and Testing *Auctoritas* — 140

FIVE · Antiquarianism II: Christian *Fasti* and Papal Connections — 151
On Superstition and Magic — 151
The Roman Academy and Anniversaries — 155
The Old and New Rome — 166
Propaganda for the Church — 175

AFTERWORD — 187

APPENDIX I · Renaissance Commentaries on Ovid's *Fasti* — 195
APPENDIX II · Comparison of Manuscript Glosses in Vat. lat. 1595, Ottob. lat. 1982, and Vat. lat. 3263 — 199
Bibliography — 205
Indices
   General Index — 227
   Index Locorum — 236
   Index Manuscriptorum — 239

ILLUSTRATIONS

FIGURE 1	January in the 1527 composite *Fasti* commentary	xiv
FIGURE 2	Pomponio Leto, *Fasti* with glosses (ca. 1469/1470)	37
FIGURE 3	*Ovidius de Fastis cum duobus commentariis* (fol. a1v.)	44
FIGURE 4	*Ovidius de Fastis cum duobus commentariis* (fol. a1r.)	66
FIGURE 5	Portrait of Pomponio Leto in *Elogia virorum literis illustrium*	76
FIGURE 6	Paolo Marsi, *editio princeps* (1482), Colophon	108
FIGURE 7	Ciriaco d'Ancona, autograph *Fasti* (1427)	122
FIGURE 8	Forum Boarium and Temple of Janus	142
FIGURE 9	Antonio Costanzi, autograph manuscript (1480)	180
FIGURE 10	Andrea Mantegna, *The Introduction of the Cult of Cybele at Rome*, 1505–6	190

ABBREVIATIONS

ANRW *Aufstieg und Niedergang der römischen Welt* (Berlin and New York: W. de Gruyter, 1972–)

CIL *Corpus Inscriptionum Latinarum* (Berlin: Deutsche Akademie der Wissenschaften, 1893–)

CTC *Catalogus Translationum et Commentariorum* (Washington, DC: Catholic University of America Press, 1960–)

DBI *Dizionario biografico degli Italiani* (Rome: Istituto della Enciclopedia Italiana, 1960–)

LTUR *Lexicon Topographicum Urbis Romae,* ed. E. M. Steinby (Rome: Quasar, 1993–2000)

RE *Pauly's Realencyclopädie der Classischen Altertumswissenschaft* (Stuttgart: J. B. Metzler and A. Druckenmüller, 1893–1980)

RIS *Rerum Italicarum Scriptores,* ed. L. A. Muratori (Milan: Ex typographia Societatis palatinae in regia curia, 1723–51)

ACKNOWLEDGMENTS

I will always be grateful to the late Jozef IJsewijn, who instilled in me a love for Neo-Latin literature and the classical tradition. My work on Renaissance commentaries would not have been possible without Ralph Hexter and Frank Coulson. They were there for me at the beginning of my project and at its end, and I thank them. I have been the fortunate recipient of a variety of support from the Knights of Columbus Vatican Film Library, the Newberry Library, the Harvard University Center for Italian Renaissance Studies (Villa I Tatti), and the American Academy in Rome, and I have benefitted from the conversations of my colleagues in these places. I would like to thank furthermore the staff and librarians at the Beinecke Rare Book and Manuscript Library, Biblioteca Angelica, Biblioteca Apostolica Vaticana, Biblioteca Comunale Ariostea, and Biblioteca Vallicelliana. For their goodwill and support I would like to mention in particular Robert Babcock, Geoffrey Eatough, Maia Gahtan, Phil Gavitt, Craig Kallendorf, Marc Laureys, Gianpiero Nasci, Mary Quinlan-McGrath, Maria Paola Saci, Barbara Shailor, and Fabio Troncarelli. My very special thanks go to Julia Gaisser, who has been both a sharp reader and my advocate; any shortcomings of my book are my own. I am grateful to my parents and to my husband Eric, who patiently helped and waited. Thank you to Tara Cyphers, Martin Boyne, and everyone at The Ohio State University Press for their invaluable assistance. Images in this book are reproduced, all rights reserved, by kind permission of the following: Biblioteca Apostolica Vaticana; Houghton Library, Harvard University; Huntington Library, San Marino, California; National Gallery Picture Library, London.

PREFACE

If Homer had hoped for ten tongues to tell his story (*Iliad* 2.489) and Vergil for a hundred (*Georgics* 2.43), then Ovid in an exaggerated ploy of inadequacy wished for a thousand (*Fasti* 2.119). Ovid might have been surprised at the multiplication of mouths not his own. Multilingual editions and translations, scholarly discussions and articles point to a resurgence in popularity of his poem on the Roman calendar year, the *Fasti*.[1] My purpose is to present a different renaissance of the poem, one that took place 500 years ago. This book examines the humanist *Fasti* commentaries by Paolo Marsi (1440–84) and Antonio Costanzi (1436–90), widely disseminated in the first age of print and extensively available in reissues, composite editions, and collected works of Ovid (see Appendix I). My argument is that Ovid's poem on the ancient festival calendar flourished in *quattrocento* Italy and in a Roman milieu. In particular, members of the Roman Academy studied Ovid's *Fasti* with a passion.

Antiquarianism is the tie that bound the fifteenth-century humanists who were involved in the Roman Academy. Restoring classical texts, reconstructing history and topography, visiting monuments and catacombs, reviving celebrations: in these pursuits and more, the Academicians brought the ancient city of Rome to life. The Academicians were professors and

---

1. See Miller (2002) for an excellent overview of scholarship.

students; they were curial officials, commissioned secretaries, poets, and diplomats; they were members of the aristocracy and dilettantes. They met in classrooms, in homes, in printing houses, and in the field. The City was an open textbook for them. In their antiquarian endeavors, they sought to return the City to its original splendor. Ovid's *Fasti* acted as interpretive guide.

With this book I hope to contribute to the history of classical scholarship and the history of ideas, with reception history as my guide. Literary encounters do not occur in isolation; instead, we are influenced by contemporary and previous societal values and constraints.[2] The positivistic approach, to discover the original meaning of a text, leads to inconclusive results. This is not to deny authorial intention, but to argue for earlier ways of reading as a complementary hermeneutical guide. In examining earlier readings we might broaden and challenge our own interpretations and in the process even arrive at a clearer definition of the meaning in the text.

Commentaries and glosses are invaluable tools for pulling together lines of thought, and they are the foundation for my arguments, as well as the very subject under consideration. Indeed, the commentary has come to be studied as a genre in its own right.[3] Notes and commentaries from previous generations yield a wealth of learning now forgotten, and continued neglect would be regrettable, considering the humanists' extensive reading in the ancients and their knowledge of classical civilization. In the balance of history we may judge some readings to be *passé*, but this is not to deny the indelible mark they have left.

Chapter 3 therefore examines the genre of the commentary, the vehicle for Renaissance study of the *Fasti*. As the transcript of a professor's lectures in class, the commentary reflects the contents of a humanist classical education. Because of its range of erudition, the *Fasti* was deemed an ideal school text, able to transmit encyclopedic knowledge as well as to provide a complete course in Roman civilization. The diligence of Ovid the researcher trying to understand the calendar provided the humanist with a model of the conscientious investigator in service of the truth. At the same time,

---

2. For a good discussion of reception theory applied to Latin poetry, see Martindale (1993).

3. Finding guides for classical authors and their editors and commentators are Maillard, Kecskeméti, and Portalier (1995); the series *Catalogus and Translationum Commentariorum* published by the Catholic University of America Press; specifically for Ovid, but with emphasis on the medieval period, Coulson and Roy (2000) and Coulson (2002; 2009). For studies on the commentary, see the volumes edited by Pade (2005a), Gibson and Kraus (2002), and Buck and Herding (1975). Digitized copies of printed texts and commentaries sometimes exist online.

the vatic or inspired Ovid gave the humanist the permission and idea to show flashes of brilliance. Finally, the commentator became a poet himself, as witnessed by the verse compositions that Antonio Costanzi and Paolo Marsi inserted into their *Fasti* glosses. The transition from manuscript to print culture, with its resultant pressures of "publish or perish," helped make the move from commentator to author complete.

I have taken as my focal point the Marsi and Costanzi composite edition of commentaries on the *Fasti,* whose presence in many rare-book libraries, not only in Europe but also in the United States (the 1527 issue is especially prevalent; see figure 1), attests to the commentaries' far-reaching impact.[4] Basing my discussion on Marsi's inventory of colleagues working on Ovid's text, I also draw on the manuscript glosses of Antonio Volsco (ca. 1440–ca. 1496) and Pomponio Leto (1428–98), and I include in my purview Leto's notes on Varro's *De lingua Latina* because of their many connections with the *Fasti*. The manuscripts contain a treasure of information and material, but there are points that I will no doubt have omitted or overlooked. Furthermore, one never knows when another manuscript will turn up.

Studies have already been written on some of the individual manuscripts, their humanist authors, or both, but no previous attempt has been made to form an overall picture of Renaissance Ovidian *Fasti* scholarship.[5] In the process of tracing the Renaissance transmitters of Ovid's poem, I introduce several less well-known figures. As a consequence, this book presents a profile of the Roman Academy and its members and their colleagues elsewhere in Italy.

Chapter 1 provides a literary and a historical context. After explaining the cultural significance of the calendar for understanding Ovid's poem, I move to a general overview of the *Fasti*'s transmission. Here I highlight the teaching and imitation of Ovid in the twelfth century. As there are countless glossed medieval manuscripts on the *Fasti* waiting to be studied, I have limited myself to what is already published. In the types of textual examinations, discussions, and quarrels among scholars in the Loire valley of France, we see precedents for the activities of the Italian humanists. Indeed, the research of the humanists cannot be separated from the

---

4. Unless otherwise noted, transcriptions are from the first, 1497 composite edition. I have standardized orthography in citations from printed works.

5. In a number of articles Accame Lanzillotta (1980; 1990; 1993) analyzed the major codex of Leto's Varro instruction. Della Torre wrote a 1903 biography of Paolo Marsi (see also the *DBI* article by Pontari 2008), while Prete was the expert on Antonio Costanzi. Lo Monaco produced an edition with introduction on the *Fasti* lectures of Angelo Poliziano in 1991, and Michael Jean is preparing a study and critical edition of Pomponio Leto's glosses on the *Fasti.*

FIGURE 1. January in the 1527 composite *Fasti* commentary. *P. Ovidii Nasonis Fastorum Libri diligenti emendatione typis impresse aptissimisque figuris ornate commentatoribus Antonio Constantio Fanensi Paulo Marso Piscinate viris clarissimis additis* (Toscolano: Alexander Paganinus, 1527), fol. a1r. *52L–479, Houghton Library, Harvard University.

work of previous generations. The case of the Alsatian humanist Beatus Rhenanus (1485–1547) will illustrate the point. Rhenanus wrote a commentary (unpublished) on the *Fasti* when he was only fourteen. In 1506, while studying in Paris, he purchased a manuscript of the *Metamorphoses* supplied with the ca. 1260 Vulgate commentary. In his procurement of a manuscript supplemented by an established earlier commentary, Rhenanus is quite representative of his time. Medieval exegesis continued to influence and inform successive scholars.[6]

Chapter 2 focuses on the development of *Fasti* interest in the latter half of the fifteenth century by analyzing the first published, 1482 *Fasti* commentary by Paolo Marsi of Pescina. Through the careful reconstruction of Marsi's student and teaching career, I delineate the group of *Fasti* scholars and their degree of interrelationship, noting in particular the guiding influence of Pomponio Leto, mentor of the Roman Academy. I explain topics of interest in Ovid's poem (all related to the profusion of knowledge in, and suggested by, the calendar), and I trace the history of a contested issue, the double dedication of the *Fasti*.

Chapter 4 investigates the core element of appeal and area of interest in the *Fasti*: Roman antiquarianism. The humanists took to heart Ovid's programmatic goal in the proemium (1.7–8), namely the survey of ancient Roman rites, customs, and civilization. In the *Fasti* the humanists saw a Rome that was still physically and culturally intact. Medieval precedents for using Ovid as a guide to the City already existed, but in the late-fifteenth-century Roman Academy of Pomponio Leto, the *Fasti* acted as a mirror of Roman civilization. After reviewing the historical evidence of the connection between Ovid's *Fasti* and antiquarian pursuits within the Roman Academy, I turn to an examination of antiquarian methodology. Advantageously situated in Rome, the humanists of Leto's Academy could investigate material evidence. As a consequence, they began to evaluate Ovid's words against their personal experiences and observations. Because ancient texts were thought to embody absolute wisdom and truth, the late-*quattrocento Fasti* commentators were not always comfortable, however, with their own empirical determinations.

Chapter 5 presents a Renaissance reading of the *Fasti* according to the Roman antiquarianism the poem was seen to encompass, and reflective of the moral purpose already inherent in antiquarian works during the Augustan restoration of state and society. Antiquarianism became a popular

---

6. The *Fasti* commentary by Rhenanus is Sélestat, Bibliothèque Humaniste, ms. 50. The *Metamorphoses* manuscript with Vulgate commentary is Sélestat, Bibliothèque Humaniste, ms. 92 (see Coulson 2011, 67).

discipline in the crisis phase of the late Republic and early Empire because it helped define what it meant to be a Roman, and the *Fasti* similarly participates in a nationalistic ardor by portraying Rome's early simplicity and purity, an age of former splendor.[7] In the proemium to Book 2, Ovid calls the *Fasti* his "military service" to Augustus (*haec mea militia est,* 2.9); poetics aside, he suggests his calendar will participate in an imperial triumph. So too did the Renaissance humanists see in the *Fasti* an image of their cultural past, a source of national pride and politics, especially useful to the papacy following its crisis and recovery from the Great Schism, when the bishops of Rome sought to re-establish the centrality and authority of the Roman church. Under Pope Pius II (1458–64), Antonio Costanzi in his *Fasti* exegesis commemorated the papal conquest of his native Fano; under Pope Sixtus IV (1471–84), Paolo Marsi redated Rome's birthday to an overtly Christian feast day, and Roman Academy members composed calendrical poems on the liturgical year in imitation of Ovid.

With the commentary as their medium, the humanists who studied Ovid's *Fasti* in the late *quattrocento* explored contemporary concerns in education, national identity, and politics. We are reminded that the work of many a commentator is "firmly bound to its intellectual and cultural milieu."[8] The localization of interest in the *Fasti* by members of or near to the Roman Academy should persuade us today to look at Ovid's poem through a prism, whereby our own readings are not absolute and our horizons are expanded.

---

7. Miller (1991, 14–15).

8. Gaisser (1993, 146), speaking here about interpretations of Catullus by Marc-Antoine de Muret, Achilles Statius, and Joseph Scaliger.

CHAPTER ONE

Reading Ovid's *Fasti*

THE AUTHOR AND HIS WORK

Ovid's *Fasti* is a religious and historical poem of the Roman year, commemorating Roman customs, heroes, and battle dates in combination with myth and astronomical lore. Ovid wrote his calendar poem in elegiac couplets and may have planned for twelve books, one for each month of the year; only six books are extant. The epicized elegy and projected twelve-month format resemble the *Metamorphoses* to a degree in spirit and style, and indeed, Ovid was working on the *Fasti* as he was writing the *Metamorphoses*. The *Fasti* is usually thought to have been intended as a tribute to the emperor Augustus and his consolidation of culture and civilization under the *Pax Romana*. In AD 8, the year he began his poem, Ovid was abruptly and irrevocably sent into exile by Augustus. The emperor banished him allegedly for the *Ars amatoria* and its undermining of morals, and for knowledge of some political intrigue (*carmen et error, Tr.* 2.207).[1] From its inception the *Fasti* was meant to draw favor, and in the hopes of recall from the Black Sea region, Ovid made revisions to his poem. Scholars disagree, however, as to whether Ovid was unable or even unwilling to complete his

---

1. See Luisi and Berrino (2008).

work in exile. Ovid's hopes for recall by Augustus or his heirs in any event were not realized, and the poet died in exile in AD 17.

As the growing body of literature on the *Fasti* shows, the poem has claimed its "deserved position" next to Ovid's other work.[2] The *Fasti*'s current promotion in the public eye began with D. E. W. Wormell, who wrote an enthusiastic essay on Ovid in 1979, the year after his contribution to the first Teubner edition found its way into print.[3] That year appears to have been a turning point, with scholars ready to reconsider the *Fasti* and divided into two camps: while Sir Ronald Syme and W. R. Johnson rated Ovid's calendrical poem a miscalculated failure, John Barsby judged it a literary creation of artistic merit deserving closer analysis.[4] From then on scholars have given the *Fasti* serious literary and historical attention.[5]

Critics had faulted the poem for its inappropriate elegiac meter, constrictive calendar format, failed attempt at praise of Augustus, and unfinished state.[6] A variety of responses has dealt with these criticisms. Stephen Hinds has challenged notions of generic category by suggesting that Ovid's self-conscious poetic stance is a creative principle rather than a confining experiment with the parameters of elegy.[7] Molly Pasco-Pranger has argued that the *Fasti* follows the generic model of aetiological elegy and the cultural model of the Roman calendar, and that the poem is a complex interaction between literature and *realia*. The calendar is not just an organizational principle but an intertext, as it were. Matthew Robinson has taken the section markers out of his edition of Book 2 of the *Fasti* because the poem itself clearly signals a movement from one calendar entry to the next; doing away with the editorial separation of days allows the reader to experience a continuous reading and can lead to "some exquisite ambiguities."[8] Mary Beard had reasoned that the Roman calendar is not a

---

2. From the introduction to the 2011 Wiseman and Wiseman translation of Ovid's *Fasti*, xxx. I will be using that as my English translation, and the 1988 Teubner edition for the Latin text.
3. Wormell (1979).
4. Syme (1978); Johnson (1978); Barsby (1978, 25).
5. For major trends see Miller (2002) and Fantham (1995a; 1995b).
6. The reader will find a bibliographical sketch and summary of these and other arguments in Newlands (1995, 1–5). The *Fasti* has also been accused of being "a jumble of astronomy ... religion ... and antiquarian lore" (Newlands 1995, 1–2, quoting Wilkinson 1955, 241–42). Gee (2000) has breathed new life into the study of the *Fasti* and astronomy. Green (2002, 71) examines religious discourse and explains the *Fasti*'s "recognizable Roman theology." For antiquarianism, see especially the work of Pasco-Pranger (2006).
7. Hinds (1987; 1992).
8. See Robinson's 2011 commentary on Book 2, 8. Herbert-Brown (2009, 130–31) agrees that the *Fasti* is, in effect, a calendar, though she feels that the *Fasti* contains even more divisions than a real calendar and therefore should not be read as a continuous text.

linear sequence of historical re-enactments but instead a series of evocative tableaux, while subsequent scholars such as Carole Newlands have viewed the *Fasti* as Ovid's manipulation of time rather than a chronological imposition on the poet.[9] By analyzing the literary and political dimensions of Ovid's exilic work together, Alessandro Barchiesi has characterized the *Fasti* as a poem of artistic tension and ambiguity, whereby the *Fasti* is no longer open to the charge of Augustan propaganda, whose success is subject to question. The encomia are never pure, but rather coded with meaning.[10] Finally, the incomplete status of the *Fasti* is often now considered a deliberate, textual maneuver by Ovid. Barchiesi in particular has stressed the perfectly thought-out termination of the work at the end of June. The poem is not incomplete but "semi-complete," as witnessed in Ovid's *sex ego Fastorum scripsi totidemque libellos* (*Tr.* 2.549), where the separated *sex totidemque* reflects the twelve books of the *Fasti*, perfectly divided in two.[11] The six books form a skillfully balanced whole, and the verbal links between the first and last books further suggest a design and integration.[12]

It is the concept of the *Fasti* as a twelve-month calendar that I will explore in this chapter. The premise of the calendar informs and sums up the very nature of Ovid's poem. It is how successive generations—particularly scholars of the twelfth-century Loire Valley in France and the humanists in late fifteenth-century Italy—viewed the *Fasti* during eras of its popularity.

Carole Newlands analyzes the *Fasti* as Ovid's manipulation of time, and she explains this as a response to Augustus's own manipulation of time.[13] The emperor had inserted himself into several dimensions of time: eter-

---

9. Beard (1987). "The calendar becomes not a chronological straitjacket, but rather a unifying framework to be exploited for artistic and thematic purposes" (Newlands 1995, 12).

10. Barchiesi (1994); translated into English as *The Poet and the Prince. Ovid and Augustan Discourse* (Berkeley and Los Angeles: University of California Press, 1997). Herbert-Brown (1994), Millar (1993), and Riedl (1989) evaluate the poem as a homage-paying participant in Augustan ideology. Newlands (1995) and Hinds (1992) read negative political overtones into the poem. Miller (1991) and McKeown (1984) do away with the issue of propaganda altogether by reading the *Fasti* as inspired by literary tradition, making it therefore apolitical. Feeney (1992) and Wallace-Hadrill (1987) have both argued convincingly that the literary and political spheres of Ovid's poetry cannot be separated and that the *Fasti* is a mirror of social reality.

11. Barchiesi (1994, 266). Cf. the caution with which others handle the poem's abrupt ending. Littlewood, in her 2006 commentary on Book 6, believes that Ovid stopped writing from a desire to expend energy on the *Tristia* and *Epistulae ex Ponto* rather than from a disinclination to continue the *Fasti* (xviii–xx). For the *Fasti*'s disruption and revisions as a process of editing on the author's own terms, free from any external considerations or outside intervention, see Martelli (2013, 104–11).

12. Holzberg (2002, 174); Miller (2002, 167).

13. Newlands (1995; 2002).

nal, celestial, and annual. In 17 BC, he ushered in the *ludi saeculares,* celebrated perhaps since the early Republic to commemorate the beginning of a new age. The dates of only two previous celebrations are known, 249 BC and 146 BC; Augustus juggled the dates so as to make 17 BC another occurrence of the festival. He found astronomers to announce this as the first year of a new *saeculum*—staged, it should be noted, to coincide with Augustus's approaching forty-sixth year, which marked a Roman's transition from youth (*iuvenis*) to senior (*senex*).[14] Exploitation of his birth sign, Capricorn, and construction of the *horologium Augusti* are examples of the emperor's control over celestial time. The *horologium* was a large sundial, its base inscription dedicating it to the god Sol evoking a connection between Apollo and Augustus, and it was erected in the Campus Martius in such a manner that its shadow fell on the Ara Pacis on the emperor's birthday. Thus Augustus's destiny as the founder of Roman peace was propagandized through stellar implications.

The *horologium* in a sense acted as a calendar. Fragments of a zodiac and Greek calendar in the surrounding pavement have also been discovered, and a Roman counterpart to them may have existed.[15] Augustus extended his influence over annual cycles. He may have modeled his actions after those of his adoptive father, who marked off the end of the month *Quintilis* with Victory Games and gave to the month the new title *mensis Julius*.[16] Augustus introduced himself into annual time with the renaming of *Sextilis,* perhaps when the Senate first proposed this in 27 BC and certainly by 8 BC. Furthermore, he inserted himself into the days of the year by adding imperial events into the Roman civil and religious calendar. The public *fasti Praenestini* (ca. AD 6–10), compiled by Verrius Flaccus, a scholar in the employ of Augustus, bears such entries as the imperium of Augustus in the consulship of Hirtius and Pansa, Augustus's closure of the gates of war in the Temple of Janus, the restoration of the Republic to the Roman people, the "black day" of Antony's birth, and the naming of Augustus, to cite but a few examples from the month of January.[17]

The timing of Ovid's composition can hardly be a coincidence, given that AD 8 was the state calendar's first year of normal function.[18] What-

---

14. Fantham (1996, 82); Galinsky (1996, 101).
15. Zanker (1988, 144); Wallace-Hadrill (1987, 224–25).
16. For the control over time started by Caesar in his reform of the Julian calendar in 46 BC, greatly enhanced and consolidated by Augustus, see Feeney (2007, 188–89), and Herbert-Brown (2009, 120–26).
17. Wallace-Hadrill (1987, 226, 229–30).
18. Herbert-Brown (1995a, 25).

ever Ovid's motivation—celebration of the emperor? a spontaneous, artistic response to the stone tablets set up at Praeneste?—his writing surely had to take into account Augustus's concurrent remodeling of the calendar. Given the number of late-medieval and early-modern manuscripts and printed editions of Ovid to which copies of inscribed calendars are appended, it certainly appears that pre-humanist and humanist scholars recognized Ovid's *Fasti* as a calendar, a verse composition modeled in part on the *fasti Praenestini*.[19]

Jörg Rüpke clarifies a matter that the medieval *magistri* and the humanists apparently knew, namely, that Ovid did not write a *fasti*, but rather a book *about fasti* (*Fastorum libri*). Rüpke cites the examples of Masurius Sabinus's *Fastorum libri* (from the reign of Tiberius) and Nisus's *Commentarii fastorum* (n.d.), both of which are commentaries on *fasti* rather than *fasti* in book form.[20] From the work of Sabinus and Nisus it is evident that in talking about *fasti* we are dealing with written calendars, not with the oral pronouncements of priests and magistrates. For a long time in early Rome, the months' civic and religious observances were announced out loud on the Capitol. This division of time was ritually acted and controlled, in contrast to the written calendars—painted or carved—which functioned as a memorial or record and were destined solely for the literate. The differentiation bolsters the theory that Ovid knew and used as a source the marble *fasti* in the forum at Praeneste. Calendars such as the *fasti Praenestini* were monuments whose function was in part ornamental. They did not fill the central role of a calendar, that is, the civic assignment of the days and their character, which needed the oral and authoritative confirmation of priests. Written calendars were open to omissions and variants, even errors. Ovid has taken this feature of written calendars and explored it at length in his poem.[21]

Furthermore, written calendars have themselves been described as commentary or exegesis. The Augustan scholar who created the *fasti Praenestini*, Verrius Flaccus, accumulated a wealth of information on cult, history, and etymology, which he added to the calendar entries. He even published a book on his *fasti* (no longer extant), which suggests how

---

19. Wallace-Hadrill (1987, 227). More generally, these manuscript and printed editions suggest an intellectually elite reading public's appreciation of chronology, an antiquarian aspect and discipline already evident in the twelfth century and peaking in the late sixteenth century. See Grafton (1995).

20. Macr. *Sat.* 1.4.6, 1.12.30; Rüpke (1995, 72).

21. Rüpke (1994; 1995, 71–73); Miller (2002, 170–74); Scheid (1992, 119–24); Wallace-Hadrill (1987, 227).

erudite the calendar was: it deserved ample study and explanation. His glossary *De verborum significatu,* preserved in the abridgment of Sextus Pompeius Festus, shows similar goals and concerns in its digressions on antiquarian topics. What is striking in the examples of entries from both the *fasti* and *De verborum significatu* is the multiple aetiological explanations. These notes added weight in not just the literal but also the figurative sense. The *fasti Praenestini* were very scholarly, and this together with its arrangement in a semicircle, facing a statue of Verrius Flaccus, emphasizes how the calendar was a tribute to its very creator.[22] Ovid's *Fasti* was similarly a vehicle of learning and opportunities for *excursus* on civilization and institutions—a definition that can be extended to commentaries in general, and to both the medieval glosses and the Renaissance commentaries on Ovid's text in particular.

Predating Verrius Flaccus, in 189 BC the consul M. Fulvius Nobilior set up a calendar in a temple dedicated to Hercules and the Muses. The format of this *fasti* with notes became canonical. It already included an etymological explanation for the months. Rüpke indicates a Greek practice of presenting calendars as offertory gifts, and he goes on to suggest that Fulvius Nobilior's calendar, painted onto the temple wall, functioned as a type of dedicatory inscription. He offers the intriguing proposition that by placing the *fasti* in a temple to the Muses, Fulvius hoped to inspire historical poems.[23] In the last line of his poem, Ovid states that the statue of Hercules played the lyre (6.812). Calendric *fasti* inspired Ovid's verse, and Ovid's *Fasti* was a springboard for further literary compositions.

A common feature of *fasti* has been the imperial sanction of the Praenestine calendar and the patrician support of a temple calendar. The calendar enjoyed aristocratic distinction, but it also had a didactic function. In part for this reason, Macrobius addressed the *Saturnalia* to his son, implying that knowledge of the calendar was an important part of an elite education.[24] A three-day symposium at the house of an upper-class Roman, the *Saturnalia* ranges over discussions on the December festivities, Roman paganism, and the calendar, much knowledge that was already diminished or lost by the time of the *Saturnalia*'s composition, ca. AD 430. Cicero had already pointed out the edifying and moral purpose of antiquarianism (*De fin.* 5.2–6) before Macrobius, and he praised Varro's *Antiquitates* for restor-

---

22. Feeney (1998, 125).
23. Rüpke (1995, 331–45). For the temple, see L. Richardson (1992, 187 ["Hercules Musarum, Aedes"]).
24. Salzman (1991, 14–16).

ing a sense of Roman identity and the past (*Academica* 1.9).²⁵ The calendar promoted this nationally shared past. Characterized as an unrolling process, with each festival dependent on the previous one and paving the way for the next, the Roman year was an unfolding narrative, an orchestration with a particular goal. Rome's goal was her history. For the sake of example, the reign of Saturn (Saturnalia) turns into the Arcadian reign of Evander (Carmentalia), which then evolves into the foundation and era of Romulus (Lupercalia) and Romulus's apotheosis (Quirinalia).²⁶ Tied to Rome's history is the preservation of a historic consciousness; Macrobius therefore stressed the calendar's study in order to commemorate and safeguard national identity for his heirs.

Indeed, to study the calendar was to reclaim one's ancestry. For just such a reason John Lydus, a sixth-century antiquarian and civil servant in Constantinople under Justinian, wrote his treatise *De mensibus,* to guard the connections and continuity between Constantinople and its Roman past.²⁷ Knowledge of the ancient calendar implied recollection and appreciation of one's heritage; in particular, it imparted a sense of Romanness. It is not surprising, then, that Ovid's *Fasti* has also been described in terms of its essential Romanness.²⁸

AETAS OVIDIANA

Ovid's *Fasti* received scholarly attention in the twelfth and thirteenth centuries, which Ludwig Traube called an *aetas Ovidiana*.²⁹ This is not to say that Ovid or specifically the *Fasti* were ignored at other times. Ovid as a poet of exile was studied by Ermold Nigellus, who himself had been banished to Strasbourg by Louis the Pious ca. 825. Influenced by the *Tristia* and *Epistulae ex Ponto,* the more obvious works in which Ovid deals with exile, Ermold compared his own situation to Ovid's. Writing *in honorem Hludowici Christianissimi Caesaris Augusti,* he acknowledged that Strasbourg and its surroundings were beautiful, and he had but praise for the bishop in whose oversight he had been placed; he admitted his punishment was not as severe as Ovid's. Of course, Ovid's own experience in Tomis was to a

---

25. Rawson (1972, 35; 1985, 235–47).
26. F. Graf (1997, 24–41).
27. Maas (1992), especially chapter 4.
28. Porte (1993).
29. Traube (1911, 113). Black (2001, 4) argues not for periodization but uniformity, a "general Italian syllabus."

degree a poetic construct, and his situation not so barren and desolate as he made it seem.³⁰ That said, the question has been raised whether in choosing Ovid over Vergil as his model, Ermold had the outcast, post-Augustan Ovid in mind instead of the Roman, Augustan one. The elegy to Louis the Pious contains references to Ovid's plea for recall from exile in the *Fasti,* echoing both the first, revised prologue to Germanicus and the second prologue to Augustus.³¹ A construct similar to Ermold's is found in the works of Henry of Settimello and Lovato Lovati. Patterning an elegy from 1193 on the *Consolatio Philosophiae* by Boethius, Henry of Settimello (Henricus Pauper) invoked Ovid as a kindred spirit.³² The prehumanist Lovato Lovati complained of an illness to a fellow Paduan in an elegy that borrows from the *Metamorphoses* but recalls Ovid's exile on the Black Sea. Lovati suggests that his own isolation and indisposition afforded him a literary opportunity.³³

The examples of Ovid's influence as an exilic author depend upon poetic reminiscences. Ovid's compositions from the end of his career were available to academics in the Middle Ages but not so easily accessible. Evidence of the *Fasti*'s existence has come down to us in a set of transmitted verses in a ninth-century *florilegium* from St. Gall.³⁴ The oldest surviving manuscript of the work (Vatican City, BAV, Reg. lat. 1709) belongs to the tenth century, and the first glossed manuscript (Brussels, Bibliothèque Royale, 5369–73) dates to the eleventh century.³⁵

Manuscripts of Ovid's *Fasti* originating from a monastic rather than classroom environment deserve special attention. They reflect a value placed on the poem's antiquarianism and erudition. One manuscript (Paris, BnF, nouv. acq. lat. 1523) of probable German, twelfth-century origin, likely dates back to a fourth- or fifth-century prototype, and it contains a calendar. Certain features have been "Christianized": the Roman eight-day week, lettered A–H, has been changed to A–G, and the wording *pontificale sacrificium* for the January 11 worship of Carmenta is glossed thus: "the *pontifex* celebrated mass on that day" (*pontifex illa die missam celebrabat*).³⁶

---

30. Holzberg (2002, 25–26, 34).
31. The full title of Ermold's poem is *in honorem Hludowici Christianissimi Caesaris Augusti Ermoldi Nigelli exulis elegiacum carmen.* See Santini (1995). For the literary topos of Ovidian exile and the "cult of sensitive friendship," see Hexter (2007).
32. *Si me commendet Naso, si musa Maronis / si tuba Lucani, vix bona fama foret* (*Elegia* 1.17–18).
33. The examples of Henry of Settimello and Lovato Lovati are discussed in Black (2011, 123–24).
34. See Rieker's 2005 edition of Arnulf of Orléans (hereafter Rieker), xxv.
35. Ibid, xxvi; Alton and Wormell (1995, 26); Peeters (1939, 254 ff).
36. Porte (1982); Boissier (1884).

The calendar is but one example of many that were appended to the *Fasti*, as noted and recorded in Merkel's 1841 edition.[37] Scholars in the Middle Ages thus recognized Ovid's *Fasti* as a calendar. From his poem, one could distill Roman dates and festivals. Of what interest would this be for the abbey, however, where the manuscript in question was probably copied? Danielle Porte suggests that the *Fasti* was prized for the sake of erudition, and that the appended calendar might have served as a type of mnemonic aid. She goes on to suggest that given the time frame, the author of the manuscript nouv. acq. lat. 1523 could have been Arnulf of Orléans or Alexander Villedieu.[38] If attributable to either schoolmaster, the authorship also highlights the didactic function of the calendar as described by Macrobius.

The scholarly value of the *Fasti* appears in the example of another monastic manuscript, Kremünster, Stiftsbibliothek, 305 from the early thirteenth century.[39] Appended to the text are verses from a poem on the zodiac of late antique or early medieval composition. The poem, in dactylic hexameters, is also found separately in a number of medieval and Renaissance *Fasti* manuscripts.[40] It can be assigned to the didactic genre of astronomical poetry originating in the Latin with Germanicus, whose incomplete didactic poem *Aratea* may have elicited feelings of kinship in Ovid and encouraged his rededication of the *Fasti*. The genre of astronomical poetry is not only a learned but also a challenging and elusive one; it has been said of Manilius, for example, that "the refinement of [his] verses, with a certain tendency to *brevitas*, the difficulty of the subjects treated, and the numerous instances of obscurity and imprecision make him one of the most difficult poets of Latin literature."[41] The presence of zodiacal compositions in *Fasti* manuscripts suggests that Ovid could impart erudition regarding star lore and that he presented a model to emulate.

The real surge of interest in Ovid's *Fasti* occurred not in a monastic setting, however, but in the city of Orléans, a hub of classical learning from ca. 1130–1230 until the rise of logic at the University of Paris.[42] In Orléans, the *Fasti* was promulgated for its didactic use. It was read and lectured on for its range of wisdom and knowledge, and it was also used by masters to

---

37. See pp. liii–lviii.
38. Porte (1982, 197).
39. See Wouters (1988).
40. The poem can be found in Baehrens (1883, 350) and has also been reconstructed in Wouters (1988, 115). Some copies separate from the *Fasti* are Munich, Bayerische Staatsbibliothek, Clm 9921, fol. 10r, and Florence, Biblioteca Medicea Laurenziana, Plut. 29.30, fol. 1r.
41. Conte (1994, 429).
42. Engelbrecht (2008, 52).

impress upon students their acumen in understanding and explaining the (sometimes abstruse) points of the poem.

The founder of the Orléans cathedral library, Bishop Theodulf (ca. 798), is known to have read Ovid. He favored manuscripts of the *Ars amatoria, Remedia amoris, Amores,* and *Heroides.* Hilary of Orléans (ca. 1075–1150) became the first schoolmaster to lecture on classical authors. Attached to the Cathedral of the Holy Cross, he must have inherited manuscripts from Theodulf as well as from the monastic order of St. Victor in Paris. The Cathedral would thus have been the first center of Ovidian studies in Orléans.[43] Successors at the Cathedral school were Fulco and William of Orléans, while other Orléanais masters include Matthew of Vendôme and Hugh Primas, as well as Arnulf of Orléans, who was affiliated with the monastery and school of St. Euverte.

Alexander Neckam praised Orléans as a center of learning greater than Mount Parnassus itself; Geoffrey of Vinsauf proclaimed that "Orléans nurses babies in cribs with the milk of the authors."[44] Neckam counseled that from Ovid's oeuvre, the *Tristia, Epistulae ex Ponto, Metamorphoses,* and *Remedia amoris* were suitable reading for schoolboys. Indeed, along with the *Heroides,* these works of Ovid predominated in the lecturers' *accessus.*[45] The number of surviving school anthologies (*libri manuales*) likewise demonstrates that the *Metamorphoses, Remedia,* and *Heroides* were the most frequently read works of Ovid. The *Fasti* comes in at number four in terms of occurrence in the *libri manuales.*[46] Neckam had given an at-best neutral recommendation for the *Fasti* (despite his own use of the poem for his writings on natural history): "some deem it good that the book about *Fasti* should not be read" (*Librum fastorum non esse legendum nonnullis placet*). Neckam's counsel appears overruled, however, by the popularity and teaching of Ovid's *Fasti,* as witnessed by its many citations during the medieval period, the *Fasti* commentary by Arnulf of Orléans, and the *Fasti* glosses by William of Orléans in the so-called *Bursarii Ovidianorum,* where *bursarius* implies a portable student guide to consult before and during lectures.[47]

The *Fasti* was, in fact, meant to instruct. This was regarded as the very reason why Ovid composed his poem. In his commentary's *accessus,* Arnulf

---

43. Ibid., 53, 56; see also Engelbrecht's 2003 edition of William of Orléans (hereafter Engelbrecht 2003), 1: 9–11.
44. Engelbrecht (2008, 52).
45. For the customary contents of the *accessus* and the systemization of knowledge described in it, see Minnis (1984), chapter 1.
46. Engelbrecht (2008, 52–55); see figs. 1 and 2.
47. Engelbrecht (2003, 1: 51–68).

of Orléans explains that the *Fasti*'s general purpose was to be a palliative for the *Ars amatoria*. Mitigating the circumstances Ovid found himself in after writing the *Ars* might seem to be a personal motive; however, Arnulf suggests it was Ovid's wish to provide the model of a good Roman citizen. With the *Fasti* before them (and not the *Ars*), the Romans would be obliging and pleasant toward each other, instead of envious and spiteful.[48] Arnulf pinpoints Germanicus's instruction, particularly in religion, as the personal reason why Ovid wrote the *Fasti* (*causa privata fuit, ut Germanicum in sacrificiis instrueret, qui futurus erat summus pontifex illius anni*).[49] In his academic prologue, William of Orléans also gives the primary purpose of the *Fasti* as one of instruction: *intencio sua est prosequi materiam vel instruere Germanicum et Romanum populum*.[50] In one passage he compares the relationship between teacher and student to that of father and son. In a gloss on fire's common dwelling place in the earth and hearth, and the flame's nourishing power (6.267), he finds a resemblance: "as for example student and teacher are almost identical, or father and son, since one is sustained by the other" (*sicut enim discipulus et magister sunt quasi idem, vel pater et filius, quia unus sustentatur ab altero*). At Ovid's "an unsleeping fire is to be found in each" (*subest vigil ignis utrique*, 6.267), William clarifies "as wisdom is for teacher and student. Indeed the teacher gives [wisdom], and the student receives it, just as the earth gives its fire, but Vesta guards it" (*sicut sapiencia magistro et discipulo. Magister enim dat, discipulus accipit, ita terra dat ignem suum, Vesta vero custodit*).[51] Knowledge dwells within everyone, yet the master elicits and conveys learning, as a father does for his son. In the transmission of knowledge we hear an echo of Macrobius and his program of educational formation.

Ovid's work was both a vessel for and a conduit to knowledge. Transmission implies an accumulation of information and research. When Ovid supplies various aetiological explanations in his poem, he may be suggesting his own series of investigative inquiries. In format, the *Fasti* permits a variety of explanations, as found in extant calendars and their notations,[52]

---

48. Rieker, xxxvii and 4: *[causa] communis, ut omnes Romanos, quos sibi invidiosos fecerat per librum de Arte amandi, per istud opus sibi gratiosos redderet, hoc opus suscepit.* Neckam felt that the *Ars amatoria* should be steered away from adolescent hands, but even it was an object of study and served a didactic purpose. See Hexter (1986, 16–18). Fulco of Orléans wrote a commentary on the *Ars*; see Coulson and Roy (2000), no. 173.

49. Rieker, xxxvii and 4. For the observation of religious customs: *Videndum est cui parti philosophie supponatur cum de sacrificiis deorum loquitur et ad deorum cultum nos inuitat et ad bonam moralitatem nos instruit . . .* (Paris, BnF, lat. 7991; no. 482a, in Coulson 2009).

50. Engelbrecht (2003, 2: 95).

51. Ibid., 2: 117; cf. 1: 290.

52. Miller (2002, 170–71).

and the medieval commentaries on Ovid's *Fasti* thus reflect the open-ended model of exegesis. Introduced by such stock phrases as *vel aliter*, divergent explanations are frequent in the glosses of William and Arnulf of Orléans. The purpose from a teacher's perspective might be to anticipate and answer student questions and even to make an unabashed display of erudition. Essentially, the object of giving alternative explanations was to capture knowledge, and Ovid's poem was ideal for such a task. It contained what a student should know: definitions, grammar, rhetoric and poetics, etymology, mythology, geography, natural history, Roman customs and institutions, and even calendrical and astronomical computation.[53]

The mini-lessons on poetics and culture are hardly surprising. No surprise either is the interest in mythology, given the medieval popularity of the *Metamorphoses,* and the fact that Arnulf wrote a commentary on it.[54] Indeed, Arnulf discreetly acknowledges Ovid as a classical authority for myth in the *Fasti*. But, ironically, Arnulf is able to pay his respect to Ovid as a source of myth in a passage where he *corrects* Ovid. In the *Ars amatoria* 1.331–32 and *Remedia amoris* 737–38, Ovid had conflated two Scyllas—one, a daughter of Nisus, transformed into a seabird (*Met.* 8.6–151), the other, a rival of Circe, turned into the sea monster opposite Charybdis (*Met.* 14.1–74). Arnulf distinguishes the Scyllas and "corrects" Ovid in a comment on the *Remedia amoris*, where the reference is to the sea monster, explaining: "there is a change to the story because the same name is used for two" (*et est mutatio fabule propter nominum equiuocationem*).[55] Through carefully articulated and impersonal phrasing, Arnulf does not draw attention to Ovid. He corrects Ovid again at *Fasti* 4.499–500, Ca[rybdi] Nisei ca[nes]. He glosses, "[Ovid] changes the story. For Scylla, daughter of Nisus, was not changed into a sea monster, but a bird, whereas Scylla, daughter of Phorcus, was changed into a monster" (*fabulam mutat. Non enim Scilla Nisi in monstrum marinum est mutata, immo in avem, sed Scilla Phorci in monstrum est mutata*).[56] Arnulf shows his brilliant grasp of mythology, but even here he does not pass critical judgment. His tone remains deferential to the *auctor* in whose shadows he is writing. Arnulf makes it appear as though authorial intent cannot be questioned.

Ovid was not surprisingly regarded as a fount of knowledge in another area, antiquarian lore. In the twelfth-century *Mirabilia urbis Romae,* the *Fasti* serves as a guide to the topography of Rome and her architecture

---

53. This is the characterization of Arnulf's commentary, specifically; see Rieker, xxxiii–xlviii.
54. For Arnulf's glosses on the *Metamorphoses,* see Coulson (1987) and Gura (2010).
55. Hexter (1986, 78–82, 80).
56. Rieker, xliv.

and institutions. The information surfaces in a *vademecum* for Christian pilgrims to the city. Although tracing the pilgrim's route to and around the churches of Rome, the author of the *Mirabilia urbis Romae* finds many occasions to point out antique sites and associations, utilizing both direct references and unacknowledged parallels to the *Fasti*. In fact, out of the *Mirabilia*'s acknowledged sources only Ovid is mentioned by name,[57] emphasizing the authority placed in Ovid as an antiquarian informant of Rome.

That Ovid's *Fasti* should be considered a guide to natural history is perhaps a bit more surprising. Arnulf draws students' attention to plants. Some manuscript witnesses, for example, detail that spikenard is a form of oil or unguent (*F.* 1.76 *spica: quedem species est ungenti*).[58] The term *species* is a twelfth-century theological combination of Aristotelian and Platonic thought, part of the theory of the evolutionary great chain of being (*scala naturae*) where the natural world fits into a designed hierarchy.[59] In terms of the value of the *Fasti*, its *pars philosophiae* classification was twofold. The poem pertained to ethics—hardly a novel medieval distinction. It also pertained to natural history; *partim subponitur ethice, partim phisice,* Arnulf writes in his *accessus*. William of Orléans similarly claims *ethice et phisice supponitur,* adding *'physis' enim Grece dicitur, 'natura' Latine.*[60] As an authority on natural history, Ovid was cited by such scholars and teachers as Vincent of Beauvais, John of Salisbury, Bernard Silvester, and Alexander Neckam, to name a few. The latter cites Ovid's description "haughtiness goes with good looks" (*F.* 1.419) when discussing the peacock in his manual of scientific knowledge, *De naturis rerum* (1.155). He acknowledges Ovid again (*F.* 2.263–64) in a remark upon the raven, who will disregard water in his preference for the nectar of the fig. This same "observation" is made by Vincent of Beauvais in his *Speculum naturale.*[61]

Arnulf expounded on the traits of the raven in the classroom while lecturing on the *Fasti*. He explains *Fasti* 2.263 "as long as the milky fig shall cling" (*dum lac[tens]*) as follows: "according to Pliny's *Natural History* [cf. 10.15], from the time that the fig begins to grow on the tree until it ripens,

---

57. Kinney (1990, 210 and 220, fn. 26).
58. The added specification *ungenti* is found in two manuscripts (Berlin, Preussische Staatsbibliothek, lat. qu. 537, and London, British Library, Harley 2489); Rieker, 16.
59. See also *F.*1.341 *costum: vocatur species picmenti; F.* 5.267 *vicie: leguminis species est.* Rieker, xlii.
60. Rieker, 5; Engelbrecht (2003, 2: 96).
61. Viarre (1966, 55); 142: *naturae placuit institutio ut corvus a potu sese abstineat quamdiu ficus dulcedine sui fructus gloriatur. Unde Ovidius: at tibi dum lactens pendebit in arbore ficus, / a nullo gelidae fonte bibentur aquae.* Cf. *Speculum naturale* 15.72 *de corvo.*

the raven has such a perforated throat that if he wants to drink water, it leaks from here and there" (*ut dicit Plinius de naturali historia, ex quo ficus apparere incipit in arbore, donec matura fiat, corvus habet pertusum adeo guttur, quod, si aquam hauriat, hac et illac effluit*).[62] Arnulf has embroidered Pliny's story of ravens who are sick and thirsty until autumn when the fig ripens. He brings in (and embellishes) an unacknowledged account from Hyginus that the raven is unable to drink because of compromised swallowing.[63] Perhaps Arnulf does not recall his actual source (Pliny or Hyginus), or he may be echoing a progression of comments from predecessors. Arnulf's comment on the *Fasti* 2.263 has the semblance of fable, but it nonetheless demonstrates that both Ovid and Pliny are founts of wisdom for natural history. Moreover, as is befitting, these two classical authors agree in their observations of the natural world.

Neckam had questioned the classroom suitability of "the book about *fasti*" (*Librum fastorum*). His formulation "book about *fasti*" shows recognition that the poem by Ovid is a commentary on the calendar. Arnulf comes to the same conclusion in his examination of the poem's title during the explanatory prologue for students, *Titulus talis est: incipit Ovidius Fastorum*. The title is a hint to the subject matter, the prescribed days to do business (*In hoc titulo denotatur materia subsequentis operis, de fastis enim et nefastis diebus agit*). After indicating the content of Ovid's work (*materia operis*), Arnulf continues: "it was custom among the Romans to mark days in the *fasti* to keep track of prosperity and adversity, so that by the annotated days they might leave an example that moves posterity to valor" (*Fuit autem consuetudo aput Romanos, ut quascumque prosperitates sive adversitates sustinerent, eas in fastis annotari facerent, ut per eas notatas exemplum posteris relinquerent et sic ad virtutem eos animarent*).[64] Arnulf makes it clear that the calendar is under investigation. He returns to the topic of the calendar again in the *accessus*, this time elaborating on categories of time, leaving nothing unexamined: "Ovid's subject matter in this work is the right and unlawful days, the rising and setting of constellations, and months, days, and the various seasons of the year: spring, summer, autumn, winter" (*Materia Ovidii est in hoc opere fasti dies et nefasti, ortus et occasus signorum et menses, dies, et diversa tempora anni: ver, estas, autumpnus, hiems*).[65] In his prologue, William of Orléans similarly describes the *materia operis* as

---

62. Rieker, xlii.
63. *De Astronomia* 40.1: *ut quamdiu fici coquerentur, corvus bibere non possit, ideo quod guttur habeat pertusum illis diebus.*
64. Rieker, 3–4.
65. Ibid., 5.

"months and days, both the rise of constellations and their setting" (*menses et dies, et ortus signorum et occasus ipsorum*).⁶⁶ He interprets Ovid's subject matter as chronological and astral time.

Given their central understanding of Ovid's poem as an investigation on time, Arnulf and William do not make their calendrical glosses brief. William relies quite a bit on Arnulf's commentary; the interdependence of their work has been proven. At *F.* 1.55, both commentators discuss the Roman counting system of Nones, Ides, and Calends. Among their observations, there is this one:

> (ARNULF): The first day of any month is called "Kalends" from [Gr.] "calo," which is "I call." For it was the ancient custom that the high priest climbed to the top of the temple and said as many times "calo," that is, "I call," as there were days from the Kalends up to the Nones.

> *Primus dies cuiuslibet mensis dicitur 'Kalende' a 'calo,' quod est 'voco.' Fuit enim consuetudo antiquitus, quod summus pontifex supra pinnaculum templi ascendebat et tociens dicebat 'calo,' id est 'voco,' quot dies erant a Kalendis usque ad Nonas.*⁶⁷

> (WILLIAM): And it is called "Kalends" from "calo" which is "I call." For it was customary on the Kalends of each and every month for the high priest to climb the top of the temple and say as many times "calo" as there were days from the Kalends up to the Nones.

> *Et dicitur 'Kalende' a 'calo' quod est 'voco.' Solebat enim in Kalendis uniuscuiusque mensis summus pontifex ascendere pinnaculum templi et dicebat tociens 'Calo,' quot dies sunt a Kalendis usque ad Nonas.*⁶⁸

William has replicated an abridged version of Arnulf's comment. In addition, the two authors share supporting evidence: Rieker has identified as sources for the comments Paul the Deacon (epitome of Festus's *De verborum significatu*), Servius (commentary on *Aeneid*), Macrobius (*Saturnalia*), Bede (*De temporum ratione*), and Papias the Lombard. From these sources we can determine the weight of medieval scholarship and the schoolmasters' areas of instruction: etymology, antiquarianism (Roman customs), and

---

66. Engelbrecht (2003, 1: 276).
67. Rieker, 14.
68. Engelbrecht (2003, 1: 283, 2: 98).

generally speaking (with Macrobius in mind) the makings of an educated young man in society.

Astral calculations (or an attempt thereat) also figure in the Orléanais commentaries on Ovid. Arnulf enters into a digression at 1.654 *toto celo* and *fulgebit nullo iam Lira nulla polo*, where he tries to reconcile the evening setting of the Lyre on January 23 with Ovid's record of the event for February 2. Most likely, Ovid is referring at 1.654 to the apparent setting of the constellation, and at 2.75–76 to the true setting.[69] Ovidian language does not take into account such things as the apparent risings and settings of stars versus their true risings and settings. Arnulf finds the passage in Book 1 perplexing: "the Lyre seems to set there [*F.* 2.76]. To this people say 'it is true, that the constellation sets both here and there, since indeed there are two lyres, namely one belonging to Arion and one to Chiron.' But this is against all astronomy, which claims there is only one Lyre" (*ibi [F. 2.76] Lira occidere videtur. Ad quod ipsi dicunt: 'verum est, quia et hic occidit et ibi. Due siquidem sunt Lire, Arionis scilicet et Chironis.' Sed hoc contra totam est astrologiam, que unam tantum asserit esse*). Arnulf opts for January 23 as the evening setting of the Lyre.[70]

The relationship between astronomy and chronology was judged to be of particularly great importance in the Middle Ages and by *Fasti* commentators. The date of the spring equinox, for example, was a source of contention. William notes at the Tubilustrium festival (*F.* 3.851 *nunc potes ad solem*), when the sun has entered the sign of the ram, "here the error of the calendars must be made note of" (*hic denotanda est falsitas Kalendariorum*). He displays his belief that Ovid's *Fasti* can be viewed as a calendar, and he acknowledges that sources for computational comparison are in conflict. Demonstrating his understanding of the Roman months and method of counting days, William insists, "it is firm and established that the sun cannot stay in a sign of the zodiac beyond thirty one days. If the sun were indeed to enter the zodiac before March 22, then thirty two days would go by from the day when it entered Pisces" (*certum est et constans, quod sol non potest morari in signo, nisi per .xxx. et unum diem ad plus. Si vero sol ingrederetur ante diem .XI. Kalendas Aprilis, invenirentur .xxx. et .ii. dies ab illa die, in qua ingressus est Pisces*). He manages to pinpoint the spring equinox to March 20 and to preserve Ovid's reliability by conflating the Quinquatrus, a festival for Minerva, with a day sacred to Mars, as befits a mythological fable about a ram:

---

69. See Green's 2004 edition (hereafter Green), 300.
70. Rieker, 40–42.

In my opinion, this then should be read thus: <u>now</u>, namely while the festivals of Minerva are beginning, now, when they end, and this is on March 20, <u>you can say with your face raised to the sun "this,"</u> that is the sun, "<u>trod the day before,</u>" that is yesterday, namely March 20, "<u>the fleece of the sheep of Phrixus,</u>" that is the Ram, and so thirty one days go by from Pisces to Aries.

Sic ergo legendum est ex parte mea: <u>Nunc</u> [F.3.851–2], dum scilicet incipiunt fieri festa Minerve, nunc cum desinunt, et hoc est .XIIII. Kalendas, <u>vultu sublato ad solem potes dicere: 'Hic,'</u> .i. sol, '<u>pressit here</u>,' .i. heri, scilicet .XIIII. Kalendas, '<u>vellera Frixee ovis</u>,' .i. Arietem, et ita invenientur a Piscibus usque ad Arietem .xxx. et unus dies.[71]

Unwittingly or not, William of Orléans has manipulated the calendar, and in doing so he resembles Ovid. This is hardly shocking, given that the *Fasti* played a small part in the medieval debate about Easter, a moveable feast dependent on the timing of the spring equinox.

Indeed, Wilken Engelbrecht believes that the *F.* 3.163–66 digression by William does not have as much to do with the *Fasti* as it does with a thirteenth-century discussion of the date of Easter.[72] Ovid speaks of the leap year, which Caesar had introduced in 44 BC to correct the calendar. However, the priests who carried out Caesar's reforms initially added a leap day every three years—an error of counting inclusively, according to Macrobius. In 11 BC Augustus slightly modified the cycle, and in AD 4, leap years were reinstated *quinto quoque anno* (Macr. 1.14.13), which is to say every four years. In the *Fasti*, Ovid remarks that intercalation occurred every five years (*in lustrum accedere debet*, 3.165).

Intercalation, which addresses the drift of the calendar from the seasons, is the cognitive link with the computation of Easter. The First Council of Nicaea established Easter as the Sunday after the first full moon after the Spring Equinox. There were few useful guidelines, however, given the discrepancy between a lunar and a tropical (solar) year. Around 723, the Venerable Bede first put the reckoning of Easter on firmer ground (*De temporum ratione*, chapters 44–65).[73] The focus of Bede's work was the calculation of time and, specifically, the guiding principles of the Easter computus. Bede is used as a source by Arnulf at *F.* 3.161.[74]

---

71. Engelbrecht (2003, 1: 282, 2: 111).
72. Ibid., 1: 279.
73. See the Jones and Wallis editions of Bede.
74. Rieker, xxxvi.

The influence of Bede's astronomical timekeeping on William of Orléans's *Bursarii* is also apparent in the discussion of minutes and moments (where an hour is made up of 60 minutes, or 40 moments)[75] and in the carry-over of a "twice sixth-day" on February 24.[76] Increasing experimentation for the precise measurement of time took place from about 1150 on, and in the thirteenth century, computistical works by John of Sacrobosco and Robert Grosseteste dealt with not only ecclesiastical but also civil time reckoning. The *Bursarii* comments at *F.* 3.163–66 fall squarely within the debate of calendar reform and the division and subdivisions of time, in an age when clocks were not yet invented and timekeeping was rather abstract.[77] In the *Fasti* comments, ecclesiastical reckoning of time cannot be fully separated from the civil reckoning of time.

Ecclesiastical concerns aside, the *Fasti* comments do not convey a Christianizing impulse. Overtly Christian comments, when they do occur, are in the service of making Ovid's poem more accessible to the student. This is especially evident in Arnulf's glossing of Roman customs and institutions. Arnulf does not always resort to a comparative method. Sometimes, exploring the *Fasti*'s antiquarian information, he simply explains. For example, at *F.* 1.121 he makes clear that <u>pacem emit[tere]</u> "refers to a custom of the Romans, who closed the Temple of Janus in peace, but opened it in war" (*ad morem respicit Romanorum, qui in pace claudebant templum Iani, in guerra vero aperiebant*). Similarly, at *F.* 1.358 <u>erit quod possit spar[gi] in tua cor[nua]</u> he writes, "this touches on a custom of the ancients, who poured wine between the horns of their sacrificial victims" (*morem tangit antiquorum, qui vina infundebant inter cornua victime*).[78] But at *F.* 1.176 <u>damus pre[ces] et ac[cipimus]</u>, he adds "like in the litany" (*ut in letaniis*), since this is something his audience can more immediately relate to; at *F.* 5.725, he compares lustrations (*lustria*) to Church petitions (*rogationes*).[79] At *F.* 1.669 Arnulf glosses with a secondary lexicographic motive: "*pagus:* a village, from which comes 'country man,' 'villager.' We also call those people 'pagans' who are a long way from the City of God" (*villa, inde 'paganus' 'villanus.' Paganos quoque dicimus illos, qui longe sunt a civitate Dei*).[80] In this example, Arnulf reveals as well the medieval convention of laying out the title of a

---

75. See the gloss *videndum est ergo, quid sit 'bisse' et quid 'momentum'* at *F.* 3.163; compare Bede chapter 3, *De minutissimis temporum spatiis*.

76. *vel 'bissextus' dicitur, quia bis computatur sextus dies unius Kalendas Martii;* compare Bede chapter 38, *De ratione bissexti*. Engelbrecht (2003, 1: 278–79).

77. Ibid., 1: 279–80.

78. Rieker, 19, 28.

79. Ibid., xlvi, 21.

80. Ibid., 42.

work in an authorial prologue, since his gloss alludes to the full title of Augustine's book *De Civitate Dei contra Paganos*.

Nor does Arnulf shy away from moralizing comments, even if these are not his emphasis. At *F.* 1.213 <u>*ut absumant q[uerere]*</u>, "to acquire in order to spend," Arnulf cautions, "this is a moral vice. Not to spend is a virtue" (*est vicium morale, non ut expendant, quid est virtus*).[81] William tends to moralize more, though even so, he manifests a fixation on a "Roman," "non-Christianizing" interpretation of Ovid, as Arnulf does. When William forms opinions, it is often in the context of possible textual variants in Ovid's *Fasti*. Here we can observe another shade of meaning for *bursarius*. In the sense that a pocketbook or purse has many folds, the *Bursarii Ovidianorum* was intended to concentrate on passages with variant readings, lines that were ambiguous and gave rise to problems of interpretation.[82]

While William was aware of textual problems and checked variants in the manuscripts available to him, he passed judgment only on moral grounds. He was conscientious toward his audience of young students. A good example occurs at *F.* 3.772: "<u>Wild boys</u>, that is, wanton and thus, from too much wantonness, <u>wild</u>. Or: <u>almost boys</u>, that is, adolescents, who are called almost boys, because they are between the age of children and young men" (<u>*Feris pueris*</u>, *.i. lascivis et ita ex nimia lascivia <u>feris</u>. Vel: <u>Fere pueris</u>, .i. adolescentibus, qui fere pueri dicuntur, quia inter puericiam et iuventutem scilicet*).[83] William gives his students not only interpretive but also behavioral choices in the *bursarius*, which they are to carry with them before and during the lectures on Ovid. An even stronger personal opinion on William's part surfaces at *F.* 3.829, again in the context of an alternative reading (*vel aliter:* <u>*Nec vos, turba fere sensu fraudata, magistri, / spernite*</u>). William interprets, and perhaps even warns competing Orléanais masters, "construe: O <u>schoolmasters</u>, <u>crowd nearly deprived of your senses</u>, because you think you know more than you do know" (*Construe: O <u>magistri</u>, scilicet <u>turba fere fraudata a sensu</u>, quia plura putatis scire quam sciatis*).[84]

This latter comment by William raises the question of collegiality among *magistri*. What was the professional rapport between Arnulf and William of Orléans, or, for that matter—one that has been investigated—between Arnulf and the rest of his contemporaries? Engelbrecht has suggested that

---

81. Ibid., 22.
82. We can infer that because he was a successor to the Cathedral school and library of Orléans, William had access to manuscripts for consultation. Engelbrecht (2003, 1: 107–8, 322, 345–51).
83. Ibid., 2: 110.
84. Ibid., 2: 111.

the relationship of teacher and student as father to son, remarked upon at *F.* 6.267–68, was characteristic of William but not so much of Arnulf, who was more self-absorbed.[85] Arnulf was conscious of his position in such a worldwide center of teaching and learning as Orléans. He was mindful of the resources available to him in Orléans, at the end of his *Fasti* commentary giving an etymological account of the city's name as "gold for foreigners," *aurea alienis,* a sentiment echoed in a letter by Stephen of Tournai: "most of the citizens of Orléans are accustomed to being as gold among foreigners, who were not even silver among their own people" (*solent plerique Aurelianensium aurei inter alios esse, qui nec argentei fuerant inter suos*).[86] In Orléans, Arnulf found his métier. He etymologizes his own name at the end of the *Fasti* thus: "fleeing no difficulty," *ardua nulla fugiens.* It is no accident that the comment occurs in a gloss on Alcides. Here, too, Arnulf provides an etymology: Hercules is called Alcides because of "aspiring to the heights of heaven" (*alta celi desiderans*).[87] By association Arnulf implies his own Herculean (and quasi-divine) effort at the task of teaching the *Fasti.* Ovid's *Fasti* confers erudition, as does the very center of learning, Orléans. Arnulf felt he was in an exalted academic position, and he wanted to protect it. He did so scornfully and aggressively.

The self-important Arnulf was "not a patient man." "Some nod off" (*quidam somniant*), he says in Ovid's *Fasti* about scholars he disagrees with (*F.* 2.326), and elsewhere he calls Ovid's commentators "bleary-eyed men and barbers" (*lippi et tonsores, F.* 2.44).[88] He alludes to gossips who sit in barbershops and pharmacies and who play audience to men engaged in verbal battles (Horace, *Sat.* 1.7.3). The commentators on Ovid are not even worth trading barbs with, Arnulf implies; they are relegated to the sidelines of invective. Certainly, Arnulf had his own enemies. For example, he railed against Fulco of Orléans, perhaps because Fulco blocked rivals from

---

85. Ibid., 1: 290.
86. Ibid., 1: 22.
87. See Marti's 1958 edition of Arnulf (hereafter Marti 1958), xxiii. Etymologizing proper names was but part of a larger pedagogical system emblematized by Isidore of Seville's late-sixth-century encyclopedia of all human knowledge, the *Origines,* or *Etymologiarum libri.* And at the root of such category of thought may have been Ovid himself, who in the *Fasti,* for example, comes up with multiple etymological explanations for the Agonalia, a sacrificial festival of various animals for one or more deities (1.317–32: "the priest asks should he go on," *agatne*; "the sheep are goaded," *agantur*; "festival [of lambs]," *Agnalia*; a Greek name from games, [*agones*]; an ancient word for sheep, *agonia*). In the Renaissance, Pomponio Leto's lectures on Varro's *De lingua latina* and humanist citations of Festus Pompeius in the *Fasti* commentaries exhibit an ongoing educative interest in etymology, as well as an understanding of Ovid's models and sources in addition to the lessons in morphology one could learn from the poet himself.
88. Marti (1955, 236).

entrance and access to the Cathedral School's library.[89] Arnulf came into further conflict with Hugh Primas, who was probably also a *magister scolarum* in Orléans. Hugo refers to Arnulf "not by name" (but then says *Rufus*, a reference to Arnulf's red hair and quick temper) in a poem satirizing his host, who plied him with food and wine, and then cheated him at a game of dice.[90]

A great deal of Arnulf's reputation comes from remarks by Hugh Primas's own teacher, and Arnulf's rival, Matthew of Vendôme. Matthew's venom toward Arnulf was such that he declared Arnulf's mother a prostitute.[91] Matthew was contentedly ensconced as professor in Orléans until the arrival of Arnulf, whose popularity as a teacher around 1175 caused Matthew to yield his position and move to Paris for ten years.[92] Matthew condemns a certain *Arnulfus de Sancto Evurtio* (after the monastery of St. Euverte in Orléans) at the end of his *Ars Versificatoria*.[93] This work on the principles of poetry and poetic composition, of a sort that was quite prevalent in the age of the *ars dictaminis* and owed much in inspiration, if not style, to Ovid, was the fruit of Matthew's teaching in Orléans. It reveals his method and where his heart lay: not in glosses or allegories but in creative artistry.[94] But with the increasing professionalization and specialization of knowledge, Orléans was becoming known as the center of study for classical authors.[95]

It is the *Fasti* in particular that pitched Arnulf into the battle for the liberal arts. He came under fire from Alexander Villedieu, whose *Doctrinale*, together with Everard of Béthune's *Graecismus*, became a standard school text heralding the dominance of dialectics.[96] Arnulf appears as the thinly veiled antagonist in Alexander Villedieu's *Ecclesiale*; he is generally recognized as the "fool" of lines 55–56, "Let the fool read what is false about the calendar; let the true knowledge of the church calendar be dear to us" (*Falsum de fastis fatuus legat; ecclesialis / Vera kalendaris sit cara scientia nobis*).[97] The passage appears in a description of the liturgical year, which in form imitates and tries to outdo Ovid's *Fasti* while at the same time condemn-

---

89. Cf. Engelbrecht (2008, 57–58). See also Rieker, xxx on Arnulf's rivalry with Fulco, who was called *imperitus*, and for a possible jab at Fulco in the *Fasti* commentary.
90. Engelbrecht (2003, 1: 19–20); Marti (1955, 237).
91. Engelbrecht (2008, 58).
92. Harbert (1975, 225–26).
93. Marti (1958, xviii–xix).
94. Ghisalberti (1932, 160).
95. Rieker, xxvii.
96. Alton and Wormell (1995, 35).
97. *The Ecclesiale of Alexander of Villa Dei*, 66.

ing it as pagan. The order in which the pagan gods are named in line 15 has also been noted as closely following that in the *Fasti*.[98] Ironically, Arnulf's *Fasti* and Ovid's *Fasti* received widespread fame in a work that had set out to destroy both.

As it turns out, Arnulf linked his fame not only to erudition like Ovid's, but also to original poetic talent like Ovid's. He compared himself to Ovid not only in the *Fasti* commentary (6.812: <u>ardua nulla fugiens</u>) but also in his notes at *Metamorphoses* 15.876: "the soul of Arnulf of Orléans, who has produced these glosses, should not be lamented, if he has glossed well; on the contrary, 'if there is truth in poets' prophecies, I will live' with Ovid" (<u>Indeflebile</u>: . . . *et anima RUFI ARNULFI qui has glosulas fecit Aurelianis defleri non debet si eas bene fecit, immo "si quid habent ueri uatum praesagia, uiuam" [Met. 15.879] cum Ovidio*).[99] Ovid's *vates operosus* or "hardworking poet" (*F.* 1.101; 3.177) implies an avid and inspired investigative researcher, a model for the commentator digging into the calendar. But Ovid's prophetic self-proclamation at the end of the *Metamorphoses* emphasizes lasting creative genius, an equally strong self-identification for Arnulf. He seems to chafe at the tradition of generations of commentators in whose shadow he stands. The subordinate function of the commentator to the classical author is manifest in the frequently cited dictum by Bernard of Chartres of men seeing themselves as dwarves on the shoulders of giants.[100]

In a way, Arnulf of Orléans did achieve long-term fame and become an acknowledged authority. His catena commentary on the *Metamorphoses*—a commentary unaccompanied by the main text of Ovid and a mirror of Arnulf's public instruction and private study—was transmitted and preserved by the Italian Zomino di Pistoia (1378–1458) and the German Amplonius Rating de Berka (1363–1435). The catena or freestanding lemmatic commentary showed the commentator's comfort with his material, and it visually prioritized his thoughts over the text itself. Arnulf's use of the format and its revival by scholars in the fourteenth and fifteenth centuries signal knowledge and authority in a specific field.[101] Arnulf's catena commentary was further disseminated as interlinear and marginal commentaries. His glosses became so imbedded in later commentaries as to be frequently indistinguishable and unidentifiable. In these instances, we see Arnulf being used by grammar masters as a source for authoritative read-

---

98. Ibid., 104.
99. Rieker, xxxi.
100. Minnis (1984, 12). See also the remarks by Schmidt (2008).
101. Gura (2010); see also Copeland (2012, 177–79).

ings, which could be plumbed and chosen to address the age and level of sophistication of the audience.[102]

THE FATE OF OVID'S SEVERED BOOK

Implicit in reading the *Fasti* is the question of the work's completeness. Given the popularity of Ovid's *Fasti* in the Middle Ages and *aetas Ovidiana*, in monastic and classroom environments, there was understandably speculation and reaction regarding the whereabouts or existence of all twelve books.[103] The humanists inherited from their predecessors the notion that Ovid had indeed written all twelve books of the *Fasti*. However, the fact that the seventh book, July, would have given seeming tribute to a non-Christian conveniently answered many questions as to what had happened to the second half of Ovid's work.

Early Christian writers, still schooled in rhetoric, showed a classicizing style of writing (and thinking) which they themselves did not consider incongruous with their faith. One need only remember Lactantius, tutor to Constantine's son in 317, an apologist dubbed the "Christian Cicero." Lactantius cited from Ovid's *Metamorphoses* and *Fasti* for his studies in polytheism. He regarded Ovid as an authority (*ut in Fastis docet*) and held that in the evolution from error to truth, and from philosophy to religion, Ovid would have been Christian.[104] In fact, what "saved" Ovid often had a lot to do with the *Fasti:* one medieval tradition has it that Ovid returned to Rome, certainly signifying redemption, and that back in Rome the last six books of the *Fasti* were burned. In a mystical way, then, with the loss of the most incriminating half of the poem starting with July and August, Ovid

---

102. Coulson (2011, 51, 65).
103. Many scholars currently agree that Ovid had, at the very least, intended to publish twelve books; he had planned and perhaps even sketched out a draft. Littlewood, in her 2006 commentary, finds it unlikely that in AD 8, some six years into the project, Ovid did not know what the entire year would look like (xviii–xix). Pasco-Pranger (2006) believes that the martial and generational patterns in the first six books prepare the way for a continuation of themes in the last six books (63, 116–119). Miller (2002) also finds that the careful structure of the first six books and the straightforward praises of the imperial family at 6.801–810 "hardly rule out a balancing final half" (167). Finally, Herbert-Brown (2002) suggests not only that Ovid had planned the second half of the *Fasti*, but that he later removed the material, because Augustus' edict of AD 11 curbed astrology and divination; the poem "bears the scars of the [stellar] surgery inflicted upon it by its author" (127). I mention in contrast the view that Ovid's last six books remained unwritten when he was sent into exile, and that the "pot does not need to be stirred further" if we emend the hexameter line of *Tr.* 2.549 to *sex ego conscripsi menses totidemque libellos:* see Trappes-Lomax (2006).
104. Le Bonniec (1989, 159–72).

both earned his just reward and was purified, thereby making it permissible for later generations to read him.[105]

In his prologue to his *Expositio* on the *Metamorphoses* from the 1320s, Giovanni del Virgilio wrote that Ovid composed a work in honor of Germanicus Caesar

> in which there are twelve books, just as there are twelve months in the year.... Only six are extant, however, and it is said the Church severed the other six, and did so setting the boundary at July and August, months that at the time were named after Julius Caesar and Augustus. Ovid assigned many portents in actual fact of Christ to Julius Caesar and Augustus.

> *in quo sunt 12 libri, sicut 12 menses sunt anni.... Sed non inveniuntur nisi sex. Et dicitur quod Ecclesia alios sex abstulit, eo quod cum determinarent de mense Julii et Augusti, qui tunc nominabantur a Cesare Julio et Augusto, ipse posuit multa signa de Christo applicando ipsa Cesari Julio et Augusto.*[106]

Most likely Giovanni del Virgilio alludes to Suetonius's account of omens such as comets and other astrological phenomena before and at the birth of Augustus, and of visions of a ruler holding thunder and scepter and the other insignia of Jupiter Optimus Maximus (*Augustus* 94–97). The allegation that the Church destroyed the second half of the *Fasti* is repeated by Arnulf of Orléans, where he claims that St. Jerome had thrown the offending books into the fire.[107] Such claims helped save the reputation of Ovid, as we have seen. Giovanni del Virgilio also hypothesized that Ovid returned to Rome but was suffocated by the welcoming crowd;[108] his manner of death presumably justified the subsequent reading of his works. Ovid's recall to Rome would also have explained the presence of the entire *Fasti* in the city. The medieval glosses all agree in their presupposition that Ovid in stating *sex ego Fastorum scripsi totidemque libellos* was telling the truth. And so Sicco Polenton, a *quattrocento* successor of the Paduan prehumanists, thought that Ovid "published twelve books on the *Fasti*" (*de fastis XII edidit*); an anonymous contemporary went further in his belief that the poet "cor-

---

105. The virulent anonymous fourteenth-century poetic tract *Antiovidianus* can be considered atypical. Note the comment *"Libri Fastorum condidit Ouidius ut scirent idolotrae deos suos..."* in Venice, Biblioteca nazionale Marciana, Marc. lat. XII.15 (4008); no. 232g.; see Coulson (2009).
106. Peeters (1939, 67).
107. *Dies XII sufficerent libris Fastorum recitandis, qui duodecim revera fuerunt, sed a beato Ieronimo incensi fuerunt propter nimium idolatrie cultum, de quo tractabant.* Rieker, xxxix.
108. Ghisalberti (1946, 25).

rected and published twelve books of the *Fasti*, six of which are missing" (*XII fastorum libros emendavit, et edidit, quorum sex desiderantur*),[109] emphasizing not only that Ovid had finished writing his work, but that he had finished revising it (*emendavit* in the perfect tense in Latin).

Speculation on the fate of the missing books revolved around disappearance by intervention or the ravages of time. A *quattrocento* Italian, a certain Francesco from Pesaro, penned a *Conquestio de amissis sex ultimis libris Fastorum Ovidii*, lamenting that he would never be able to see or read the second half of the *Fasti*, lost to the devouring jaws of time.[110] He goes on to inquire of the fates, "was it not enough to have distressed and contributed to the death of the poet in exile?" (fol. 109v: *non ne satis fuerat celebrem lacerasse poetam, / non ne sat exilio contribuisse necem?*). The author's choice of words, *lacerasse*, is noteworthy, since its meaning to mangle or mutilate can be applied to the body of the poet's work. The expression reflects the understanding that Ovid's work had been amputated, that it had been violently cut short, as well as that it needed completing. At the end of his poem, Francesco calls upon Jupiter and Apollo to bring their counsel and resources to the entire poem of Ovid's, whereby the work might be recovered and restored (fol. 110r: *Iuppiter huc venias, divum placidissime semper, / tuque pater musis mitis Apollo veni, / conscilium concti superum tribuatis opemque / sacriloquum vatis quo reparetur opus / conctaque Peligni florescant carmina divi / nostraque sint illis pectora plena sonis*). *Reparetur* conveys the yearning for "repair." How can Jupiter or Apollo help? While Jupiter may signify divine intervention, Apollo suggests the possibility of artistic inspiration to restore or renew Ovid's *Fasti*.

The theory that the last six books of the *Fasti* had been lost spurred many humanists to look for them. Antonio Costanzi tells secondhand of the poem's sighting in its entirety. In the 1480 autograph manuscript of his commentary and the 1489 *editio princeps*, he reports Francesco Veneto's testimony that he had seen and even read the last six books of Ovid's work

---

109. Peeters (1939, 76), from Landi's edition of Book 6 (hereafter Landi), 220.
110.
Hei mihi non valeo tristes retinere querelas,
hei mihi singultus non cohibere graves.
Sex equidem relego fastorum saepe libellos
mellifluis plenos dulcisonisque modis,
sex alios nequeo (dolor o dolor!) ipse videre
temporis ex esu qui periere fero.

incipit, Franciscus de Magistris Pisaurius, *Conquestio de amissis sex ultimis libris Fastorum Ovidii ad M. Matheum Gipsum* (Vatican City, BAV, Reg. lat. 1826, fols. 109v-110r). The text is catalogued in Coulson and Roy (2000), no. 131.

in the library of the King of France.¹¹¹ The comment has dropped out of the later, printed *Fasti* commentaries, the hopes of the accuracy of the report in all probability having been dashed. Of course, some humanists were not beyond inventing rumors. Poking fun at a friend's credulity, Baptista Mantuanus allegedly maintained that relatives of his in Spain owned a complete edition of the *Fasti*.¹¹² Perhaps Mantuanus was referring to his own *Fasti*, a composition he wrote on the liturgical year in imitation of Ovid, published in 1516.¹¹³ Similarly, Conrad Celtis led the Venetian publisher Aldo Manuzio to think that he possessed a copy of the lost books of the *Fasti*, although it is possible that Celtis was also circulating his own composition under Ovid's name, for Manuzio had his suspicions about Celtis's claim.¹¹⁴

The examples of Mantuanus and Celtis support the idea that the *Fasti* was felt to be incomplete, and that its deficient state elicited a desire for full repair. If the humanists could not find the remainder of Ovid's poem, then they could restore it in flattering imitations, or they could fill in the lacunae with supplements. The desire to do the latter already manifested itself in the Middle Ages; for example, an anonymous eleventh-century scribe penned the opening verses of Book 7 of the *Fasti*, and these were copied in many subsequent manuscripts.¹¹⁵ Because they were supposedly a transcription, these verses could have been accepted as genuine. They are perhaps best thought of as pseudepigrapha, passages that are not intentionally deceptive.¹¹⁶ They were not a forgery designed to rival or imitate Ovid. Rather, their composition may have been motivated by the simple desire to fill in

---

111. . . . *reliquum huius operis quod Franciscus Venetus, totius pene orbis terrarum peragrator, nobis iureiurando firmavit vidisse ac legisse apud inclytum regem Gallorum* (*editio princeps*, Romae: Eucharius Silber, 1489, fol. 156v). This remark no longer appears in the 1497, composite edition of the *Fasti*. The discovery of the lost books has been wrongly attributed to Costanzi directly, by Peeters (1939, 77), and Landi, 220. Landi in fact had quoted from the collected works of Ovid edition by N. Lemaire, vol. 8 (Paris: N. E. Lemaire, 1824), 368: *Eos [= reliquos Fastorum] etiam in Bibl. Regis Galliae exstare falso scripsit Antonius Constantius de Fano*.

112. Peeters (1939, 76); Landi, 219.

113. See Trümpy (1979) for the text, translation, and commentary.

114. Spitz (1957, 9). For the correspondence, see *Der Briefwechsel des Konrad Celtis*, ed. by H. Rupprich (Munich: Beck, 1934), no. 315.

115. Vatican City, BAV, Vat. lat. 3262:

> *Si no[v]us a Jani sacris numerabitur annus,*
> *Quintilis falso nomine dictus erit.*
> *Si facis, ut fuerant, primas a Marte kalendas,*
> *tempora constabunt ordine data suo.*

Peeters (no folio number cited), 75.

116. See Speyer 1971, 13 and 138; also Grafton 1990, 5–6.

the acknowledged lacunae in a respected author's work; Diogenes Laertius (2.42) similarly "quotes" verses that Socrates reportedly wrote (*Phaedo* 60D).[117] The attempt at beginning a seventh book of the *Fasti* reflects the medieval understanding that Ovid's work had been cut short, and that it needed completing.

Perhaps it was the same medieval set of opening verses to Book 7 that C. Celtes Protacius (1459–1518) saw and transcribed, and apparently treated as real. In the seventeenth century, Nicolaus Heinsius felt that Celtes had not so much been out to deceive others as he had been deceived himself, and Heinsius moreover scoffed at Gronovius's (1611–71) report that the last six books of the *Fasti* were preserved at the house of a presbyter in a village near Ulm.[118] Like the anonymous eleventh-century scribe, Celtes, by his transcription, showed the desire for an intact text. Where a work was felt to be incomplete, a transmitter of texts could begin to fill the gaps. Behind the persona of the so-called scribe or transcriber there lurks an author of supplements. And as witnessed by Heinsius, in the seventeenth century a recognition of fake or forged Ovids replaced blind belief in, or a hope for, the discovery of the last six books; this liberation allowed supplements to flourish on their own as a literary genre. No longer were only a few verses added to the *Fasti*; authors now fabricated the entire second half of Ovid. And so it is that in 1649 the *P. Ovidii Nasonis Fastorum libri duodecim, quorum sex posteriores a Claudio Bartholomae Morisoto . . . substituti sunt* appeared in Dijon. The Frenchman openly claimed to have written the last six books of the *Fasti* himself.[119]

The era of Claude Morisot has been outlined as the burgeoning literary phase for supplements,[120] but this is not to ignore the 1428 composition of a

---

117. Speyer, 137. Speyer lists one reason, or opportunity, for creating forgeries as filling out a tradition (Ergänzung der Überlieferung), but when the motive is pure, i.e., no more than the wish to replace or compensate for a literary loss, he distinguishes the new writing as pseudepigraphic (138).

118. Peeters (1939, 75–76); Landi, 219 (quoting from the 1841 Berlin edition by R. Merkel, 303): *Noribergae vidi antiquam editionem, cui adscriptum erat: reliqui sex libri servantur apud presbyterum in pago prope Ulmam. Principium septimi:*

Tu quoque mutati causas et nomina mensis
a te qui sequitur, maxime Caesar, habes.

Scriptum manu C. Celtis Protacii.—J. F. Gronovius. Heinsius responding to Gronovius' account: *sed opinor Celtem . . . non tam decipisse quam fuisse ab aliis deceptum.*

119. BN128.601; my thanks to Ralph Hexter for providing this reference.

120. Note the supplements to Livy (1648–54), Curtius Rufus (1654), and Lucan (1639), as well as Maffeo Vegio's thirteenth book of the *Aeneid* (1428). It is in the first half of the seventeenth century that the composition of supplements reached its peak. See Schmidt (1964, 51). Maffeo Vegio has been edited and translated by Putnam and Hankins (2004).

thirteenth book of the *Aeneid* by Maffeo Vegio. Richard Thomas reads into Vegio's impulse and writing the same unsatisfying feeling about the *Aeneid*'s ending recognizable to many modern scholars and students.[121] Perhaps Vergil's privately vengeful, unwed Aeneas needed redeeming in order to restore his place and value within the rest of the Augustan epic. As for the *Fasti*'s incomplete status, this is often now considered a deliberate tactic on Ovid's part. The termination of the work at the end of June seems too perfectly thought out. The poem is not incomplete but clearly and methodically half-complete, as suggested by the separation of *sex* and *totidemque* (*sex ego Fastorum scripsi totidemque libellos, Tr.* 2.549).[122] Moreover, since Ovid broke off the *Fasti* just before the most obviously significant months of July and August, one can't help wondering if Ovid's false claim of completion was intended "to make Augustus feel responsible for the loss of the part of the work that would have done him most honor."[123] What, then, does an invented second half of the *Fasti* say about un-silencing an anti-Augustan Ovid? In the end, it is wise to remember that Ovid's complaints about his exile are to a certain degree a literary conceit, and that the genre of supplements can stand on its own as a literary creation, meant to imitate and emulate an ingenious classical author.

---

121. Thomas (2001, 280–84).

122. Barchiesi (1994, 266). Newlands (1995), chapter 6, agrees that the poem's final suspension is a literary tactic, the inevitable result of a progressive denouement; but cf. the caution with which others handle not only the assertions that the poet broke off but also the reasons why (see Volk 1997).

123. See Fantham's 1998 edition (hereafter Fantham 1998), 2; see also Fantham (2002, 231).

CHAPTER TWO

Fifteenth-Century Revival

TIME AND PLACE

Interest in Ovid's *Fasti* re-emerged in Renaissance Italy, with widespread and long-term results. The late-fifteenth-century revival and popularity of the *Fasti* is attested by a composite volume of commentaries edited by Bartolomeo Merula and published in Venice by the firm of Giovanni Tacuino on June 12, 1497.[1] Joining under one cover the commentaries of Paolo Marsi of Pescina and Antonio Costanzi of Fano, whose first editions had appeared in 1482[2] and 1489 respectively, the Merula issue quickly became a standard. It flourished on the Italian market for thirty years in six reprints. Pirated versions also found their way into France. After the final 1527 edition (a large print-run, judging from the number of copies that can be found in rare-book libraries in the United States and across Europe), the Marsi and Costanzi *Fasti* commentaries made their

---

1. In the prefatory letter Merula makes the point *haud invitus et carmen correxi et enarrationes curavique ut Antonii Fanensis et Marsi interpretationes una imprimerentur a diligentissimo ac solertissimo bibliopola Ioanne Tacuino nostro, ne quid ad carminis intelligentiam deesset.* Bartolomeo Merula edited a number of Latin texts for Tacuino's press, and Tacuino published various commentaries by Merula, among them one on Ovid's *Tristia* in 1499 (discussed in Gabriel Fuchs's 2013 Ohio State University dissertation "Renaissance Receptions of Ovid's *Tristia*").

2. The 1480 edition (HC 12151) mentioned by Peeters (1939, 183) is apocryphal; having made a search for it, Bianchi (1981) concludes that it is a spurious work (71, fn.1).

way into later composite works, notably volume three of Ovid's *opera omnia* published in Basel in 1550, and volume two published in Frankfurt in 1601. We should also note that Paolo Marsi's commentary was reprinted separately four times at the end of the fifteenth century, and that a copy traveled with an Italian tradesman to the Low Countries, where it was transcribed by the Flemish manuscript workshop of the abbot Raphael de Marcatellis and owned by the private library of St. Bavon in Ghent.[3] Part of Marsi's commentary was likewise copied out by the humanist, reformer, and classical scholar Beatus Rhenanus in 1498.[4] In Ovidian *Fasti* studies, the work of Paolo Marsi and Antonio Costanzi ruled the field in the Renaissance.

The commentaries are in origin an Italian, humanist project. For the further localization of and context for the *Fasti*'s popularity, the best evidence comes from Paolo Marsi himself. In a characteristically self-referential manner, Marsi informs his audience of the chronology of his study and teaching of the *Fasti*, and he gives a history of recent *Fasti* commentaries. Piecing together details from the prefatory and end material of the *editio princeps* of his work, we learn that Marsi's commentary had its genesis with the patrician Cornaro family in Venice but came to fruition in Rome.[5]

The lengthy dedication of the 1482 edition, as well as the alternating prose and verse prefaces to Books 2–6 of the *Fasti,* is addressed to Giorgio Cornaro, son of the wealthy Marco Cornaro. In all likelihood Marsi had been introduced to the Cornari by his friend and mentor, the famous antiquarian Pomponio Leto, who had taught in the household from 1461–64.[6] Before taking up permanent residence in Rome in 1474, and perhaps beginning as early as 1471, Marsi tutored Giorgio.[7] Marsi's *Fasti* commentary was printed by the firm of Baptista de Tortis in Venice on December 24, 1482, at the behest and expense of Giorgio Cornaro; in the *Emendatio locorum* at the end of the volume, Marsi explains:

---

3. This is Ghent, Bisschoppelijke Bibliotheek, Cath. 12 (no. 28), fols. 16r–212r (modern foliation), described in Derolez, (1979, 161–68). The *terminus post quem* for the manuscript is 1482, and the *terminus ante quem* is 1507, the end of de Mercatellis's service as abbot and a year before he died. See also Derolez (2002, 557).

4. Sélestat, Bibliothèque Humaniste, ms. 50, fols. 102r–195r contain Books 3–6 of the *Fasti* with glosses, copied by Beatus Rhenanus. Fol. 195 is dated 1498. An *Interpretatio V libri Fastorum per Paulum Marsum* begins on fol. 153v. Description in Kristeller, *Iter Italicum,* vol. 3 (1983), 345 (I have not seen this manuscript). See furthermore Adam (1973, esp. 18).

5. The following paragraphs clarify and correct some of the analysis in the della Torre (1903) biography of Marsi.

6. Accame (2008, 44).

7. Pontari (2008, 742).

These are the things, Giorgio Cornelio, which I had written on Ovid's *Fasti* with great care and diligence eight years ago and were dedicated to you from the start. It seemed wise counsel to hold on to the work until now, lest a hasty publication be a mark of disgrace rather than praise. But now, since I have at last been permitted to come over to you in Venice from Rome, I have placed the final touch on these studies over which I have toiled at night by candlelight, and I have given them for printing to that man whom you yourself mandated.

Haec illa sunt, Georgi Corneli, quae nos octo antea annis in Ovidianos Fastos magna cura ac diligentia scripseramus et a principio tibi dicata. Visum est illud inire consilium ut in hoc usque tempus pressa teneremus, ne editio praecipitata dedecori potius quam laudi esset. Nunc vero cum tandem ex urbe Venetias ad te venire licuerit his lucubrationibus nostris extremam modo manum imposuimus et cui tu ipse mandasti dedimus imprimendas.

In other words, Marsi departed for Venice in 1482 to supervise personally the publication of his commentary, which had first begun to take shape in 1474. Furthermore, the Venetian business trip seems to have come after the recently completed academic year 1481–82, when Marsi was Professor of Eloquence at the University of Rome; in 1482, he was lecturing on the *Fasti*, as revealed by this gloss at *F.* 2.389:

Albula: The Tiber had flooded, as I have seen currently also, twice in particular on January 7, 1482, while I was lecturing on these lines and the Tiber was then so overrunning its banks that, swollen by winter rains, it flooded over them completely.

Albula: *inundaverat Tybris, ut vidimus hoc quoque tempore bis maxime septimo idus ianuarias anno salutis Mccclxxxii, dum haec profitebamur cum Tybris omnes ripas excederet ita et tunc auctus hymbribus* [sic] *supra ripas eruperat.*

While he was in Venice, Marsi wrote and added to his commentary the prefaces for his patron. They have been composed in a clearly linear, chronological order. In the dedication proper, Marsi remarks that he and Antonio Volsco were unable to co-produce a *Fasti* commentary, because the latter "became busy with his tome on Propertius, and I left the City" *(occupato illo in Propertianis monumentis et me ab urbe digresso)*; the year referred to is again 1482, for at the beginning of the year Volsco's edition of Propertius without commentary was published in Rome.[8] In the prose preface to Book 4, Marsi says that his efforts to write in Venice have begun to flag. He complains that "the report of a most acute disaster has somewhat called away from its initiative, Cornelio, this work dedicated to you, growing in size and at the half-way mark already speeding into port" (*Destinatum tibi scilicet, Corneli, opus maturantem et e medio cursu iam in portum accelerantem acerbissimae calamitatis meae nuntius paulum ab instituto revocavit*). He proceeds to lament the recent death of his one surviving brother Angelo, struck down by a Turkish soldier in Toscolano during the War of Ferrara (1482–84).[9] By the sixth book with the end in sight, Marsi is ready to return to Rome, where he is awaited at his teaching post by his colleagues and friends. "Behold, I swiftly traverse a vast ocean for you" (*Ecce tibi celeres vastum percurrimus aequor*, l. 8), Marsi says to his patron in literal and figurative language,

> in a very generous bay most of my work has now been completed.
> Now my bark seeks port with full sail
> and has loosened the rope from a safe bulwark.
> I shall set off and search again companions who equal me in affection,
> who are fostered by Rome and summon me hence,
> for I have long been absent while writing for you, Cornelio,
> the legacies of my toil on Venetian waters.
> A most loyal army awaits my discourse,
> though it has venerable leaders in Marsi's absence.

> *Liberiore sinu, iam pars exacta laboris*
> *maxima, ianque ratis pleno petet hostia velo*
> *quae simul a tuto religaverit aggere funem.*
> *Discedam repetamque pares in amore sodales*
> *quos nunc Roma fovet, quibus hinc revocamur ab isdem*
> *nanque diu abfuimus, tibi dum monumenta laborum*
> *nostrorum in Venetis Corneli ex[s]cripsimus undis.*
> *Militia ex[s]pectat nostram fidissima vocem*
> *quanquam habet illa duces pro Marso absente verendos.* (ll. 9–17)

Among those expecting his return, Marsi mentions in particular Pomponio Leto, Antonio Volsco, and Pietro Marsi, all professors in Rome and the

---

8. Sextus Aurelius Propertius, *Elegiae*, recognovit Antonius Volscus. Romae: Eucharius Silber, MCCCCLXXXII ante id. Ianuar.

9. della Torre (1903, 13–18).

latter two, members of Leto's circle of intellectuals known as the Roman Academy. Therefore Paolo Marsi's early teaching of the *Fasti* took place in the Venetian Cornaro family household, which would later subsidize the cost of the commentary's publication; but Marsi's career with respect to the *Fasti* would come into full swing in Rome and find its context specifically within the circle of Pomponio Leto.

Certain features of Marsi's commentary do betray its Venetian origin. There is a trace of Marsi's teaching to a young Cornaro at 2.312, a gloss that is intended to make the text come alive. The princess Omphale has set Hercules female tasks such as carrying her parasol. Marsi glosses *sustinuere manus Herculeae:* "the hands of Hercules, for he was holding [the parasol] aloft with his own hand, just as it is now the custom to hold over the heads of great lords a curtained shade, which the Venetians call umbrellas, but are better called awnings" (*manus Herculis, nam ipse sua manu sustentabat, velut nunc de more est supra magnorum dominorum capita pallia ferre, quas Veneti umbrellas vocant, melius umbracula dicuntur*).[10]

As we will see, there are many comments in Marsi's *Fasti* that also make reference to Rome. In the dedication, Marsi explains how his work on the *Fasti* evolved in Rome. He begins on an apologetic note: "After it was finally admissible (I beg your pardon) for me to go from a long Venetian deferment back to that Rome I had left ten years before, headed as for a port and hoped-for repose, I resumed those studies, Giorgio Cornelio, which I had put aside for the length of my absence from native soil" (*Postquam mihi ex longa peregrinatione redire tandem tua quoque pace e Venetiis Romam unde decennio antecesseram velut in portum et optatam quietem licuit, rettuli me, Georgi Corneli, ad ea studia quae tam longo tempore intermiseram quam longo a patriis sedibus abfueram*). Della Torre has suggested that this ten-year hiatus from Rome occurred from 1463–73, or as I would modify it slightly, 1464–74.[11] Despite tutoring Giorgio Cornaro in Ovid, Marsi began composing and organizing his notes in Rome in 1474, counting perhaps on a bit of scholarly seclusion. But this leisure was not to remain, for Marsi continues (with a dash of false modesty):

> The domain of teaching was publicly entrusted to me, although I was neither wanting nor seeking it. I would have gladly refused it as an arduous and very difficult task in so great a company of learned men, if long-

---

10. Compare Marsi's remark concerning the aspirated "h" at *F.* 6.300, for why Greek Ἑστία became Roman Vesta: *ea aspiratio vertitur in vocabulum nostrum, sicut ab hespero Vespero, ab Henetis Venetis dicimus.*

11. della Torre (1903, 22).

standing friendship (compelled, as I was, by its daily reproach) had not deflected me from that plan. At last I took up this teaching, and in the first year I very assiduously interpreted the poems of Horace and Ovid's *Tristia*. The next year I taught before a crowd of listeners with great care and prudence that sublime work, the *Fasti*.

Traditaque publice nec optanti nec petenti mihi profitendi provincia fuit, quam ut arduam ac perdifficilem in tanto doctissimorum hominum coetu libentissime repudiassem, nisi me vetus amicitia ab instituto reppulisset, cuius quotidiano quodam convicio compulsus. Eam tandem aggressus, lyricos primo quidem anno Horatianos ac Ovidii Tristia diligentissime interpretatus sum, proximo vero divinum illud Fastorum opus . . .

It appears that in 1474 Marsi was hired as a professor in Rome. The date of his appointment has been commonly accepted as 1480; in conferring this date, della Torre based himself on Bertolotti, who, like Egmont Lee after him, had studied archival records of university payments.[12] Indeed, Marsi's wages for the years 1481–84 are documented.[13] No payroll accounts for the years 1475 and 1476 exist,[14] but this does not mean that Marsi was not hired. In 1474–75 he taught Horace and the exilic poetry of Ovid; in 1475–76 he taught the *Fasti*. The latter is confirmed by Marsi's gloss on intercalation at *F.* 3.164: "I lectured on this passage on that very day which was added to February in AD 1476" (*eo enim die hunc locum legimus, qui quidem dies ad intercalationem Februario superadditus est anno salutis Mccccxxvi*).

After the academic year ended, Marsi continued with his research on Ovid. In the preface Marsi admits to having expended little energy on astronomy while teaching, complaining "for truly, when there are as yet few lecturers in astronomy who have the proper command of it . . . how can a professor of the humanities master that which [he has] never even dabbled in?" (*Etenim si ex his ipsis qui astrorum scientiam profitentur pauci admodum sunt qui eam ipsam recte teneant . . . quo pacto nos humanitatis professores eam tenebimus quam ne unquam quidem delibavimus?*).[15] By 1479

---

12. Ibid., 265; Bertolotti (1883, 89–90); Lee (1978, 184).
13. Lee (1978, 251–52; 1984, 134, fn. 17).
14. Lee (1984, 142).
15. Compare Piero Valeriano's assessment of his profession in his inaugural lecture on Catullus in Rome in 1521: "there is no discipline that anyone can understand completely, and yet the *grammaticus* alone is expected to accomplish everything. . . . [he must] know something even of trivial things, so that not even the smallest detail can escape him" (Gaisser 1993, 115).

Marsi tried to make up for his lack of knowledge about the stars. At 3.406, glossing the constellation of the Great Bear, Marsi advises the reader, "all that pertains to the stars' rising and setting will be more clearly explained at the end of this work; there I will take everything up again" (*Haec omnia quae ad ortum et occasum siderum pertinent in fine operis lucidius explicabuntur; ibi omnia repetemus*). Indeed, at the end of the 1482 edition Marsi appended a letter entitled "Reckoning of the Stars" (*Ratio Astrologiae*) that can be dated internally to 1479 through a discussion of the precession of the equinoxes, wherein Marsi proposes a theory to account for the slow drift of the stars 1422 years after Ovid's birth. Although he in fact adds nothing to an essentially medieval concept of an oscillating eighth and ninth sphere, Marsi appeals to the authority of his "teacher Rigius Adriacus," the astronomer and mathematician Johannes Regiomontanus.[16] At 3.852 he calls the German his most intimate friend.[17] The two may have already been acquainted by 1463, when Regiomontanus left Rome to accompany Bessarion, the new papal legate to the Venetian Republic (accounting for the epithet "Adriacus"). If not, then surely Marsi met the astronomer when the latter was summoned to Rome to reform the calendar (a project interrupted by Regiomontanus's untimely death in 1476 from the plague).[18]

In Rome, Marsi's thoughts on Ovid had a chance to mature. In addition to recounting the development of his *Fasti* studies there, Marsi sketches the relationship of his work to that of his colleagues and competitors. In the dedication, before moving to a declaration of his pre-eminence in the field of *Fasti* commentaries, Marsi catalogues his predecessors, beginning at the top of the list with his "own friend Pomponio Leto, the most faithful interpreter of antiquity and all Latinity, [who] many years before had written a few things on the *Fasti*" (*Scripserat in Fastos pluribus ante me annis pauca tamen fidelissimus antiquitatis et totius latinitatis interpres Pomponius noster*). Della Torre suggests that Marsi may have been introduced to the *Fasti* through private instruction by Leto after 1457;[19] Leto was possibly initiated

---

16. *Ne videar penitus (ut rumpatur livor) huius rationis expers, utor enim praeceptore Rigio nostro Adriaco astrologorum principe ut nemo dicere me possit erraturum, eaque erit nobis quaestio cur illud sit quod poetae Nasonis et Augusti temporibus sol arietis principium inibat undecimo calendas apriles. Nunc vero id fit quinto idus Martias. Fecit hoc quidem differentia motuum corporum caelestium illorum et nostrorum temporum, nam ab eo anno quo natus est Ovidius usque in hunc annum defluxere anni mille quingenti et xxii.*

17. *Inus, scilicet novercae Phrixi, quae cum aperte fabula videatur, princeps tamen astrologorum Ioannes Germanus, familiarissimus noster, omnia ad effectus ipsius arietis refert.*

18. Malpangotto (2008, 28–31); Rosen (1975).

19. della Torre (1903, 21).

himself by his teacher, Pietro Odi da Montopoli.[20] Three manuscripts of Leto's notes on the *Fasti* are known to be extant. The lengthiest, Vatican City, BAV, Vat. lat. 3263, is from the late 1480s (Zabughin more narrowly dates it post-1488) and reflects Leto's life-long study of the *Fasti*.[21] Vat. lat. 3264 is a deluxe manuscript of the *Fasti* with glosses on the first five folio pages, produced circa 1469/70 for a private pupil of Leto's and member of his Academy, Fabio Mazzatosta (see figure 2).

Ferrara, Biblioteca Comunale Ariostea, II.141, is another deluxe manuscript, containing glosses on the *Fasti* among several other of Ovid's works (the *Nux, Ibis, Medicamina faciei femineae,* and *Amores*); it bears the coat of arms of Agostino Maffei, again a member of the Academy. The manuscript, whose ownership went unnoticed but whose writing was first identified as autograph by Francesco Lo Monaco, is as yet undated; it may stem from the same period in which Leto dedicated his edition of Sallust to Maffei, that is to say in 1490.[22] Leto's vigorous scholarly activity on Ovid's poem is evident, as well as the presumably strong importance attached to the *Fasti* in the Roman Academy, a topic that will be discussed at more length in chapter 4. It should be noted here that glossed notes to the *Fasti* also exist on fols. 71v–73v of Vatican City, BAV, Ottob. lat. 1982, a manuscript consisting of classical extracts, humanist texts, and correspondence, which Wouter Bracke has attributed to the cultural ambience of Leto's circle.[23] Of the textual witnesses to Leto's comments (that we know of), Marsi apparently means the Mazzatosta manuscript when he refers to the "few things" that Leto had written on the *Fasti,* but it is not inconceivable that an even earlier set of scattered notes existed.

After the deferential bow to his master, Marsi continues: "I followed afterwards, running over the entire gamut of Ovid's work, leaving nothing

---

20. Vatican City, BAV, Vat. lat. 1595 contains glosses and corrections in Pietro Odi di Montopoli's hand to Ovid's *Ars amatoria, Remedia amoris, Amores, Tristia, Fasti, Epistulae ex Ponto, Ibis,* and *Heroides (epistula* XV): see Buonocore (1995, 108).

21. Zabughin (1909/1910–12), 2: 153; for a full discussion of the Vatican manuscripts, see pages 146–55. For a more recent description of the manuscripts accompanied by bibliography, see Buonocore (1995, 111–12; 1994, 207–8). Lo Monaco (1992b, 854 fn. 22) identifies Naples, Biblioteca Nazionale, IV F 8, as a manuscript copy of Vat. lat. 3263. However, the online source REMACCLA (*Repertorium Manuscriptorum et Commentariorum Auctorum Classicorum Latinorum / Repertorio dei Manoscritti e dei Commenti degli Autori Classici Latini*) calls the author of the commentary Antonio Costanzi. I have not seen the manuscript.

22. Lo Monaco (1992b, 854 fn. 22); on the edition of Sallust, see Osmond and Ulery (2003), Lunelli (1987, 193), and Ullman (1955). In conversation, Francesco Lo Monaco did seem to be of the opinion that the well-constructed manuscript now in Ferrara dates to late in Leto's career with respect to the other *Fasti* glosses.

23. Bracke (1992b, 21).

FIGURE 2. Pomponio Leto, *Fasti* with glosses (ca. 1469/1470). Vatican City, BAV, MS Vat. lat. 3264, fol. 1r. Reproduced with permission of the Biblioteca Apostolica Vaticana.

unconsidered or undiscussed. Thereafter Anacliterius of Perugia, a man very distinguished in both Greek and Latin literature and eminent in both kinds of speaking, commented on the *Fasti*" (*Postea nos secuti provinciam omnem percurrimus, nihil intactum nihilque indiscussum relinquentes. Deinde Perusiae Anaclyterius meus vir, tum graecis tum latinis litteris ornatissimus et utroque dicendi genere illustris, Fastos et ipse interpretatus est.*) Anaclyterius is Francesco Maturanzio; if Marsi's commentary on the *Fasti* first took written shape in 1474, then according to his chronology, a commentary by Maturanzio must be dated post-1474. The classicization, indeed Hellenization, of Maturanzio's name by Marsi, who favored such practices due to his affiliations with the Roman Academy, confirms this post-1474 date, as does Maturanzio's return from a much anticipated trip to Greece in June 1474. Maturanzio spent nearly two years in Greece with the specific aim of improving his facility in the Greek language, and he procured manuscripts as well (a treatise on grammar, tragedies by Aeschylus, and comedies by Aristophanes, among other works). For various years between 1475 and 1486, Maturanzio occupied the chair of eloquence in Perugia.[24]

Marsi continues:

> Somewhat earlier, Antonio Volsco, a most learned and scholarly young man and a very careful interpreter, performed the same activity. So great was the friendship and good will between us, that we planned to publish under one common title the studies which we toiled over by candlelight. This has not been accomplished to date, because he became busy with his tome on Propertius, and I left the City.
>
> *Idem paulo ante fecit doctissimus et eruditissimus iuvenis interpresque diligentissimus Antonius Volscus, cum quo est mihi tanta necessitudo et mutua benivolentia ut communi utriusque titulo lucubrationes nostras essemus edituri, quod occupato illo in Propertianis monumentis et me ab urbe digresso non est in praesentia factum.*

Even by contemporaries, Volsco was most known for his work on Propertius, as well as for that on Ovid's *Heroides;* in an essay on the merits of commentators, Battista Guarino does not make mention of Volsco's *Fasti*.[25]

---

24. See Falzone (2009).

25. *Acutior in poetis explicandis cultiorque meo iudicio Antonius Volscus et ipse Pomponii auditor, diligens in Nasonis Heroidibus, sed in Propertio diligentior.—Baptistae Guarini dissertatio,* in Lo Monaco (1992a, 144). Volsco published a commentary on the *Heroides,* without the text, in 1481. His commentary on Propertius appeared in his 1488, second edition of the poet (the *editio princeps,* without commentary, is from 1482). See Thomson (2011, 164, 210, 219–20).

Little is known about Volsco's early life or even the date of his birth. He was probably born between 1440 and 1450, which could correspond to the description of *iuvenis* not only by Marsi but also by Pomponio Leto in 1468.[26] Since Marsi was born in 1440, it seems more likely that Volsco was born near the end of that decade in order for Marsi to call his peer *iuvenis*. His commentary on the *Fasti* is preserved in Rome, Biblioteca Vallicelliana, MS R. 59. The commentary at 218 folio pages is extensive. From the length of the commentary and the level of detail, we can infer that Volsco had been working on the *Fasti* for a long time, perhaps starting already in 1468, when he was in the orbit of Pomponio Leto. It is worth noting again that Volsco was a member of Leto's Academy, as witnessed by surviving correspondence and the inscription of his name on the walls of the catacomb of Ss. Marcellino e Pietro, in addition to his authorship of a *De antiquitate Latii*.[27]

The Vallicelliana manuscript is a set of student lecture notes; it is a running commentary where an excursus, long or short, follows a lemma from a word or phrase from Ovid. The commentary reflects the influence of Pomponio Leto's teaching and Volsco's own conclusions, which he most likely reached when he was a professor in Rome post-1473.[28] The wealth of mythological detail furthermore suggests cross-fertilization with the study of Propertius and Ovid's *Heroides*. Leto's teaching on the *Fasti* is evident in several places in the Vallicelliana manuscript. On numerous occasions Volsco refers to Tiberius as the dedicatee of the *Fasti* (fols. 2v, 3r, 3v, 4r, 5r, 21v, 29v, 31v, 112r, 112v, 151v, and 214v); in Vat. lat. 3264, dating to 1469/70, Leto also refers to Tiberius as the dedicatee, whereas he had changed his mind in favor of Germanicus in Vat. lat. 3263, dated after 1488. Another Pomponian influence can be seen at *F.* 2.109–110, *dura penna*, the hard shaft that pierces the brow of the swan who sings most sweetly before dying. Volsco's comment, *senili quae durior est,* states that the shaft is a feather, namely, a harder feather that appears in older swans. Here he

---

26. Maillard, Kecskeméti, and Portalier (1995, 427) give 1450 as the year of birth; basing the results on the evidence cited, Thomson settles for a date ca. 1440 and refutes earlier testimony for a date ca. 1424–25 (2011, 219).

27. Volsco's correspondence with Giuliano Marasca is preserved in the Pomponian manuscript in Vatican City, BAV, Ottob. lat. 1982; see Bracke (1992b, 91–92). For the catacomb inscription see Lumbroso (1890, 216). The *De antiquitate Latii,* preserved in London, British Library, Harley 5050, was composed after 1477; see Pincelli's 2000 edition of Martino Filetico (hereafter Pincelli), xxxvi. Description in Kristeller, *Iter Italicum,* vol. 6 (1989), 183b. Pincelli believes the manuscript gives proof that Leto and Volsco were among those who quarreled with Martino Filetico on his reading of "Lavinia" for "Lavinaque" in Vergil *Aen.* 1.2.

28. There are surviving records of Volsco's professorship for 1481–83 and 1494–96; Thomson (2011) suggests that Volsco might have taught in Rome from 1473 onwards (219).

summarizes Leto's gloss (Vat. lat. 3263, fol. 22v) *cyncis senescentibus penna exigua dura in pluma frontis innascitur,* "a small but hard feather that grows in among the brow feathers of aging swans." Leto goes on to state that he had listened to the songs of such dying swans on his trip to Eastern Europe (*audivi ego canentis cycnos in paludibus ScyΘarum*), a journey that is thought to have occurred in 1479 or 1480.[29] Volsco was then obviously still working on his *Fasti* commentary in 1480, if he was able to include Leto's observation on natural history.

Paolo Marsi refers twice in Book 6 of his commentary to information he received from Volsco, or at least with which he was in agreement. For *Fasti* 6.711, Marsi remarks,

> The poet said Thyene from Dodona, but the better reading is Dodonian Thyene so that it is in the vocative case. And lest I deprive someone of due praise, my friend Volsco was the first at Rome to claim it should be said like this; indeed I approved of his opinion.
>
> *Poeta Dodona Thyene dixit, sed melius leges Dodoni Thyene, ut sit vocandi casus; et ne cui sua laus detrahatur, Volscus noster Romae primus fuit qui ita dicendum asseret, cuius quidem sententiam approbavi.*

We see that Volsco in his comment on the same line corrected the reading, using a mythological detail from Hyginus that the Hyades, of whom Thyene, or Thyone, was one, were called Dodonian nymphs (*Vocandi casus est. Ferecides Iadas Dodonidas ninphas appellat quoniam in Dodone silva Epiri nate sunt*).[30] Marsi attributes the innovative reading to Volsco, and by borrowing it for his own commentary he gives some weight to his prefatory remark that "so great was the friendship and good will between us, that we planned to publish under one common title the studies which we toiled over by candlelight."[31] Moreover, the statement that Volsco was pre-

---

29. On the date of Pomponio's journey: Bracke (1989, 298); cf. Accame (2011, 39–40). Leto's use of the letter *theta* became commonplace after 1470, when he had begun learning Greek (Steinmann 1988, 53).

30. Rome, Biblioteca Vallicelliana, MS R. 59, fol. 212r. Hyginus, *De Astronomia* 2.21: . . . *Hyades appellantur. Has autem Pherecydes Atheniensis Liberi nutrices esse demonstrat, numero septem, quas etiam antea nymphas Dodonidas appellatas. Harum nomina sunt haec: Ambrosia, Eudora, Pedile, Coronis, Polyxo, Phyto, Thyone.* Volsco might also be echoing the scholiasts on Lucan (*BC* 6.27): *Dodona silva est Epiri.* See Keseling (1908, 98).

31. At 6.809, Marsi tries to clear up doubt as to who is meant by the *matertera Caesaris,* the mother's sister, or aunt, of Caesar: *videtur hic dubium an habuerit sororem matris C. Caesaris an sororem Acciae matris Augusti an sororem Liviae. Sed cum poeta rationem habeat uxoris quae apud materteram Caesaris, ut diximus paulo ante, fuerit, inque suis habuit matertera Caesaris ante, puto*

occupied with Propertius when Marsi left to oversee the 1482 publication of his commentary is consistent with what we know: Volsco's edition of Propertius, accompanied by only a Vita, was published in Rome in 1482.

Volsco for his part considered Marsi one of his closest friends and a luminary of their era (*vir nostri temporis litteratissimus mihique summa benevolentia convinctissimus*).³² The same connection cannot be said to have existed, as we shall see later, between Paolo Marsi and Antonio Costanzi. Marsi concludes his list of *Fasti* commentators with the final mention of his competitor: "but not to cheat him of anything," Marsi insists,

> He who bestows most on the Latin language deserves high praise in every field of studies. Antonio from Fano also, a man unique for his talent and learning and incomparable in Greek and Latin, has already spent many years examining the plan of the *Fasti*.

> *Sed ne quaequam defraudemus, plurimum linguae latinae conferens magnam ille laudem in omni studiorum genere meretur. Antonius praeterea Phanensis, vir et ingenio et doctrina singularis et in utraque eloquentia summus, in indaganda ratione Fastorum pluribus iam annis occupatur.*

It is possible that Marsi encountered Costanzi or at least news about his work during the latter's trip to Rome in the summer of 1481.³³ Indeed, Costanzi had been studying and teaching the *Fasti* well before the first publication of his commentary in 1489. Comments on the *Fasti* are preserved in Vatican City, BAV, Chig. H. VI. 204, fols. 1r–74v, a codex with a modicum of notes and autobiographical details permitting a date circa 1470; and Vatican City, BAV, Urb. lat. 360, fols. 1r–198v, a deluxe manuscript presented to Federico, the duke of Urbino, with the subscription Fano, 1480.³⁴ While the latter commentary was written for conspicuous consumption and private use, it in fact represents Costanzi's public teaching, which transpired in his native Fano from the end of 1463 until the

---

de eadem hoc in loco dicere. Sic intelligemus de sorore Liviae, quae matertera erat Tyberii longe maior natu quam Livia Drusilla, quod Volscus quoque noster asserebat. Here again Marsi stands by a claim that Volsco made (fol. 216v: *Livia maior huic Drusille soror, Caesaris Tiberii matertera, qui filius fuit Livie Drusille ex Tiberio Nerone*).

32. Thomson (2011, 214, 215).
33. For evidence of the trip see Prete (1991, 215).
34. For a description of the manuscripts with bibliography see Buonocore (1994, 84–85, 165) (the Chigiano codex is also cited in Buonocore 1995, 102–3); for their attribution, dating, and interrelationship, Campana (1950, 236–56).

year of his death in 1490.³⁵ Costanzi himself had grown up reading Ovid as a boy, schooled in the *Fasti* by his noted humanist instructors, Guarino of Verona (gloss at 1.316: *Qui versus cum me adulescente Ferrariae inter discipulos celeberrimi viri Guarini Veronensis varie iactaretur*) and Ciriaco d'Ancona (gloss at 4.954: *portae [Fanensis] titulum . . . Cyriacus ille Anconites, vir inclytus et vetustarum rerum solertissimus indagator, magno Fanensium civium conventu legit nobis pueris atque interpretatus est*).

Other Italian humanists besides those catalogued by Marsi were also concerned with Ovid's *Fasti*. In his funeral oration for Antonio Costanzi, Francesco Ottavio ("Cleofilo") speaks of approaching Domizio Calderini and Niccolò Perotti in Rome on his master's behalf and consulting them about difficult passages in the *Fasti*.³⁶ In the dedicatory letter of his 1495 edition and emendations of Catullus, Girolamo Avanzi also alludes to a commentary on the *Fasti* written or at least begun by Calderini; he had noticed it in the deceased Calderini's library in the summer of 1491.³⁷

Nothing by Perotti or Calderini on the *Fasti* seems to have survived, but a localization of interest in Rome is evident. Another important commentary on the *Fasti* that did survive is the *Collectanea* of Poliziano.³⁸ Poliziano delivered his course on the *Fasti* in the same year that Marsi did. Promoted by Lorenzo de' Medici to the professorship of Greek and Latin in 1480, Poliziano lectured on Ovid during the first two years of his academic appointment at the Florentine Studio. While *Heroides* 15, the *Epistula* of Sappho to Phaon,³⁹ constituted the partial subject matter for 1480–81, the *Fasti* was the topic for 1481–82.⁴⁰ The significance of interpretation by the progressive Florentine textual scholar and critic

---

35. Evidence for Costanzi's teaching from the communal archives of Fano is given in Castaldi (1916, 277, fn.4).

36. Prete (1993, 47). The passage reads: *Eram enim et tempore in urbe Roma, ubi optimi praeceptoris mei litteras accipiens, quibus me eruditorum perquirere sententias iubebat, optimi discipuli fungebar officio. Itaque quid Domitius, quid Sypontinus, quid caeteri eruditi sentirent ipsemet et perquirebam, et ad praeceptorem meum Antonium scribebam . . . perquirebat Antonius non indoctus, non rerum ignarus, non ut ab aliis sciret quod ipse nesciret, sed ut ponderatis omnium sententiis quae esset optima iudicaret.* (*Octavii Cleophili Fanensis Oratio ad senatum Fanensem* in *Antonii Constantii Epigrammatum libellus* [Fano: Hier. Soncino, 1502]).

37. Lo Monaco (1992b, 858–59). *Hieronymi Avancii Veronensis . . . in Valerium Catullum et in Priapeas Emendationes . . .* (Venice: Giovanni Tacuino, 1495), fol. 5v: *Iisdem diebus Ciceronis ad Atticum epistolas non nobis minus quam Attico fuerant cognobiles reddebat, itidem commentaria in Silium Italicum, libros Fastorum Nasonis, politica Ciceronis officia, ac plaeraque alia praesertim fere absoluerat, praesertim inchoauerat.* See also J. Ramminger, "Calderini, Domizio," *Repertorium Pomponianum* (URL: www.repertoriumpomponianum.it/pomponiani/calderini.htm, accessed 22 July 2010).

38. See Lo Monaco's 1991 edition (hereafter Lo Monaco 1991).

39. This also has been published. See Lazzeri's 1971 edition.

40. Lo Monaco (1991, xii).

cannot be underestimated. Copies of Poliziano's notes were transcribed by his students,[41] and surely it is owing to Poliziano that Michele Verino held Ovid in such esteem; citing a possible versified *Fasti* commentary for inclusion among Poliziano's *Silvae*, Verino calls Ovid's *Fasti* "the fairest work of that divine poet" (*illius divini vatis liber pulcherrimus*).[42] Furthermore, Poliziano's influence can possibly be traced in the art of his contemporary Botticelli, who depicted a scene from the *Fasti* in the *Primavera*, the transformation of Chloris into the goddess of spring (*F.* 5.195–222).[43]

Poliziano was careful in the classical authors he selected for study and instruction, as he was anxious to impress the Medici as his career commenced.[44] Surely Poliziano was aware of Calderini's work on the *Fasti* in Rome,[45] and it is not hard to imagine his knowledge of the contemporary study of the *Fasti* within the Roman Academy as well, given his association with Pomponio Leto and their mutual interest in stone calendars.[46] During his 1482 trip to Venice, Marsi wanted to stop in Florence to visit Poliziano. He was prohibited from entering the city for fear that he was carrying a rumored contagion from Rome, and a versified appeal to Poliziano to intercede and help open the doors of Florence apparently met with either no response or no luck.[47] Even without direct association with Paolo Marsi, it is safe to assume that Poliziano wished to keep abreast of scholarly trends in Rome as he embarked on his own professorship in Florence.[48]

---

41. For instance, Poliziano's *Fasti* was preserved by Francesco Pucci, a student of Poliziano's, as in Oxford, Bodleian Library, Auct. P II 2. See Lo Monaco (1991, xvii).

42. F. O. Mencken, *Historia vitae Angeli Politiani* (1736), 609; quoted in Wind (1968, 114, fn. 5).

43. See Dempsey (1992, 30–33). On the other hand Hope and McGrath (1996, 177–78) firmly disavow humanist involvement in the *Primavera*. It might also be noted that at the 1998 annual meeting of the Renaissance Society of America in College Park, Maryland, Dempsey dated the *Primavera* to ca. 1478.

44. Martinelli (1978).

45. See the veiled reference at *F.* 1.20 and Lo Monaco's (1991) discussion on xxxv.

46. Leto sent a copy of the *Fasti Venusini* to Poliziano; see their 1488 correspondence in Poliziano's *epistolario*, I.15 and I.16. In 1487 Leto had also loaned a manuscript of Lucretius's *De Rerum Natura* to Poliziano (see Solaro's 1993 edition of *Lucrezio*, 23).

47. The verse letter to Poliziano is Florence, Biblioteca Medicea Laurenziana, XC sup. 37, fol. 133r (Pontari 2008, 743; recorded in della Torre 1903, 271–73). Poliziano made his first trip to Rome in December 1484 and no longer would have been able to meet Marsi, who had died in February of that year.

48. Is it possible that Poliziano was dissuaded by the Florentine elite from too much contact with the Roman humanists? Robert Black makes the case that there were scarcely any professional humanists in Florence until the end of the fifteenth century, because Florentine society, with its emphasis on mercantilism, had given preference to the pre-university abacus schools rather than Latin grammar schools. By the last decades of the fifteenth century, the Florentine upper class tried to distinguish itself from the bourgeois through private tutors and a Latin school education. See the preface to Black (2007).

> ita cecinit: Eſſe quoqʒ faus reminiſcif affore tēpus. Quo mare: quo tellus correptaqʒ regia cœli A tde
> at:& mūdi proles operoſa laboret. Seneca ēt in libro de cōſolatiōe ad Martiā idē ita refert:& quū tēpus
> aduenerit:quo ſe mūdus renouaturus extinguat:uiribus iſta ſe ſuis cedēt: & ſydera ſyderibus ieurrent
> & oī flagrāte materia uno igne quicquid nūc ex diſpoſito lucet ardebit:& Lucanus libro ſeptimo inquit
> Cōmūis mūdo ſupereſt rogus oſſibus aſtra Miſturus:& Auguſtinus libro.xx.de ciuitate dei ſcribit fi
> gurā huius mūdi cōflagratione periturā:ſicuti factū eſt aquaʀ iundatione diluuii. Nunc poſtea q̄ litte
> ris tuis reſpōdi:& tibi moregeſſi :ne ī imēſū creſcat epiſtola: dicēdi ſinē faciā. ſi te prius monuero:ut Ma
> gnifico patrono tuo Victori Minoto homini nobiliſſimo:& perpulchre docto me cōmendare nō deſi-
> nas. Vale Venetiis. Anno. Mccccxcvi. Calendis Aprilibus.
>   Domici Palladii Sorani tetraſtichon ad Antonium Cōſtātiū poetam illuſtrem.
>   Sulmo tumet naſone ſuo:uerona catullo.
>   Gloria romani magna tibulle laris.
>   Vmbria callimacho gaudet:cos ipſa philetha.
>   Lætentur patriæ mœnia clara tuæ.

FIGURE 3. *Ovidius de Fastis cum duobus commentariis* (Venice: Joannes Tacuinus de Tridino, 1497), fol. aIv. Inc 5447 (24.4), Houghton Library, Harvard University.

Poliziano's study of Ovid in Florence and the financial support of Marsi's commentary in Venice notwithstanding, the major *locus* and inspiration for Renaissance Italian *Fasti* studies does appear to have been Rome, and Pomponio Leto's Academy specifically. For that reason, even though Antonio Costanzi was not a Roman humanist, his commentary was very consciously associated with that of Paolo Marsi and the whole environment of the Academy by the time of the first composite edition of 1497. In this volume and its reprints, Merula's preface is followed by a four-line verse panegyric of Costanzi by Domizio Palladio of Sora (see figure 3). Palladio had recently come to Venice from Senigallia, where his sponsorship by Giovanni della Rovere—the duke of Sora and of Senigallia, Fano, and Ascoli Piceno—inevitably indicates his acquaintance and association with Costanzi.[49] However, earlier in 1480 Palladio had been a disciple of Leto in Rome; he dedicated impassioned verses to both Leto and the Roman Academy, and in 1484 he participated in one of the Academy's annual celebrations on the day of the city's founding.[50] Palladio's testimony in the 1497 composite edition connects Costanzi to Marsi, and it

---

49. Martini (1988, 238–39).

50. *Ad Pomponium Laetum excellentissimum* and *Ad Academiam* are both published in *Domici Palladii Sorani Epigrammaton libelli. Libellus elegiarum, Genethliacon Urbis Romae, In locutelium* (Paris: Georg Wolf and Thielmann Kerver for Jean Petit, ca. 1499). Palladio's participation in the celebration of Rome's birthday and the *Genethliacon* composed for the event are examined by Tournoy-Thoen (1972). For Palladio's discipleship under Leto and biography in general, see Martini (1979; 1969).

makes both commentators' affiliation with a peculiarly Roman environment explicit and outspoken.

TEACHING PARTICULARS

Three Vatican manuscripts provide a synoptic overview of the period of *Fasti* studies under discussion. Together, Vat. lat. 1595, Ottob. lat. 1982, and Vat. lat. 3263 reveal the timeframe when the *Fasti* was popular and the manner in which it was taught. Vat. lat. 1595 is a deluxe manuscript of Ovid's *opera omnia* datable to ca. 1450 and owned by Pope Pius II.[51] It has been instrumental in the recension of texts. La Penna, for example, notes its readings for the *Ibis* and claims the manuscript to be the best representative of a group that served as the source of the poem's 1471 *editio princeps*.[52] The manuscript contains corrections and variants, rubrics, and some glosses, mostly in the hand of Pietro Odi di Montopoli. An admired poet and a professor at the University of Rome since 1450, Pietro Odi was Pomponio Leto's teacher after Lorenzo Valla; such was his influence that Leto's grammatical exegesis is thought to reflect his style instead of the philosophical bent of Valla.[53] The text of the *Fasti* appears on fols. 254r–331v.

Ottob. lat. 1982 has been described as a kind of miscellany. It contains a variety of classical and humanistic texts in Latin and in Italian. Despite the assortment and fragments of texts, it is a unified whole, with selections made for a specific purpose in accordance with humanistic, pedagogical ideals. Names of Roman Academy members recur, whether as authors (Paolo Pompilio, for example: *Framea*, fol. 13ff; life and comments on Catullus, fol. 171ff; epitaph for Aesop, fol. 215v) or as addressees (in the letters on fols. 24r–50v, for example).[54] The manuscript clearly belongs to a Roman Academy and University setting. An epitaph for Andrea Brenta, who died at the beginning of 1484, and a watermark datable to 1485–95, suggest an *ante quem* of 1500 for the manuscript, and, in all likelihood, a date closer to 1485, not long after Brenta's death. Most of the humanist texts were therefore probably composed in Rome in the 1470s and 1480s.[55]

---

51. Description in Pellegrin III.1 (1991), 179–81; Buonocore (1995, 108).
52. Publi Ovidi Nasonis *Ibis,* ed. A. La Penna (Florence: La Nuova Italia, 1957), cxxx–cxxxvi; cited by R. J. Tarrant, "Ovid, *Ibis,*" in L. D. Reynolds (1983, 274, fn.8).
53. Accame (2008, 38). See furthermore Donati (2000, 50–65).
54. Bracke (1990, 27, 37).
55. Ibid., 38.

Comments on the *Fasti,* Book 1, appear on fols. 71v–73v under the title *Fastorum collecta ex me ipso,* although the author is unknown.

Vat. lat. 3263, described earlier, is the lengthiest version of the preserved notes by Pomponio Leto on the *Fasti.* By comparing a selection of comments on Book 1 from Vat. lat. 1595, Ottob. lat. 1982, and Vat. lat. 3263, we can better understand the teaching of the *Fasti* in the latter half of the fifteenth century (Appendix II). The first two manuscripts have more rubrics than comments. The rubrics and glosses correspond quite closely to the captions that Pomponio Leto uses in Vat. lat. 3263 to divide the text of the *Fasti,* text that is then surrounded by commentary. Clearly, the hierarchical division of a text made it easier for a teacher to organize his lecture and to focus students on the important issues. Leto's headings are a sort of summary of the *Fasti.* They reflect the contents of Ovid's poem; as signposts, they also suggest contemporary interest in and insights on the poem. The topics that are treated in the three manuscripts include Ovid's life and the recipient of the *Fasti,* the foundation dates of temples, the history of battles, Roman customs, astronomy, and etymology (the definition for *scorta,* harlots, is an example at 1.629 in Vat. lat. 1595).

The *Fasti,* of course, is regarded as a calendar, as the expression *Fastor[um] Lib[er]* on fol. 1r of Vat. lat. 3263 makes clear.[56] As a calendar, Ovid's *Fasti* contains both temporal (ceremonial) and astral information. We might note the discrepancy among *Fasti* lecturers in the attribution of dates, whether these be commemorative dates or the risings and settings of stars. The January 11 celebration in honor of the deities Carmenta and Juturna is recorded incorrectly as *iiii idus [Januarii]* in Vat. lat. 1595 and correctly as *tertio idus Januarii* in Ottob. lat. 1982 and *ante iii eid. [Januarii]* in Vat. lat. 3263. A miscalculation in the date of a star's rising or setting could throw off calendrical computations completely. The repercussions would then be felt in the reconstruction of chronological dates, as perhaps happened for the January 11 Juturnalia in Pietro Odi's note.

The sun passing through Aquarius on January 17 is quoted as *xv kalendas Februarias* in Vat. lat. 1595, *x kalendas* in Ottob. lat. 1982, and (in agreement with Ovid) *xvi kal[endas]* in Vat. lat. 3263.[57] Ovid records the

---

56. Vat. lat. 3264 (Leto's *Fasti* for Fabio Mazzatosta) contains a "kalendarium Ianuarius-Iunius" on fols. 86v–89v and "kalendarium Ianuarius-December" on fols. 90r–96v (Buonocore 1995, 112). The Ferrarese manuscript II.141, Leto's *Fasti* for Agostino Maffei, has a calendar on fols. 1r–6v. See also the calendar by Ciriaco d'Ancona—Antonio Costanzi's teacher—on fols. 67v–68v in Vat. lat. 10672 (ibid., 113).

57. The date (*xvi kalendas*) corresponds with Pliny, *NH* 18.235, although Columella places the setting a day earlier. See Bömer's 1957–58 edition of the *Fasti* (hereafter Bömer), II: 73.

evening setting of the Lyre as January 23 (*x kalendas Februarias*), which is emulated again in Leto's manuscript, Vat. lat. 3263, but cited as *ix kalendas Fe[bruarias]* in Vat. lat. 1595. In fact, the apparent evening setting of the constellation of the Lyre occurred on January 28, the true setting on February 9. At the root of all this confusion lies the fact that ordinary language did not distinguish between the apparent risings and settings of stars, based on empirical observation, and the true risings and settings of stars, determined by mathematical calculation. This is to say nothing of the distinction between a morning or evening rising or setting. It is unlikely that Ovid made his own astronomical calculations, and a contemporary reader would not have turned to him for information[58]—a point that may have been lost on medieval and Renaissance commentators.

For calendrical computations, humanists normally limited themselves to relevant remarks from literary sources such as Varro, Festus, Gellius, Macrobius, Solinus, and Plutarch, and they would have looked to previous generations of commentators as well. Anthony Grafton declares that Paolo Marsi and Antonio Costanzi floundered in the "difficult astronomical [points in the *Fasti*], confronted with which they closed their eyes and called for Macrobius."[59] Costanzi exhibits exactly this inclination in his comment on March 23 for the Tubilustrium, when the sun had already entered the sign of the Ram at the vernal equinox—a passage also of great interest and some discomfort for the *Bursarii* author, William of Orléans. The calendrical holiday preceding the Tubilustrium is the Quinquatrus, a feast day for Minerva on March 19 that popularly came to include the four days following as well, thus ending on the Tubilustrium. Ovid had given these details about the two holidays at lines 809–10 and 849–50. For Ovid, the horoscope of Aries at lines 851–52 was a chance to retell the myth of the golden-fleeced ram who tried to rescue Helle and Phrixus from their stepmother Ino, and nothing more. But it is in the horoscope that Costanzi gets mired. He works his way backwards and forwards from the sun's entrance into Pisces in February.[60] Like William

---

58. For astronomical phenomena Ovid could have picked from a variety of dates in his sources. But perhaps Ovid intentionally positioned the wandering stars in such a way as to link them with festivals and themes, being more concerned with literary allusions than with technical accuracy. Thus he could introduce Greek myths into the Roman calendar using aetiological stories of the constellations (see Robinson's 2011 edition [hereafter Robinson], 13, 16–17).

59. See Grafton's *Joseph Scaliger*, vol. 2 (1993), 45, 56.

60. *Si enim putares fieri posse ut penultimo Quinquatruum die ix calendas Apriles Sol in Arietem transitum faceret, quem supra legimus xiiii calendas Martias inisse Piscium signum, procul dubio fatereris solem quinque ac triginta dies fere in Piscibus absumpsisse, quod si esset solstitialis annus constaret diebus pene xx supra cccc cum et reliquis signis zodiaci nullum non tantumdem sibi temporis vendicaret.*

of Orléans, he attaches a date of March 20 to the spring equinox, in the end simply justifying "and so it must be said that on March 20 the sun passes over into the sign of the Ram, and this part of the zodiac relates to the sun's nature, as Macrobius writes" (*dicendum igitur est xiii calendas Aprilis solem transire in Arietis signum, quae pars zodiaci ad naturam solis refertur, ut Macrobius scribit*). Costanzi has dealt with a technical subject in a way "that had satisfied non-specialist commentators and reassured non-specialist readers since ancient times: define the hard words, argue about etymologies, and shut off discussion before some pertinacious student asks how to apply a given technique in practice."[61] It is no wonder, then, that the non-specialist Paolo Marsi put off a computation of the stars until 1479 with the disclaimer of even a passing knowledge of astronomy (*quo pacto nos humanitatis professores eam tenebimus quam ne unquam quidem delibavimus?*).[62]

While the attribution of dates posed a concern for the exegetes of Ovid's *Fasti*, festivals and rites themselves did not. The interest in ceremonies *per se* is abundantly clear in the humanist glosses. The consideration of ancient customs and their causes is likewise obvious. Pietro Odi flags Ovid's explanation of the sacrifice of birds (fol. 260v: *qua causa volucres mactantur*), and Pomponio Leto draws attention to the reason for the slaying of cows (Vat. lat. 3263, fol. 10v: *caussa mactati bovis*). The *Fasti* contained all kinds of lessons in Roman culture.

Indeed, the *Fasti*'s perceived cultural stockpile was considerable. The anonymous author in Ottob. lat. 1982 summarizes Ovid's information on offerings and aromatics sprinkled at the altars: "the ancients sacrificed with spelt and salt; soon frankincense, myrrh, costum, and saffron were obtained from Arabia and Cilicia," he writes for 1.337–42. He includes one aetiology: "myrrh drops are called 'weeping,' because they sweat from the tree bark" (fol. 72r: *Lacrimate mirre apellantur quod e cortice sudant*). The addendum restates Ovid's "myrrh, produced as tears from its bark" (*lacrimatas cortice murras*, 1.340), and its inclusion reveals the humanists' interest and belief in the *Fasti* as a guide for natural history. We might compare Leto's heading *de avibus* (Vat. lat. 3263, fol. 12v) with the reminiscent entry

---

61. Grafton, vol. 2 (1993), 40.
62. The Renaissance *Fasti* commentators generally conceded the subject of celestial phenomena to others. Even so, Ovid's work was envisioned as a source of astronomical wisdom and lore. Many humanists composed didactic poems on astronomy. These humanists often had a direct affiliation with the Roman Academy, as did Lorenzo Bonincontri, who wrote a *De rebus coelestibus*. Sometimes the writers were associated with the Roman Academy, such as Giovanni Pontano, who wrote a *Urania* praised by Ludovico Lazzarelli. See Soldati (1903) and de Nichilo (1975).

de corvo in the encyclopedic *De naturis rerum* by Alexander Neckam or *Speculum naturale* by Vincent of Beauvais.

For the humanists, as for the scholars of earlier generations, natural history was bound up with story and myth. Myrrh is sap from the myrrh tree; it oozes from the incision made in the tree's bark. Pliny the Elder had made reference to the process and described the tree as "sweating" (*sudant*).[63] Variations of *lacrimate* and *sudant* in Ottob. lat. 1982 also appear in the Myrrha episode in Ovid's *Metamorphoses,* in which Myrrha, having surrendered to her unnatural love for her father, was turned into a weeping tree that labored and cracked in delivery.[64] Ovid's fable was in the minds of humanists who annotated the *Fasti,* even as they plumbed it for natural history.[65]

For the fifteenth-century reader, the poem also contained mini-lessons in history. The *Fasti* glosses are often brief, descriptive lists of names and events; their sequence is not chronological but Ovidian. As a register, the glosses betray a desire for the systemization of the past—a starting point for *continuity* with the past. Beginning with Book 1, Pietro Odi and the anonymous writer in Ottob. lat. 1982 draw attention to the "Restoration of the Republic," when on January 13, 27 BC the Senate bestowed on Octavian the title "Augustus" and Octavian handed his provinces over to the people (1.589–90; fol. 263r and fol. 72v in the two manuscripts, respectively). Ovid continues his verses in Book 1 with allusions to famous *cognomina*; the humanist manuscript glosses explain not only who the individuals are, but also the victories for which they won their titles. The commentators give P. Cornelius Scipio the Elder, who overcame Hannibal at Zama in 202 BC, the nickname "Africanus" at 1.593.[66] Manuscripts Vat. lat. 1595 and Ottob. lat. 1982 both correctly ascribe the long battle and 69 BC victory against Crete to Q. Caecilius Metellus. Pietro Odi alludes to Gaius Marius's *cognomen* "Numidicus" for the triumph of Numidia in 109 BC and

---

63. *inciduntur bis et ipsae isdemque temporibus, sed a radice usque ad ramos qui valent. sudant autem sponte prius quam incidantur stacte dicta, cui nulla [murra] praefertur. NH* 12.35.

64. *gratulor huic terrae, quod abest regionibus illis / quae tantum genuere nefas: sit dives amomo / cinnamaque costumque suum sudataque ligno / tura ferat floresque alios Panchaia tellus, / dum ferat et murram: tanti nova non fuit arbor* [*Met.* 10.306–10]; *non tulit illa moram venientique obvia ligno / subsedit mersitque suos in cortice vultus / quae quamquam amisit veteres cum corpore sensus, flet tamen, et tepidae manant ex arbore guttae. / Est honor et lacrimis, stillataque cortice murra / nomen erile tenet nulloque tacebitur aevo* [10.497–502]; *nitenti tamen est similis curvataque crebros / dat gemitus arbor lacrimisque cadentibus umet* [10.609–11].

65. For the transmission of Ovid's fable, see Coulson (2008).

66. The victory over Nysauros in Ottob. lat. 1982 is left uncredited, due to a manuscript variant or misreading. Ovid's reference is to the defeat of the Isauri, a mountain tribe in Cilicia, by the general P. Servilius Vatia "Isauricus."

correctly attributes the *cognomen* "Numantinus" to Scipio Africanus minor (132 BC). While Pietro Odi is silent on Drusus, the student in Leto's circle specifies Germany as the origin of the name "Germanicus" for Tiberius's brother, who died on the field in AD 9. But Pietro Odi finishes the list of famous individuals, correctly citing T. Manlius as the winner of a collar and the name "Torquatus" in 367 or 361 BC; M. Valerius as the recipient of the *cognomen* "Corvus," after a crow that settled on his helmet during battle in 349 BC; "Magnus" as Pompey the Great; and the "Maximi" as the Fabii (Paullus Fabius Maximus and Q. Fabius Maximus Rullianus).[67] In manuscripts Vat. lat. 1595 and Ottob. lat. 1982 not every person is identified, and not every one correctly. The fact nevertheless remains that the *Fasti* was an inventory of history, and the events therein gave the humanist a fuller view of the Roman past.

THE DEDICATION OF THE *FASTI*

The fact that the *Fasti* contains a double dedication did not trouble the humanists; they seem to have understood that full well. The proemium to Book 2 functions as the original dedication to Augustus. Ovid moved it to the second book, writing a new proemium and dedication to Germanicus at the beginning of Book 1, after the death of the emperor.[68] Like their medieval predecessors, the humanists recognized that there was a complication in the compositional evolution of Ovid's work. After all, in his exilic elegy Ermold Nigellus had incorporated allusions from *both* the revised proemium to Germanicus and the original proemium to Augustus.[69] If Paolo Marsi is our example, the humanists recognized both the panegyrics to Augustus and Ovid's appeal to a new imperial protector after AD 14.

Why would the dedication of a work matter to the humanists? Perhaps the answer lies in the fact that they themselves needed patronage, which once obtained was not always secure. Just like the poets from earlier centuries, the humanists could be subject to political whims and circumstances, vagaries that dictated a search for a new Maecenas.[70] Ovid's chal-

---

67. The "glossary" of names is found in Bömer II: 67–68.

68. Braun (1981: 2346–52), on the other hand, argues that the proemium to Book 2 is in its (original) position for the sake of compositional balance. For the topic of the *Fasti*'s dedications see especially Fantham (1985, 243–81); also Robinson, 51–54.

69. Santini's statement (1995, 162–63) that except for Ermold Nigellus the issue of a double dedication was not realized before 1727, and had gone unnoticed by Marsi, is unfounded.

70. See the example of Ludovico Lazzarelli in Fritsen (2001). For literary patronage as discourse with ancient literary patronage, see de Beer (2013).

lenge of finding the best recipient for the *Fasti* would have been a subject of intrigue and interest, and it would have struck a personal chord with the *Fasti* commentators.

Delving into the matter of the two dedications, Marsi writes:

> People claim that these books of the *Fasti* were written under the principate of Augustus, and I allow that writing to Augustus in the first year of his exile, [Ovid] says that he had composed twelve books. . . . This must be believed and maintained, that these were written at Rome for the most part, but that the first six books (the only ones published) were revised in Pontus, and that while [Ovid] was revising, he took away and he added many things. He did not change what he had written about Augustus while the emperor was alive, [but] he added what seemed to relate to praise of Germanicus.

> *Asserunt hos Fastorum libros sub Augusto principe scriptos, et ego fateor primo enim anno exilii ad Augustum scribens dicit se xii libros Fastorum scripsisse. . . . hoc credendum et asserendum est, scriptos fuisse Romae magna ex parte, sed in Ponto emendatos sex priores libros tantum editos dumque emendaret multa sustulisse multaque addidisse. Quae de Augusto vivente scripserat non immutavit . . . addebat quae ad laudem Germanici pertinere videbantur.*

Marsi argues that Germanicus was the final patron whom Ovid invoked. In the *accessus* to his commentary, Marsi furthermore declares that Ovid "dedicated [his] work not to Tiberius Augustus, as many claim, but to Germanicus, the son of Drusus, brother of Tiberius, that Drusus, who died in Germany" (*dicavitque hoc opus non Tiberio Augusto ut multi afferunt, sed Germanico Drusi fratris Tiberii filio, illius Drusi, qui in Germania oppetiit*).

The root of the debate (*ut multi afferunt*) is whether Ovid finally chose Tiberius or Germanicus to receive the *Fasti*.[71] The dispute was due to a confusion and conflation of the persons' identities. The first six books of Tacitus's *Annales,* which contained the narrative of events from the death of

---

71. Tiberius was adopted by Augustus in AD 4, and Ovid honored Tiberius at *F.* 1.533, 615–16, 645–50, and 707. Consensus has it that Germanicus, whom Augustus made Tiberius adopt, is the intended recipient of the revised *Fasti*. Ovid and the prince shared common literary ground, since Germanicus may have composed an astronomical *Phaenomena* and was therefore a skilled fellow poet (see Fantham 1985, 387–91; for a note of caution about shared literary talent see Green, 147–48). In any event, there is no doubt as to the bid for the approval of Germanicus, "who was becoming [an] increasingly successful" heir to Augustus and could potentially secure Ovid's recall from Tomis (Green 15–17, 31–44; quotation at 17).

Augustus to that of Tiberius, would have helped solve the mystery, but this portion of the *Annales* was not available until its 1508 discovery and subsequent 1515 publication in Rome.[72] Therefore, controversy swirled around names and mistaken identities in the *quattrocento*. At one time, Pomponio Leto glossed the *Fasti*'s opening invocation "Germanicus Caesar, receive this work with tranquil countenance" (*excipe pacato, Caesar Germanice, vultu / hoc opus; F.* 1.3–4) as "Germanicus Tiberius who conquered Germany" (*Germanicus Tiberius qui Germaniam vicit*; Vat. lat. 3264, fol. 1r); much later in his career, he glossed the same line "Germanicus, son of Drusus, adopted by Tiberius by order of Augustus" (*Germanicus, Drusi filius, adoptatus a Tiberio iubente Augusto*; Vat. lat. 3263, fol. 1r). Here is a small sampling of humanists who make a claim about the *Fasti*'s dedication, with their commentaries given in chronological order:

Tiberius
Ciriaco d'Ancona
>Teacher of Antonio Costanzi
>Vatican City, BAV, Vat. lat. 10672

Pomponio Leto
>Vatican City, BAV, Vat. lat. 3264

Anonymous student of Leto
>Vatican City, BAV, Ottob. lat. 1982

Antonio Volsco, student of Leto
>Rome, Biblioteca Vallicelliana, R. 59

Germanicus
Pietro Odi di Montopoli
>Teacher of Pomponio Leto
>Vatican City, BAV, Vat. lat. 1595

Guarino da Verona
>Testimony of Antonio Costanzi

---

72. R. J. Tarrant, "Tacitus. *Annales,* 1–6" in L. D. Reynolds (1983, 406–7).

Antonio Costanzi
    Vatican City, BAV, Chig. H. VI. (ca. 1470);
    1489 *Fasti* commentary

Paolo Marsi
    Student of Pomponio Leto
    1482 *Fasti* commentary

Pomponio Leto
    Vatican City, BAV, Vat. lat. 3263

Antonio Costanzi argued his side in a long letter to his friend Giovanni Battista Almadiano of Viterbo. The letter, dated Fano, November 12, 1471 (*Fani pridie id. Novembris MCCCCLXXI*), appears in a posthumous collection of his poetic and prose works, the *Epigrammatum libellus*.[73] In the *argumentum* of his 1489 printed *Fasti* commentary, Costanzi summarizes in a few sentences the content of the letter, stating that "when Naso was exiled to Pontus and had added and changed many things, he dedicated this work not to Tiberius, as I will explain, but to Germanicus, the son of Drusus, [who was] the stepson of Augustus (*Naso relegatus in Pontum plerisque additis ac mutatis inscripsit hoc opus non Tiberio, ut docebimus, sed Germanico Drusi privigni Augusti filio*). The issue of the *Fasti*'s dedication obviously consumed Costanzi for quite some time, for the letter to Almadiano appears in its entirety in Chig. H.VI.204 (fols. 76v–77v), where otherwise the glosses are either minor or few. A sardonic epigram appears at the end:[74]

Germanicus, if Naso could speak [his mind] to Tiberius,
    he didn't want to have written the *Fasti* for an undeserving Nero.
With that label removed, why was he so brief?
    The son has the rewards of the title which he deserved.

Dicere si potuit Tiberio Germanice Naso
    noluit immerito fastos scripsisse Neroni.
Nomine cur dempto tam brevis ille fuit?
    Natus habet tituli munera qui meruit.

---

73. Fano: Hieronymus Soncino, 1502.
74. Here on folio 77v, Costanzi has left his signature (*Ant. Const. phanensis*) and signed the date *phani die xii november 1471*.

In epigrammatic style, Costanzi plays with the words *immerito* and *meruit*. *Titulus* is also a pun. Germanicus, Tiberius' adopted son, has received both the title of the book, that is to say the *Fasti* itself, and a title of honor. His name Germanicus was inherited from his real father Nero Drusus, who was awarded the name posthumously for his successful campaigns against the Germans (an appellation not similarly granted to Tiberius).

In his letter Costanzi is more reserved, offering rational advice to Almadiano. He begins by apologizing for not responding sooner to the inquiry about his adamant position on the *Fasti*'s dedicatee:

> It had not slipped my mind what I had promised you the previous summer in Rome, that I would write as soon as possible why I think Ovid's *Fasti* was written to Germanicus, the son of Drusus Germanicus, and not to Tiberius Nero. But both private and public affairs which envelop me everywhere had the effect of not being able to fulfill my promise until today.
>
> *Non exciderat a memoria quod aestate proxima Romae tibi pollicitus fueram, scripturum me quam primum cur Ovidii Fastos ad Germanicum Drusi Germanici filium, non ad Tiberium Neronem scriptos existimarem. Sed et privata et publica negocia quae me undique circumsaepiunt, effecere ut in hunc usque diem promissum implere distulerim.*

It is possible that Costanzi is talking about his trip to Rome as Fano's ambassador to the College of Cardinals upon the death of Pope Paul II on July 26, 1471. Costanzi spent several months in curial circles, and on September 1 he was joined by two other prominent orators to congratulate the newly elected Sixtus IV.[75] Writing to Almadiano in early November, Costanzi did not put off his promise as long as he makes it seem.

The argument of Costanzi's letter can be outlined as follows: *A*.) In reading Ovid's letters from exile and the *Fasti,* many people have confused the identities of Tiberius and Germanicus.[76] *B*.) Ovid revised the *Fasti*

---

75. Castaldi (1916, 287–88). Cf. Costanzi's remark in the *Fasti* (*cum ad urbem me contulissem orator missus a senatu Fanensi ad Sixtum Quartum Pontificem Maximum*) with communal records from August 23, 1471, noting that *omnes . . . comendaverunt solertiam et diligentiam oratoris predicti* (ibid., 288, fn. 2).

76. In fact, note the incipits of two fifteenth-century *Fasti* manuscripts: *Germanicum plerique Tiberium intelligunt* (Milan, Biblioteca Ambrosiana, C 140 inf., fol. 51v, and San Daniele del Friuli, Biblioteca civica Guarneriana, 90); *Ovidius scribit hoc opus ad Tiberium Caesarem Germanicum a Germania devicta in qua periit cognominatus* (Vatican City, BAV, Vat. lat. 1603, fols. 1r–2v). The manuscripts are no. 123 and no. 328 in Coulson and Roy (2000).

in exile and, aware of the political circumstances, sought Germanicus's patronage after Augustus's death. *C.*) For this reason Ovid directs his words to Germanicus, addressing his military victories. *D.*) Only once does Ovid address Tiberius. One instance does not mean the whole poem is dedicated to him. *E.*) Notice Ovid's titles and terms for members of Augustus's family. Everywhere, Ovid makes reference to Germanicus. A correct understanding of family history will demonstrate that Ovid wrote the *Fasti* not for Tiberius, the son of Augustus, but for Germanicus, the grandson of Augustus.

Costanzi credits his teacher Guarino da Verona with explaining beyond a doubt that the *Fasti* was written for Germanicus rather than Tiberius (*accipe . . . quam recte celeberrimus vir Guarinus Veronensis ceterique illum sequentes sine ulla dubitatione docuerint Fastos inscriptos esse Germanico, non Tiberio*), and continues:

> Very many have read those letters the *Tristia* and *ex Ponto*, nearly all of which, we know, Ovid wrote after he had been exiled to Pontus, while Augustus was still alive, but a few immediately after the emperor's death. In these letters, because Ovid made mention of Germanicus's triumph and one time beseeched Tiberius to take revenge for the death of his brother Drusus, that "thus in the near future as the purple-clad avenger of [his] brother's death he would drive snow-white steeds" and because he often inserted the name of Germanicus in his verses, people have been deceived, thinking that Tiberius was called Germanicus by Ovid.

> *Legerunt plerique epistolas illas Tristium ac de Ponto, quas Ovidium scripsisse constat postea quam est relegatus in Pontum omnes fere vivente Augusto, paucas statim post eius interitum. In his cum Ovidius Germanici triumphi fecerit mentionem [E. P. 2.1] et aliquando precatus fuerit ut Tiberius fraternam in Drusi mortem ulcisceretur ut "sic tibi mature fraterni funeris ultor / purpureus niveis filius instet equis" [E. P. 2.8.49–50], cumque Germanici nomen saepenumero suis versibus inseruerit, decepti sunt, existimantes Tiberium a Nasone Germanicum appellari.*

In other words, many believed that Tiberius was meant each time Germanicus was mentioned; Tiberius was but another name for Germanicus. The episode from history to which Costanzi refers in *E. P.* 2.1 is the triumph decreed to Tiberius in AD 9 for his victory over the Illyrians. It was finally held on October 23, AD 12, when Germanicus shared the triumphal insignia and rode in the procession with Tiberius. In the intervening time,

Tiberius had subdued the German rebels who had killed Varus and his three legions. Ovid's letter from exile *is,* however, addressed to Germanicus (*Germanice,* l. 49); he promises to praise a future triumph of Germanicus in verse (ll. 57–68; *Hunc quoque carminibus referam fortasse triumphum, / sufficiet nostris si modo uita malis,* ll. 63–64, especially).[77] Apparently, this was enough to mislead readers into thinking that by Germanicus, Ovid meant Tiberius. Their belief was bolstered by *E. P.* 2.8, which contains an appeal to Tiberius (ll. 37–42) and an expression of hope for his triumphant victory over Germany (*sic fera quam primum pavido Germania vultu / ante triumphantis serva feratur equos,* 2.8.39–40). Ovid alludes to the death of Nero Drusus, killed in Germany by a fall from his horse, and in this context anticipates that Tiberius will receive due honors for justice done to his dead brother: that "thus in the near future the purple-clad avenger of [his] brother's death might drive snow-white steeds" (*sic tibi mature fraterni funeris ultor / purpureus niveis filius instet equis, E. P.* 2.8.49–50).

The collapsing of identities explained, Costanzi details in his letter that the *Fasti* itself contains confirmation of its dedication to Tiberius for those who have misread:

> Besides, they have read those verses in the first book of the *Fasti* "a new reason is better: Germany has marked her disheveled hair / for your command, estimable general. / And so you offered up the spoils of the nation that ordained a triumph / and built a temple for the goddess whom you yourself honor. / Your mother supported this with actions and an altar." In these verses the error not only of those less knowledgeable but also of the most learned men has been reinforced.

> *Legerunt praeterea versus illos in primo Fastorum "causa recens melior: sparsos Germania crines / corrigit auspiciis, dux venerande, tuis. / Inde triumphatae libasti munera gentis / templaque fecisti, quam colis ipse, deae. / Haec tua constituit genetrix et rebus et ara" [F. 1.645–49]. Quibus versibus non solum eorum qui pauca viderunt, verum et eruditissimorum virorum error confirmatus est.*

Here Costanzi is referring to Tiberius's dedication of a temple to Augustan Concord on January 16, AD 10. Tiberius had already vowed to rebuild this temple in 7 BC in the joint names of his deceased brother Nero Drusus and

---

77. The predicted triumph of Germanicus may be the one recorded in *Fasti* 1.285–86; see Green, 131.

himself, using the spoils of the German wars for which he was about to celebrate a triumph (Dio Cassius, 55.8.2). The pledge coincides with the joint dedication with his mother of a shrine to Concord in the Porticus Liviae, also in 7 BC. The *dux venerande* in line 646 most certainly then refers to Tiberius recently returned from the German field, a point to which we shall return shortly.[78]

Costanzi states that many have misinterpreted Ovid's verses regarding the temple of Concord (*F.* 1.645–49). Indeed this is so. The student of the *Fasti* in Ottob. lat. 1982 cites Suetonius (*Tiberius* 20) for extra evidence that Tiberius rebuilt the Temple of Concord with the spoils of his German campaign and dedicated it to his name and that of his dead brother Drusus.[79] The oddity, however, is the point of emphasis: "[this] proves that this work of Ovid's was written for Tiberius" (fol. 73r: *quod probat ho[c] opus Ovidii ad Tiberium scribi*).

Costanzi next reminds Almadiano that Ovid did not write the *Fasti* from exile but rather revised it there. He sought a new protector, someone to press his case now that Augustus had sent him to Pontus:

> And so driven into exile, Ovid changed his mind and dedicated the *Fasti* to Germanicus, hoping it would happen that his work at some point in time would result in a more lenient place of exile or a pardon to return. For indeed, Germanicus was not impious and cruel, as it is agreed Tiberius was, but so mild and harmless, according to Suetonius, that Augustus had nearly decided to make him his successor, impressed by his virtues.

> *pulsus itaque in exilium Naso mutavit sententiam eosque inscripsit Germanico, sperans fore ut aliquando eius opera vel clementiorem locum exilii consequeretur vel veniam redeundi. Fuit enim Germanicus non impius et crudelis, qualem constat fuisse Tiberium, sed adeo lenis atque innoxius teste Suetonio [Cal. 3.3],*[80] *ut eius virtutibus motus Augustus fere statuerit eum sibi facere successorem.*

Here too he cites as evidence of revision from exile Ovid's complaint of homesickness to Germanicus at *F.* 4.82.[81]

---

78. Fantham (1985, 262–63). Tiberius celebrated a triumph over the German tribes west of the Elbe on January 1, 7 BC. For a history of the temples to Concord and a different interpretation of the shrine in the Porticus Liviae, see Green, 290–93 and 297–98.

79. Suetonius erroneously gives the year as AD 12.

80. *lenius adeo et innoxius,* Suet. *Cal.* 3.3.

81. *ut igitur scripti sunt Fasti ante relegationem autoris ita nunquam editi nisi vel cum Ovidius exularet in Ponto vel forte post eius interitum additis prius ab eodem autore nonnullis carminibus et*

The point of revision in the name of Germanicus made, Costanzi returns to his discussion of military triumphs.

> Since these things are so, and Ovid mentions a victory each in the *Fasti*, namely "There was peace, Germanicus, and the Rhine, the reason for your triumph, had already surrendered its waters to serve you" and "Germany offers her hair unbound," and once directs his words to Tiberius (just as he often addresses Augustus and even more often Germanicus; this is a habit most used by both poets and orators), many have strayed into error thinking that the *Fasti* was dedicated to Tiberius, and how true this is can easily be judged from this, that when he directs his words to Tiberius he does not call him Germanicus, but says "under your auspices, venerated leader, Germany offers her hair unbound."

> *Quae cum ita sint, et Ovidius in Fastis utriusque victoriae faciat mentionem ut "pax erat et vestri Germanice causa triumphi / tradiderat gelidas iam tibi Rhenus aquas" [1.285–86] et "sparsos Germania crines corrigit" [1.645–46] semelque ad Tiberium suum vertat sermonem (sicuti et saepe ad Augustum et ad Germanicum saepius: qui mos et poetarum et oratorum est usitatissimus), multi in errorem inciderunt Fastorum opus Tiberio inscriptum existimantes, quod quam verum sit vel hinc facile iudicari potest, quod ubi ad Tiberium vertit sermonem eum Germanicum non appellat, sed ait "sparsos Germania crines corrigit auspiciis dux venerande tuis."*

There seems to be no doubt in the minds of Costanzi and others that the *dux venerande* (F. 1.646), "venerated leader," represented anyone but Tiberius. The *dux* was not named by Ovid, however, and presumably readers made their identification by working their way backwards, since Germanicus was not addressed directly here as in so many other examples. The error in reasoning was then converting every occurrence of the name Germanicus to Tiberius, that is, considering them one and the same person. Costanzi's quarrel on this point is not his invention; several surviving humanist glosses on "there was peace, Germanicus, and the Rhine, the reason for your triumph, had already surrendered its waters to serve you" (*pax erat et vestri Germanice causa triumphi / tradiderat gelidas iam tibi Rhenus aquas*, F. 1.285–86) bear him out. The Antonio Volsco manuscript has the gloss <u>*O Germanice*</u>: *O Tiberi* (fol. 5r; on fol. 5v he continues:

---

mutatis ut libuit, quod hi versus testantur: "Sulmonis gelidi patriae Germanice nostrae, / me miserum Scythico quam procul ille solo est. / Ergo age tam longas iam supprime musa querelas" . . . .

Tiberius Bellum Germanicum gessit), and in the margin of the Ferrarese ms. II.141, Pomponio Leto writes: *Triumphaverat de Germania Tiberius* (fol. 11v).[82] Costanzi's point is that if Ovid turns to Tiberius once, this does not mean that the whole *Fasti* is dedicated to Tiberius, nor that each time Germanicus is mentioned, Tiberius should be read in his stead. It is the same complaint Costanzi made about erroneous interpretation of the *Epistulae ex Ponto*.

Costanzi then enumerates instances where Ovid addresses Germanicus, and explains how in doing so, Ovid hints at and tries to create a bond with Germanicus. He refers again to Ovid's exilic poetry, *E. P.* 4.8, a letter to Suillus Rufus, a member of Germanicus's staff:

> ... read, I ask you, that letter which Ovid wrote to Suillus after the death of Augustus, where he promised to place all his talent at the disposition of Germanicus, Germanicus I say, not Tiberius, and he called Germanicus a poet just like he did in the *Fasti*, as in: "but now, Caesar, in some measure your verses have sanctified your grandfather, / whose virtue added him to the stars. / If any life still resides in my talent, Germanicus, / all of it will serve you. / You as poet cannot spurn the tribute of a poet, / for that has value in your judgment."

> ... *lege, quaeso, eam epistolam quam post mortem Augusti Ovidius scripsit ad Suillum, ubi Germanico, Germanico inquam, non Tiberio pollicetur omne suum ingenium serviturum et Germanicum vatem appellat quemadmodum et in Fastis, ut "et modo, Caesar, avum quem virtus addidit astris, / sacrarunt*

---

82. The triumph reported in *Fasti* 1.285–86 took place on May 26, AD 17. Already in AD 15, Tiberius had accelerated a decree of triumph for Germanicus, in order to recall him from the front between the Rhine and the Elbe. Fantham (1985, 250) and Green, 131, claim that Ovid anticipates Germanicus's triumph but did not live to record its actual celebration in May, AD 17. This may explain Leto's slightly different gloss on *vestri causa triumphi* in Vat. lat. 3263: *non Germanici per Germanicum, sed familie suae, nisi ii versus post fuerint additi* (fol. 3v)—the triumph does not apply to Germanicus, but to his family (*vestri* vs. *tui;* cf. Green, 131)—unless these two verses were added after Ovid's death! Paolo Marsi had yet a different take. At *F.* 1.285 in his 1482 commentary he declares that Ovid was still alive for Germanicus's triumph, asserting, "listen closely now, for I have said what you least expect" (*Arrigite nunc aures, nam id dixi quod minime expectabatis*). Going over evidence from Ovid, *E. P.* 4.13.45–46; Suetonius, *Cal.* 1.1; Strabo 7.1.4; and Eusebius (perhaps in confusion with Jerome, *Chronicon* Abr. 2033), he sums up: "from these things which I have said it may now at last be agreed upon that Germanicus triumphed while Ovid was still living" (*Ex his igitur quae diximus iam tandem constet Germanicum Ovidio adhuc vivente triumphasse*). The author of the article on Ovid in Pauly's RE 18.2 (1949), col. 1920, believes that Ovid was at least still alive on October 17, AD 17, because at *F.* 1.233ff. he refers to the dedication of the renovated temple of Janus "ad theatrum Marcelli" which occurred on that date.

aliqua carmina parte tuum. / Siquid adhuc ergo vivi, Germanice, nostro / restat in ingenio, serviet omne tibi. / Non potes officium vatis contemnere vates, / iudicio pretium res habet ista tuo" [E. P. 4.8.63–68].

Ovid suggests such is the talent of Germanicus that, as author of a *Phaenomena*, he has even honored his deified grandfather in the heavens above. The Latin *vates* connotes prophetic inspiration, appropriately enough. At the same time that he flatters Germanicus, Ovid also uses the term *vates* for himself. Costanzi draws a comparison to the *Fasti*, alluding to 1.25: "if it is lawful and right, as a bard yourself control a bard's reins" (*si licet et fas est, vates rege vatis habenas*), and earlier, 1.19–20: "ready to undergo the judgment of a learned prince, my page shakes as if dispatched for the god of Claros to read" (*pagina iudicium docti subitura movetur / principis, ut Clario missa legenda deo*).[83] Costanzi emphasizes Ovid's argument of the poetic ties which bind him to Germanicus and offers this as more proof of his directing his literary output to Germanicus.

From there, Costanzi clears up questions of genealogy. He clarifies Ovid's "Caesar, in some measure your verses have sanctified your grandfather" as follows:

> But here someone might object that "grandfather" refers to Julius Caesar, and where (Ovid) says "Caesar Germanicus," it is not Germanicus the son of Drusus, but Tiberius who must be understood. Someone so objecting errs completely. In fact, Ovid says that the grandfather is Augustus, not Julius Caesar, and Germanicus, not Tiberius, is the son of Drusus.
>
> *sed hic mihi quispiam forte obiecerit avum dici Iulium Caesarem, et ubi ait Caesar Germanice, non Germanicum Drusi filium accipiendum esse sed Tiberium. Errat tota via siquis ita obiicit. Avum enim Augustum non Iulium Caesarem et Germanicum Drusi filium non Tiberium dicit.*

Costanzi is of course right to connect the vocatives *Caesar* and *Germanice*, which then leaves Augustus as the correct interpretation of *avus*. Costanzi also connects *E. P.* 4.8 with *E. P.* 4.6 and 4.9:

---

83. In Vat. lat. 3264 from earlier in his career, Leto takes the "learned prince" at 1.19–20 to refer to Tiberius (fol. 1r: *Cornelius Tacitus libro xiii ait "Tiberius artem quoque callebat qua verba expendere* [sic] *tum validus sensibus aut consulto ambiguus"* [Ann. 13.3]. *Valuit Tiberius aut poetice.*) However, at the same passage in Vat. lat. 3263 dating from the latter part of his career, Leto identifies the prince as Germanicus (fol. 1v: *Suetonius Tranquillus in Vita Caesarum* [Cal. 3.1; 3.2] *de Germanico: "ingenium in utroque eloquentiae doctrineque genere praecellens" et pene statim: "oravit causas etiam triumphales; atque inter cetera studiorum monimenta reliquit etiam comedias Grecas"*).

For in the letter which comes a bit earlier and which Ovid writes to Brutus, these are his words: "Augustus had begun to pardon the misinformed mistake; / he left in abandonment my hopes and world together. / Still, such poem about the recent deified as I could send / from my distant abode, I sent for your reading." Likewise, in the letter to Graecinus (he writes): "Perhaps those poems which I wrote about you, a newly made god, and sent, will reach you even there." Therefore the grandfather is Augustus, and Germanicus, son of Drusus, is Augustus' grandson, not Tiberius.

Nam in epistola paulo ante precedenti quam Ovidius scribit ad Brutum, verba haec sunt: "ceperat Augustus deceptae ignoscere culpae; / spem nostram terras deseruitque simul. / Quale tamen potui de caelite, Brute, recenti / vestra procul positis carmen in ora dedi" [E. P. 4.6.15–18]. Item in epistola ad Grecinum: "pervenient illuc et carmina forsitan illa, / quae de te misi caelite facta novo" [E. P. 4.9.131–32]. Avus ergo Augustus est, et Germanicus, Drusi filius, Augusti nepos est, non Tiberius.

For evidence of a poem Ovid may have written upon the death and apotheosis of Augustus—none is extant—Costanzi refers to more outspoken Ovidian testimony in letters 4.6 and 4.9. The circle of personal identifications complete, Costanzi proclaims nothing is more obvious (*Quid hoc apertius, quid manifestius est*), and "always and everywhere that Ovid says Germanicus, he means the one whom I think, and not even once in all of his works does he describe Tiberius using the name Germanicus" (*qui semper ubicumque Germanicum dicit illum significat quem ego sentio et ne semel quidem in omnibus suis operibus Germanici nomine Tiberium exprimit*).

Costanzi even adds one final quote of proof from the *Fasti* (1.589–90) as a postscript to his letter, since it comes after the subscription. Yet the very polite Almadiano was not convinced. In his reply, dated Fano, February 28, 1472 (*Fani pridie kalendas Martias MCCCCLXXII*, published likewise in the 1502 *Epigrammatum libellus*), he claims to base his opinion on logic and *auctoritas* (*Hoc enim assidue me praestiturum polliceor, ne minimum quidem verbum prolaturum quod non aut ab evidenti ratione aut a veterum auctoritate proficiscatur*). His refutation is brief and, once under way, to the point. Almadiano observes that "indeed, throughout these demonstrations Ovid does not seem to have written to Germanicus son of Drusus at all, but to Tiberius Caesar Germanicus, for truly, nowhere do I find that Germanicus, Drusus's son, ever founded or dedicated any temples" (*Videtur enim*

Ovidius his demonstratibus nullo pacto ad Germanicum Drusi filium verum ad Tiberium Caesarem Germanicum inscripsisse, etenim Germanicum Drusi nulla unquam templa condidisse et dedicasse comperimus). Of course, this reflects a common current of thought that we have already seen, apparent in the notes to the first book of the *Fasti* by a student in Leto's circle, claiming the dedication of a temple, especially *Tiberius*'s dedication of a temple, as proof of Ovid's affiliation with Tiberius (on the temple of Augustan Concord, January 16, AD 10: *quod probat ho[c] opus Ovidii ad Tiberium scribi;* Ottob. lat. 1982, fol. 73r). Moreover, Almadiano has just done what Costanzi had so cautioned against: he has created one person out of two (*Tiberius Caesar Germanicus*). Truly, in the late fifteenth century, controversy swirled over the *Fasti*'s dedicatee. The heat of the debate is obvious in Paolo Marsi's commentary, where he says that even in the classroom he was assailed by his own students for rejecting accepted opinion.[84] It is precisely in the classroom and as commentators that both Paolo Marsi and Antonio Costanzi were trying to make a mark.

---

84. At *F.* 1.285: *Sed longius quam fuerit nostrum institum progressi sumus. Coacti quidem fecimus ad reprimendos eorum obstinatos animos, qui dum haec profitemur, maledictis assidue nos incessunt, quoniam ab eorum sententiis abhorrere videar cum a veritate abstrahere me non possint.*

CHAPTER THREE

Commentary and Professional Identity

AN INVITATION TO COMMENT

Chapters 1 and 2 have already indicated how easily Ovid's *Fasti* lent itself to comments. As a composition on the calendar, Ovid's poem is itself a commentary. Ovid used as one of his sources Verrius Flaccus, the Augustan scholar behind the *Fasti Praenestini* and a (lost) monograph on the calendar. Ovid frankly acknowledges his debt to calendars and to Verrius Flaccus. He consults a calendar for the first time at *F.* 1.289–90, when he declares "something I've been allowed to discover from [it]—on this day the Fathers dedicated two temples" (*quod tamen ex ipsis licuit mihi discere fastis, / sacravere patres hac duo templa die*). The temples are to Aesculapius and Ve(d)iovis, consecrated in 290 BC and 194 BC, respectively. Both the *Fasti Antiates Maiores* and *Fasti Praenestini* mention the two temples under January 1. However, the Verrian *Fasti Praenestini* is the likeliest source for Ovid, given its inscription *(fastus Aescu)lapio Vediovi in Insula* and Ovid's notice of the dual temple location on the Tiber Island (*insula, dividua quam premit amnis aqua, F.* 1.292).[1] The enjambment of *insula* (line 292) and the linguistic emphases on the neighboring, analogous monuments suggest that "Verrius' four-word notice sparks a rich Ovidian

---

1. Green, 133; for the inscription, see Degrassi (1963, 2).

meditation, albeit [brief], on the shrines and their divine inhabitants."[2] Verrius Flaccus is not just a source, but an intertext.

By the time that Ovid was writing, the calendar had become increasingly unintelligible with its mass of accretions, and the stone *fasti* set up at Praeneste was more an ornament to the power of its sponsor, Augustus, than a tool of instruction. Verrius Flaccus was a prominent antiquarian known for his treatise *De verborum significatu,* which not only explored obsolete terms, but also digressed on ancient Rome in general. He was a learned specialist, just the sort whom Augustus liked to cultivate as part of his influential circle, displacing the traditional aristocracy in what has been called a "cultural revolution."[3] The Roman calendar subsequently became an object for the initiated and elite. To the ordinary observer, it would seem mystifying.

The connections between the calendar and the commentary are again striking. Not only is the calendar a model for the commentary, but it can also be considered the text in need of elucidation, the primary text whose secrets are asking to be unlocked. It thus begs for an antiquarian researcher. Note by way of definition that the text that requires a commentary "is always an authority" (and the Augustan control over time had certainly made the calendar an authority). Furthermore, "the authority in question is not self-explanatory: the traces in which its wisdom is lodged are ambiguous, scanty, lacunose, difficult. . . . If the authority could explain itself, it would presumably not require that a commentator come along to do so for it."[4] It is little wonder, then, that the *Fasti* by Ovid invited commentary in the Renaissance.

Ovid's calendrical poem became the perfect text for the Renaissance commentator to investigate for its arcane wisdom. Furthermore, just as the calendar retained its aristocratic distinction, so too did the poem find favor among the elite. And so the history and content of both were revealed to young men and boys with social status. Macrobius in the fourth century had written the *Saturnalia* to benefit his son, recounting for him the antiquarian discussions that had taken place at the house of an upper-class Roman. In addressing his son, Macrobius indicated that knowledge of the calendar was necessary in order to be highly educated. In a similar vein, in 1480 Antonio Costanzi hoped that his patron the Duke of Urbino would pass on the *Fasti* commentary to his son Guido-

---

2. Miller (2002, 172–74).
3. Wallace-Hadrill (1997, 16–18).
4. Most (1999, viii).

baldo to read.⁵ The *quattrocento Fasti* commentaries were destined as gifts for private individuals; but they were also the lecture notes of professors. The poem was regarded as an essential component of the humanist curriculum, as specified in the 1459 educational treatise by Battista Guarino—son of Guarino da Verona, Antonio Costanzi's teacher. He writes that in addition to the *Metamorphoses,* students

> should at least have the *Fasti* at their disposal, in which certain lesser-known myths and histories and an account of the calendar are treated in considerable detail. . . . There is no other text which informs us more fully about the customs and religious rites of the ancients.
>
> *illud tamen unum* De fastis *in promptu habebunt, in quo et fabulae quaedam ignotiores et historiae et fastorum ratio satis abunde pertractatur*. . . . *Nullum enim haberemus, ex quo plenius et mores et sacra veterum perspiceremus.*⁶

Ovid's *Fasti* was thus regarded as a kind of compendium of learning. By taking notes on the *Fasti,* students were putting together a compilation they could later use for reference and perhaps even plumb for their own compositions, as Guarino's phrase *in promptu* suggests.⁷

Indeed, the *Fasti* presented an ideal topic of study in that it taught everything. Ovid's poem was a lesson not only in Latin language and grammar, but on the whole of Roman culture as well. The content of the *Fasti* (as well as, generally speaking, all ancient texts) allowed the commentator to amass a wealth of information. The commentator functioned as a polymath, decoding every word of the classical author. In unlocking meaning, he employed the line-by-line method of glossing dating back to Servius's commentary on Vergil.⁸ The printed commentaries of Marsi and Costanzi are typical of the times in format: lemmatized remarks surround the verses of Ovid, leaving no doubt as to the central text. Also, in their glosses Marsi and Costanzi borrowed and collected from previous generations of commentators. By delving, digging, and adding—he did not omit alternative explanations or parallel stories from the body of ancient literature—the commentator was regarded as unveiling all the mysteries and hidden learning of the classical author. The 1497 composite edition

---

5. *quaeso uti hoc opusculum illustri principi Guidoni Ubaldo filio tuo, cui summa omnia debentur, aliquando legendum tradere non dedigneris*; Vatican City, BAV, Urb. lat. 360, fol. 198r.

6. From *De Ordine Docendi et Studendi,* ed. and trans. Kallendorf (2002), 288–89.

7. With the help of their teachers, students could use Ovid's *Fasti* to create a book of commonplaces; on the genre, see Moss (1996); Vogel (2000); Havens (2001).

8. See Grafton (1977), as well as "The Paraphrase-Commentary" in Grendler (1989, 244–50).

FIGURE 4. *Ovidius de Fastis cum duobus commentariis* (Venice: Joannes Tacuinus de Tridino, 1497), fol. a1r. Inc 5447 (24.4), Houghton Library, Harvard University.

of commentaries shows Marsi and Costanzi writing in scholarly seclusion, but they are seated around the central figure of Ovid like pupils on either side of their master (see figure 4).

The practice of treating all topics and minutiae was expected of commentators, as we can tell from an essay written in the commentator's defense by Battista Guarino.[9] In his *dissertatio,* all the major interpreters of classical texts from 1474 to the end of the 1480s are enumerated and extolled. Profiling humanists who have admirably performed their task, Guarino notes that Domizio Calderini and Ubertino Crescentino could explain the impenetrable.[10] Arriving at Paolo Marsi, Guarino praises him for an encyclopedic knowledge that matches Ovid's:

> What can be said to exist in the poet's repertoire that he did not set before the eyes of readers? I would almost dare to say that reading his work

---

9. The *dissertatio* first appeared at the end of the 1494 *editio princeps* of Marc Antonio Sabellico's *De Latinae linguae reparatione* (Lo Monaco 1992a, 140).

10. Of the former: *nihil erat tam arduum et difficile quod de se natura illa non sponte polliceri posset.* Of the latter: *Nulla lectio est in qua teneriora ingenia facilius coalescant, sed multa prius . . . ignoratione rerum subobscura, multae dicendi virtutes parum intellectae, quae res in causa fuit ut qui omnia altius scrutari solent diu non temere eam lectionem adierint.* Ibid., 143, 145.

confers more learning than does the reading of Ovid, whose interpreter he designated himself.

> *Quid in poetices apparatum dici potest, quod ille legentium oculis non subiecerit? ut ausim propemodum affirmare plus illius lectionem quam Nasonis, cuius se interpretem exhibuit, ad eruditionem conferre.*[11]

Indeed, this is how Marsi represents himself in the preface to his commentary: as a genius at uncovering and understanding Ovid, that well-spring of recondite learning "in which so many mysteries of the ancients, so many in terms of myth and science, are very enigmatically hidden" (*divinum illud Fastorum opus, in quo tot veterum mysteria, tot mythice physiceque, obscurius recondita sunt*). In fact, Marsi confers a religious quality on the *Fasti*. He calls it a "divine work" because it contains knowledge of ancient rites and customs, and in the catasterisms, or star myths, stories of the gods are joined together with science.[12] It would take a clairvoyant to gain understanding of such secrets "enigmatically hidden," but Marsi declares success in "leaving no topic untouched or undiscussed" (*nihil intactum nihilque indiscussum relinquentes*). He announces to the reader that in his comprehensiveness, he has satisfied expectations: "This one thing I dare profess, that I have fulfilled the requirements of my office. A fair reader would judge there is nothing that can further be desired" (*Hoc unum ausim dicere me in hoc opere et militiae meae morem gessisse et aequum lectorem nihil esse in eo quod ulterius desiderari queat iudicaturum*). Marsi portrays himself in this manner as a representative of the commentary tradition. He also patterns himself after the well-known commentator Niccolò Perotti, whose *Cornu Copiae* on Martial essentially turned into an encyclopedia. A modern critical edition of the *Cornu Copiae* takes up eight volumes.[13] Marsi's phrase *nihil intactum nihilque indiscussum relinquentes*

---

11. Ibid., 144.

12. Cf. Lilio Giraldi on Vulcan's eponym Iunonigena (the underlining is mine): *Hac eadem ratione Ouidius Vulcanum Iunonigenam uocauit.* [Met. 4.167–89] *Ex Iunone enim uel* <u>mythice</u>, *uel* <u>physice</u> *gigni uidetur. Scribit Seruius, Vulcanum e coelo in Lemnum cecidisse: idque fingi ea ratione, quia Vulcanus uidetur esse fulminis ignis, qui crebro in Lemno insula cadit.* Lilius Gregorius Gyraldus, *Historiae Deorum Gentilium* (Basileae: Oporinus, 1548), Syntagma 13. The fusion of the nomenclature and features of Greek and Roman gods with astral bodies is discussed by Seznec (1972), Chapter 2: "The Physical Tradition." In his remark, Marsi also alludes to Varro's tripartite division of religion in which the system of poets (*mythikon / fabulosum*) and philosophers (*physikon / naturale*) differs from that of the people, that is, a priestly community (*civile*). For Varro's tripartite theory, see Pépin (1956); for its use by Ovid, see Green (2002).

13. *Cornu Copiae, seu linguae Latinae commentarii*, ed. J.-L. Charlet et al. (Sassoferrato: Istituto Internazionale di Studi Piceni, 1989–2001).

echoes Perotti's claim *ita hunc Poetam exposuit ut ne verbum quidem reliquerit intactum.*[14]

As the impact of the polymath system of knowledge and transference of knowledge was felt, commentaries began to bulge. In his *Elegantiae,* Valla defined the word commentary (*Commentaria quid sint,* 4.21), and he distinguished two meanings, a *libellus* or short treatment of a topic, and a full-length discussion (*expositio et interpretatio auctorum*).[15] In practice, the short treatment was never followed, at least not until more specialized terms and publications such as *Adnotationes, Observationes,* and *Miscellanea* appeared. In the sixteenth century, the humanist J. L. Vives made moderation and relevance to theme the key elements in his definition of the commentary.[16] Even at the end of the fifteenth century, there were already those who preferred brevity. Giovanni Calfurnio, for example, thought that many commentators were verbose and that they overly quoted parallel authorities.[17] Codro Urceo satirized the minutiae in which commentators immersed themselves.[18] Paolo Marsi, however, did not think that over-zealousness detracted from his explanations. He defends himself for packing so much into his commentary, and in the preface he outlines his position as follows:

> Although plain brevity has always pleased me in other matters, I did not want to confine myself in this work to the narrow bounds customary for many, who very often confuse the matter and render less apparent that which must be made clear.
>
> *Quanquam in ceteris dilucida brevitas semper placuit, in eo tamen opere nolui me continere terminis ut multi solent angustis qui rem plerumque confundunt et quod ad diluciditatem redigendum est, minus perspicuum reddunt.*

In the 1482 preface to the second book of the *Fasti,* Marsi's stated approach turns into an apology. The role of the commentator is being brought into question; Marsi's accounting of himself reflects the equivocal status of his profession:

---

14. Pade (2005b, 52–54). Perotti died in 1480. Although published posthumously in 1489, the *Cornu Copiae* dates to 1478 in manuscript form. Perotti's phrase *ne verbum quidem reliquerit intactum* predates that of Marsi in print.

15. Ramminger (2005, 78).

16. Lo Monaco (1992a, 105, 137–38).

17. Monfasani (1988, 40).

18. Blanchard (1990, 107).

I might seem to have exceeded the code of law of the good interpreter, which is principally not to insist on details and silently to ignore things which can be understood from daily usage. But if they consider where and for whom I put my services on display, they will judge my prolixity completely forgivable. For indeed, I did not write a commentary in my study or in pleasant seclusion, for my own enjoyment and of my own free will. Rather, I lectured in the middle of Rome, mistress of the world, and in the public gymnasium, for the untutored as well as the learned, and for young boys as well as older students. . . . Add to this the fact that I had to linger over the enormity of the work and its antiquity, nearly consigned to oblivion, in order to explain the one thing and to dig out the other from the deepest shadows. Therefore the just reader will consider my effort praiseworthy, rather than censure it for any prolixity.

Videar quidem boni interpretis legem excessisse, cuius illud praecipuum est in minimis non insistere et quae ex quotidiano usu percipiuntur silentio praeterire. Sane si quo in loco et quibus id nostri muneris exhibetur animadvertent, dignam profecto venia prolixitatem hanc meam iudicabunt. Non enim haec in nostro cubiculo aut in amoeno secessu nobis ipsis et nostro arbitrio commentamur, sed in media urbe Roma, terrarum et gentium domina, et in publico gymnasio, tam rudibus quam eruditis, tam pueris quam grandioribus natu profitemur. . . . Adde et rerum magnitudinem et antiquitatem pene obliteratam ut alteri explanandae, alteri ab imis tenebris eruendae omnino fuerit a nobis immorandum. Laudandum igitur industriam meam duxerit aequus lector potius quam ullius prolixitatis arguendam.

Marsi excuses himself for belaboring well-known points on the basis of his listening audience; his classroom is filled with both beginners and advanced students.[19]

Many comments do seem to cater to the younger student and help make Ovid's poem more accessible; for example, at 2.342, on the wayfarer who recoils from a snake in his path, Marsi makes the rather self-evident remark, "this is natural. We usually tremble when we have either seen or stepped on a snake, because of its poison and cold touch" (*naturale est. Solemus enim expavescere aut visum aut calcatum anguem ob venenum et frigiditatem*). This use of the personal voice, as well as the evocation of common experience, allows a student to identify with what he is studying.[20] His

---

19. Grafton and Jardine (1986, 64).
20. Campanelli and Pincelli (2000, 144–45).

comment on 3.122–26 provides an opportunity to elaborate on counting with ten as the base of the decimal numeral system (perhaps Marsi held up ten fingers): "when we count, we go up to ten, then one added to the tenth number resumes the series, such as ten, then eleven; twenty, then twenty one; and so forth for the rest" (*cum numeramus, ascendimus usque ad decem, postea resumitur primus numerus decimo additus, ut decem, postea undecim; viginti, postea viginti unum; sic de reliquis*). Compare the higher-reaching explanation of magistracies or "ancient offices" (*honores veteres*, 3.147): "for an 'office,' as the jurist Callistratus says, 'is the municipal administration of the Republic'" (*honor enim, ut Callistratus Iurisconsultus inquit, est municipalis administratio reipublicae*; cf. *Dig.* 50.4.14). The types of exegesis in Marsi's commentary do support his complaint that he gave his lectures "for the untutored as well as the learned, and for young boys as well as older students." His teaching on the *Fasti* was destined for a reading public only after it had been taught to a wide audience (several times, in fact). In 1498, Josse Bade's solution to the common predicament of a mixed audience was to publish other, more learned commentaries next to his own, easy ones. He recognized a need in the market for books that had commentaries for more than one level of student.[21]

Marsi's self-acknowledged verbosity, which goes beyond the mere number and variety of remarks he felt compelled to make, is apparent throughout his commentary. After digressions of a historical, mythological, or even autobiographical nature, he often ends with an admission such as "but I've said enough now"[22] or "let's return to Ovid."[23] Or again, his comments become so endless and repetitive that he cross-references himself,[24] sometimes not even remembering exactly where he had made a previous

---

21. See White (2013, 88–90).

22. *Sed de his hactenus* (1.579); *Sed haec hactenus, quae ideo retuli, ut his quoque commentariis adderem morem creandorum regum* (3.153–54).

23. *Sed ad poetam redeamus* (3.55); *plura et clarissima oppida in eadem regione silentio praetereo, ut Talacotium, Albammaleam, Haveianum, sed ea commemoravi quae Asiatica nomina retinent, ut illud mihi persuadeam Marsiam magnum fuisse regem in Asia, unde tot loca in nostris regionibus nomen acceperint. Sed ad poetam redeamus* (6.703); and in a continuing strain to return to the text: *Sed satis sit. Quamvis et illud tragicum adduci queat, domi lycissam quid pavisse profuit, ut illa rostro sanguinem hauriret truci? Sed redeamus ad rem. . . . Sed prosequemur iter institutum* (4.11).

24. *nam Atlas fingitur caelum humeris sustinere, de quo inferius dicemus* (2.490); . . . *et alia quae mox dicemus* (2.497); *et hoc propter metum quasi riguerant, nam naturale est ut timore deficiente sanguine a partibus exterioribus contrahitur cutis, et ex ipsa contractione pili rigescunt, de hoc disseruimus superiore libro in eo versu "obstupui sensique metu riguisse capillos"* (2.502), and again: *propter cedentem sanguinem cute contracta. Inde rigent hirsuti crines, ut in primo quoque libro diximus* (3.333); *de Vesta omnia quae ad rem faciunt in sexto libro dicemus, et aliquid superius attigimus* (3.417); *quid autem intersit inter disertum et eloquentem, diximus in tertio libro* (4.112); . . . *ut in primo libro diximus* (4.412).

similar remark.²⁵ The same sort of internal referencing system occurs in the one witness to Marsi's Lucan commentary.²⁶ Marsi's profuse written and verbal expression was familiar to his colleagues, and his signature style took on mythic proportions. Paolo Cortesi left an anecdote that Marsi died shortly after he had given the funeral oration for Andrea Brenta and received criticism for the stiff and labored eulogy.²⁷

By contrast, Antonio Costanzi is self-consciously to the point in his *Fasti* commentary. Of course, this brevity is only relative, since his commentary is in fact no less bulky than Marsi's. However, Costanzi does portray himself as a concise interpreter. The twelve-line prefatory poem entitled *Ad Posteros* in the 1489 *editio princeps* of his commentary reads as follows:

> If one day you read the small volumes I have written on
>   the *Fasti*, take them, posterity, because they are few.
> I had no ambition but to write what was necessary.
>   I did not want to weave here a great Aristotle,
> nor do you need to fear a divine ancestral genealogy
> . . . .
> my little book could only have grown
>   to become a burden to its student.

> *Scripta mihi in Fastos si parva volumina quondam*
>   *legeris, haec paucis accipe posteritas.*
> *Nulla mihi ambitio, scripsi quodcunque necesse est.*
>   *Nec volui hic magnum texere Aristotelem,*
> *nec tibi divorum proavos seriemque verendam*
> . . . .
> *Nanque meus tantum potuit crevisse libellus*
>   *ut fieret cuius sarcina discipulo.*

Costanzi's sentiment recalls Ovid, who clarifies that even though he has introduced an "epicized" elegy, the *Fasti* is fundamentally elegiac in

---

25. *hoc est decimo mense, de quo plura circa principium primi libri diximus* (2.124); *Castoris et Pollucis, de quo templo diximus circa finem primi libri* (3.791).

26. Bianchi (1981, 73).

27. *Hunc defunctum Paulus Marsus quum laudavisset, fuissetque in ea laudatione a multitudine quasi explosus, propterea quod nimia contentione vocis pronunciasset, tantum animo accepit dolorem, ut paucis interpositis diebus, quum ad animi sollicitudinem morbus accessit, moreretur.* Paulus Cortesius (Paolo Cortese), *De hominibus doctis dialogus*, cited and discussed (with *gravitas*) by Colantoni (1911, 245).

nature.²⁸ Costanzi professes to have kept his remarks on Ovid brief, and this because he feared becoming monotonous. E. H. Alton has found similar language in a thirteenth-century *Fasti* commentary that belonged to a lecturer: "lest the audience's hearing be dulled by loathsome loquacity, let us see briefly and succinctly what the author treats in this work and how and to what purpose" (*ne prolixitatis fastidio aures audientium obscurentur, breviter et compendiose de quo et ad quid et qualiter auctor agit in hoc opere videamus*).²⁹ The remark reveals the lecturer's concern to hold the attention of his students.

We can also see in Costanzi the desire to avoid making mistakes in front of his class. Costanzi sympathizes from his own student days. Explaining that a lustrum is five years, which should not be confused with an Olympiad (*F.* 2.183), he says: "pay careful attention to this passage, reader . . . I do not want any error to lead you down the path that quite a few boys in Ferrara travelled, when I was at school" (*tu lector hoc loco diligenter adverte . . . nolo error quidam te ducat inde via, in quo me puero nonnulli iuvenes Ferrariae versabantur*).³⁰ The unintentional consequence of spreading mistakes was the discouragement of student interest. Though trying to bolster the reputation of the commentator, Battista Guarino echoes the concerns of critics on precisely this point:

> . . . [commentators] fill miserable youths with many absurdities, and what is worst of all, through their false opinions (they seem in agreement to have taught something), they force youths to hate those writers before they are at an age to understand them.

> . . . *imbuntque miseros adolescentes multis ineptiis, quod omnium pessimum est, cogunt etiam falsis opinionibus (ut aliquid docuisse videantur assentire) ac scriptores ipsos prius odisse quam per aetatem possint intelligere haec illi.*³¹

Trying to explain Augustus's reform of the calendar (*F.* 3.155), Costanzi states: "I would not be disinclined to report the various errors of those fixing the intercalary days, if I were not afraid of making my own mis-

---

28. *Caesaris arma canant alii* (*F.* 1.13). See Miller (1991, 12).

29. Alton (1930, 123). The manuscript is Copenhagen, Kongelige Bibliotek, GKS 2010; it is listed as no. 23 in Alton, Wormell, and Courtney (1977).

30. Cf. Costanzi's comment at *F.* 3.849: *sunt qui legant "tuba lustrare canoram," existimantes consuevisse Romanos hoc tempore tubarum cantu lustrare universam civitatem ultimo, videlicet, quinquatruum die, quod quidam non indocti olim nobis pueris tradiderunt. Nos autem legendum esse non dubitamus "tubam lustrare canoram"*. . . .

31. Lo Monaco (1992a, 141).

takes along the way and rousing loathing in the reader" (*non pigeret varios intercalantium errores referre nisi vereremur ne et ipsi obiter erraremus lectori fastidium afferentes*). Costanzi probably refers to the errors made by those who regulated the Republican and then the Julian calendar, and who misunderstood the intercalation rules explained by Macrobius. Costanzi acknowledges that it is impossible to know everything, and he intimates that one looks like a fool pretending otherwise; he therefore intentionally leaves out any celestial computation. His attempts to clarify astral calculations would only bore his audience.[32] The hands-off approach is quite the opposite from that taken by Paolo Marsi, who appended a *Ratio Astrologiae* to his *Fasti* commentary, all the while complaining that a humanities professor should not be expected to understand astronomy. Interestingly enough, Marsi thereby fell into the category of teacher so frowned upon by his associate Regiomontanus (*familiarissimus noster*, F. 3.852). Regiomontanus declared in the 1464 inaugural lecture of his course that teachers were continuing to pass on superficial knowledge to students because they had never learned the science of astronomy.[33] More than one humanist bemoaned the limitless drive for universal knowledge. A generation later still, Caelio Calcagnini inveighed against erudition for erudition's sake in his essay "That studies should be moderated" (*Quod studia sunt moderanda*).[34]

AGGRAVATIONS OF PRINT

Commentators were at a critical impasse in their work. Battista Guarino wrote his *dissertatio* at the end of the *quattrocento*, exactly at a time when commentators were under attack because their product was ill-defined and their professional profile was so difficult to establish.[35] All commentaries were beginning to look alike as lectures in *Altertumswissenschaft*. When every commentator was supposed to be exhaustive, how was one distinguishable from the other? Furthermore, was a commentator an author in his own right? Did he contribute an original literary product? One must

---

32. Compare Costanzi's similar comment at F. 1.1 *cum causis:* . . . *lege libellum qui Sphaera inscribitur* [Johannes de Sacrobosco's thirteenth-century *Tractatus de Sphaera*]. *Neque enim quaecunque vel pueri norunt huic operi placet inserere, ne crescat in immensum et nos, quod minime sumus, ampulosi atque ostentatores videamur, qui magis eos probare consuevimus qui multa breviter quam qui pauca dicerent copiose.*
33. Malpangotto (2008, 91).
34. Blanchard (1990, 99–101).
35. Lo Monaco (1992a, 113).

also remember that the humanist did not have the luxury of pondering and penning philological insights in moments of privacy and quiet, "in [his] study or in pleasant seclusion, for [his] own enjoyment and of [his] own free will" in Marsi's words. Commentators were *grammatici*. Their academic positions were precarious; jobs were often scarce, and competition was fierce.[36]

In Rome, those with the most job security were also employed in some fashion by the Curia. However, Pomponio Leto was an exception to the rule, rejecting the advice of his friend the humanist-bishop Giannantonio Campano to look for a clerical appointment. Leto preferred to live a life of frugality, and he supplemented his salary from the *Studium Urbis* with private lessons, which helped him afford his house on the Quirinal hill.[37] Paolo Marsi actually renounced his post in the College of papal abbreviators in Rome, in or around 1463. He commemorates the day of his "release" in a gloss at *F.* 2.852 (the *Regifugium*):

> The poet has dwelled long on the expulsion of the kings and freedom borne Rome, and I have dwelled perhaps too long in my interpretation. But the digression and the analogy in this history writer were the sweeter for that freedom itself is more pleasing to me: I who have celebrated the commemorative day of my freedom on the third of September for the same number of years after my liberation nine years ago, and I who have decided that [the day] must be celebrated for as long as I live.[38]

> *Et multum poeta ipse et nimis forte nos in eo interpretando ad eiectionem regum et partam Romanae urbi libertatem immorati sumus, sed eo mihi fuit dulcior ipsa immoratio et in hunc historiographum collatio, quo gratior est ipsa libertas qui, posteaquam mihi me ipsi nono abhinc anno vindicavi, celebravi quot annis festum libertatis tertio nonas septembres celebrandumque quoad vixero institui.*

An additional financial consideration is that one professor's stipend did not equal another's but depended on his prestige and the number of students in his course. Leto had the ability to enthrall an audience. He

---

36. Cf. Lee (1984, 127–46).
37. On Leto's correspondence with Campano, see de Beer (2008, 181–84, 199–200); for his house on the Quirinal, see Campanelli and Pincelli (2000, 105–6).
38. Marsi made a special point to observe this anniversary in 1468 while on the ambassadorial voyage with Bernardo Bembo, and he wrote a poem, "The annual celebration of his freedom in Collo, an African hamlet in Numidia" *("Annua libertatis sue celebratio apud Colium villulam Aphricae in Numidia")*. See Fritsen (2000b, 372, fn. 46).

related to his times the texts he was explaining, and his eloquence was so great that he was able to overcome his stuttering when lecturing. Students waited for Leto's arrival before sunrise, lanterns in hand—a testament to their teacher's popularity. The *Studium Urbis* afterwards "institutionalized" the dawn hours as an instruction time. Still, even Leto's popularity fluctuated. His reputation suffered in the 1470s after his release from prison; by this time his competitor Calderini had won over many pupils[39] (see figure 5).

Paolo Marsi's career can be charted against Leto's to some degree. Marsi was a devoted and true student of Leto, a fact he wished to impress upon others; he wanted to capitalize on Leto's fame. Marsi tried to create a line of succession in which he was the latest heir of knowledge and wisdom. He saw himself as following Valla in a direct line after Leto as professor of rhetoric in Rome; this becomes apparent in his gloss on *F.* 2.685 as to whether Tarquinius Superbus was the son or the grandson of Tarquinius Priscus: "this has been sufficiently discussed long ago by Valla and much later by my dear Leto and on another occasion by myself" (*satis et a Valla iampridem et longe post a Pomponio nostro et alias a nobis disputatum est*). Marsi seemingly wished to establish a new pedigree, *Lorenzo Valla—Pomponio Leto—Paolo Marsi,* that would parallel or equal the one *Lorenzo Valla—Pietro Odo da Montopoli—Pomponio Leto.* The latter arrangement was already acknowledged and accepted by Marsi's contemporaries.[40]

But while Marsi was carving out his professional identity, he was also dealing with financial struggles. We have already seen that he did not have a curial employment to fall back on. In 1482 he traveled between Venice, seeing to the publication of his commentary, and Rome, where he was teaching. That same year, he invoked the pope's help in difficult economic times and pleaded for a subsidy. His elegiac petition "Father Sixtus, have pity on me, and have pity on my household / which will fall in disrepair if your support is lacking / . . . / and do not let me die from hunger" (*Sixte pater, miserere mei, miserere domusque / quae ruet, auxilio si caret ipsa tuo, / . . . / nec patiare mori corpora nostra fame*) may reflect the situation expressed in the prefaces recently attached to his *Fasti* commentary, namely the death of his last surviving brother Angelo, in whom (along with Angelo's new bride and the prospect of children) Marsi had placed the hope of his old age.[41] In response to his plea, he was given the church benefice of

---

39. Campanelli and Pincelli (2000, 118, 125, 140, 142–45).
40. On the latter arrangement see Donati (2000, 22–27, 62–65); Accame (2008, 38).
41. In the 1482 *Praefatio in quartum librum Fastorum cum declamatione orbitatis morte fratrum* Marsi laments: *Angelum nuncupatum, quem ego ipse educaveram et bonis moribus institueram, et in*

FIGURE 5. Portrait of Pomponio Leto in Paolo Giovio, *Elogia virorum literis illustrium* (Basel: Petrus Perna, 1577), p. 78. IC5 G4395 B575v, Houghton Library, Harvard University.

quo spem omnem futurae senectae ... tuendae collocaveram, et cui sociam nuper thalami dederam, ut ex eo mihi esset illa sobolem paritura, o me miserum! O me infelicem! Latinum [bellum] sustulit. The poem to Sixtus IV (and attributed date) is given in della Torre (1903, 278–79); the manuscript is Rome, Biblioteca Angelica, MS 1350 (fol. 342r–v). I see no reason to doubt della Torre's date of 1482, *pace* Campanelli and Pincelli (2000, 112).

S. Maria de Ortuncula in the Marsi diocese on December 10, 1483.[42] One can look for comparison to the precarious academic position and financial worries of Antonio Costanzi, who in 1486 threatened to take a teaching position in Cesena. His alert resulted in a pay raise from the city fathers of Fano.[43]

Francesco Lo Monaco and W. Scott Blanchard identify a new source of strain in the challenging quest for employment: the printing press. They regard the advent of print as grounds for pressure for the *criticus* and *grammaticus* to define their professional identity. Indeed, not all humanists were happy with the news of the printing press. Niccolò Perotti, although he took great advantage of the invention, initially saw only the medium's negatives for the Latin language, as books would become corrupted through poor editing.[44] Little of Codro Urceo's work survives, perhaps intentionally; he may have shunned publication in order to avoid having his words in print and available for scrutiny by his peers.[45] Antonio Costanzi may have suffered from print anxiety for the same reason as Codro Urceo. His comment "I would not be disinclined to report the various errors of those fixing the intercalary days, if I were not afraid of making my own mistakes along the way and arousing loathing in the reader" (*non pigeret varios intercalantium errores referre nisi vereremur ne et ipsi obiter erraremus lectori fastidium afferentes*) does raise the question of whether he wished to put his reputation on the line. The chance of a tarnished reputation because of publication was a real possibility: some professors took students on excursions to the typesetters and incidentally pointed out adversaries' imminent mistakes; others went to a bookseller to give their students a spontaneous lesson on the latest release and its (laughable) contents.[46]

Nevertheless, Bartolomeo Fonte found that printers deserved praise because they conferred immortality on writers both ancient and modern.[47] Many, if not most, humanists rushed to fashion a reputation and make a name for themselves in print. In the prefatory letter to the 1497 composite *Fasti* commentaries, the editor Bartolomeo Merula made sure to advertise

---

42. Lee (1978, 184).
43. Formichetti (1984, 372). Chambers (1976, 77–81) mentions occurrences of witheld or reduced salaries in Rome and the resulting protests by teachers there.
44. Blanchard (1990, 104).
45. Ibid., 111–12.
46. In the first example, Calderini pointed out a mistake by Perotti; in the second, Pietro Marsi and Sulpizio da Veroli critiqued a poem by Giovanni Battista Cantalicio. See Campanelli and Pincelli (2000, 136–39).
47. B. Richardson (1999, 80).

his commentary on the *Tristia,* which would appear in 1499 but which he proclaimed was well on its way to being finished.[48] Humanists craved elevated professional status and authorial identity, and Paolo Marsi is a case in point: he embraced the print medium already in its early stages. At the beginning of 1469, Marsi set off with the *condottiere* Nicolò Canal to the East in order to record his deeds as Captain General against the Turks. This was Marsi's second journey from the port of Venice in the space of two years. He had already accompanied the ambassador Bernardo Bembo on a mission to Seville in 1468. Both trips were Marsi's attempts to leave behind the scene of Pomponio Leto's extradition to Rome. Leto, as head of the Roman Academy, was imprisoned along with other members in Castel Sant'Angelo by papal decree, on the various charges of sodomy, paganism, and republican plots.[49] Marsi sought escape from his sorrow, and undoubtedly he also felt safer abroad.[50] While on tour with Nicolò Canal, Marsi witnessed the June 15, 1470, fall of Negropont, a debacle that the admiral had helped to create. Marsi recounted the disaster in a poem written for Paul II, *Lamentatio de crudeli Eurapontinae urbis excidio,* which he completed while he was still at sea on August 26, 1470.[51] Back in Venice, Marsi immediately handed his work to the printer Federico de' Conti. The *Lamentatio* enjoyed only a very limited print run, however, as Conti's business fell victim to the Venetian printing crash. A second edition printed anonymously in Rome in 1471 also would have had a limited circulation, since by the end of 1472 thirst for news from Negropont and first-hand accounts of its fall to the Turks had dried up.[52] Nonetheless, the speed with which Marsi publicized his poem reflects his desire to take full advantage of the printing industry. The same confidence and haste would mark the later publication of his lecture notes and commentary on the *Fasti.*

One reason for the humanist to expedite the printing of his work at the end of the *quattrocento* was to avoid plagiarism. It was all too common to have one's research appear under somebody else's name. Codro Urceo, in

---

48. *Ovidium enim de Tristibus ac Plynium de Animalibus opus sane arduum ac perdifficile interpretamur, cuius provinciae magnam partem absoluimus.* There is no documentation that I have found for a commentary on Pliny.

49. On the suppression of the Roman Academy in 1468 see Lowe (1994), Masotti (1982), Palermino (1980), and Dunston (1973).

50. For the story of Marsi's first trip with Bernardo Bembo and the poetic log he produced (*Bembica peregrina* or simply *Bembice:* Vatican City, BAV, Reg. lat. 1385; Ferrara, Biblioteca Comunale Ariostea, II.162; Windsor, Eton College Library, 156), see Fritsen (2000b).

51. Marsi must have wanted to ingratiate himself with Paul II, in light of the pope's distrust of the Roman Academy. The poem is printed in della Torre (1903, 287–95) and discussed by Meserve (2006, 458–60), as an early news event to be printed and circulated.

52. Meserve (2006, 459–60).

his satire on the grammarian's profession, given as a *praelectio* to a course on Aristophanes (1494–95), informs his audience of a student who had appropriated material from him. After copying lecture notes and allegedly going through Codro's library, the student "when the time was right embellished himself with these discoveries, and provided himself a reputation with them" (*cum tempus erat, his se honestabat, his sibi nomen parabat*).[53] It did in fact happen that volumes were produced with the wrong attribution and without the real writer's knowledge or consent. A little-known humanist might publish his own work under the name of someone else, who was far more famous and sometimes no longer alive. In 1482 the obscure Brescian humanist Pellacinus made public his commentary on Valerius Maximus under the name of Ognibene da Lonigo, who was long since dead.[54] In fact, Ognibene's name was frequently used to cover up the identity of a real author.[55] Certainly the printers themselves were complicit in these acts of forgery. In the dedication of his 1490 edition of Sallust, Pomponio Leto took on a menacing tone to ward off those who would plagiarize and attach their own name as author.[56] To keep matters under his control, Leto collaborated very closely with printers.[57]

It was especially a teacher's lecture notes that were fodder for the hungry publishing hordes, as remarked upon in Codro Urceo's satire. In the preface to his *Fasti* commentary, Paolo Marsi reported that he had carefully expounded Ovid in a crowded classroom of listeners (*magna cura ac vigilantia auditorumque frequentia professi sumus*) where

> the more [one] has to elaborate, the more he cannot even utter a word but that it is taken down by [the students] to whom the service is offered, and once taken down, every word is published with a sudden and brash impulse.

> *in quo nobis eo magis elaborandum fuit, quo ne verbum quidem unum efferri potest, quod non ab his quibus id praestatur muneris excipiatur exceptumque temerario quodam impetu vulgetur.*

---

53. Blanchard (1990, 109).
54. Monfasani (1994, 35).
55. Monfasani (ibid.) calls this "something of a cottage industry at Venice." Ulery (2005) has even found a medieval commentary printed in the Renaissance under Ognibene's name.
56. Farenga (1994, 64).
57. Besides Farenga's article, see also Scapecchi, who cites Leto's collaboration with and reliance on Georg Lauer to produce texts for university courses or texts written by Roman Academy members (2005, 122–23) and traces all the different printers Leto worked with (2007, 41–46).

However, the circulation of notes could also simplify matters, so that the humanist professor often took a copy of his lectures to the printer.[58] While Marsi appears exasperated by the way students not only held on to every spoken word but also organized their notes at home, he goes on to say that he could at least borrow his students' copies in order to publish his lecture in the same methodical arrangement he gave it.[59] Domizio Calderini commented that all he had to do was polish what his students had written before sending it off to the printer.[60]

The catch to the practice was that once a transcription was in circulation, it was there for anyone to publish. Multiple copies of a lecture might be in existence. Pomponio Leto's lecture notes on Vergil, for example, were shared in the same way that students make copies of each other's notes today.[61] Notes that floated around made plagiarism tempting, and the concept that the owner of written material was the person who had it in his physical possession was still popular. Privileges granting exclusive rights for a number of years to printers, editors, translators, and even to authors themselves, did not become common until at least 1492 in Venice, and even then almost exclusively in that city.[62] Therefore, speed was of the essence in getting a work out in one's name. Marsi reveals his concern to get his commentary out and established as the first and primary one in the field, when he boasts in the preface

> how quickly I have completed this work. Indeed, there were others who displayed many years' worth of effort at the same task and still in those years did not finish. I actually brought my work to its conclusion within a few months' time . . .

---

58. Battista Guarino saw private notetaking, on the other hand, as having the distinct added benefit of future self-publication. In his treatise on education, he advised searching the writings of the ancients for maxims for one's own, personal commonplace book, and he added: "Writing glosses in books is also extremely profitable, the more so if [students] have some hope of publishing them someday, for we are more careful with such things when we are in pursuit of praise" (*Explanationes quoque in libros scribere vehementer conducet, sed tamen magis si sperabunt eas in lucem aliquando prodituras*). From *De Ordine Docendi et Studendi* in Kallendorf (2002, 294–95). This passage is also cited by A. Buck, in the introduction to Buck and Herding (1975, 8).

59. In the preface to his second book of the 1482 *Fasti* commentary: *at nullum pene profertur verbum quin ab illis omne protinus excipiatur, excepta domum referunt, relata in suum ordinem digeruntur. Ab illis deinde, si quid edituri sumus, labores nostros mutuamur et quo ordine a nobis omnia prolata sunt.* See also Campanelli and Pincelli (2000, 129–30).

60. Grafton and Jardine (1986, 65); Marsi's use of student notes for publication is also discussed (64–65).

61. Dunston (1967).

62. Richardson (1999, 38–43, 69–74); Chartier (1994, 32–37); Gerulaitis (1976, 32); Kristeller (1992, 22).

> *qua celeritate fuerit a nobis hoc opus absolutum. Fuere enim alii qui cum plurium annorum in hoc ipso operam exhibuissent non tamen pluribus annis absoluerunt. Nos vero paucis mensibus ad finem deduximus . . .*

Marsi felt he had bragging rights, and his insistence on thoroughness and completion is understandable in the face of possible competition. Just as Leto left a warning to others in the dedication of his 1490 Sallust not to attach their name to his work, so Marsi insisted that he was the sole expert on Ovid. Not only did he turn out his product quickly, but he also reigned supreme in the field of *Fasti* studies.

The following claim, again from the preface, reveals how Marsi wished to be regarded as the acknowledged authority with the final say-so:

> I won't mention the uncommon talent which my nature has given me and the hard work I applied. Because of these two things I judge that I am able to prevail both in consulted and final opinion. This is confirmed also by the testimony of others, who have sought my opinion in many things and once it was sought, fully maintained it. And so let me speak without boasting, so that genuine praise will not be detracted from the one who deserves it, for I am the first to have crossed this enormous ocean on a bold skiff and to have revealed to others what was previously unknown, and to have so revealed it that I have eliminated the burden of further research from everyone.

> *Taceo de ingenio quod mihi non mediocre natura suggessit et de ea quam ego industriam adhibuerim, in quo et consilio valere et iudicio simul me posse existimo, quod aliorum quoque testimonio comprobatur qui iudicium meum in multis expetivere et expetitum sunt omnino secuti. Liceat ita sine arrogantia loqui ne cuiquam benemerenti vera laus detrahatur, cum primus ego per totum hoc ingens pelagus audenti cimba cucurrerim et quae prius incognita erant ceteris aperuerim et ita aperuerim ut ulterius inquirendi laborem omnibus ademerim.*

Marsi's transparent aim is to so dazzle his audience with his learning that he will convince his successors that there is no more work on Ovid's *Fasti* left for them to do. He is clearly telling others to stay away. Moreover, calling his commentary a "skiff" (*cimba / cymba*) is meant to convey how effortless the exegesis of Ovid was for a man of his talent. The metaphor of the writing project as a sea voyage is taken directly from Ovid (*F.* 1.4 and 466; 2.3 and 863–64; 3.790; 4.18 and 729–30). "Enormous ocean" (*ingens pelagus*) indicates the immensity of Marsi's task,[63] while "skiff" (*cimba / cymba*) is appropriate to suggest Marsi has avoided shipwreck.[64] In addition, Marsi's skiff is "bold" (*audenti*), for it has made the dangerous crossing. Marsi echoes the initial nervousness of Ovid setting out on his poetic journey (*timidae navis*, 1.4) and his sense of accomplishment in reaching a goal when he has entered port at the end of Book 2 (*venimus in portum*, 2.863).[65] Marsi clearly understands the "epicized elegy" that is Ovid's poem by including references to the deep ocean that is epic and the coastal waters that are elegy, and he imitates and emulates Ovid, a point to which we shall return shortly. Marsi has completed his maritime journey: the writing and, more importantly, the publishing of his commentary. This leaves no further research to be done, and future generations need only read his work. This sentiment appears at *F.* 3.824, where Marsi has made a textual emendation, correcting the name of the world's first cobbler. The inventor of shoe-making is Tychius; Marsi rejects the readings "Batius" by some scholars and "Pythius" by others, both of which were in fact mistaken conjectures.[66] Around the same time of Marsi's *Fasti* publication, Poliziano determined the critically accepted reading "Tychius," and in 1488, Filippo Beroaldo similarly recorded "Tychius" in his *Annotationes centum*.[67] But in 1482, undoubtedly aware of competition, Marsi proclaimed himself as the *Fasti* champion. He gives a wholly different appraisal and states "but I

---

63. Compare Vergil's use of *aequor*, modified by such adjectives as *magnum, vastum,* and *immensum,* to describe the enormity of his undertaking (*magnum: Georgics* 4.388, *Aen.* 9.101; *vastum: Aen.* 3.191, 2.780, 10.693; *immensum: Aen.* 11.355). See Lieberg (1969, 234–35). Marsi also employs the phrase *vastum aequor* in his verse preface to *Fasti* Book 6.

64. Propertius uses *cumba* (3.3.22) to signify that he is hugging the coast and playing it safe with his lighter verse, namely love elegy; Lieberg (1969, 235). He wants to avoid drowning in the deep waters of epic.

65. See Green, 32–33 (on *F.* 1.4) and 215 (on *F.* 1.466), and Robinson, 58–59 (on *F.* 2.3) on Ovid's representation of the progress of his poem as a sea voyage. Marsi adopts the imagery as well throughout his commentary. He is spreading the sails in the 1482 verse preface to Book 3 (*iam tempus adest, iam pandere vela*); the death of his brother suddenly stays the journey in the preface to Book 4 (*opus maturantem et e medio cursu iam in portum . . . accelerantem . . . revocavit*). Giorgio Cornaro sees the commentary reaching port and coming to conclusion in the verse preface to Book 6 (*Ecce tibi celeres vastum percurrimus aequor / liberiore sinu, iam pars exacta laboris / maxima, ianque ratis pleno petet hostia velo*).

66. *Aliqui legunt "sit Batio doctior," ex eo quod Plinius dicat Batium invenisse sutrinam; alii legunt "Pythio," quod qua ratione dicant nescio, nisi referant ad Apollinem sandalarium*. The correct reading of Pliny, *NH* 7.196 is actually [*invenit*] *sutrinam* **Tychius** *Boeotius*.

67. Poliziano's correct reading was based on a passage of Homer's *Iliad* (7.219–23); see Lo Monaco (1991, 306). Filippo Beroaldo's reading is cited in the 1978 Teubner. Compare Leto's *Fasti* manuscript for his pupil Agostino Maffei (Ferrara, Bib. Com. Ariostea, II.141): *Phitio* appears on fol. 54r but has been corrected to *Titio*. On fol. 60v in Vat. lat. 3263 Leto writes: *Tychius Aiacis clypeum fecit ex corio, cuius rei meminit Homerus in vij Iliados*.

have read, as those who have followed me, <u>sit Titio</u>" (*ego autem legi, et qui me secuti sunt idem fecere, sit Titio*). In claiming that there are adherents to his emendation, Marsi portrays himself as leader. One might compare this with his emendation of *palam Stygias,* changed to *Palaestinas* at *F.* 4.236.[68] He prefaces his correction with the remark:

> Allow me now to humbly look after my interests, so that no one will want to rob me of my praise. For truly, this passage has never been understood in my time by anyone but me. I was the first one to explain it, and whatever exegetes came after me either maintained my opinion or else were mistaken in their understanding.

> *Liceat nunc mihi sine arrogantia rem meam tueri, ne quis me mea laude defraudatum ire velit. Hic enim locus a nullis unquam nostrae aetatis viris intellectus est, praeterquam a nobis. Primus ego explicui, et quicunque sunt postea interpretati aut sententiam meam secuti sunt aut non recte intellexerunt.*

The precariousness of academic positions, the ill-defined nature of the role of the teacher-commentator, the advent of print and rush for self-advertisement—all contributed to what is a staple of humanist rhetoric, especially evident in the late *quattrocento*: invective.[69] Publishing one's commentary theoretically meant staking a claim and outrivaling others in professional knowledge of a classical author. Publication increased status, unless of course one's commentary became corrupted (for this reason Pomponio Leto distanced himself from his printed lectures on Vergil)[70] or was forged under another name. But publishing also meant leaving oneself open to attack and dealing with colleagues' criticism.

Polemics were certainly a part of the life of the Roman Academy, whose members taught at the *Studium Urbis.* Paolo Pompilio, for example, debated about prosody and diglossia in ancient Rome, exchanging rancorous words with Sulpizio da Veroli, who had published works on metrics and on grammar.[71] Antonio Volsco quarreled with Pietro Marsi about

---

68. The passage has long been considered a *locus desperatus.* Frazer, in his 1929 edition *ad loc.*, notes that some anonymous commentators chose Palaestinas, with the meaning "of or pertaining to the [seaport] Paeleste." This in fact is Marsi's conjecture: Palaeste in Epirus, where Caesar records he landed during the war with Pompey (*Paleste locus est in ora Epiri apud Oricon, quo e navibus descendit Caesar cum iret cum exercitu adversus Pompeium.* Cf. *BC* 3.6.) See Butrica (2004).
69. See Rao (1988–90); Laureys (2003).
70. Grafton and Jardine (1986, 65).
71. See Bracke (1992a).

errors he had found in the latter's printed commentary of Silius Italicus.[72] Pomponio Leto, Antonio Volsco, and Paolo Marsi teamed up and took issue with Martino Filetico on his reading of "Lavinia" for "Lavinaque" in the second line of Vergil's *Aeneid*, prompting Filetico to defend himself and write an invective in the 1480s against his detractors, the first of his *In Corruptores Latinitatis*.[73] In the second *In Corruptores Latinitatis*, he tells how *Samothraica*, his explanation for the provenance of the Trojan *penates* (*victosque penates* at *Aen*. 1.68), was misheard and misunderstood by a pupil, becoming *Sandra* or *Salamandra* in the transcribed lecture notes. This fell into his adversaries' hands and was taken to be Filetico's own grammatical mistake.[74] On a later occasion, when Filetico was expounding on *populosque feroces contundet* (*Aen*. 1.263), members of the Roman Academy were in the audience and stood up to attack him in front of his students.[75] Filetico counter-attacked in his invective, accusing the Roman Academy of low moral standards and of putting on banquets and festivities, such as the revived Palilia, in order to curry favor with students.[76]

Paolo Marsi was not an innocent bystander in the controversy surrounding Martino Filetico. Marsi also had his own personal enemies to deal with, however, as defensive remarks within the body of his own *Fasti* commentary make clear. At *F.* 2.571, glossing the rites of the Mute Goddess, who was identified with the Mother of the Lares and invoked during the Feralia to silence enemies, Marsi says to his students:

> I wish I both knew and could use the spell for stifling the barks of a Cerberus, who although he wants to profess wisdom, is completely lacking in every gift of wisdom, who although he advises others to contain themselves, is not able to contain himself, who has other people's vices before his eyes, but keeps his own behind his back. I will not answer him back, lest I set before you the same example of verbal abuse.

> *Quo utinam et nos sciremus et possemus uti ad allatratus Cerberi reprimendos, qui cum sapientiam profiteri velit ab omni sapientiae munere profecto*

---

72. Rose (2001, 395–98).

73. See Pincelli, esp. xxvii–xlv, where she explains the manuscript evidence and historical context of the quarrels.

74. *In corruptores Latinitatis* II.8, discussed in Pincelli, xxxviii; also in Campanelli and Pincelli (2000, 135).

75. *In corruptores Latinitatis* II.40 (Pincelli, 22, 106–11); also Campanelli and Pincelli (2000, 140).

76. *In corruptores Latinitatis* II.47: *Adolescentulorum animos pollicitis muneribus, blanditiis et opipari coena decipiunt, Bacchanalia domi colunt, alia multa facitant, quae pro honesti officio dici non possunt* (Pincelli, 23, 116).

vacat, qui cum alios contineri moneat se ipsum continere non potest, qui aliena vitia habet ante oculos, sua autem a tergo reiecit. Non obloquar ne maledicentiae vobis ut ille praebeam exemplum.

Marsi does not name his enemy, standard practice taken from Petrarch's invectives. Following Petrarch as model, Marsi furthermore refers to his enemy as an animal, a dog from hell. Filetico himself had called the Academicians who stood up and ridiculed him in the audience *canes*.[77] Marsi repeats the canine slur at *Fasti* 4.11, pretending to take the moral high ground while he exposes his rivals' overreaction. They act as though he has committed treason, *lèse majesté* he says, because he redefined *cum causis* as *cum originibus*:

> Some have very recently inveighed against me as if in using that word I violated the majesty of nature—me, a most faithful interpreter, a pious man who utterly abhors every curse. Though they carp at me in puerile jests and bark at my reputation indiscriminately, they will not succeed in tearing me away from my initiative. . . . Not yet have I learned to curse, nor if it is in any way possible, will I reply with any note of slander.[78]

> *Nescio qui in interprem fidelissimum, virum pium et ab omni maledicentia penitus abhorrentem, nuperrime fuerint invecti, quasi fuerit in eo verbo maiestas naturae laesa. Carpant licet in puerilibus ludis et in nomen meum passim allatrent, non tamen efficient ut ab instituto divellar. . . . Nondum enim maledicere didici, nec si quid fieri potest, sine ulla maledicentiae nota respondebo.*

It is especially as his commentary went to print that Marsi found himself in trouble. In his elegiac preface to Book 5 of the *Fasti*, he tells Giorgio Cornaro,

> When sure gratitude was my due for service,
>   someone began to malign my ability;
> and while both young and old were endorsing and honoring
>   my name, and all Venetians bearing it aloft to the stars,

---

77. Marsh (2003, xii–xv); *In corruptores Latinitatis* II.40 (Pincelli, 22).
78. The *lèse majesté* joke appears again at *Fasti* 3.837: *Ego autem, nisi a detractoribus laesae maiestatis arguerer, dicerem "captam Minervam," quod illi eo die, eo in loco legitime constituto, auctoritate senatus a pontificibus consecrato, potissimum sacrificetur, nam Pompeio Festo teste* [Fest. p. 65 Müll] *captum locum dicimus ad sacrificandum legitime constitutum.*

a certain somebody, alas! inflamed by unjust jealousy, broke in,
    and barked liked a cur against my deeds.

Dum certa officio debetur gratia nostro,
    nescio quis nostras carpere coepit opes,
cumque probent celebrentque meum iuvenesque senesque
    Adriacique omnes nomen ad astra ferant,
rumpitur heu! quidam livore accensus iniquo
    latratusque refert in mea facta canum. (ll. 5–10)

While personally supervising the printing of his *editio princeps*, Marsi came under attack by a Venetian (the only clue he gives to his detractor's identity).[79] This man blamed Marsi for the lack of care shown his work and for his poor command of extemporaneous speech, an especially sore point for Marsi, as the time spent on verse in his own defense suggests.[80] One can almost believe the anecdote that Marsi died shortly after hearing the criticism leveled against him for Andrea Brenta's eulogy. Responding to this Venetian (a person with immediate access to his work) and to other general nay-sayers, Marsi appended both an *Emendatio quorundam locorum* and a *Ratio Astrologiae* to his volume.[81] Blaming passages that needed correction on printers' haste,[82] he told Cornaro, "I therefore wanted to add these things, so that no one can rightly say that Marsi has either made a mistake or disregarded anything" *(Haec nos ideo voluimus addere, ne quis dicere aut errasse Marsum aut aliquid praeteriisse iure possit)*. Congratula-

---

79. *Non tamen Adriaco est genitus de sanguine claro / impia nam Veneti non didicere loqui.* (ll. 33–34 of *Praefatio in V Librum Fastorum et contra invidum*, 1482 *editio princeps*).

80. *Nunc vigilem damnat furiali murmure curam* (l. 11); *Hic modo quod rarum est dicentem ex tempore damnat, / sive agar ad numeros sive solutus eam, / at dedit hoc natura mihi atque industria munus, / hoc vigiles noctes hoc peperere dies. / Ille quidem fructus studiorum maximus, ille / unus iudicio, Quintiliane, tuo,* [cf. *Inst.* 10.7.1] */ illa etiam longi sunt praemia certa laboris / verus et ingenii fertilioris honos: / pectore facundo dicendi ex tempore vires, / quas qui non habeat non petat, ille forum / diffugiat populum, tacito se condat in antro / et scribat versus per duo lustra duos.* (ll. 17–28).

81. In the *Emendatio quorundam locorum* Marsi notes that because his commentary had met with approval in Rome, he had dared to hope for the same in Venice; however, a "Tisiphone" (in mythology, one of the Furies) had unofficially seen his published work before corrections (*Sed cum sperandum mihi esse ducerem neminem fore illud opus, quod Romana censura probavit, Venetiis damnaturum, nescio qua Thessyphone factum sit ut contineri non potuerit invidiae furor et ante inspectum opus inofficiosum hunc laborem meum coeperit allatrare.*) In the *Ratio Astrologiae*, Marsi claims that his maligner will no longer besmirch his professional reputation or stand in the way of his fame: "but the more his fury rages at the bit, the brighter my glory will be" (*sed quo magis illius saeviet in frenis rabies, eo dilucidior erit laus nostra*).

82. *loci quidam in commentariis nostris paululum immutati, ne dixerim depravati, et hoc non mea culpa factum sed celeritate illorum qui caracteres imprimendos contexunt.*

tory verses for an erudite and eloquent Marsi appear on the 1482 commentary's colophon page. The jurist poet Roberto Orsi remarks that Marsi undertook his project with disregard for snooty critics, those "who have the nose of a rhinoceros" (*qui nasum rhinocerontis habent*, l. 8; quoting Martial 1.3.6).

PRIMACY AND PRINT

The new world of publish or perish could be termed publish *and* perish, when one's reputation was clearly on the line; such were the pressures that the humanist commentators felt. In this age of print, Paolo Marsi and Antonio Costanzi also argued with each other. Their controversy did not reach the heights of invective, yet each referred to the other with great anxiety, to say the least. Their dispute revolved around whose commentary was first. Although Costanzi's *Fasti* commentary came off the press in 1489, he already had a finished manuscript in 1480, two years before the appearance of Marsi's *editio princeps*. Marsi was not unaware of Costanzi's work; his exclamation that "Antonio from Fano . . . has already spent many years examining the plan of the *Fasti*. I do not know if he has reached the end" (*Antonius praeterea Phanensis . . . in indaganda ratione Fastorum pluribus iam annis occupatur. Nescio si illi ad finem perventum est*) seems too consciously offhand for him not to have known something. Marsi follows the remark with what seems to him a self-evident reason for the advancement of his work, namely that "not everybody has at home that store of books which I have in Rome; therefore things which are very easy for me are more difficult for others" (*non enim omnes quae nobis est Romae eam domi librorum supellectilem habent; ita quae nobis facillima sunt redduntur aliis difficiliora*). His presence in Rome, *caput mundi*, gave him a distinct advantage over the humanist in Fano, we may surmise; it is why, he says a bit earlier in the preface,

> I brought my work to its conclusion within a few months' time, which nonetheless should surprise no one. For indeed, I am in that City where the study of the humanities has always flourished, and where a greater supply of books can be accessed than in the rest of Italy, in fact than anywhere in the entire world. Add to this the company of most learned men who flock to the City as though to a common home, so that on all points where there is some doubt, you immediately have someone to consult, which in other places is not at all the case.

> *Nos vero paucis mensibus ad finem deduximus, quod tamen admirationi debet esse nemini. Sumus enim in ea urbe in qua humanitatis studia semper floruerunt, ubi et maior librorum copia quam in cetera Ausonia, immo in toto orbe, posset comperiri. Adde et doctissimorum hominum frequentiam qui in urbem tanquam in communem patriam confluunt, ita ut in omnibus in quibus aliqua oriretur dubitatio, statim quem consulas occurrit, quod in ceteris locis minime erit.*

Indeed, Rome was a book collector's haven. German printers set up shop first in Rome, with its large transient population and ready consumer market.[83] Books were available not only for purchase but also for loan. With Sixtus IV's formal creation of the Vatican Library in 1475, and his appointment of Platina as prefect, books and manuscripts could be borrowed. Many professors at the *Studium Urbis,* such as Andrea Brenta, Domizio Calderini, Sulpizio da Veroli, and Pomponio Leto, took advantage of borrowing privileges, as their names on loan registers show. Leto put his house and his own collection of codices at the disposal of his friends, so that his residence on the Quirinal became just the sort of gathering place Marsi mentions, where intellectuals could converse with one another.[84]

Yet Antonio Costanzi was certainly not shut off from the rest of the scholarly world, even if he did not reside in Rome. The colophon of his autograph manuscript of the *Fasti* reads *Finis anno MCCCCLXXX.* Since 1480, the commentary had been housed in the library of Federico of Urbino, the dedicatee. But the fact that there was only one copy of his finished product proved problematic for Costanzi. Because his commentary was in manuscript form, it did not know widespread circulation.

Federico da Montefeltro, the duke of Urbino, preferred manuscripts over printed books. He directly commissioned deluxe manuscripts with elegant handwriting, few abbreviations, ample white margins, and decorations. He also asked the bookseller Vespasiano da Bisticci to keep a special eye out for such manuscripts, in order to furnish his cultural monument, the lavish library in Urbino.[85] Federico purposefully portrayed himself as a refined and intellectual humanist prince, and manuscripts, which were more costly than new books, lent status and conveyed exclusivity.[86] In its

---

83. Modigliani (2005, 75–76).
84. Vircillofranklin (2002, 375–77); Campanelli and Pincelli (2000, 119–20); Accame Lanzillotta (2000, 78).
85. Peruzzi (2004, 27, 76–78).
86. Modigliani (2005, 67), states that a manuscript leaf cost about ten times the price of a printed leaf (or six to eight times as much, if the printed leaf were from a second-hand book). As for the exclusivity associated with owning a manuscript, see B. Richardson (2009, 1, 12).

architectural design and in what it housed, the library formed an integral part of Federico's resplendent ducal palace. In the preface of his *Fasti* commentary, Costanzi praises this

> grandest library with its ceiling pendents, staircases, and stone floor buttressed underneath by some wondrous system; the fresco work, the extravagant gold, the emblems, the paintings, fashioned together at last at such great expense and with such cleverness and skill, that no one would willingly leave the sight of it.
>
> *amplissima bibliotheca, pensilibus, scalis et admirabili quadam ratione suffultis pavimentis, tectorio, auro nimio, signis, picturis, tanta demum impensa, tanta solertia et artificio condita, ut nemo ab eius spectaculo, nisi invitus, abscedat.*[87]

Despite this tribute to the duke of Urbino, the knowledge that his manuscript was not widely known agitated Costanzi, all the more when Marsi's *Fasti* commentary was emerging. In his 1489 *editio princeps*, Costanzi lays claim to the primacy of his work through an appended letter to a student of his, Zagarello Gambitelli:[88]

> It does not annoy me, as I see you suspect, that you write "Marsi of Pescina is a most acclaimed poet and a friend of mine." You know indeed that I precede him in the edition of his work and that I have always spurned those profits which many seek from printers: I am more than rich enough in the gifts and abundance of immortal God and, something better, in my generosity of spirit—things which Marsi has customarily spurned. And you know that I published my commentary long before he began his, as can witness all of Urbino, whose royal library displays my work, almost brittle from age and use. There (to name but a few) Lodovico Odasio of Padua, a most learned young man in Latin and Greek, Lorenzo Astemio of Macerata, a most lettered man and long since prefect of the library for the illustrious emperor Federico, and leading citizen Ottaviano, most eminent and remarkable in knowledge of all the liberal arts, have rendered the studies which I toiled over by candlelight so illustrious with their praise, that I can justly disregard the glory which the publishers could spread abroad for me.

---

87. While the 1497 edition has *auro nimio*, the 1489 *ed. princeps* reads *auro minio*—"the gold, the vermillion." The passage is also cited in Peruzzi (2004, 150–51).

88. Cf. Formichetti (1984, 373).

Non est nobis molestum, ut te video suspicari, quod scribis Marsum Piscinatem poetam clarissimum ac nobis familiaritate coniunctum. Praevertere nos impressione operis sui nosti enim et contempsisse nos semper eos quaestus quos multi ab impressoribus aucupantur, cum immortalis Dei munere satis superque divitiis abundemus, et (quod melius est) animi magnitudine. Qui eas spernere consuevit, et edidisse commentarios nostros multo antequam is aggrederetur suos, uti omne Urbinum testari potest, cuius regia Bibliotheca nostrum opus paene attritum et inveteratum ostendit, ubi, ut alios omittam, Ludovicus Odoaxius Patavinus, iuvenis utriusque linguae doctissimus, et Laurentius Abstemius Maceratensis, vir litteratissimus ac Praefectus Bibliothecae iampridem apud inclytum Imperatorem Federicum et Octavianum principem, eminentissimum omniumque liberalium artium cognitione praestantem, lucubrationes nostras tantum in modum suis laudibus illustrarunt, ut merito eam gloriam neglexerimus quam disseminare nobis poterunt impressores.

The date of the letter is June 1482, in other words, when Marsi's commentary was going to press. At the time Zagarello was also in Venice, and he apparently conferred with Marsi, as Costanzi's reference, "most acclaimed poet and a friend of [yours]," suggests. At the end of his letter, Costanzi invites Zagarello back to Fano (*Vale, et si Venetiis avelli potes tandem in patriam redi. Fani Idibus Iuniis Mccclxxxii*).

The contents of Costanzi's letter and Marsi's *Emendatio quorundam locorum* both make clear that Zagarello acted as a sort of go-between, who informed Costanzi about certain points of Ovidian exegesis that Marsi was making and vice versa. The main issue was the identification of *spica Cilissa*, which ancient Romans burned on the hearth on January 1. At *F.* 1.76, Marsi claims this is not Cilician saffron, a blossom, but rather Cilician nard or spikenard, a plant identifiable by its bristly top. "Indeed, the poet does not talk about a Cilician *flower* (*flos*)," Marsi points out, attentive to Ovid's words, "but a Cilician *bristle* (*spica*), and from this we must understand nard, of which Pliny says 'all kinds have a pleasing scent'" (*non enim dixit flos Cilissus, sed spica Cilissa, et de nardo intelligit, de quo Plinius "odoris gratia omnibus maior"* [*NH* 12.44]). Marsi then refers to his experience from a trip along the coast of Turkey in 1469; "even if you do not read in Pliny about the nard of Cilicia," he explains,

> that does not matter. For truly, Pliny does not say that nard does not grow in Cilicia.... Moreover, I picked spikenard on the coast of Cilicia with my very own hands, and I showed it to my audience when I lectured

on this line. Besides, although saffron has a substantial scent, it still is not burned for its scent, but is for other use.

> *Etsi Cilissum nardum non legas apud Plinium, non refert. Non enim inquit Plinius non nasci in Cilicia nardum. . . . Ego autem in ora Ciliciae spicam meis manibus legi et auditoribus meis ostendi, cum haec legerem. Praeterea crocus, cum sit magni odoris, ad odorem tamen non aduritur, sed alius usus est.*

Saffron is extracted from a species of crocus, the word that is here employed by Marsi; *crocus* can mean both the flower and the spice derived from it. Marsi notes that when he was teaching, many "were railing against me, because I wished the spikenard to be understood, while they were of the opinion that the most highly-praised saffron from Cilicia was meant" (*in me invehebantur, quoniam de spica nardi voluerim intelligi, cum ipsi de croco ex Cilicia laudatissimo provenienti intelligendum esse censerent*). This same point is taken up by Antonio Costanzi in his letter to Zagarello. Informed about Marsi's reading for *spica Cilissa*, he writes (immediately after scorning the praise that publishers could spread abroad for him):

> The fact that you indicate to me Marsi has decided *spica Cilissa* is spikenard, not saffron, because he gathered spikenard in Cilicia with his own hands, because the saffron plant does not have a bristle, because it was not customarily burned for its scent—that does not mean that I regret having made public what *I* wrote.

> *Quod autem mihi significas placere Marso spicam Cilissam nardum esse non crocum, quod ipse suis manibus nardum in Cilicia legerit, quod crocus spicam non habeat, quod ad odorem uri non consueverit, non facit ut quod scripsimus edidisse poeniteat.*

Costanzi brings in as an authoritative textual witness Pliny, who records that Cilicia is celebrated for its crocus (*scripsimus spicam cilissam crocum esse, quod prima nobilitas sit Cilicio croco, ut auctor est Plinius* [*NH* 21.16]).

For his part, Marsi quickly responded to the criticism directed at him by his colleagues in Rome and by Costanzi. In the appended *Emendatio quorundam locorum* he writes:

> I said that spikenard was to be understood [at *F.* 1.76]. Many people criticized my reading since Pliny did not mention Cilician nard—as though it can't be found elsewhere just because Pliny does not report it. But

let them finally read Dioscurides whom the most erudite young man Ermolao Barbaro, upon whom all praise of letters has been heaped, has just translated into Latin. They will positively find that nard also grows in Cilicia.[89]

Diximus enim in primo libro eo in loco et sonet accensis spica Cilissa focis de nardo intelligendum. Damnabant illud multi, ea ratione quod Cilissi nardi Plinius non meminerit, quasi alibi inveniri non possit, quod a Plinio non referatur. Sed legant tandem Diascoridem, quem eruditissimus iuvenis et omni litterarum laude cumulatissimus Hermolaus Barbarus modo Latinum fecit. Invenient certe et in Cilicia nasci nardum [*De Materia Medica* 1.8].

Since the weight of classical authorities cannot be ignored, Marsi brings in the latest author to be "discovered," the Greek pharmacologist and botanist Pedanius Dioscorides. Again, Marsi uses the press to his advantage. He has put into print the first, unpublicized bits of Ermolao Barbaro's Latin translation of Dioscorides from 1481/82.[90]

In his letter dated 1482, Costanzi cited as witnesses to his *Fasti* manuscript Lodovico Odasio, tutor to Federico's son Guidobaldo, and Lorenzo Astemio, official court librarian. Astemio arrived in Urbino at the end of 1476, when Federico's collection of manuscripts had already begun to take shape, and he compiled the first inventory of the collection; his catalogue does include Costanzi's 1480 autograph *Fasti* commentary, Urb. lat. 360.[91] However, Costanzi's declaration that his manuscript is "almost brittle from age and use" (*paene attritum et inveteratum*) is fiction, a statement made for rhetorical effect, as the manuscript's still beautiful condition indicates.

Augusto Campana advanced the hypothesis that perhaps Costanzi was not referring to his 1480 autograph manuscript as "brittle from age and use," but to an even earlier exemplar, an archetype from which all other copies (including the printer's) might be derived. If so, that archetype is now lost.[92] Counter to this hypothesis is Costanzi's disdain for print, at

---

89. *De Materia Medica,* Book 1, chapter 8 *de montana nardo*, from the 1518 Aldine edition: *Montanam vero nardum, quae quibusdam thylacitis et niris dicta est, Cilicia gignit et Syria.*

90. A completed version of Ermolao Barbaro's Dioscorides with commentary (the *Corollarium*) was ready ca. 1489 and published posthumously in 1517. Marsi's borrowing and announcement of his friend's work is evidence for when Barbaro began his translation (1481/82). Marsi probably met Barbaro for the first time in Venice in 1471 (Pontari 2008, 742). For the genesis and development of Barbaro's work, see Ramminger (1999).

91. Peruzzi (2004, 32–34); Campana (1950, 246). Astemio's inventory is Vatican City, BAV, Urb. lat. 1761.

92. Campana (1950, 249, fn. 1).

least initially: his work has already garnered such attention in the court of Urbino that he could "justly disregard the glory which the publishers could spread abroad for [him]" (*ut merito eam gloriam neglexerimus quam disseminare nobis poterunt impressores*). For Costanzi, scribal publication *was* publication. This sentiment recurs, but with an ironic twist, in a later epigram, where Costanzi repeats that the ducal library is his witness:

> I was the first among Italians to uncover the *Fasti*'s secrets,
> > as the ancient library at Urbino proves.
> The printer has spread the news that my work is published,
> > the poor printer, more impoverished than Codrus.
> Still they will come to light, and the censor will see,
> > how worthwhile my toils by candlelight are.

> *Primus ego Ausonidum Fastorum arcana retexi,*
> > *ut vetus Urbini bibliotheca probat.*
> *Distulit impressor nostros vulgare labores,*
> > *impressor Codro pauper pauperior.*
> *Hi tamen in lucem venient, censorque videbit*
> > *quidnam operae pretii nostra lucerna ferat.* (ll. 7–12)[93]

Costanzi suggests that because he is mentioned in Paolo Marsi's *editio princeps*, the world now knows of his work. He slights Marsi's printer by comparing him to the Juvenalian character Codrus, whose poverty was proverbial; Costanzi perhaps implies that unsold copies of Marsi's *Fasti* commentary will lead to the printer's financial ruin.[94] By the time of this epigram, Costanzi had more than likely personally seen Marsi's first edition, as *censor* suggests. Marsi held the Roman Academy title of censor in 1482, and it appears in the colophon of the 1482 printed *Fasti* commentary.

Despite all his protestations, Antonio Costanzi realized a little late that he, too, needed to take advantage of innovation and circulate his work in print. The person who most likely convinced him of the

---

93. The poem from Costanzi's 1502 *Epigrammatum libellus* is no. 94 (*Ad Franciscum Ubertum Caesenatem*) in Castaldi (1916, 332). It is also discussed by Campana, who notes that Costanzi's son-in-law Giovanni Antonio Torelli repeated the lines *Ausonidum primus Fastorum arcana retexit, / ut vetus Urbini bibliotheca probat* in his own epigram, composed in 1490 for Costanzi's death (1950, 247–48).

94. *Nil habuit Codrus;* Juvenal, *Sat.* 3.208. For the proverb *Codro pauperior* see Erasmus, *Adage* I.vi.76, in *The Collected Works of Erasmus*. Vol. 32: *Adages I.vi.1 to I.x.100*, ed. R. A. B. Mynors (Toronto: University of Toronto Press, 1989), 51–52. For the economic hurdles printers faced, see B. Richardson (1999, 25–38).

urgency to publish in 1489 was Lorenzo Astemio, the very friend whom he invokes on his behalf in the letter to Gambitelli. Astemio had entered the duke of Urbino's employ in late 1476, but had previously been editor in the printing house recently established in Cagli. Astemio had dedicated two works to Ottaviano Ubaldini, who was Federico's right-hand man. Costanzi calls Ottaviano "leading citizen," a gentle pun on the name Octavian to indicate his close bond and identification with the "emperor" Augustus, that is, Federico Montefeltro (*inclytum Imperatorem Federicum et Octavianum principem*).[95] Not only was Ottaviano Federico's "double," ruling Urbino in Federico's absence; he was also Urbino's cultural advisor, a "most eminent and remarkable [man] in knowledge of all the liberal arts" (*eminentissimum omniumque liberalium artium cognitione praestantem*) in Costanzi's words. Apparently Astemio's editorial experience gave him access to Ottaviano, who would have introduced him to Federico's court. It has been suggested that Astemio and Ottaviano shared a "clandestine" interest in typography, considering Cagli's location only a little to Urbino's south.[96]

It appears that even after Costanzi's death in 1490, Astemio had a hand in publishing his work. We can infer this from the subsequent pattern of Astemio's involvements. In 1499, Astemio left his post as chief librarian in Urbino to become a teacher of grammar in Costanzi's native Fano. In 1501 the printer Gerson Soncino moved to Fano, and soon thereafter "Astemio exhorted all who had unpublished manuscripts of good Latinity to send them to . . . Soncinus, so that being printed by so well-known a man" their names would be remembered by posterity.[97] One of the first works to come off Soncino's press was Costanzi's own *Epigrammatum libellus,* published posthumously in 1502 under the direction of Costanzi's son Giacomo.[98]

In the end, perhaps the 1489 first and only stand-alone printing of Costanzi's commentary had some advantage. Marsi's work had already been republished by that time. In the 1497 composite edition, Antonio Costanzi's commentary is privileged typographically, with his lemmatized remarks preceding Marsi's; and in 1527, the *Fasti* edition came to be known as *commentatoribus Antonio Constantio Fanensi, Paulo Marso Piscinate viris clarissimis additis,* where Costanzi is named first.

---

95. Federico may have been the natural son of Bernardino Ubaldini, which would mean Federico and Ottaviano were quite literally brothers. See de Beer (2013, 268–71).
96. Castellani (1929, 416); Tocci (1986, 16).
97. Amram (1909, 89, 93).
98. Formichetti (1984, 373).

AUTHORSHIP

In the *Fasti,* Ovid twice uses the phrase *vates operosus* (1.101–2 and 3.177) to refer to himself. In the first instance, the god Janus thus addresses the terrified poet, who is searching for the necessary information and inspiration at the beginning of the year, in other words, at the beginning of his literary enterprise. The term *vates operosus,* hard-working and inspired poet, seems contradictory. However, the idea of a poet-seer who must nevertheless toil away has its roots in antiquarian writers such as Cicero and Varro, and it culminates in the creative poetry under Augustus. It is precisely in the age of Augustus and the spirit of nationalism that *vates,* the old Roman word for poet-seer, was revived, displacing the Greek loan word *poeta,* which simply means maker and does not have the visionary association of *vates.*[99] Ovid's self-defining term *vates operosus* is a declaration both of his method, investigative antiquarian research, and of his persona, an inspired authority.

I would like to suggest that the *vates operosus* became a sort of paradigm for the Renaissance commentators on the *Fasti,* whether this was conscious or not. The antiquarian lore of the hard-working poet was a boon to the humanist professor, whose conventional role was to accumulate a wealth of information but whose professional identity was also being called into question. In Marsi and Costanzi we see commentators who find a personal voice and who shape themselves in their work as poets.

Both men were indeed looked upon as professors and poets. In his *dissertatio,* Guarino says of Costanzi (whose *editio princeps* had not yet been printed): "great is the expectation that surrounds Antonio of Fano for his commentary on the six books of the *Fasti,* even though this man is likewise a supreme poet and the most elegant author of epigrams and elegiac verse" (*magna est de Antonio Phanense in sex Fastorum libros expectatio etsi poeta hic idem optimus epigrammatumque et elegiarum scriptor elegantissimus*).[100] As for Marsi, "who has so weightily explained all the Roman rites in his account of the *Fasti*" (*qui tam significanter omnes Romanos ritus in Fastorum enarratione explicavit*), Guarino says,

> There is no more extemporaneous poet alive. His poem has been inserted in the *Fasti,* whereby we are given to understand how great he would have been at the art, had he chosen to temper his disposition.

---

99. Fantham (1996, 89).
100. In Lo Monaco (1992a, 146).

> *Nulla nostra tempestate extemporalior poeta. Illius carmen est Fastis insertum, ex eo datur intelligi quantus in poetica futurus fuisset, si temperare voluisset ingenio.*[101]

The composition referred to by Guarino and which won Marsi such high acclaim is a *Genethliacon* or birthday poem for the city of Rome. Introduced at *F.* 4.31, on Romulus's descent from Venus and Mars and the entire origin of the Roman race, Marsi's poem rivals Ovid's genealogical account.[102] It consists of 285 lines of verse, but Marsi impresses on his audience that even this is just an abbreviated version.[103] Not only does he quote from the poem extensively at *F.* 4.31, but he drops other internal references to it in his commentary, most notably at 4.812, 816, and 818.[104] Undoubtedly it is Marsi's *Genethliacon* that Costanzi refers to in his 1489 poem *Ad Posteros,* when he tells his readers to expect brevity "and not fear a divine ancestral genealogy" (*nec tibi divorum proavos seriemque verendam*).

Marsi draws his audience's attention to his poetic talents when he alludes to yet other of his compositions. For instance, on the origins of the *paraklausithyron* at *F.* 4.109, Marsi remarks, "I would talk here about the first inventors of poetry, if I had not done so at another passage and also in verses of my own" (*dicerem hoc loco de primis carminum inventoribus, nisi alio loco dixissem et carmine quoque cecinissem*).[105] At 4.280 he says about Tenedos, "I have written a poem on the location and fertility of this island" (*nos in ea ipsa insula de situ et fertilitate eius carmen scripsimus*). Marsi probably means his poem about Malta, "lying between the Phoenicians and the Sicilians" (*Sidonios inter Trinacriosque iacens*, l. 4) and "formerly bountiful; now the island remains barren / . . . / and no rain shower has fallen" (*Fertilis hec quondam nunc infecunda quiescit / . . . / et nullus pluviae decidit hymber aque*, ll. 13–16). Marsi visited Malta in 1468 with Bernardo Bembo and probably misremembers the island as Tenedos from his travels the following year in the entourage of Nicolò Canal, Captain General against the Turks in the battle of Negropont.[106]

---

101. Ibid., 144.

102. See the next chapter for the context of this poem. I have not reprinted the *Genethliacon,* since it is fully reproduced with a critical apparatus by Bianchi (1981, 85–95).

103. *Hactenus iuvet haec de Romulo dixisse, quoniam eo natali nos longius progressi sumus ad Augusti tempora.*

104. Bianchi (1981, 76, 94).

105. I have not been able to trace this poem. As Horace offers a lament in front of the closed door in *Ode* 3.10, and threatens the door in *Ode* 3.26, it is possible that Marsi discussed the *paraklausithyron* when he lectured on Horace in 1474–75, and that he easily found subject matter for a composition of his own. Of course, Marsi would also have been familiar with Ovid, *Amores* 1.6.

106. The poem recording the stopover in Malta, "*Inter navigantes quod ad inclytam urbem et illius portum applicuimus,*" appears on fol. 32r–v of the *Bembice,* Vatican City, BAV, Reg. lat.

In addition to inserting self-references and lines of verse in the body of his commentary, Marsi chose to turn half the prefaces to the individual books of the *Fasti*, books 3, 5, and 6, into poems. As prefaces, these poems are in fact separate compositions, external to the text of Ovid, and they are more visible to the reader here than they would have been among the indistinguishable profusion of glosses. The poetic prefaces consequently allow Marsi to exert his own authorship. He does not shy away from imitating and competing with Ovid.

Among the end matter of the 1482 *editio princeps*, Marsi puts in a good word for his finished *Fasti*, a sort of advertisement in dactylic hexameter. The twenty lines, which begin with the charge "go forth now you labors, / go forth my verse, and proclaim abroad throughout the entire earth the finale" (*iam vos hinc ite labores, / ite mei totumque pedes efferte per orbem*, ll. 1–2), serve to attract the attention of potential book buyers. In fact, Marsi seems to have done everything right in promoting his work. His publication was underwritten by his wealthy patron, Giorgio Cornaro, to offset the costs to the printer, who might otherwise be left with overstock and not see a return on his financial investment; Cornaro lived in Venice, center of financial power and expertise in the burgeoning Italian printing industry at that time; and the *Fasti* fell into the category of "educational provision" recognized for its pool of buyers by publishers.[107] Marsi was also clever enough to advertise. He points out the lasting benefit of his work when he directs his commentary to "resonate in all homes filled with childhood years; / it will be your sacred duty to promise constant resource and benefit to youth / and to offer nourishment in grave old age" (*perque omnis resonate domos puerilibus annis; / vos certam promittere opem et prodesse iuventae / fas erit atque gravi praebere alimenta senectae*, ll. 9–11). With a pun on *fas*, Marsi avers that his *Fasti* will be of use over the course of a person's lifetime. He has taken advantage of the circumstances he described in the preface to the second book of the *Fasti*, that he "lectured . . . for the untutored as well as the learned, and young boys as well as older students" (*tam rudibus quam eruditis, tam pueris quam grandioribus natu profitemur*). Marsi now fuses his own poetry with his commentary, work that he has already done.

1385. The journey with Canal to the East is said to be getting under way in the retrospective proemium of the *Bembice*, fol. 1v (*Ipse procelloso turbine rursus agar / ductoremque sequar magnum de gente Canali*), and the trip is referenced in several passages of the *Fasti* commentary. See for example at 4.279: "at the promontory of Rhoetum in the mouth of the Hellespont, entering on the right-hand side near Troy, where I was so many times myself, there was a dock and port of the Argives" (*apud Rhoetum promontorium in faucibus Hellesponti apud Troiam ad dextram Hellespontem ingredientibus, ubi nos ipsi toties fuimus, erat navale et Archivorum portus*).

107. Pettegree (2010, 53–55, 58, 178–79).

Costanzi, for his part, had become shrewd by the time his commentary was printed. His 1489 edition reveals a telling remark on Paolo Marsi and poetry and on self-promotion. In a gloss that is not present in his 1480 autograph manuscript, Costanzi states that brevity is his principle (implying a contrast with Marsi). At *Fasti* 4.748 (*stabulis noxa repulsa meis*), he declares,

> Servius prefers the definition of *noxa* as punishment, by all means as offense. There is no doubt besides that a crime, offense, punishment, and fault are all called *noxa*. Read Festus, Nonius, Donatus, Macrobius, and Ulpian, so that if I have repeated something they record about this, you will not use that saying of Horace against me: "a leech that will not let go of the skin until he is full of blood."

> *Servius [Aen. 1.41] vult noxam poenam esse, noxam vero culpam. Caeterum et damnum, culpam et poenam ac peccatum noxae nomine appellari dubium non est. Lege Festum, Nonium, Donatum, Macrobium et Ulpianum, ne si quicquid de hoc tradunt recitavero, dicas in me illud Horatii "non missura cutem nisi plena cruoris hirudo [Ep. 2.3.476]."*

The leech that won't stop until gorged with blood is the image Horace leaves the reader with in the last line of his *Ars poetica*, and it refers to the poetaster. Given that Costanzi's comment did not appear in his 1480 manuscript, and that his distaste for Marsi's "divine ancestral genealogy" is clear, we can safely assume that the Horatian quote is a jab at Marsi.

Costanzi also drew positive attention to his own poetic *ingenium*. In the 1489 *editio princeps*, the following distinction has been added to the summary prefaces to Books 2 and 3 of the *Fasti:* "*Interpretatio Secundi / Tercii libri per Antonium Constantium Fanensem Poetam Laur[eatum]*." Already in 1468 Emperor Frederick III had bestowed the laurel crown on Costanzi in Rome; now Costanzi's Ovidian readership was reminded of his status as poet laureate in the commentary first printed by Eucharius Silber in Rome.

Two of Costanzi's epigrams appear for the first time in the 1489 Rome edition of his *Fasti* commentary. At Ovid's invocation *Bellice Mars* (*F.* 3.1), Costanzi says he finds it appropriate to include "that epigram of mine which I recently sent you, most excellent general Federico" (*nostrum illud epigramma, quod proxime ad te misimus, Federice imperatorum excellentissime*):

Harsh engine of war, the task summons you
> to make the enemy, a stranger afar, yield to Italy.
In you lies Rome's every hope and inclination;
> destiny prepares leaves for your laurel-bearing brow.

Hostis ut Hesperiis cedat procul advena terris,
> *durum Martis opus te vocat iste labor.*
In te omnis Latii spes inclinata recumbit;
> *fata parant fronti gramina laurigerae.* (ll.1–4)[108]

The epigram may very well refer to Federico's defeat of Sigismondo Malatesta in 1463 and the subsequent return of territory in the March of Ancona to the Papal States. Federico da Montefeltro died in 1482; it is all the more interesting, then, that this epigram does not appear in the autograph manuscript that Costanzi dedicated to him. The 1489 published statement "that epigram . . . recently sent to you, most excellent general Federico" again raises the question of whether or not some previous manuscript of Costanzi's existed prior to 1480, an archetype that is now lost.

With no aim but to impress and delight in his own poetic ingenuity, Costanzi appends the following at *F.* 6.176, on the pygmy: "In my time, I saw a man in Umbria who was a little taller than the pygmies. His name was Leonello, and I once wrote some playful verses about him" (*Nos paulo proceriorem pygmaeis hac aetate in Umbria vidimus hominem, cui Leonello nomen fuit, in quem lusimus olim his versibus*):

When his cloak is let down to his ankles and lifted
> mid-thigh, there is naught. What is Leonellus?
You say "nothing," but "nothing" is taller than "naught,"
> so what is he? Leonellus is "nada."

Demissa nihil est ad talos veste femurque
> *subducta ad medium. Quid Leonellus erit?*
Respondes nihilum. Nihilum sed longius ipso
> *est nihil, at quid erit? nil Leonellus erit.*[109]

---

108. Line 1: cf. *Hostis ut Ausoniis discederet advena terris* (Silius Italicus, *Punica* 17.1). Line 2: cf. *Nos vocat iste labor* (Statius, *Ach.* 1.539). The epigram, addressed *Ad Federicum inclytum ducem Urbinatum*, was published posthumously in *Antonii Constantii Epigrammatum Libellus [. . .]* (Fano: Hier. Soncino, 1502), fol. 3r.

109. *Ad Varum de Leonello pumilo*, in *Epigrammatum Libellus* fol. 4r. The third line reads

Whether to find fulfillment, please an audience, win patrons, or simply stand out from the crowd, both Marsi and Costanzi promoted their literary identity in an age of transition. Print culture gave commentators the push, if not the motivation, to publish and to distinguish themselves from everybody else.

In assuming the mantle of poet, a commentator would appear to challenge the very poet whom he was to explicate. Nevertheless a yearning for creative autonomy is expressed by Filippo Beroaldo in the dedicatory epistle to his Propertius commentary, when he pronounces: "the greatest, or better yet divine, virtue is that of poets . . . but a great virtue also is that of the interpreter" (*Maxima est vel potius divina virtus poetarum. . . . Magna etiam vis et ipsorum explanatorum*). This statement does, to a degree, reflect humility and the prolonging of the commentary tradition.[110] But given Beroaldo's habit of mind, we ought to interpret him as suggesting that while exegesis is commendable, the highest virtue still lies in the creative power itself.[111] It therefore comes as no surprise that when Poliziano was hired as professor of rhetoric at the Florentine *Studio* in 1480, he chose for his first lecture course Statius's *Silvae*, the source for his own *Stanze*. Poliziano wished to create an immediate association between himself and the author on whom he was commenting, implicit in the prefatory remarks concerning *furor poeticus*. By referring to Statius's capacity for improvisation, Poliziano wanted his audience to recall his own poetic talents and displays in the Medici household.[112] The professions of university lecturer and poet were not mutually exclusive: Poliziano's final success may very well have been his eminence as an author and poet who, like Vergil or Horace, was read in the schools—a status Marsi or Costanzi probably never could have imagined.[113]

---

respondens nihilum, sed longius ipso in the *Fasti* commentary. However, I have recorded it here as preserved in Ravenna, Biblioteca Classense, Ms. 74 fol. 30v, in Prete (1972), facing p. 2.

110. Buck, in Buck and Herding (1975, 7–8).

111. Beroaldo succeeded more than most commentators in keeping the attention of his students and making lectures lively. Furthermore, he self-consciously imitated the ancient author Apuleius and successfully promoted his work in print. See Gaisser (2005).

112. Martinelli (1978, 105).

113. In addition to the *Stanze* in *volgare*, Poliziano also wrote *Silvae* (*Manto, Rusticus, Ambra,* and *Nutricia,* 1482–86), which were the focus not only of lectures but also of commentaries. His *Silvae* "came to assume a canonical status in university courses throughout sixteenth-century Europe" (Coroleu 1999, 169). In the city of Gouda in Northern Europe, the Italian poet Baptista Mantuanus was also read by students (Hoven 1979, 551). My thanks to Terence Tunberg for pointing me to this information.

CHAPTER FOUR

Antiquarianism I

THE ROMAN ACADEMY, THE *FASTI,* AND A
NEW HISTORICISM

OVID AS GUIDE TO THE CITY

In his 1503 dialogue *De Culice,* Pietro Bembo dramatizes the corollary relationship between textual and archeological inquiry in Renaissance Rome. The interlocutor Ermolao Barbaro decries the hidden and obstructed physical layout of the City: "Not only those things which till now had been able to remain standing have been neglected," he notes,

> but also those very things which still do stand and remain. The circular Pantheon, one building of all in particular which should stand out and be seen far and wide in the surrounding cobblestoned square, they have gradually so hedged in with houses and taverns up to the very temple walls, that it is now only scarcely and poorly viewed from the north.
>
> . . . *non ea modo quae stare adhuc potuerant negliguntur, sed illa ipsa etiam quae stant quaeque permanent . . . Pantheum quidem ipsum, quae profecto aedes una omnium maxime, quoniam rotunda est, late circumstrato foro patere undique prospicique debuerat, ita paulatim domibus tabernisque ad templi parietes ex aedificatis obsepierunt, ut ab aquilone tantum nunc vix aegreque conspiciatur.*

He equally rues the fate of the Vatican Obelisk, which has also been blocked from view, and he inquires of his friend Pomponio Leto:

> What about writings which have been lost from sight, which are not just a pleasure and a delight, but also relief and medicine, food and drink for the soul as it were? Such a large number indeed in every genre of learned ancient authors whether Greek or Roman, the Poets especially—how must they be made public?[1]

> *Quid illa vero, Pomponi, quae non oblectamenta modo et delectamenta sed levatio etiam et medicina et quasi potus aliquis cibusque animorum sunt, scripta videlicet illa tot in omni quidem doctrinarum genere antiquorum hominum, vel Graecorum vel nostrorum, maxime autem Poetarum, quae perierunt, quomodo sunt ferenda?*

This exchange typifies Roman humanism, colored with an archeological tint.[2] Prompted by the impressive ruins that protruded everywhere and served as a reminder of the past, humanists uncovered the physical fabric of Rome and recovered the manuscripts of lost authors. The one endeavor in Rome complemented the other; nowhere better could this dual activity go on than *in* Rome.

The restoration of antiquity in both a literary and visual sense accounts for the Renaissance attraction to the *Fasti*. In treating Ovid's text—editing, emending, and glossing it—the humanists at the same time had a guide to the City. The status of the *Fasti* as an antiquarian handbook, wherein the fabric of the city and its underlying civilization might be investigated, is evoked by Antonio Costanzi. In the preface to his commentary, after a programmatic defense of the poem for its benefit to the readers' morals, Constanzi clarifies:

> Add to this that many of the most magnificent temples and buildings of Rome, once the display of Roman majesty, of which either only the ruins of the foundations remain or no traces are visible at all to today's earnest explorer, appear nearly whole and undestroyed in this work of Ovid's, so that the zealous can easily see and contemplate those things which are barely discernible to their eyes.

---

1. Pietro Bembo, *De Virgilii Culice et Terentii fabulis liber* in *Omnia quotquot reliqua, praeter Venetam Historiam et Epistolas, extant opuscula* (Argentorati, 1609), 782–83. Written in 1503, the dialogue was first published in 1530. The setting ideally dates it between June 1490 and July 1493, during Barbaro's last sojourn in Rome. See Danzi (2005, 27).

2. Stinger (1998, 1–2).

Accedit ad haec quod pleraque urbis templa magnificentissima et aedificia olim Romanam ostentantia maiestatem, e quibus hac aetate fundamentorum tantum reliquiae manent aut certe nulla vestigia vel diligenter explorantibus sese offerunt, in eodem opere paene integra et inviolata monstrantur, ut eius modi rerum studiosis quae cernere minime possunt ea facile et videre et contemplari liceat.

In his recommendation of Ovid's verbal witness to the former splendor of Rome, Costanzi has reversed a commonplace of antiquarian writing, which said that it is the ruins themselves, though but a fraction of the whole, that reveal the original. In 1411 Manuel Chrysoloras had insisted that the "heaps of stones show what great things once existed, and how enormous and beautiful were the original constructions."[3] In the *Fasti*, the humanists had a literary counterpart to tell them about the visual. The importance of Ovid's work as a manual was even more pronounced for outsiders to Rome such as Costanzi, who did not have the day-to-day experience of living in the cityscape.

For the feel of the ancient city, there is much in the *Fasti* to suggest the role of Ovid as tour guide. The poet's frequent collocation of "here where" (*hic ubi*) lends an aura of immediacy and local presence. One can imagine Ovid pointing out the site of the former *naumachia*, for example, at *F.* 2.391–92: "here you might see boats moving about where the *fora* are now, and where your valley lies, Great Circus" (*hic, ubi nunc fora sunt, lintres errare videres, / quaque iacent valles, Maxime Circe, tuae*).[4] He could be gesturing to a shrine on the slope of the Caelian hill at 3.836–37: "here where the road is not level but almost level, you may see the little shrine of Minerva Capta" (*hic, ubi non plana est, sed prope plana via, / parva licet videas Captae delubra Minervae*).

It is no surprise that before the humanists revived the *Fasti*, a precedent existed for regarding Ovid as a guide to the City. Many reminiscences, especially from Book 2, appear in Petrarch's description of the monuments of Rome (*Fam.* 6.2). Petrarch even uses Ovidian language while pointing out a Vergilian route: "here was the palace of Evander, here the temple of Carmenta, here the cave of Cacus" (*hic Evandri regia, hic Carmentis edes, hic Caci spelunca*).[5] Information from Ovid similarly

---

3. The statement by Chrysoloras is made in his *Comparison of Old and New Rome*, translated by Smith (1992, 199–215, at 200) and discussed pp. 158–59. Note the echo in Angelo Decembrio's dialogue *De politia litteraria*; see Curran and Grafton (1995, 239).

4. Volk (1997, 299–300).

5. See Marcozzi (2010, 183–85). See also how Ovid points out landmarks in *Tristia* 3.1.27–34, where Ovid's book timidly asks for the way in Rome from a passerby. For the itinerary when Evander takes Aeneas on a tour of future Rome, see *Aen.* 8.314–69.

appears in topographical treatises of the Middle Ages. The twelfth-century *Mirabilia urbis Romae*, written ca. 1143 by a "Benedictus Canonicus" of St. Peter's, contains several allusions and many unacknowledged parallels to Ovid's *Fasti*.[6] Although it was the standard medieval handbook for pilgrims to the Eternal City, the *Mirabilia*'s itinerary of churches is in reality a chart to the ancient monuments and aims less to infuse the devout with religious fervor than to point out former temples and palaces.[7] The *Fasti*'s function and influence are evident, considering the fact that the author of the *Mirabilia* seems to have had little or no acquaintance with the classics or the "classical," other than Ovid's work.[8] The early fifteenth-century *Tractatus de rebus antiquis et situ Urbis Romae*, a topographical catalogue by an "Anonymus Magliabechianus," likewise cites the *Fasti* as a literary source. The *Fasti* serves as a handy reference work for the Roman monuments that are no longer clearly recognizable in the late Middle Ages. For example, the author directs the reader to Ovid for the ruined apsidal hall known as the Temple of Venus and Cupid off to the left of the basilica of Santa Croce in Gerusalemme:

> At Santa Croce in Gerusalemme there was a temple of Venus and Cupid. It is not right for me to speak of these temples otherwise or expound on them further, since pointing them out is not acceptable for a presbyter of the Lord. But may those who read Ovid on the *Fasti* be able to forgive me, since he treats them at length in his work.
>
> *Ad Sanctam Crucem in Iherusalem fuit templum Veneris et Cupidinis, de quibus templis non licet me aliter dicere nec largius extendere, quia non esset dominis presbyteris grata ostensio, sed legentes Ovidium de Fastis possent me habere excusatum, in suo volumine tractantem ad plenum.*[9]

The allusion is vague, since Ovid does not specifically discuss the Temple of Venus and Cupid. As in the similar cases in the *Mirabilia*, what we see here is the general recognition and appreciation of the *Fasti* as a repository of information on Roman monuments, their location and meaning. The *Fasti* was a *vademecum* of sorts.

Ovid was essential for the newly transformative guide to Roman topography by Flavio Biondo, who was more precise in his citations. His

---

6. Kinney (1990, 210 and 220, fn. 26).
7. See Nichols's 1986 edition of the *Mirabilia* (hereafter Nichols), xxviii.
8. Kinney (1990, 210).
9. Quoted by Weiss 1988, 61.

Roma Instaurata of 1446 is interdisciplinary in method; Biondo correlated the history, regions, and landmarks of Rome with the sources available to him. He still greatly depended on literature, however. Biondo favored Livy, but he had frequent recourse to Ovid, and the *Fasti* is cited thirty times in the *Roma Instaurata*.[10] In deliberating and solving problems of topography, Biondo often says that an ancient author "shows," "imparts," or "makes apparent" (*ostendit, edocet, manifestum facit*) a location or the identity of a building. These are turns of phrase he also applies to Ovid.[11] Ovid maps out the city; he "shows that the temple of Vesta was near the Tiber" (*Vestae templum Tyberi propinquum fuisse ostendit, R. I.* 2.56; *F.* 2.11), for example, and "in Book 3 clearly shows that the Asylum was at the foot of the Tarpeian Rock" (*in III clare ostendit Asylum fuisse sub saxo rupis Tarpeiae, R. I.* 2. 69; cf. *F.* 3.431). This sentiment that the *Fasti* can be read as a blueprint of Rome is still echoed by Pomponio Leto, who uses vocabulary similar to Biondo's. Commenting on the gated temple of Janus, which served as an index of peace and war, Leto told his students in 1484, "Ovid instructs where the gate was" (*docet Ovidius ubi porta erat*; cf. *F.* 1.257 ff.).[12]

Ovid was read not only as a guide to the City's physical landmarks and history. Indeed, Ovid assumes more than this simple role in the *Fasti*. Christian Hülsen many years ago pointed out Ovid's debt to Varro, whose *De lingua Latina,* Book 6, Ovid consulted in particular for its etymologies and aetiological approach.[13] As the "father of modern antiquarian studies," Varro left his trace on Ovid: Varro codified the word "antiquarianism" in his systematic survey of Roman life documented through language, literature, and custom, the *Antiquitates Rerum humanarum et divinarum* (AD 47);[14] and Ovid's reconstruction of Roman society, his portrait of religious rites and political protocol, is developed with the Varronian framework in mind. In fact, Ovid is justifiably called "a kind of poetic Varro."[15] Subsequently, it is not just the topography of Rome—the seven hills, the locations and descriptions of altars and temples, physical traces and tangible remains—that the humanists sought in the *Fasti*, but the entire legacy of society. The twofold nature and historical meaning

---

10. *R. I.* (as published in D'Onofrio 1989, 99–266): Book 1, ch. 2, 9, 75, 76; Book 2, ch. 46, 48, 50, 52, 55, 56, 57, 59, 66, 72, 78; Book 3, ch. 27, 29, 32, 61.

11. Brizzolara (1979–80, 36).

12. The statement appears in a student's transcription of Leto's lecture on Varro, *De Lingua Latina,* Vatican City, BAV, Vat. lat. 3415, fol. 75r.

13. *Varronianae doctrinae quaenam in Ovidii Fastis vestigia extent* (Berlin: Goetsch & Mann, 1880).

14. Momigliano (1950, 288).

15. Miller (1991, 10).

of antiquarianism was understood by the humanists. It was reflected in their own antiquarian works, such as Biondo's *Roma instaurata* (1446) and *Roma triumphans* (1459), complementary in nature; the analysis of ancient structures in the one treatise and of public administration and private institutions in the other has been said to reflect two halves of a Varronian ideal. Similarly, in the foreword to his *De Urbe Roma,* a description of classical monuments in Rome, Bernardo Rucellai promised a future series of studies on Roman institutions.[16] The evidence of archeological remains helped antiquarians better understand the society that they were trying to reconstruct, and it was this total objective that the humanists brought to their reading of the *Fasti*.

CONTEXT: THE ROMAN ACADEMY

In his twofold scholarly approach to the city which he so loved, studied, and explored, Pomponio Leto well fits the description of the Renaissance antiquarian. He composed a regionary catalogue of Rome, gave walking tours of the ancient sites, and carried with him a field notebook for recording classical inscriptions, some of which he also collected and displayed in his home on the Quirinal hill.[17] These activities all testify to Leto's interest in Rome's physical feel and form. But Leto was no less interested in the fabric of Roman society; he compiled a survey of the Republican legal and political system (*De Romanis magistratibus, sacerdotiis, iurisperitis et legibus*), revived the ancient custom of the Palilia or celebration of Rome's founding on April 21, and made visits to the paleo-Christian catacombs on the Via Appia with members of his Academy. He reportedly was so enthusiastic about the former civilization of the city that he dressed in a toga and gardened according to the precepts of Columella. Much of the information about the city he gleaned from its writers. Among the authors Leto edited, emended, or taught were Frontinus, Sallust, Varro, Columella, Festus, Vergil, Lucan, and Ovid. His commentary on Sallust, in its explanation of the City's founding and the glosses on the names *Roma,*

---

16. See Mazzocco (1985, 124–28). See more generally Mazzocco (1987), and for parallel philosophical approaches between Leto and Biondo, Mazzocco (2011).

17. For the catalogue see de Rossi (1882, 49–87), also in Valentini and Zucchetti, *Codice topografico* vol. 1 (1940), 193–258. The walking tour, recorded by a student (*Excerpta a Pomponio dum inter ambulandum cuidam domino ultramontano reliquias ac ruinas urbis ostenderet*), has been published in *Codice topografico* vol. 4 (1953), 423–36, and again in D'Onofrio (1989, 273–90). Surviving fragments of Leto's inscriptions are in Vatican City, BAV, Vat. lat. 3311.

Troiani, Aeneas, and *Aborigines,* celebrates Roman *virtus.*[18] Antiquarianism was Pomponio Leto's domain, and it is therefore not surprising to discover that Ovid's *Fasti* was a particularly seminal text for both Leto and the circle of humanists who gathered around him.

The Renaissance context for study of the *Fasti* was indeed Pomponio Leto's Roman Academy, as suggested by the historical evidence given in the colophon of Paolo Marsi's 1482 printed commentary (see figure 6):

> Litterariae sodalitati viminali et universae academiae Latinae ad viventium posteror[um]q[ue] usum Pau[li] Marsi Piscin[natis] Poe[tae] Romani fideliss[imam] Fast[orum] Interpretationem Baptista Tortius a Neocastro Venetiis imprimendam curavit anno salutis MCCCCLXXXII et a constituta sodalitate an[no] IIII D[omenico] R[uverio] car[dinali] divi Clemen[tis] Protectore Pont[ifice] Firman[o] et Nestore Malvis[io] Praefectis Pomponio Laeto P[ublio] Astreo et Paolo Marso Censorib[us] IX. Cal. Ianuar.

It is well known that Pomponio Leto in his position as head of the Academy assumed the title "Pontifex Maximus."[19] Apparently, similar titles were bestowed on other members of the Academy during the appropriate years of their tenure. Arnaldo Della Torre has identified the prefect "Pontifex Firmanus," someone of ecclesiastical rank (*pontifex*), as Giovanni Battista Capranica, who was appointed bishop of Fermo on July 27, 1478;[20] his name can also be found under the pseudonym "Pantagathus sacerdos achademiae [sic] Romanae," scratched on the catacomb walls of San Callisto.[21] At the annual observance of Rome's birthday in 1484, Capranica's colleagues mourned his recent and violent death (*Infelix etiam non aequa sorte peremptus / Panthagatus*).[22] The prefect Malvisius is Nestore Malvezzi, a Bolognese nobleman and chamberlain to Pope Sixtus IV, and close friend of Fausto Andrelini, the first Academy member to be awarded the laurel crown at the Palilia or birthday celebration in 1483. Malvezzi most likely helped Andrelini to his appointment of service to the bishop

---

18. See Osmond (2011).
19. POMPONIV.PONT.MAX. is found on the walls of the catacombs of San Callisto; Lumbroso (1890, 218).
20. della Torre (1903, 245). See also Conrad Eubel, ed., *Hierarchia Catholica Medii Aevi sive Summorum Pontificum, S. R. E. Cardinalium, Ecclesiarum Antistitum Series ab anno 1431 usque ad annum 1503 perducta,* vol. 2 (Münster: Typis librariae Regensbergianae, 1914), 154.
21. Lumbroso (1890, 218), and Palermino (1980, 141, fn. 71).
22. Miglio, (1976, 156–57); Tournoy-Thoen (1982, 17–19; 1972, 216–18, 222).

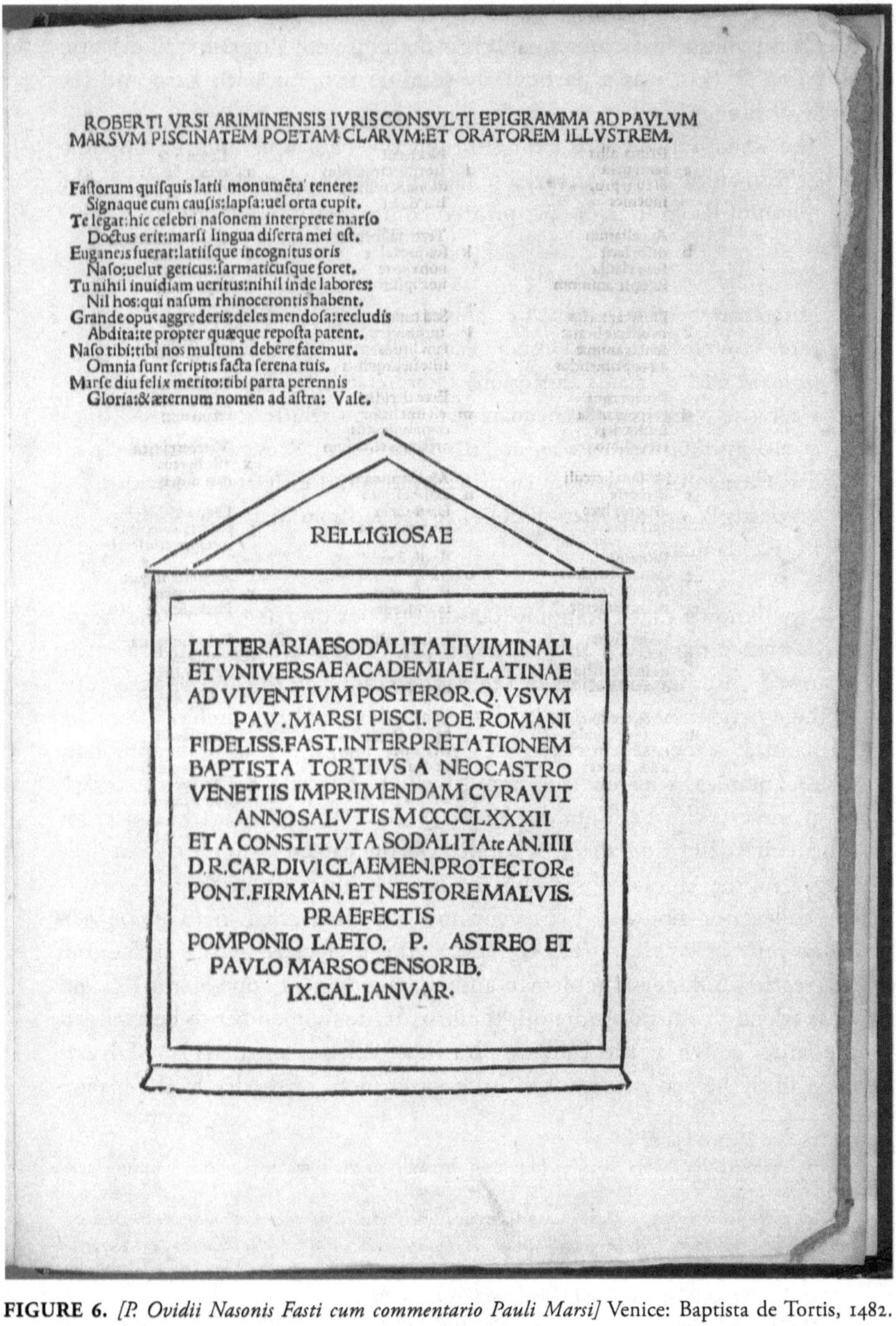

ROBERTI VRSI ARIMINENSIS IVRIS CONSVLTI EPIGRAMMA AD PAVLVM
MARSVM PISCINATEM POETAM CLARVM:ET ORATOREM ILLVSTREM.

Fastorum quisquis latii monumēta tenere:
  Signaque cum causis:lapsa:uel orta cupit.
Te legat:hic celebri nasonem interprete marso
  Doctus erit:marsi lingua diserta mei est.
Euganeis fuerat:latiisque incognitus oris
  Naso:uelut geticus:farmaticusque foret.
Tu nihil inuidiam ueritus:nihil in de labores:
  Nil hos:qui nasum rhinocerontis habent.
Grande opus aggrederis:deles mendosa:recludis
  Abdita:te propter quæque reposta patent.
Naso tibi:tibi nos multum debere fatemur.
  Omnia sunt scriptis facta serena tuis.
Marse diu felix merito:tibi parta perennis
  Gloria:&æternum nomen ad astra: Vale.

RELLIGIOSAE

LITTERARIAE SODALITATI VIMINALI
ET VNIVERSAE ACADEMIAE LATINAE
AD VIVENTIVM POSTEROR. Q. VSVM
PAV. MARSI PISCI. POE. ROMANI
FIDELISS. FAST. INTERPRETATIONEM
BAPTISTA TORTIVS A NEOCASTRO
VENETIIS IMPRIMENDAM CVRAVIT
ANNO SALVTIS M CCCCLXXXII
ET A CONSTITVTA SODALITAte AN. IIII
D.R.CAR.DIVI CLAEMEN. PROTECTORe
PONT. FIRMAN. ET NESTORE MALVIS.
PRAEFECTIS
POMPONIO LAETO. P. ASTREO ET
PAVLO MARSO CENSORIB,
IX. CAL. IANVAR.

FIGURE 6. *[P. Ovidii Nasonis Fasti cum commentario Pauli Marsi]* Venice: Baptista de Tortis, 1482. Colophon. Reproduction courtesy of the Huntington Library, San Marino, California.

of Mantua, Ludovico Gonzaga, then resident in Rome.[23] Domenico della Rovere, cardinal and brother of Sixtus IV, we are told acted as guardian of the Academy after its reinstatement along papal lines in 1479. He was awarded the titular church of San Clemente on August 13 of that year.[24] Finally, the censors of the Academy in 1482 were Leto, Marsi, and Publio Astreo. We know the latter, a Perusine poet, as a collegial member of the sodality. In 1476 he was in Rome at Pacifico Massimo's birthday celebration, which was attended by many humanists from Leto's circle. Astreo's correspondence with Marsi (either Paolo or Pietro) is preserved in Vatican City, BAV, Ottob. lat. 1982, a manuscript attributed to a Pomponian "ambience." Furthermore, he recited the funeral elegy for the academician Bartolomeo Platina.[25] Quite clearly from the evidence that Marsi has left behind in the colophon, his scholarship on the *Fasti* can be situated within the context and pursuits of the Roman Academy.

Although he was not a Roman humanist, even Costanzi was tied to and indirectly honored by the Roman Academy because of his *Fasti* commentary. In the 1497 and later composite editions of the commentaries, the editor's preface is followed by a poem composed by Domizio Palladio and dedicated to Costanzi.[26] Among the epigrams that form Palladio's *oeuvre*,[27] we find one addressed *Ad Pomponium Laetum excellentissimum* and another full of unbridled enthusiasm *Ad Academiam*.[28] Palladio was a student of Leto's and an avid member and supporter of the Academy, and when Leto reinstated the rite of the Palilia, Palladio composed a *Carmen in Romae Urbis Genethliacon* for the 1484 celebration.[29] Palladio may even have tried to initiate similar annual, antiquarian proceedings for Venice.[30]

---

23. della Torre (2003, 245); Tournoy-Thoen (1982, 17–19); Weiss (1961, 138).

24. Eubel (1914, 62, 65; see fn. 20 above); see also Dykmans (1988, 17, fn. 43). Della Rovere was made cardinal on February 10, 1478 (Lovito 2005, 69).

25. Massimo's poem about his birthday has been published in Desjardins (1986, 366–67), with commentary on 453–54. For the correspondence between Astreo and Marsi, see Bracke 1992b, 77–78, 130–31. The funeral oration is reported in Lee (1978, 199–200).

26. *Domici Palladii Sorani tetrastichon ad Antonium Constantium poetam illustrem.*

> Sulmo tumet Nasone suo, Verona Catullo.
> Gloria Romani magna Tibulle laris,
> Umbria Callimacho gaudet, Cos ipsa Philetha
> laetentur patriae moenia clara tuae.

27. On Palladio see Martini (1969). Palladio also wrote an epitaph for Leto, found at the end of Leto's *Romanae historiae compendium* (Venetiis: Bernardinus Venetus, 1499) and reprinted on p. 79 of Paolo Giovio's *Elogia Virorum literis illustrium* (Basil: Petrus Perna, 1577).

28. In *Domici Palladii Sorani Epigrammaton libelli. Libellus elegiarum, Genethliacon Urbis Romae, In locutelium* (Paris: Georg Wolf and Thielmann Kerver for Jean Petit, ca. 1499).

29. See Tournoy-Thoen (1972, 213).

30. Jacks (1993, 153).

While it is true that the Roman Academy "was probably a rather loosely organized group of humanists, acquaintances and students" with fluid boundaries and changing participation, many who belonged to the group, especially those in Leto's inner circle, felt that they were part of the initiated, or "members."[31] Paolo Marsi is certainly one such man with a strong personal affiliation. From the colophon's "in the fourth year from the sodality's foundation" (*a constituta sodalitate anno IIII*) it is evident that Paolo Marsi was a member of the so-called second Roman Academy, dating from 1479. Although associated with the Academy earlier, he had no direct involvement before the 1479 phase. Marsi courted the patronage of Paul II,[32] who had outlawed the group in 1468 on the dubious charges of sodomy, paganism, and republican plots.[33] More to the point, Marsi was out of Rome from about 1464 to 1474; at the moment of the Academy's suppression, he was in Venice, where Leto most likely had helped him to opportunities of academic instruction.[34]

But the Roman Academy in this first period was already dear to Paolo Marsi's heart. Leto taught privately in Venice in 1467–68, and in the summer of 1468 he was ready to embark for the East. Marsi had planned to accompany Leto on this journey exploring monuments and culture, until Leto's unforeseen extradition from Venice by papal decree. The turn of events so affected Marsi that he accepted a secretarial commission to foreign parts, setting sail for Spain in the middle of August with the ambassador Bernardo Bembo. In his poetic travelogue, the *Bembica Peregrina* or *Bembice,* Marsi expresses his thoughts on the Roman imprisonment of his friends, whom he calls *fratres academici.* He laments Leto's seizure and incarceration in Castel Sant'Angelo, and he describes the imprisonment of other Academy members.[35] Marsi mentions that from the group

---

31. See de Beer (2008, 192; 2013, 159–60).

32. Marsi dedicated his *De crudeli Europontinae urbis excidio* to Paul II, about the debacle of June 15, 1470, the wasting of the Adriatic island of Negropont by the Turks. Printed in della Torre (2003, 287–95); see furthermore Ventura (1974, 666).

33. A readable and dramatic tale of the conspiracy (but a not entirely scholarly account) is provided by D'Elia (2009). A summary of the events and a review of Platina's role is given in the introduction to *De Honesta Voluptate et Valetudine* in Milham's 1998 edition, 18–23.

34. See della Torre (1903, 52) on the school that Marsi may have established in Venice prior to 1468. Leto may have also introduced Marsi to the Cornaro family.

35.

> *Heu! meus a Venetis fuerat Pomponius undis*
> *raptus, et Iliacas tractus adusque domos*
> *abditaque in tristi doctissima pectora cella,*
> *et secum in Stygio docta caterva sinu.*

Lines 7–10 of *Ad fratres Academicos Romae captivos*; see della Torre (1899, 64–65). For a full discus-

Then Campano, sweet child of the Muses, was
    confined: woe! tender petitions were of no avail.

Cumque hoc Pieridum Campanus dulcis alumnus
    clauditur: heu! mites nil potuere preces. (ll. 13–14)

In his commentary on the *Fasti*, Marsi interrupts his gloss on the Janiculum hill at 1.246 with

> . . . there is the church of S. Onofrio, well-known for both its crowd of worshippers and for the tomb of my brother Antonio Campano the younger. If the fates had advanced him to a riper age, he would have equaled the fame of the ancient poets with his verse, but envious of his talents, fortune snatched him away from us while he was still in his youth.

> . . . *ubi est templum divi Onophrii clarum tum ipsa religione et hominum frequentia, tum etiam Antonii Campani iunioris fratris mei sepulchro, quem si in maturiorem aetatem fata provexissent, suo carmine antiquorum poetarum famam adaequasset, sed fortuna bonis invidens eum nobis in ipsa adulescentia surripuit.*

Antonio Settimuleio Campano, called "il Campanino" (to distinguish him from Giannantonio Campano, also affiliated with the Roman Academy), was one of the major suspects of the "conspiracy." A talented poet, he composed sixty-eight epigrams, some of them addressed during his incarceration to such kindred Academy members as Platina, Lucido Fosforo Fazino, and Lucilio.[36] While in prison he also acted as copyist for Leto,[37] who later composed an epitaph for him, which was placed in the church of Sant'Onofrio.[38] Campano died at the age of twenty, allegedly because of the tortures he was submitted to while in Castel Sant'Angelo. Platina writes, "Campano, a most surpassing youth and a unique adornment to the times, when you consider his literary talent, was tortured; I dare believe that he died afterwards from his wounds and grief-stricken spirit" (*torquebatur . . . Campanus, optimus adolescens et unicum saeculi nostri decus, si ingenium et litteraturam inspicis; quibus cruciatibus et dolore animi mortuum*

---

sion of the *Bembica Peregrina* (or *Bembice*), see Fritsen (2000b). Marsi's autograph manuscript is preserved in Vatican City, BAV, Reg. lat. 1385 (my source).

36. Masotti (1984, 458).
37. Ibid., 456; Masotti (1987, 170–71); Campanelli (1993, 17).
38. Recorded in della Torre (1903, 99–100).

postea crediderim).³⁹ By referring to this whole episode in his Ovid commentary, Marsi reveals how closely he himself was associated with the first Roman Academy and the influence its setting and milieu had on his study of the *Fasti*.

In the first four reprints of Marsi's commentary, the reference to the re-established sodality is maintained in some form in the colophon, a fairly common type of occurrence in books by Academy members at this time.⁴⁰ Maria Grazia Blasio has made note of the fact that the humanists teaching in Rome at the end of the *quattrocento*—these were for the most part Pomponio Leto and his colleagues in the renovated Academy—influenced the editorial choices and production of books.⁴¹ The humanists worked closely with printers, delivering to them transcriptions of lectures, which were often course notes taken by the students. The *Fasti* was therefore not simply a subject for study in the Academy, but for pupils at the Studium Urbis as well.

The boundary between the Academy and students at the university was a fine one, not so surprising perhaps in light of recent scholarship by intellectual historians, who question the very idea of the academy. While the existence of Leto's Academy, for which we have specific and first-hand accounts, is proven and recognized, the notion of a Platonic Academy in Florence has been discredited. James Hankins dissects the Latin meaning of *academia* and notes the word's application not only to regular gatherings of Renaissance literary intellectuals, but also to humanist schools, the *gymnasium*.⁴² Concetta Bianca argues that the identification of *academia* with a school as well as a coterie began in the 1470s. Pomponio Leto may have associated *academia* with his and his fellows' imprisonment in 1468 (cf. Marsi's poem written that year *Ad fratres Academicos Romae captivos*). However, the encyclopedist and humanist Raffaele Maffei records that it was Leto who implemented the distinctive term *sodalitas* to refer to the group of intellectuals and friends who gathered around him (*domunculam in Quirinali sibi paraverat, ubi sodalitatem litteratorum, ut ipse appellabat, instituit*). *Academia*, perhaps as a result, became synonymous with public

---

39. In Garin (1952, 702). Doubt has been cast on the supposition that Campano died as a direct result of his tortures; he lived for another year after he had been freed from prison. See di Bernardo (1969, 219).

40. Usually the initial phrase *Litterariae Sodalitati Viminali* . . . is repeated, although in the 1485 Venetian edition even the information about the Academy's membership is replicated.

41. Blasio (1986); see also Bracke (1992a).

42. Hankins (1991, 433–35); Hankins's article is evaluated by Chambers (1995). The definition and the history of academies were first considered by Frances Yates; see in particular "The Italian Academies" (Yates 1983).

(and private) instruction. Richardus Graman de Nekenich, a German pupil of Pomponio Leto, marks his 1480 transcriptions of a course on Sallust as completed in Pomponio's Roman Academy (*Pomponii Achademie romane principis in Salustii Iugurthinum Bellum explanationes finiunt*).[43]

The distinction between *sodalitas* and *academia* is clear in the colophon of Marsi's 1482 *Fasti* commentary, where we find the statement that the commentary was produced *Litterariae sodalitati viminali et universae academiae Latinae*.[44] However, the two "institutions" are grammatically linked and not designed to be mutually exclusive. There was surely a conflation of the activities of intellectual exchange and teaching, of social gathering and instruction. The identification of *academia* with *gymnasium* (or *Studium*) sometimes confused the humanists themselves, as we see in the complaint of Paolo Pompilio to Sulpizio da Veroli, both members of Leto's circle; Pompilio reproaches his colleague for his inattention to proper nomenclature "when," he says, "you publicly lecture at the *gymnasium*, which you ineptly call the *academia*" (*at etiam palam cum profiteris in gymnasio, quod tu ineptissime academiam appellas*).[45] This statement bears witness to an overlap of terms and also an overlap in the composition of two scholarly establishments. Students *were*, as a matter of fact, sometimes present at Roman Academy gatherings. The observance of the Palilia, for example, was a university-wide celebration. The diarist Jacopo Gherardi da Volterra has left a record of the day's events for the year 1483. Paolo Marsi read the opening speech; Fausto Andrelini was awarded the laurel crown; and in the church of San Salvatore "the sodality had prepared a sumptuous banquet for the lettered men and university students" (*Pransum est apud Salvatoris sacellum, ubi sodalitas litteratis viris et studiorum studiosis elegans convivium paraverat*).[46]

Ovid's poem was a subject of study for Leto's pupils and Academy members in a frequently overlapping context, as we know from a witness to Leto's work on the *Fasti*, Vat. lat. 3264. The recipient of the codex, Fabio

---

43. Bianca (2008, 30, 32, 36–44).
44. Pomponio Leto purchased his house on the Quirinal hill in 1479. Academicians confused the Quirinal and Esquiline hills and the smaller Viminal in between, as witnessed by Marsi's excursus at *Fasti* 1.259, correspondence between Academy members, and even Leto's own writings. See Dykmans (1987, 106–7); Bracke (1992b, 59, 124); Magister (1998, 167–96); Accame (2007, 19–20).
45. Chambers (1995, 8 fn. 49).
46. *Il Diario romano di Jacopo Gherardi da Volterra* in *RIS* 23.3. Academy and university functions coincided likewise during the Pasquinalia. The Pasquinalia included a poetic contest in which students attached epigrams to the "talking statue" of Pasquino (actually Menelaus holding the body of Patroclus), who was dressed up each year as a thematic Roman divinity. Reynolds (1985, 179); D'Onofrio (1990, 49, 54).

Mazzatosta, was a wealthy young man tutored by Leto, though not a student at the university. Leto produced other fine manuscripts of ancient authors for Mazzatosta, notably a Lucan, Statius, Martial, and Silius Italicus.[47] The educational intent of the group of manuscripts is obvious from the remark at the end of the Lucan, in which Leto hopes to have assisted Mazzatosta's intellectual growth.[48] In a letter in 1471, Giovanni Antonio Campano had expressed his personal hope that Mazzatosta would take in the precepts of Leto.[49] Mazzatosta's interest in illuminated manuscripts and the extent to which he himself was involved in their production were seen as the mark of an antiquarian and a reason for congratulations by Academy member Filippo Buonaccorsi ("Callimachus Experiens").[50] Mazzatosta was also a member of the Roman Academy. The classicized version of his name, "Fabius Ambustus," has been found scratched on the catacomb walls of Ss. Marcellino e Pietro. (Giovanni Antonio Campano can be found there as "Antistes Percutinus").[51]

The importance of the *Fasti* as text for the Roman Academy—students, members, and all—is also testified by the ownership of Leto's glossed manuscript, today II. 141 in the communal library of Ferrara. The coat of arms, a gold deer rampant against a blue background with gold and blue bands underneath, identifies it as having belonged to Agostino Maffei. José Ruysschaert, who had indirect testimony that in 1581 the manuscript existed, lists it as number 115 in his inventory of the famous library of the Maffei family in Rome.[52] A glance at this catalogue reveals that Leto himself borrowed many of the codices of classical authors that the Maffei possessed, and other codices were annotated by Academy members. Maffei was one of the first Academy members to be imprisoned with Leto, commemorated in the verses of the *Bembice* by Paolo Marsi. After lamenting, "Woe! My Pomponio was seized from Venetian waters / and hauled all the way to the Ilian abode" (*Heu! meus a Venetis fuerat Pomponius undis / raptus, et Iliacas tractus adusque domos*), Marsi continues a few lines later,

---

47. Lucan, *Bellum Civile*: Vatican City, BAV, Vat. lat. 3285; Statius, *Thebaid*: Vat. lat. 3279; Martial, *Epigrammata*: London, British Library, King's 32 (with the collaboration of Niccolò Perotti); Silius Italicus, *Bellum Civile*: Vat. lat. 3302. See Pade (2011); Maddalo (1991); Zabughin (1909/1910–12), vol. 2 (1910), 18–27; Zabughin (1906, 228–34); Ussani (1904). Piacenti (2007) attributes seven deluxe codices to Mazzatosta (103, fn. 32).

48. Maddalo (1991, 56); Zabughin (1906, 231).

49. Maddalo (1991, 57); Zabughin (1906, 230). The letter is reproduced in F. R. Haussman, *Giovanni Antonio Campano (1429–1477). Erläuterungen und Ergänzungen zu seinen Briefen* (publ. Dissertation Freiburg i. Br., 1968), 203–4.

50. Pontari (2009, 544).

51. Lumbroso (1890, 216); di Bernardo (1969, 222).

52. Ruysschaert (1958, 354).

"the young and venerable Agostino Maffei / now also has been oppressed in a murky dwelling" (*atque Augustini juvenis veneranda Maphaei / pectora in obscura nunc quoque pressa domo*).[53] Leto addressed epigrams to Maffei while both were in prison;[54] Maffei was finally released from Castel Sant'Angelo in July, 1470.[55]

Although the date of composition of the Ferrara manuscript is uncertain, it may have been produced ca. 1490, in the period when Leto dedicated his edition of Sallust to Agostino Maffei.[56] Maffei has been called "one of the leading antiquarians of the Roman Academy." In addition to his bibliophile leanings, he owned an impressive collection of coins, sculptures, and other antiquities.[57] The discussion of ancient Roman sites and topography was of special interest to him; he had Giovanni Tortelli's section about Rome in the 1449 *De Orthographia* separately transcribed as a book for him.[58]

Pomponio Leto's house, the *Studium Urbis*, the collection of the Maffei family—all came to be established in the same *rione*.[59] Add to this the creation of the Vatican library by Pope Sixtus IV in 1475 and the very accessibility of the topographical landscape of Rome, and it is no wonder that Paolo Marsi would boast about the swift completion of his work in the preface of his *Fasti* commentary.

While Marsi had the good fortune to live and work in Rome, and to avail himself of the ruins that lay all around him, Antonio Costanzi had to take in what he could during visits to the City. He found the time for a guided tour in 1471, while serving as ambassador of Fano among curial circles; at *Fasti* 1.245, he notes: "the shrine of [the] god [Janus] was pointed out to me on the Janiculum, when I went to the City on an oratorical mission from the senate of Fano to Pope Sixtus IV" (*Ostensum enim mihi est in Ianiculo huius dei sacellum, cum ad Urbem me contulissem orator missus a senatu Fanensi ad Sixtum Quartum Pontificem Maximum*). Costanzi's schedule allowed for only a glance at the major attractions, but he again eagerly took in what he could, as is apparent at *F.* 1.709 on the Ara Pacis (for the Templum Pacis):

---

53. della Torre (1899, 64–65) (revised).
54. Two compositions, one to Maffei, another to Platina and Maffei *in tandem*, have been published by Masotti (1982, 202).
55. Zabughin (1909/1910–12), vol. 1 (1909), 181.
56. On the edition of Sallust, see Osmond and Ulery (2003).
57. Weiss (1988, 72, 194); P. Osmond, "Agostino Maffei," *Repertorium Pomponianum*, URL: www.repertoriumpomponianum.it/pomponiani/maffei_agostino.htm, accessed 8 July 2012.
58. Weiss (1988, 72).
59. Chambers 1976, 69; Bedon (1991, 11–15). The Sant'Eustachio region also became the home of the della Valle collection and display of antique sculptures.

where, as Josephus says, "all rarities were collected as men in their zeal previously wandered all over the world to see." When I was on the Via Sacra in Rome I wanted to gaze on the temple's enormous ruins, from which I could not be torn away, even though I was encumbered by the most serious business. I could not satisfy my curiosity, and in my contemplation of the ruins grew angry that fortune had allowed the sight of such a great thing to be stolen from us.

quo ut inquit Iosephus [Bellum Iud. 7.5.7] "omnia collata sunt quorum visendorum studio antea per totum orbem homines vagabantur." Eius ego ruinas ingentes cum essem Romae in Via Sacra volui contemplari, unde avelli non poteram, quamvis gravissimis negociis impeditus, cum expleri mentem nequirem exardesceremque tuendo tantum licet ut fortunae tantae rei nobis spectaculum subtraxisset.

The enormous ruins of the Basilica of Constantine—commonly known as the Templum Pacis—were majestic and awe-inspiring to Costanzi, who wanted to linger upon the sight or marvel (*spectaculum*).⁶⁰ Costanzi's survey of the ruins was hurried, as he sorrowfully admits; one can picture him being rushed around by a local guide, as happened to the traveler Giovanni Tolentino in 1490, who had only four days in Rome and left errors in his travelogue. As a papal diplomat and visitor to Rome, Costanzi did not have the time for indulgent wanderings that Leto and his group did. Costanzi was interested in both the physical layout of Rome and the writing of Ovid, as his interjections in his *Fasti* commentary suggest; the one corroborated the other. Ovid's *Fasti* would have to stand in for the monuments when Costanzi could not see them firsthand.

THE EARLIER GENERATION OF ANTIQUARIANS

To understand the humanists' nostalgia for ancient Rome in general, and the Roman Academy members' methods of antiquarian study in particular, one must take a look back at their cultural inheritance, beginning with Petrarch (1304–74). Petrarch wandered among the ruins of Rome in 1337

---

60. Costanzi glossed *Ara Pacis,* but *ara* and *templum* were evidently interchangeable terms. Note Antonio Volsco's gloss at *Fasti* 1.709: *deduxit nos ad aram: ad templum Pacis* (fol. 30v). The Temple of Peace was built after the capture of Jerusalem in AD 71 and filled with the spoils of the Jewish war. Its identification with the contiguous Basilica of Constantine was common in the Middle Ages and Renaissance; see Shofield (1980, 253, fn. 55).

with his friend Giovanni Colonna. Petrarch's Rome, however, was one of the literary imagination. His letter to Colonna recalling their stroll is not as much a descriptive account of the monuments as it is an evocation of Rome's glorious past seen through literature. When he writes to Colonna, "here was the palace of Evander, here the temple of Carmenta, here the cave of Cacus" (*hic Evandri regia, hic Carmentis edes, hic Caci spelunca*), he echoes passages from Book 8 of Vergil's *Aeneid* where Evander conducts Aeneas to his home and shows him places that will become famous. The overlay of routes only points out how diminished the existing Rome is in Petrarch's eyes. Petrarch trusted literary sources more than monuments, for "search out the entire City: you will find either nothing, or the faintest traces of such great buildings" (*quaere Urbem totam, aut nihil invenies, aut perexigua tantorum operum vestigia*) as the Baths of Diocletian or the Septizonium.[61]

Petrarch's "digging" into the past would instruct and inspire a new generation of antiquarians, who compared text with object: Poggio Bracciolini, Ciriaco d'Ancona, Leon Battista Alberti, and Flavio Biondo. These humanists were in turn the precursors of Pomponio Leto and his circle, and of Antonio Costanzi. Despite the urge to strike out a new path, the antiquarians often replicated each other's mistakes, repeated information from medieval sources, relied on common opinion and folklore, and ignored the physical evidence that confronted them. There was no direct line of development in what was a "lively, rapidly evolving discipline."[62]

Poggio Bracciolini's inspection of Roman ruins from close at hand has been said "to [mark] the beginnings of systematic field archeology in Rome," and his *De varietate fortunae*, a treatise on the ruins of Rome written between 1431 and 1448, was "a charter of the new scholarship."[63] Poggio's words in the opening of his *De varietate fortunae* invite comparison with Petrarch's. Poggio reminds his interlocutor, Antonio Loschi, with whom he shared excursions in Rome, of their astonishment over

> the mutability of fortune, completely astounding and a thing to be deplored, whether on account of the erstwhile enormity of fallen structures and vast ruins of the ancient city, or the immense decay of such a great empire.

---

61. The quotation is from *De Remediis utriusque fortunae* 1.118. See Weiss (1964); Mazzocco (1975, esp. 355–56); Greene (1982, esp. 88–93). In the *Mirabilia*, baths were mistakenly regarded as the ruins of palaces, and the Septizonium was the so-called seat of the seven sciences or a temple of the sun and the moon (Stinger 1998, 67).
62. Grafton (2000, 230).
63. Grafton (1993, 93; 2000, 228).

> *tum ob veterem collapsorum aedificiorum magnitudinem et vastas urbis antiquae ruinas, tum ob tanti imperii ingentem stragem, stupendam profecto ac deplorandam fortunae varietate.*

After dismounting their horses and taking in the view from the Tarpeian Rock, Loschi had lamented

> how different the Capitol Hill [was] from the one which Vergil prophesied, "golden now, formerly bristling with forested thickets;" indeed, how the verse [could] deservedly be changed to the Capitol "once golden, now squalid, filled with thorn and briar-bushes."

> *Quantum . . . haec Capitolia ab illis distant, quae noster Maro cecinit, "Aurea nunc, olim silvestribus horrida dumis"* [Aen. 8.348]. *Ut quidem is versus merito possit converti: "Aurea quondam, nunc squalida, spinetis vepribusque referta."*[64]

Like Petrarch, Poggio evokes the grandeur of Augustan Rome. Citing from the same passage in the *Aeneid* about Evander's survey of the landscape, Poggio is similarly nostalgic for the classical past and distressed over time out of joint. Rome is now a wilderness, and the ruins are a symbol of decay, not only of buildings but also of humankind. The degeneration of the body here hinted at is just the reverse of the anthropomorphic vocabulary of architecture. Poggio decries how Rome "stripped naked of all ornament, [was lying] prostrate like a giant rotten corpse" (*ut nunc omni decore nudata, prostrata iaceat instar gigantei cadaveris corrupti*). In applying the metaphor of the body, Poggio emphasizes his aversion to deterioration.[65]

Poggio ventured into that wilderness and urban decay, however, in order to scrutinize monuments and copy down inscriptions, and in this investigative approach he foreshadowed the practices of Pomponio Leto. In the *De varietate fortunae* Poggio identifies the pyramid near the Porta Ostiense as the tomb of Caius Cestius from the carved letters that were revealed when he swept aside the brambles. Since the inscription was nearly intact, Poggio is surprised that "the most learned Francesco Petrarca wrote

---

64. Latin extracts (and facing Italian translation) of *De varietate fortunae* can be found in D'Onofrio (1989, 67–90, here 67). For all four books of *De varietate fortunae*, whose date of composition and method of compilation are troublesome, see *Poggio Bracciolini. De varietate fortunae*, ed. O. Merisalo (Helsinki: Suomalainen Tiedeakatemia, 1993).

65. The common belief that the air close to ruins was unhealthy is thereby more understandable. Hansen (1996, 100–101 and 114, fn. 97). See furthermore de Caprio (1991).

in a certain letter of his that this was the tomb of Remus" (*doctissimum virum Franciscum Petrarcham in quadam sua epistola scribere, id esse sepulcrum Remi;* cf. *Fam.* 6.2), and he supposes that by "adopting popular opinion, [Petrarch] had not given much weight to careful investigation of the inscription" (*secutum vulgi opinionem, non magni fecisse epigramma perquirere*).[66] The medieval *Mirabilia urbis Romae* had conveyed the information that the pyramid was the tomb of Remus, and it was this tradition that Petrarch followed but Poggio corrected by inspection.

Poggio himself repeated some stories about the ruins of Rome. Nonetheless, he was among the first to collect inscriptions as well as to transcribe those of others, and his *sylloge* (or epigraphical compilations) were in turn consulted, tested, and added to by his successors.[67] Poggio also used recently discovered classical texts for his antiquarian enterprise. He learned about the Roman system of aqueducts after locating a manuscript of Frontinus's *De aquis urbis Romae* in 1429, and he put the new knowledge to use in the *De varietate fortunae*.[68] Pomponio Leto himself co-edited the *editio princeps* of Frontinus post-1483.[69] Literary sources would always continue to complement field work.

The adventure-seeking antiquarian Ciriaco d'Ancona embraced the ideals of Petrarch and Poggio both. According to his friend Francesco Scalamonti, in 1424 Ciriaco "eagerly set out for the famous city of Rome in order to view the world's greatest and most significant historical monuments" (*se statim Romam inclytam ad urbem, ut ex ea primum maxima rerum atque potissima nobilium in orbe monumenta videret, quam avidissime contulit*). On a return trip in 1433, Ciriaco again visited the ruins and told the Holy Roman Emperor that "these are the shining witnesses the ancients left behind them, and they possess particular power to fire the minds of noblemen to the greatest deeds and to the pursuit of undying glory" (*ea praeclara sunt veterum monumenta, virorumque nobilis praesertim animos ad res maximas gerendas et ad gloriae et immortalitatis studium vehementer accendunt*).[70] Ciriaco emerges as a wide-eyed enthusiast for the past, who believes that relics are *sigilla historiarum* or "validating seals of history."[71]

---

66. D'Onofrio (1989, 69).
67. Grafton (1993, 93).
68. Goodhart Gordan (1991, 146–47); D'Onofrio (1989, 77).
69. Frontinus, *De Aquaeductu Urbis Romae*, ed. R. H. Rodgers (Cambridge: Cambridge University Press, 2009), 360.
70. See Mitchell and Bodnar's 1996 edition of Scalamonti (hereafter Mitchell and Bodnar), 15, 17, 47, 68, 117, 131.
71. Brown (1996, 81 and 306, fn. 44), quoting correspondence between the antiquarian Jacopo Rizzoni and Ciriaco.

These relics are "as for Petrarch, . . . living voices crying across the waste for the torn fabric of the empire to be reknit."[72] It was not just the political past that needed saving but the physical past. Ciriaco complained to the emperor how ancient sculptures and fragments were being destroyed by Rome's citizens as scrap material for the lime kilns.[73] He wanted to see Rome whole again; his drawings of monuments from his travels show them complete, staving off erosion and decay, as it were.[74] Flavio Biondo memorialized Ciriaco thus: "by his investigation of ancient monuments [Ciriaco d'Ancona] restored the dead to the memory of the living, as he used to put it" (*qui monumenta investigando vetustissima mortuos, ut dicere erat solitus, vivorum memoriae restituebat*).[75]

Ciriaco took advantage of travel from a young age from his home on the Adriatic coast. He sojourned not just in Italy but all around the Aegean and in the Levant as well. He "converted" to antiquarianism after viewing the inscription and images on Trajan's arch in the Ancona harbor in 1421, and documenting ancient monuments soon became his life's passion. Examining the ruins of Rome in 1424, it seemed

> that the stones themselves afforded to modern spectators much more trustworthy information about their splendid history than was to be found in books. He accordingly resolved to see for himself and to record whatever other antiquities remained scattered about the world.
>
> *lapides et ipsi magnarum rerum gestarum maiorem longe quam ipsi libri fidem et notitiam spectantibus praebere videbantur. Quam ob rem et reliqua per orbem diffusa videre atque litteris mandare praeposuit.*[76]

Everywhere he went, he copied inscriptions, coins, gems, sculpture, and architecture into his sketchbooks, which numbered six large volumes by the time of his death.[77] In this way, Ciriaco preserved testimony from the past. However, it would be incorrect to think that he turned his back

---

72. Mitchell (1960, 471).
73. Mitchell and Bodnar, 18, 68, 131.
74. Hansen (1996, 85). See the drawings by Ciriaco, or copies made of them, by Giuliano da Sangallo in the front plates of Bodnar and Foss's 2003 edition of Ciriaco (hereafter Bodnar and Foss).
75. *Italia Illustrata* 3.5.15, in White's 2005 edition of Flavio Biondo (hereafter White 2005), 260–61.
76. Mitchell and Bodnar, 48, 117.
77. Ibid, 15; Brown (1996, 82–83). For Ciriaco's epigraphy, see especially the essays in Paci and Sconocchia (1998).

on literary tradition. On his journeys he looked for manuscripts too, and along with his sketchbooks he carried his own copies of Pliny, Thucydides, Ptolemy, Pomponius, and Strabo, essential aids for the study of natural history and geography.[78] Finally, ancient texts could be just as much a source of inspiration as physical remains. In his personal manuscript of Ovid's *Fasti*, dated May 13, 1427, Ciriaco recorded inscriptions which he saw in Philippi. Scalamonti writes,

> I know that what particularly inspired the young man to visit this region was the passage he had read in Ovid's *Fasti* about the death of Julius Caesar: "Be witnesses, Philippi, / and those whose scattered bones make the ground white."

> *quae potissimum loca visere nobilem iuvenis animum incitasse cognovimus, quod apud Nasonem in Fastis de morte divi Caesaris lectitarat: "testes estote Philippi et quorum sparsis ossibus habet humus"* [*F.* 3.707–8].[79]

Ovid could be not only a guide to the monuments of Rome, but also a guidebook more generally, an inspiration and complementary source for the study of the ancient past. Significantly, Antonio Costanzi received his early schooling in Ancona from Ciriaco, who had finished copying out Ovid's *Fasti* (with calendar) in 1427 (see figure 7).[80]

Leon Battista Alberti's interest in carved inscriptions is in large part attributable to Poggio and Ciriaco as well.[81] As with his friends, his experiential knowledge cannot be separated from his literary background. Alberti was steeped in classical learning, and in his technical writings he wove in quotes from ancient authors, often refashioning them.[82] But he proclaimed his intention to put equal weight on the close reading of ancient monuments. In his *De re aedificatoria*, completed ca. 1452, he describes his antiquarian method thus:

> No building of the ancients that had attracted praise, wherever it might be, but I immediately examined it carefully, to see what I could learn from it. Therefore I never stopped exploring, considering, and measuring everything, and comparing the information through line drawings . . .

---

78. Bodnar and Foss, xii–xiii.
79. Mitchell and Bodnar, 58, 125, 154. The inscriptions from Philippi are *CIL* III, 647 and 7337.
80. Buonocore (1994, 226); Formichetti (1984, 370); Mitchell and Bodnar, 15.
81. Grafton (2000, 235–39).
82. Regoliosi (2005).

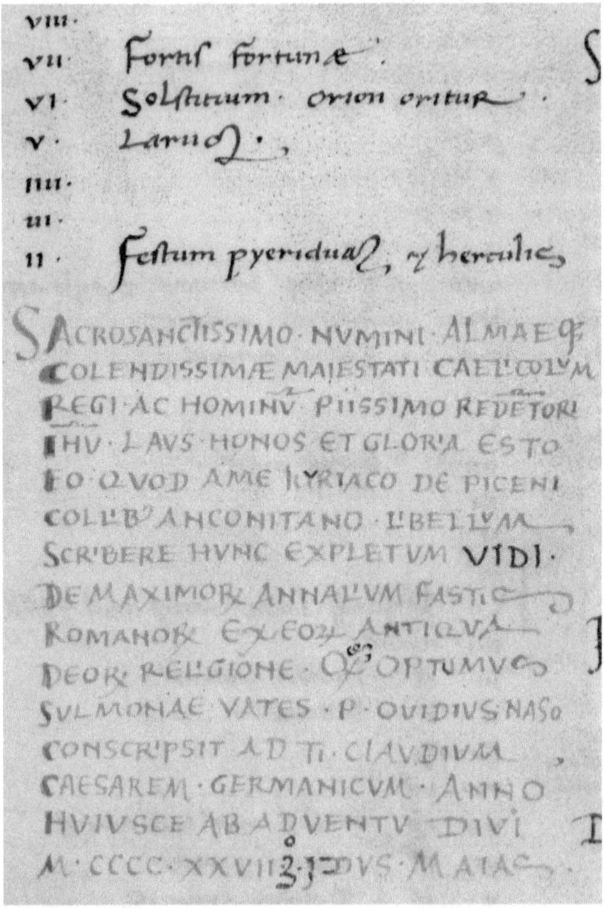
viii·
vii· Fornis fortunae·
vi· Solstitium· orion oritur·
v· Larus·
iiii·
iii·
ii· Festum pyeridum, et herculis
SACROSANCTISSIMO· NVMINI· ALMAEQ
COLENDISSIMAE MAIESTATI CAELICOLVM
REGI· AC HOMINV· PIISSIMO REDETORI
IHV· LAVS HONOS ET GLORIA ESTO
EO QVOD AME KYRIACO DE PICENI
COLLIB ANCONITANO· LIBELLVM
SCRIBERE HVNC EXPLETVM VIDI·
DE MAXIMOR ANNALIVM FASTIS
ROMANOR EX EOR ANTIQVA
DEOR RELIGIONE· QVOS OPTVMVS
SVLMONAE VATES· P· OVIDIVS NASO
CONSCRIPSIT AD TI· CLAVDIVM
CAESAREM· GERMANICVM· ANNO
HVIVSCE AB ADVENTV DIVI
M·CCCC·XXVII· IDVS· MAIAS·

FIGURE 7. Ciriaco d'Ancona, autograph *Fasti.* Part of calendar and subscription with date (1427). Vatican City, BAV, MS Vat. lat. 10672, fol. 68v. Reproduced with permission of the Biblioteca Apostolica Vaticana.

Nihil usque erat antiquorum operum in quo aliqua laus elucesceret quin ilico ex eo pervestigarem siquid possem perdiscere. Ergo rimari omnia, considerare, metiri, lineamentis picturae colligere, nusquam intermittebam . . .[83]

83. *De re aed.* 6.1. English translation: *On the Art of Building in Ten Books,* by J. Rykwert, N. Leach, and R. Tavernor (Cambridge, MA: MIT Press, 1988), 154–55; Latin from *Leonis Baptiste Alberti De re aedificatoria* (Florentiae: Impressum Nicolai Laurentii, 1485), 182.

Elsewhere in the *De re aedificatoria,* however, he remarks with regards to engineering methods:

> We shall ... deal with the materials suitable for constructing buildings, and we shall relate the advice handed down to us by the learned men of the past, in particular Theophrastus, Aristotle, Cato, Varro, Pliny, and Vitruvius: for such knowledge is better gained through long experience than through any artifice of invention; it should be sought therefore from those who have made the most diligent observations on the matter.

> *Atqui nos quidem in huiusmodi rebus quae ad opus aedificiorum commoda sunt recensendis ea referamus quae docti veteres tradidere, praesertim Theophrastus, Aristoteles, Cato, Varro, Plinius Vitruviusque. Nam ea quidem longa observatione magis quae ullis ingenii artibus cognoscuntur, ut ab his qui istius modi summa diligentia adnotarunt petenda sint.*[84]

Ancient writers thus do more than provide a textual frame of reference; they are sources of inspiration and themselves models for the practice of direct study and observation (*longa observatione*), even though a slightly pejorative tone toward the discussion taken up by the ancients does intrude (*istius*). Alberti continues by proposing to compare personal field work and modern techniques to authoritative texts: "we shall add whatever observations are in any way relevant to the discussion from those which we have made ourselves by studying the works of our ancestors or by listening to the advice of artists with experience" (*Addemus ... siqua ipsi ex maiorum operibus aut ex peritorum artificum monitis adnotarimus quae ulla ex parte dicendis conferant*).[85]

With his combination of classical learning and technical skills, Alberti was able to be something of a personal tour guide. He gave walking tours of Rome to his Florentine patrons the Rucellai. From the records left behind by Giovanni and Bernardo Rucellai, it is evident not only that father and son were shown famous sites in Rome, but also that they themselves took part in measuring structures and examining inscriptions up close. Giovanni Rucellai spent the mornings of the Jubilee year 1450 in church, but in the afternoon he inspected antiquities.[86] Every evening, he wrote down what had left an impression on him. His diary varies in accordance with his pilgrimage, from a description of the relics of saints and of marvels such

---
84. *De re aed.* 2.4. *On the Art of Building,* 38–39; *De re aedificatoria,* 44.
85. Note here also Alberti's confidence in craftsmen (Grafton 2000, 76–83).
86. Ibid., 258.

as the *Scala Sancta,* to classical monuments such as the *meta Romuli* near Castel Sant'Angelo. Giovanni gives measurements for the *meta Romuli,* but the very name for this pyramid, thought to be the tomb of Romulus, reveals the influence of the *Mirabilia urbis Romae.*[87] The information on the *meta Romuli* reflects the counsel of Alberti, who had set out problems of measurement and developed surveying techniques in his *Ludi matematici,* but who could not combat long-held opinion and who also surely retold some of the oral traditions passed along by Rome's inhabitants.[88]

Antonio Costanzi would have relished the time and opportunity for such a tour as Alberti might give. His devotion to the classical past was reinforced, if not awakened, by Ciriaco. But arguably the greatest influence on Costanzi, Paolo Marsi, and Pomponio Leto was the antiquarian scholarship of Flavio Biondo. An extraordinary number of traces and direct quotations of his thought and work appear in the *Fasti* comments written by Pomponian scholars. Biondo's tools for uncovering antiquity included coins, inscriptions and *sylloge,* toponyms, and literature. He made a very conscious attempt to distance himself from the *Mirabilia urbis Romae,* and he set out to repudiate the medieval treatise in his attempts to correct the names and locations of monuments.[89] In fact, in the 1446 *Roma Instaurata* he is unique in his analysis of toponyms.

For Biondo, place names were a key to the history associated with places. We can take as a case study the Theater of Pompey complex. Poggio had already detected some of the ruins of the Theater of Pompey lying underneath private homes (because of local lore, he had known to look in the Campo de' Fiori neighborhood). Further ruins—fallen columns of a portico—were visible slightly to the east, in a small area then called Piazza Satro or Satrio, probably from two statues of satyrs discovered there. Next to the portico, which served as a park and a shelter from rain for theater-goers, was a curia. The latter site, better known today as the site of Julius Caesar's assassination, was used into Augustus's time for pleasant strolls. In *Roma Instaurata* 2.112 Biondo writes about the area: "we ought

---

87. See the "Descrizione delle bellezze e antichità di Roma," in *Giovanni Rucellai ed il suo Zibaldone,* vol. 1, ed. A. Perosa (London: The Warburg Institute, 1960), 67–78; page 72: "la meta di Romolo, ritratta a modo d'uno diamante punta, gira da piè braccia 160, cioè 40 per ogni faccia, alta braccia 40, tutta coperta di marmi, in su che si dice essere la cenere dell' ossa del detto Romulo." Cf. Nichols, 35, 86.

88. Grafton (2000, 83, 125, 252–53); for Alberti's writings on mathematical and geometrical principles, in Latin with English translation and commentary and including the *Ludi matematici,* see *The Mathematical Works of Leon Battista Alberti,* ed. by K. Williams, L. March, and S. Wassell (Basel: Birkhäuser, 2010).

89. Fubini (1968, 547–48); Brizzolara (1979–80, 30).

to believe the atrium of Pompeii was there, where it is now commonly known through a corruption of language as Satrum and where now a semi-intact portico is discernible" (*Atriumque vero Pompei credere debemus fuisse ubi nunc corrupte Satrum vulgo appellant et porticus est nunc semiintegrata cernitur*).[90] Popular nomenclature has become a capable antiquarian tool, for Biondo is able to correctly relocate the Theater from San Lorenzo in Damaso, its position in the *Mirabilia urbis Romae*.

By using toponyms as a type of evidence, Biondo could refute common misconceptions, but etymology could also be misleading. From several literary sources Biondo knew the legend of Romulus's extension of asylum to fugitives. In the *Fasti*, Ovid had located the Asylum *sub rupis Tarpeiae* (3.43). Combining this reference with an area of Rome occupied by prostitutes, a place of refuge for runaway women (*nunc asylum institutum*), Biondo incorrectly put the Asylum in the Forum Boarium, at the Temple of Portunus (converted to a church and rededicated at the end of the *quattrocento* to Santa Maria Egiziaca, patron saint of penitent prostitutes).[91] Etymology did not always yield successful results, although we do see the attempt by Biondo to untangle strands of legend.

Moreover, this example shows that Biondo employed not only toponymy but also philology in his investigations. He consulted many authors, including but not limited to Cicero, Varro, Livy, Ovid, Pliny, and Suetonius, along with writers of the late antique and early Christian era. His familiarity with the classics began at an early age under the Veronese Guarino Guarini, who promoted the circulation and dissemination of texts, and who was Biondo's lifelong mentor. Biondo gained a reputation of his own among the humanists in northern Italy, and accordingly he was entrusted with transcribing a manuscript of Cicero's rhetorical works in 1442 (discovered in the cathedral library in Lodi in 1421).[92] Because of Poggio's generosity, Biondo could make use of the recently discovered work of Frontinus on aqueducts for his *Roma Instaurata*.[93] And, of course, Biondo drew upon the *Fasti* for both sides of the antiquarian enterprise, the investigation of monuments on the one hand, and of customs and institutions on the other. The *Fasti* confirmed the location of the temple of Venus outside the Porta Collina and bore witness to the magnificence of the temple of Mars in the Campus Martius. It provided information for the religious festivals of the Agonalia and Februa. As we have seen, it also helped Biondo

---

90. Günther (1981, esp. 359–67); Brizzolara (1979–80, 46–47); Robathan (1970, 207–8).
91. *R. I.* 1.57–59 (D'Onofrio 1989, 185–86); see also Robathan (1970, 209–10).
92. See Castner's 2005 edition of Biondo (hereafter Castner 2005), xv.
93. Brizzolara (1979–80, 34).

identify (if inaccurately) both the location and the custom of the *Asylum Romani*.[94]

Biondo has been noted for his "devotion to collecting and preserving the textual monuments of antiquity."[95] As with so many of the well-trained and well-versed humanists, he often paraphrased his literary sources from memory (the more citations the better), and the lapses in memory, when he has paraphrased incorrectly, do not undercut the overall impression of his powerful knowledge and recall.[96] The manifold references to ancient authors reveal Biondo's trust in *auctoritas*: the perfect wisdom and eternal truths of the *auctores*, the writers of the Greeks and Roman world. But such dependence on the ancients could certainly stifle creativity. Indeed, where there was no answer to a vexing question of archeology or topography, Biondo often deferred to authority. Only where there was a disagreement between sources or where a tradition was obviously erroneous or untrustworthy did he engage in a critical assessment by comparing the textual witness with outside evidence. Even then, he did not always try to resolve a problem. Either older *auctores* were given preference to more recent ones, or Biondo sometimes recorded divergent written opinions without taking a position.[97] An example from *Roma Instaurata*, on the development of Rome's topographical layout, is typical. Biondo begins by asserting,

> It is thereupon a well-known fact that only the Capitoline or Tarpeian mount and the Palatine and Aventine hills, with those valleys which we see in between, had encompassed the city, because Livy shows that all five other mountains and hills were added. For these are the words on the matter in Book 1 about the deeds of Tullius Hostilius: "Rome meanwhile grows on the ruins of Alba; the number of citizens is doubled. The Caelian hill is added to the town and that it might become more populated, Tullus chose it for the site of his palace and lived there."

> *Eam Capitolinum sive Tarpeium et Pallatinum Aventinumque montes solum, cum iis quas intercedere videmus convallibus comprehendisse hinc constat, quod omnes alios quinque montes et colles additos Titus Livius ostendit. Sunt*

---

94. Tommasini (1985, 35).

95. Tommasini gives an exhaustive list of authors cited by Biondo in the *Roma Triumphans* in the appendix on pages 79–80. Scholars have also remarked on the way in which Biondo *detached* sources from their context, so that they became moveable pieces disposed of at will for his antiquarian work. This observation has been made in particular with reference to the *Italia Illustrata*, Biondo's attempt to do for all of Italy what he had done in the *Roma Instaurata*. Castner (2005, xviii [for quotation], xxi); White (2005, xv).

96. White (2005, xiv–xv).

97. Brizzolara (1979–80, 41, 43); Clavuot (1990, 182, 185).

enim illius de Tulii Hostilii rebus gestis haec verba libro primo "Roma interim crescit Albae ruinis, duplicatur civium numerus. Caelius additur urbi mons, et quo frequentius habitaretur eam sedem Tullus regiae capit, ibique habitavit" [1.30].

Biondo goes on with "the second hill added to the new city was the Janiculum" (*secundus novae urbi additus mons fuit Ianiculensis*) and quotes from Livy 1.33, and in similar fashion continues, "the other three were afterwards added by King Servius all at the same time" (*alii tres postea simul a Servio rege additi*), quoting from Livy 1.44. Biondo next remarks without concern, "Tacitus seems to think differently about the borders of the first town; these are his words: 'from the forum Boarium the trench for marking out the town was begun . . . and the Capitoline was added not by Romulus, but by Titus Tatius'" (*sed Cornelius Tacitus aliter de urbis primae ambitu sentire videtur; cuius sunt haec verba: "A foro Boario . . . sulcus designandi oppidi coeptus . . . et Capitolium non a Romulo, sed a Tito Tacio additum"*). He cites from Tacitus's *Annales* 12.24 in full. Nothing about the discrepancy over how the city and its boundaries grew is further said. Biondo simply ignores the variance in the accounts, and he shows no preference for one textual authority over the other. He switches to an immediate "let's continue," announcing his intention to discuss what are now the eight hills and the points of interest on them (*progressuri ad eam inquam tendimus aedificiorum locorumque urbis descriptionen, qui nunc sunt octo montes*).[98]

While this methodology of giving equal weight to ancient testimony is fairly standard for Biondo, there are plenty of instances where Biondo cites the testimony of authors who had lived at the time of construction of a particular monument. Along with his allegiance to ancient texts is the realization that the city-plan of Rome is not static. Certainly this sense of history enabled him to compare material objects with textual sources, which we see him doing throughout his work.[99]

Finally, in 1444 Biondo accompanied Cardinal Prospero Colonna, an admirer and collector of antiquities, to see some remains from two ships that had belonged to the emperor Caligula. Colonna later commissioned the salvage of the galleys from the bottom of Lake Nemi in a move called "the first attempt at archeological recovery." Biondo was able to closely inspect one of the ships, which was raised from the waters under Alberti's supervision.[100]

---

98. *R. I.* 1.72, punctuation and orthography slightly adapted from D'Onofrio (1989, 137).
99. Brizzolara (1979–80, 40–41, 51); for Biondo as a historian, see Hay (1959).
100. Grafton (2000, 248).

Biondo shared with his humanist friends the antiquarian practice of book study and examination of physical evidence. However, just like the men of his generation, and much like Pomponio Leto after him, Biondo employed a method that was not a perfect blend of textual and visual comparison. Perhaps nowhere can this better be seen than in the 1474 historical geography *Italia Illustrata*. One revision to this work shows Biondo relying entirely on his own recently discovered fragment of Ammianus Marcellinus for a description of the Umbrian settlement Ocriculum. Ocriculum had been rebuilt closer to the Tiber river in Roman times, but Biondo neglected first-hand evidence of the ruins at Ocriculum and on the Via Flaminia nearby. Biondo cites classical authors for the existence of a lethal spring on Mount Soracte, but he proves it through personal observation:

> I believe this all the more, since the Most Eminent Roman Cardinal Prospero Colonna and I together wandered all through the ruins of the city of Antium. When we had entered the woods there, we came upon a small spring and on its edge two little birds lay dead, apparently from drinking the water.

> *Quod quidem nos certius ea ratione credimus, quia cum vir summus Prosper cardinalis de Columna Romanus nosque simul Antiatis urbis ruinas perlustraremus, silvas ibi quibus ingressi fonticulum offendimus, in cuius labris aviculae duae post gustatam, ut apparebat, aquam occubuerant.*[101]

Scholars have commented on Biondo's indiscriminate method in the *Italia Illustrata*.[102] Perhaps he was simply faced with where to put his trust most: the wisdom of the ancients, or his own senses.

THE *FASTI* AND FIRST-HAND OBSERVATION IN ROME

The influence of the previous generations of antiquarian scholars on members of the Roman Academy cannot be underestimated. Flavio Biondo was honored directly as a shining light. In his *oratio* for the celebration of the 1484 Palilia, Alessandro Farnese pays special tribute to the two recipi-

---

101. Castner (1998, 97).
102. The seemingly random method may have been due to Biondo's haste (the *Italia Illustrata* was an overwhelming project) and Biondo's unsteady source of livelihood in the Roman Curia (Castner 1998, 101). Cf. White (2005, xiv–xvii) for a gentler view.

ents of that year's *laurea poetica,* Pomponio Leto and "Gaspare Biondo, son of Flavio [Biondo]. The prefect of our sodality, [Gaspare] adorns the name and deeds of his famous father with all his study of the liberal arts" (*Gaspari B[londo] Flavii filio, nostre sodalitati praefecto, qui praeclari genitoris sui nomen et acta omni bonarum artium studio exornat*).[103] Gaspare Biondo, apostolic secretary, oversaw the publication of his father's works, as he says in a prefatory letter of the Rome 1474 *editio princeps* of the *Italia Illustrata.*[104] Both Gaspare Biondo and his father held a place of honor among those in Pomponio Leto's circle; even Leto's daughter Nigella read the *Roma Instaurata.*[105] Antiquarianism—Flavio Biondo's domain—suffuses the intense study of Ovid's *Fasti* by Leto and his colleagues.

Walks around Rome by humanists who were both students of Leto and teachers themselves are quite obvious in the Fasti *commentaries.* Often the Christian churches in Rome acted as markers for the topography and ancient edifices which the Academicians saw, and which they wanted to make come alive for their students in lectures. In a gloss on *Fasti* 3.522, Volsco identifies the Caelian hill as the site of Santo Stefano Rotondo (*Celius Mons ubi est S. Stefanus Rotunnus,* fol. 94v), echoing Leto as well as his predecessor Flavio Biondo, and ultimately, the *Mirabilia Urbis Romae:* "the Caelian [is] where the Church of Santo Stefano in Monte Caelio is" (*Celius mons ubi est ecclesia sancti Stephani in Celio monte*).[106]

Christian landmarks are again pointed out at *Fasti* 4.345, in a passage about the heroine Claudia Quinta, who escorted the goddess Cybele through the Capene gate after drawing the ship with the divinity's statue up the Tiber river. Antonio Volsco clarifies, "through the porta Capena, which goes to the church of San Paolo" (*per Portam Capenam quae itur ad templum divi Pauli,* fol. 127v). He also glosses "Porta Capena is the gate which leads to Porta San Paolo" (*Porta Capena est quae ducit ad Portam divi Pauli*), echoing the identification made by Pomponio Leto in his *Excerpta,* a record of his walking tours.[107] Paolo Marsi mentions the same church at

---

103. The *oratio* is reproduced in Tournoy-Thoen (1972, 226–28, here 228).

104. Fanelli (1968), Castner (2005, xxxiv). Regarding Gaspare's textual interventions, see White (2005, 357–61).

105. Zabughin (1906, 234).

106. Latin in Parthey's 1869 edition (hereafter Parthey), 3; trans. in Nichols, 8. Cf. *Roma Instaurata* 1.80 *ecclesia sancti Stephani rotunda de ipso monte Caelio cognomen habens,* in D'Onofrio (1989, 151). Leto's *Excerpta* is less verbatim: *Caelius mons . . . est magni ambitus; et includit ecclesias Quatuor Coronatorum, Sancti Stephani Rotundi, Sancti Ioannis et Pauli* (D'Onofrio 1989, 286); at *DLL* 5.45–46 he comments: *Mons Celius est ubi nunc est Basilica Lateranensis et Sancti Stephani.* Rome, Biblioteca Angelica, MS 1348, fol. 25v.

107. *ubi est porta Capena, et ad moenia ubi est porta Sancti Pauli* (D'Onofrio 1989, 288).

Fasti 2.601 when he glosses "Almo," a tributary of the Tiber, as "the stream is a little outside the city, along the Via Ostiense; its source is the basin not far from the church of San Paolo" (*Almo fluvius est paulo extra urbem Via Hostiensi, qui ex paludibus oritur non longe a templo divi Pauli*).

Christian churches are the modern landmarks of ancient Roman sites. Their inclusion in *Fasti* comments does not differ in purpose from the parallels Leto draws (for example) between Catholic bishops, prelates, and abbots, and ancient *flamines* in the *De lingua Latina*. Modern equivalents, in fact, make the classical world more recognizable.[108] The Christian references also attest to the paleo-Christian interests of the Roman Academy, whose members made excursions to the catacombs. Perhaps Leto even led visits to churches, if we take into consideration his Latin poem on the succession of Lenten Station Churches of Rome.[109] Certainly Biondo's love for the City was great enough to incorporate Christian Rome and modern monuments in his *Roma Instaurata*,[110] and the inclusion of churches was part and parcel of the *Mirabilia urbis Romae* as well.

Comparative methodology can be seen at work in Marsi's *Fasti* gloss at 6.396. After recording information from Varro (*DLL* 5.43) and Plutarch (*Camillus* 14.2) on the Via Nova, Marsi notes that the street

> connected to the Forum and the Via Sacra and passed along the Palatine, where even now there is the church of Santa Maria in Via Nova. By linguistic corruption people call [the church] Santa Maria Nova, since it is on the Via Nova.

> *iungebatur foro et viae Sacrae tendebatque prope Palatium, ubi et nunc aedes est sub appellatione divae Mariae in Via Nova, quamquam vulgus corrupte divam Mariam Novam vocat, cum in Via Nova sit.*

Varro and Ovid suggest that a slope or staircase joined the Via Nova to the Forum Romanum on the forum's southwest side, and Marsi paraphrases Varro correctly on this account.[111] In the fashion of Flavio Biondo, Marsi cites *auctores* on the matter before he adds modern evidence as proof. And

---

108. *DLL* 5.84: *Flamines: sunt quemadmodum nostro tempore episcopi, protonotarii, et abates.* Rome, Biblioteca Angelica, MS 1348, fol. 54v.

109. The poem is reproduced in Morin (1923). See Stinger (1998, 49 and 347, fn. 126).

110. A point made by Weiss (1963, 339).

111. *qua Via Nova: per quam a Velabro ad Romam ascendebant, ut Varro ostendit*; cf. *DLL* 5.43: *Velabrum, et unde escendebant ad infimam Novam Viam.* In the late Republican and Augustan period, this stretch of the street was obliterated. Even modern attempts to correlate literary evidence with archeological remnants of the Nova are frustrating; see Wiseman (2004).

also in the manner of Biondo he uses place names, but these ultimately fail him in this example. The church Marsi has identified is Santa Francesca Romana, which impinges on the Temple of Venus and Rome on the northeast side of the Forum and is also known as Santa Maria Nova, to distinguish it from Santa Maria Antiqua, which was abandoned due to structural damage in AD 847.[112] The church is indeed close to the Via Sacra, a street that had a more reliable archeological history than the Via Nova. Marsi mentions the Via Sacra in his gloss; perhaps he was hearing an echo of Horace's "by chance I was walking along the Sacred Way" (*ibam forte Sacra Via*; *Sat.* 1.9.1) in Ovid's "by chance I was returning [on the route] which now joins the New Way to the Roman Forum" (*forte revertebar . . . illa / quae Nova Romano nunc Via iuncta foro est*, 6.395–96). However, the church in question did go by the name Santa Maria Nova, which Marsi himself notes is common parlance. This is how we find it called in the *Mirabilia*, Poggio's *De varietate fortunae*, and Leto's *Excerpta*.[113] Marsi miscorrects when he emphasizes that the church is S. Maria *in* Nova, but like Biondo he uses philology as a tool; he believes that the church shares an integral connection with its location, instead of with its foundation history.

Of course, neither the antiquarians of Marsi's generation nor the antiquarians of the previous one were archeologists. They were not involved in excavations (the raising of a galley from Lake Nemi notwithstanding), and they limited themselves to what they could see on and above ground. Entire structures could therefore be confused. For example, Marsi misidentifies the temple of the Mater Matuta or Portunus (*F.* 6.479), occupied in his time by the church of Santa Maria Egiziaca, when he tells his audience "that the temple, circular in form and with upright columns around it, still intact, is on the very bank of the Tiber and on the edge of the Forum [Boarium]—the church of Saint Stephen Martyr" (*Quod templum rotundae formae erectis in ambitu columnis integrum adhuc est in ipsa ripa in extrema parte fori sub titulo divi Stephani martyris*). From the description, it is clear that Marsi has in mind the round temple of Hercules Victor, dedicated to Santo Stefano alle Carozze.[114]

---

112. Francesca de' Ponziani was buried in S. Maria Nova in 1440; however, the name change to S. Francesca Romana did not occur until after the saint's canonization in 1608 (Hülsen 1927, 352).

113. The *Mirabilia* states: *palatium Romuli inter sanctam Mariam novam et sanctum Cosmatem* as well as *arcus Titi et Vespasiani ad sanctam Mariam novam* (Parthey, 5, 6). From *De Var. fortunae* Book 1: *loco edito in Via Sacra, altera occidentem, altera orientem versus, hodie Mariam Novam appellant . . .* (D'Onofrio 1989, 70). See Leto's *Excerpta: In horto Sanctae Mariae Novae est vestigium templi Aesculapii et Concordiae* (ibid., 273).

114. Compare Poggio, *De var. fortunae* Book 1: *Extat et Vestae templum iuxta Tiberis ripam ad*

Still, sometimes archeological discoveries were made, or rather, stumbled upon; it was to the antiquarian's advantage to be alert. From the previous example, it appears that the Forum Boarium was an area of particular interest and activity for Marsi. He gives news of the recent unearthing of a prized ancient artifact at *F.* 1.582 on the legend of Hercules Victor, so named because Hercules had slain Cacus and his divinity had consequently been recognized by Evander:

> Who would believe, now that so many ages have passed since that altar was famous, that in my time, while I was teaching in Rome, the marble quarriers found the Ara Maxima in a far corner of the forum Boarium, and they dug up the bronze statue of Hercules, along with various inscriptions. These were all immediately taken to the Capitoline and placed in the Palazzo dei Conservatori, so that everyone could see them.

> *Verum quis crederet tot iam elapsis saeculis ab eo tempore quo celebris erat illa ara, illis diebus quo haec Romae profitebar, in ultimo angulo fori Boarii ab his qui marmora inquirebant reperta est ara Maxima, et effossa aerea Herculis statua, cum multis circa eam epigrammatibus, quae omnia delata mox fuere in Capitolium et in atrio dominorum Conservatorum collocata, atque omnibus visenda patent?*

The colossal bronze statue of the demi-god was found during the demolition of the remains of a round temple near the Ara Maxima (which Marsi seems to confuse with the Ara Maxima itself). The destruction of the temple and subsequent unearthing of the bronze Hercules occurred during the pontificate of Sixtus IV and has been dated to ca. 1474, which was the first year of Marsi's teaching.[115] The excavation caused a stir in the Roman Academy, as the reports by both Leto and Marsi attest. Moreover, several second- through fourth-century inscriptions dedicated to Hercules were found in the area and transferred along with the bronze statue to the Palazzo dei Conservatori.[116] Both Marsi and Leto refer to their discovery,

---

initium montis Aventini, rotundum ac patens undique nullo muro, frequentibus tantum suffultum columnis, id posteri martyri Stephano dedicarunt (ibid., 72).

115. Pomponio Leto had not dated the discovery to anything more specific than the papacy of Sixtus IV: *Post muros aedificiorum scolae Graecae statim non longe fuit templum Herculis in foro Boario, rotundum cum multis antiquitatum vestigiis et dirutum tempore Xisti IIII* (Excerpta in D'Onofrio 1989, 288). On the basis of Marsi's account I have modified the date *prima del 1474* as suggested by Presicce (2000, 195). See furthermore Richardson (1992, 188–89; "Hercules Victor, Aedes"); Bober and Rubinstein (2010, 129–30); and Michaelis (1891, 15).

116. *CIL* VI, 312–18; Platner and Ashby (1926, 253).

as well. One can imagine Academy members hurrying over to the dig in the Forum Boarium as news travelled. About fifteen years later, tourists to Rome were still breathlessly reporting on the statue of Hercules that was part of Sixtus IV's collection.[117]

The excitement over the unearthing of the bronze Hercules is reminiscent of another spectacle that caused a big stir: the discovery of a preserved body of a Roman girl in a sarcophagus along the Via Appia on April 16, 1485. At least twelve contemporary accounts of the incident remain, among them one by Roman Academy member Paolo Pompilio, who characterized the event as truly prodigious. Leto conjectured that the body was Tulliola, daughter of Cicero. As with the statue of Hercules, the corpse was brought over to the Palazzo dei Conservatori.[118] Such finds were the stuff of legend, and in the late-*quattrocento Fasti* notes and commentaries, we frequently see a will to believe, a hope to turn up something unexpected. A revealing example occurs at *Fasti* 1.521, *care nepos Palla*, where Marsi remarks: "yet I never saw any tomb of Pallas at Rome, nor was I able to find out anything about the Parentalia or anything else from the customary rites, such as raised altars etc. for Evander and other heroes and Carmenta" (*ego tamen neque sepulchrum Romae Pallantis ullum vidi, neque parentalia neque aliud ex consuetis sacris cognoscere quicquam potui, velut Evandro et aliis heroibus et Carmenti aras erectas et reliqua*). Marsi's declaration exemplifies the two corresponding aspects of antiquarianism: the search for material remains and the reconstruction of society. Marsi wants to find a relic, the tomb of Pallas (Marsi was no longer living when the sarcophagus with the female corpse was discovered), and because Pallas was the grandson of Carmenta (her prophecy of his death occurs at *F.* 1.521), he wants to know more about Roman family funeral rites. The Parentalia was especially significant as an annual ceremony at family tombs lining the roads. Of course, it is specifically noble and well-augured Roman families in whom Marsi is interested. We can infer this not only by his reference to heroes (*heroibus*) but also from the Ovidian context, a prophecy that culminates in the house of Augustus (529–36) and echoes Vergil's *Aeneid*.[119] Rome's mythic origins and destined glory are the subtext of Marsi's *Fasti* excursus, and his search is for the "embodiment" of the past.

---

117. Shofield (1980).
118. Lanciani (1892, 294–301); Mercati (1937); Barkan (1999, 57–60); *Bartolomeo Fonzio. Letters to Friends*, ed. by A. Daneloni, trans. by M. Davies (Cambridge, MA: Harvard University Press, 2011), 92–95.
119. Green, 234–35.

Marsi was presumably not the only person to have looked for Pallas. He clearly knew the story recounted by William of Malmesbury that in the preceding eleventh century a farmer digging in his fields found the colossal body of Pallas, an eternal lamp still burning inside the coffin by his head. The supposed epitaph read:

> Here lies Pallas, son of Evander, whom the soldier
> Turnus killed after his fashion, with a spear.

> *Filius Evandri Pallas, quem lancea Turni*
> *militis occidit more suo, iacet hic.*[120]

Popular legend left its imprint on the humanist Paolo Marsi. Moreover, the idea of an authenticating inscription may have inspired him. Of final note are the elements of a perfect, undecomposed body and an eternal flame. The desire is to find a Rome that is whole, whether it be through her visual or literary monuments.

Traditional lore still had its hold on the Renaissance antiquarians. Indeed, what was Costanzi looking at when he was shown a temple of Janus during his tour of Rome in 1471? Costanzi's gloss at *Fasti* 1.245 that "there are some who read <u>my altar is on a hill</u>, which is agreeable" (*sunt qui legant <u>ara mea est colli</u>, quod non displicet*) is revealing. At this same juncture, Marsi explains:

> Some read <u>my hill is a citadel</u>; but the better reading is <u>my altar is on a hill</u>, for the words make sense, since a shrine dedicated to this divinity is still supposed to stand on that hill, which he inhabited and was called the Janiculum after him.

> *Aliqui legunt <u>arx mea collis erat</u>; melius <u>ara mea est colli</u>, nam fidem facit verbis suis, quod sacellum suo numini dedicatum adhuc extet in eo colle quem incoluit et qui ab eo Ianiculus nuncupatur.*

According to the critical apparatus of the Teubner edition of the *Fasti*, the reading *ara mea est colli* for *arx mea collis erat* does indeed occur in some manuscripts that follow the tradition of the eleventh-century Ursianus codex (Vatican City, BAV, Vat. lat. 3262). However, Marsi appears to

---

120. *Willelmi Malmesbiriensis monachi De Gestis Regum Anglorum libri quinque* vol. 1, ed. W. Stubbs (London: H. M. Stationery Office, 1887), 258; see also A. Graf (1882, 93) and Barkan (1999, 56–57).

have consulted popular legend rather than manuscripts. Leto's reading of the *Fasti* also shows *ara mea est colli* (Vat. lat. 3263, fol. 7r; Vat. lat. 3264, fol. 5r).

Modern topographers have debated whether or not there was a cult of Janus on the Janiculum.[121] There is no archeological evidence, yet etymology has led to speculation. *Ianus* and *colo* together would suggest the Janiculum as "the place where Janus lives" and substantiate the accepted reading of *Fasti* 1.245, *arx mea*. A variety of classical sources also report that Janus ruled as king from a citadel on the hill.[122] Through analogy with terms such as *terricola, caelicola,* and *monticola,* however, one could interpret the compound of *Ianus* and *colo* to mean "Janus worshipper" and infer the presence of a Janus temple on the hill, rather than a stronghold.[123] Marsi himself interprets according to sense: *fidem facit verbis suis,* he says; therefore there must be a shrine on Janus's hill. He agrees with Flavio Biondo, who asserts that

> the principal name of the more established place in the region [Trastevere] deceived even many of the most learned men of our age, who do not know that on the crest of that hill, where now nuns live, there was a temple of Janus.

> *fallit vero plaerosque etiam aetatis nostrae doctissimos editioris ea in regione loci prima appellatio, quod ipso in collis cacumine ubi nunc sacrae inhabitant virgines, Iani templum fuerit.*[124]

Intuition counted, and a layperson was sometimes a more trusted source of information than the pedant. Biondo had a convent in mind for the Janus temple, possibly the contemporary San Pancrazio, a monastery for Cistercian nuns, and this is perhaps the site Costanzi was shown.[125] While the existence of a temple to Janus on the Janiculum is fantasy, it still appears in illustrated Renaissance topographies of Rome, most notably Marco Fabio Calvo's *Antiquae urbis Romae cum regionibus Simulachrum* (*editio princeps* 1527), where one finds a *templum Iani* depicted on the *mons Janiculus*.[126]

---

121. Preller (1881, 1:176) still assumed the existence of a Janus temple.
122. Among others Vergil *Aen.* 8.357 and Servius; Pliny *NH* 3.68; Macrobius *Sat.* 1.7.23. See Holland (1961, 230).
123. Ibid.
124. *R. I.* 1.22, in D'Onofrio (1989, 113).
125. *Codice topografico,* ed. Valentini and Zucchetti, vol. 4 (1953), 265, fn. 3.
126. See Jacks (1993, 198, 204).

The influence of Biondo and his methodology—reliance on literary sources, visible remains, and traditional lore—are evident again in Marsi's comment at *Fasti* 2.201 (*Carmentis portae dextro est via proxima iano*), where Biondo's suppositions are continued. The passage is cited as a *locus difficilior* in the Teubner edition of the *Fasti*.[127] Biondo had equated the Porta Carmentalis (or Scelerata), which Ovid refers to, with the right-hand arch (or western face) of the Janus Quadrifons. On the Janus Geminus, a temple with a double doorway, founded at the lowest point of the Argiletum by Numa as an index of peace and war, Biondo says:

> That is now the temple which, constructed of white marble with its four open-sided gates, stands nearly whole next to San Giorgo in Velabro. From elsewhere: Livy mentions the temple when he says "the Fabii set out from the right-hand arch."

> *Id est nunc templum quod candido marmore extructum patentibus quadrifariam portis ad sanctum Georgium in velo aureo extat pene integrum, cuius alio loco diximus Livium meminisse quom Fabios dextro Iano profectos dicit.*[128]

Biondo confuses the no longer extant Janus Geminus with the visible ruins of the Janus Quadrifons in the Forum Boarium. He recalls the passage in Livy 2.49.8 where the ill-fated Fabii march through the Carmental Gate to meet the Veii (*Infelici via, dextro iano portae Carmentalis, profecti*). The line of reasoning and mistaken identity, conflating the arch of the Carmental gate with that of the Janus Quadrifons on the authority of Livy, is echoed by Marsi. He explains Ovid's *dextro iano* in the passage on the routing of the Fabii at *F.* 2.201 as follows:

> <u>On the right-hand</u>: because he considers it to be near the right side. In many manuscripts it is written "the right-hand road is the nearest path," but "from the right-hand arch" is better. According to Livy "they set out from the right-hand arch of the Carmental gate." You should not understand this as applying to the Janiculum, which was outside the city boundary, but to the temple of Janus, which was situated between the two fora, as I have said above.

> <u>*Dextro*</u>: *quod ad dextra habet. In multis codicibus scriptum "dextra est via proxima," melius est dextro iano, nam et Livius inquit de hoc eodem "a dextro*

---

127. The Alton, Wormell, and Courtney edition (1988, xx).
128. *R. I.* 2.46 in D'Onofrio (1989, 180).

iano portae Carmentalis profecti," nec intelligas de Ianiculo monte, quod erat extra urbem, sed de templo Iani quod erat inter duo fora, ut supra.

Marsi instructs his audience not to confuse the Janus arch mentioned in this verse with the "temple of Janus" on the Janiculum, but rather to identify it with the Janus Quadrifons discussed at *F.* 1.258 (*iuncta foris templa duobus*):

> Numa had founded the Janus temple at the lowest point of the Argiletum, and it was ... where now those four enormous, marble arches stand, facing the four poles of the earth. There also is the church of San Giorgio in Velabro.

> *Iani templum ad infimum argiletum Numa condiderat, eratque ... ubi et nunc sunt quattuor illi ingentes et marmorei arcus, in quatuor mundi partes respicientes. Ibi quoque et templum divi Georgii ad Velabrum.*

The confusion between the Janus Geminus and Quadrifons, and the Porta Carmentalis as one of its arches, first appears in Biondo. The mistake is repeated by Marsi, who similarly quotes Livy as evidence. Biondo's antiquarianism carried such weight that its influence was still felt. Biondo was not quite upstaged by the later humanists, and he was held in esteem by Leto's circle.

Biondo did resort to epigraphy as a source for critical historical inquiry. He utilized inscriptions which for the most part were already well-known. Here he was surpassed by Leto and his generation of antiquarians, whose works display a fascination with epigraphy. We might note to begin with the colophon to the 1482 *editio princeps* of Marsi's *Fasti* commentary, where the information about Leto's sodality is rendered in Roman capitals in a structure with a pediment. Ovid could be considered paradigmatic for the antiquarian researcher consulting epigraphical sources, since in the *Fasti* he himself four times refers to ancient calendars and once to an inscription.[129] Leto copied inscriptions into a notebook, fragments of which still survive. He discovered a Roman rustic calendar on stone, now known as the *Menologium rusticum vallense,* which was printed by Jacopo Mazzochi ca. 1509. Leto furthermore kept a sizeable epigraphical collection in his house on the Quirinal hill, whether in the garden or lodged in the walls.[130] He purportedly wished to be buried on the Via Appia with a

---

129. *F.* 1.7, 1.657, 3.87–96, and 3.844.
130. Grafton (1993, 96–97); Magister (1998; 2003).

classical epitaph, and composing epitaphs was, in fact, a nostalgic exercise in his circle.[131] The Academician Giovanni Antonio Campano composed an epigram about a sleeping nymph, not only inspired by, but possibly written for, a sculpture to be set in a Roman statuary garden.[132]

Adopting ancient customs and (re)inventing inscriptions made their way into Leto's *Fasti* commentary and his collection of epigraphy. On fol. 90v of Vat. lat. 3263, at *F.* 5.294, Leto glosses *Publiciumque* as follows: "The Publician road is on the Quirinal, facing west. Better said, it is northwest. At the lower end there is the temple of Apollo and Clatra, at the upper end there was the Capitol in antiquity. . . ." (*Clivus PUBLICIVS in Quirinali colle est occasum versus. Melius inter occasum et boream. Ex parte inferiore habet templum Apollinis et Clatrae, ex superiore Capitolinum vetus. . . .*). The single word in Ovid prompts Leto to make a topographical and archeological excursus. The so-called temple of Apollo and Clatra appears in Leto's regionary catalogue of Rome and (with an alternate spelling) in the record of his walking tours of the ancient sites of the city. It is a monument of Leto's own imagination and the result of error; there is, after all, no known goddess *Clatra*.[133] However, Leto may have found on the Quirinal the fragment of an inscription that contained (in some form) the words *fores clatratae*, which are known from actual epigraphical collections. Perhaps Leto then turned the *fores clatratae* (barred / latticed gates: from *clathro*) of a temple of Apollo into a goddess affiliated with Apollo. In fact, a stone slab with Apollo and Clatra was owned by Angelo Colocci, who had inherited Leto's collection in the first half of the sixteenth century. Somewhat later the antiquarian Pirro Ligorio documented a more fanciful inscription, perhaps inspired by Leto's "find."[134] Leto believed in his fragment: he told students about it not only in his lectures on Ovid's *Fasti*, but also in the course on Varro's *De lingua Latina*, and he seems to have pointed out the site of a destroyed temple associated with the divinities Apollo and Clatra on walking tours.[135] The inscription was no conscious forgery on Leto's part; rather, we see evidence of the desire to see Rome reconstructed and whole again. And indeed, the epigraphical label

---

131. N. Petrucci (1994).

132. Wren (2006, 108–10).

133. De Rossi (1882, 72–76); . . . *mons a sinistris habet domum cardinalis Neapolitani* [Oliviero Carafa], *et est pars Quirinalis montis, et vocatur mons Clatiae et Apollinis* (Leto's *Excerpta* in D'Onofrio 1989, 280).

134. de Spirito (1993; 1996); Hackens (1960–61, 185–96). See also Fanelli (1979). Cf. the false inscription recorded in *CIL* VI, 5, 128*.

135. Leto's reference to the temple of Apollo and Clatra appears in a gloss to *DLL* 5.51 (Accame 2007, 19, fn. 44).

and toponym lasted: *Mons cum templo Clatrae et Apollinis* appears in the 1551 Bufalini map of Rome.

Leto's *Fasti* manuscript Vat. lat. 3263 shows additional, even direct, evidence of manufacturing inscriptions. On folio 68r, in a passage on the envoys sent to ask for the cult statue of Cybele from Attalus I of Pergamum (*F.* 4.265–66), Leto has inserted the gloss: INTERPRAETATIO ex libro xxix T.Livii. ·M· VAL· LEVINVS· COSRIS M· CAECIL· METEL· PR¯ RIVS ·L· SVLPICIVS GALBA AEDŁCAVS C. TREMEL. FLAC M· VAL· FALCO QRII. Leto makes reference to Livy 29.11.3, where the five members of the delegation to King Attalus are named (a former consul, praetor, aedile, and two quaestors). However, rather than paraphrase Livy, Leto has written the names and ranks of the ambassadors as if in a classical inscription; no doubt Leto is creating a visual counterpart to Livy.[136] In another example, Leto more realistically balances Livy and stone carvings to illustrate grammar and spelling (*F.* 4.223): "*Attis, Attinis,* found on marble and in Livy, is written in Latin with two letters *t* and an *i*" (*Attis, Attinis, ut marmora testantur et Livius utitur et scribitur per duplex T et i Latinum;* fol. 67r of Vat. lat. 3263). We see Leto calling upon material witness to support philology. The observation of what the Romans left behind—not in manuscripts but in inscriptions, a more tactile and immediate form—appears as well at *Fasti* 3.667. Here, Leto's gloss is in the first person, increasing the appeal to the senses. On Anna of Bovillae, Leto writes: "Bovillae is twelve miles distant from Rome. On the left side of the Via Appia I saw a marble with the inscription S. P.Q:Bovillanus" (*Bovillae oppidum distans ab urbe duodecim milia passuum. Ego a sinistra parte viae Appiae vidi marmur in quo scriptum erat S. P.Q:Bovillanus;* fol. 57r of Vat. lat. 3263).[137]

But possibly the most interesting piece of epigraphical evidence in Leto's *Fasti* occurs at 2.119–148, the February 5 anniversary of the day when the Senate conferred upon Augustus the title *Pater Patriae*. A temple to Concord was dedicated on this day in 216 BC, and in witness of this fact Leto draws upon a fragment of the calendar of Praeneste (modern Palestrina), quoting "CONCORDIAE IN ARCE."[138] Leto and other members of the

---

136. For another example of Leto's illustrative antiquarian techniques, see Gwynne (1995). The author demonstrates how Leto may have had at his disposal a coin of Jupiter Stator from the reign of Antoninus Pius, and drawn the figure from this coin in the margin of a Cicero manuscript.

137. Cf. *CIL* XIV, 2408, a dedicatory inscription found in the area around Bovillae, and once owned by Leto (according to P. Ligorio); Magister (1998, 188 [no. 81]).

138. The full gloss on fol. 22v of Vat. lat. 3263 reads: Nonis Febr. die nefasto sacrificia in monumentum Augusti sacrificia fiebant in arce in templo Concordiae, cuius rei memoria legitur Praeneste in marmore: NON NP CONCORDIAE IN ARCE FERIAE EX S C QVOD EO DIE IMPERATOR CAESAR AVGVSTVS PONTIFEX MAXIMVS TRIB POTEST XXI COS XIII A

Academy, it turns out, participated in active searches for the Roman antiquities at Praeneste, and they were among the first to "discover" this ancient city of Latium. In his *De antiquitate Latii,* Antonio Volsco documents having seen the mosaic of the Nile from the Temple of Fortune in Praeneste, which redates the mosaic's discovery in the 1620s to at least 1507.[139]

TRAVEL AND TESTING *AUCTORITAS*

The humanists engaged in an interdisciplinary scholarship: text and object updated the known ancient world; empirical observation both clarified and substantiated what was read. The disparity between classical texts and antiquities could be disquieting, however. Scholars, including teachers and examiners of Ovid's *Fasti,* were often uncomfortable contradicting *auctores.* The regard for Pliny the Elder is a case in point. Admired for his encyclopedic thirty-seven books on natural history, Pliny was the model and source *par excellence* for first-hand, empirical observation, but it was Pliny who was often more trusted than the kind of science he represented. Moreover, the restoration of a correct text of Pliny was of as great importance as his approach.[140]

Much of what Pliny mentioned verged on the marvelous. His scrutinizing words stimulated the imagination; he made the unimaginable seem possible. Flavio Biondo certainly put his faith in Pliny. He believed in the powerful and toxic effect of a spring on Mt. Soracte, as discussed above, because in his own observations, "on [the spring's] edge two little birds lay dead, apparently from drinking the water" (*in cuius labris aviculae duae post gustatam, ut apparebat, aquam occubuerant*). This corroborated Pliny, who said: "Varro claims that at Soracte there was a spring, four feet wide, which at sunrise pours forth steam as if it is boiling. And birds which had drunk from it lay dead next to it" (*Plinius 'ad Soractem Varro asserit fontem esse, cuius sit latitudo quattuor pedum, soleque oriente eum exundare ferventi similem. Avesque quae gustaverint iuxta mortuas iacere.'* [*NH* 31.27]).[141]

SENATV POPVLO QUE ROMANO PATER PATRIAE APPELLATVS. Cf. *CIL* I,314, cited in Zabughin (1910–12), vol. 2 (1910), 152.

139. See La Malfa (2003).

140. Nicolò Leoniceno found himself in the middle of a debate in 1492 when he claimed that many of Pliny's errors, especially in the medical and pharmacological books, were due to Pliny himself instead of technical faults introduced by copyists, editors, and printers. See Tateo (1995), Nauert (1979), Reeds (1976), Castiglioni (1953), and Thorndike (1934).

141. Castner (1998, 96–97); White (2005, 108–9).

On the mysterious effects of a spring, one might compare Biondo's remark with something similar by Paolo Marsi. In an excursus at *Fasti* 1.708 Marsi argues for the location of the *lacus Iuturnae,* no longer visible in the Roman forum as it had been in antiquity. Even though he knew from Dionysius of Halicarnassus (6.13.4), Livy (2.20.12; 2.42.5), and Valerius Maximus (1.8.1) that the spring-fed pool "where Castor and Pollux were seen bathing the sweat from their horses" (*in quo Castor et Pollux abluere sudorem equorum visi sunt*) was near the temple of Vesta, Marsi places it in the Forum Boarium. "Later generations can now see [the pool] a little further away" (*quae nunc paulo illinc remotior cernitur a posteris*), he says,

> For indeed, at the church of San Giorgio under a half-ruined tower is that very spring with its healing waters. I wanted to test this and make sure this was the spring of Juturna, particularly since Varro spoke of "the nymph of Juturna who gives aid, and therefore many who are ill customarily seek her water, on account of that name." And so five times I took one of my students with dermatitis to bathe there, and immediately he was relieved of all his infection.

> *Est enim apud templum divi Georgii turris semiruta sub qua est ipse fons et aquae quidem salubres. Quod ego experiri volui, quo certior fierem an ea esset aqua Iuturnae, praesertim cum Varro diceret "nympha Iuturna quae iuvaret itaque multi aegroti propter id nomen hinc aquam petere solent"* [cf. *DLL* 5.71]. *Duxi igitur illuc ad abluendum quinquies discipulum scabidum, protinusque ab omni scabie liberatus est.*

Marsi has put together several literary sources to discover a site mentioned in Ovid, and he substantiates the textual evidence with external, "scientific" proof. Through Varro's etymological explanation that Juturna (like the twins Castor and Pollux) was a helper of men, Marsi finds the additional authoritative link that he needs. He then tests the salubrious powers which, according to Varro, the fountain of Juturna possessed. He tests the restorative effects of a spring in front of San Giorgio in Velabro, the conduit of an ancient, underground aqueduct, where women still came to do their wash (see figure 8).[142] A marginal note in a manuscript of Leto's Varro lectures also locates Juturna's pool at the same church (*hec fons est*

---

142. Marsi's passage is also noted in Grafton and Jardine (1986, 84–85) and Muecke (2003, 220, fn. 43).

FIGURE 8. Forum Boarium. Temple of Janus, San Giorgio in Velabro, and laundry basin in Etienne Du Pérac, *I vestigi dell'antichità di Roma raccolti et ritratti in perspettiva con ogni diligentia* (Rome: Lorenzo della Vaccheria, 1575.) Parte prima [1600], plate 12. Typ 625 00.342, Houghton Library, Harvard University.

prope templum Sancti Georgii; Rome, Biblioteca Angelica, MS 1348, fol. 42v), and the identification also appears in Bufalini's 1551 map of Rome.

In unraveling Ovid's *lacus Iuturnae* by assembling and comparing literary sources on the one hand, Marsi was able to distinguish between the *lacus Iuturnae* near the Temple of Castor and Pollux and the *Aedes Iuturnae* in the Campus Martius.[143] By an appeal to personal experience on the other hand, Marsi was able to verify what he believed to be the actual *lacus Iuturnae*, even if it had oddly moved location. Direct observation and authoritative truth could co-exist; they had to. But what happened when the antiquarians' beliefs were more greatly challenged? What happened when classically trained humanists travelled outside of Rome, outside of Latium, and outside of Italy? What did exposure to the customs, cultures, and landscapes foreign to their own teach the humanists? In the generation before Leto, Ciriaco already travelled extensively, and his experiences still led him in essence to "restore the dead."[144]

Pomponio Leto travelled relatively little, preferring his life in Rome and at the *Studium urbis*. He had planned to go to the East in 1468 to learn Arabic and Greek, a plan that was disrupted by his extradition from Venice. Leto made only two voyages subsequently: to Eastern Europe in 1480 (included on his itinerary were Germany, Hungary, and Russia), and to Germany again in the winter of late 1482 / early 1483, when he received the privilege to crown poets from the emperor Frederick III. Leto referred to his 1480 trip as his *iter Scythicum*, and many "Scythian notes" appear in his manuscripts on classical authors.[145] The Scythian notes reflect Leto's curiosity and interest in what he saw.[146] Thus, at Vergil *Geor.* 3.461–62, Leto paused to consider the Tartar custom of drinking the blood of horses, mixed with or without milk; at *Geor.* 3.383 (and in his Sallust commentary), Leto marvelled on the use of fox pelts for warm clothing. He comments on a porridge eaten throughout the Black Sea region (Valerius Flaccus *Arg.* 2.448), as well as on a fermented beer made

---

143. Marsi anticipated Andrea Fulvio in the *Antiquaria Urbis* (Rome, 1513); see Muecke (2003, 220, fn. 43). See also Laureys (2006, 212).

144. In the *Italia Illustrata,* Biondo rued the passing of Ciriaco of Ancona, "who by his investigation of ancient monuments restored the dead to the memory of the living, as he used to put it" *(qui monumenta investigando vetustissima mortuos, ut dicere erat solitus, vivorum memoriae restituebat)*; White (2005, 260–61). See further Mitchell (1960, 470); Neuhausen (1996).

145. Accame (2011; 2008, 42–43, 68–71, 118–23); cf. Bracke (1989, 293–99).

146. Toward the end of his life, Leto enjoyed an active correspondence with Peter Martyr, who provided him with information about voyages to the New World and answered questions about new lands and their inhabitants. Leto continued to be interested in cultures not his own despite his own limited travels. See Eatough (1998, 3, 18, 509–16).

by the addition of milk to the porridge (*Georg.* 1.154). He refers to what he observed in Russia at *Fasti* 1.693 (Vat. lat. 3263, fol. 18v), inserting the first-person singular in his gloss. He comments on the method of grinding and toasting spelt (*farra:* QUOMODO FAR TORRETVR . . .): "the Scythians do the same thing for oats and wheat . . . I saw it, I was there and I tasted it" (*sciθae idem faciunt in avena et tritico . . . vidi ego interfuique et gustavi*), he says. Leto draws on personal experience to expand upon what Ovid mentions in the *Fasti*. At the same time, there is a wariness of overstepping boundaries. At *Fasti* 4.409 (fol. 71v) Leto glosses *farra deae*, "spelt for the goddess," as "salted flour, of which I spoke in Book 1, on the authority of Pliny (*mola salsa est de quo diximus libro primo ex Plinii auctoritate*).[147] Direct observation could not replace the mantle of wisdom of *auctoritas*.

The introduction of empirical observation is also apparent in the exegesis of Leto's pupils. First let us look at Leto's gloss on Arion and his lyre in *Fasti* 2.79–118, where Arion's strumming is compared to the mournful notes of a dying swan. Leto writes (Vat. lat. 3263, fol. 22v):

> Pierced with a feather: aging swans have a small, hard, inborn feather in the down on their forehead. Some write that the swan's brain is injured by this feather; they are of the opinion that the swan then sings most sweetly, when he is about to die. I myself have heard the swans singing in the Scythian marshes. The inhabitants of Scythia do not know that the singing swan is about to die.

> Traiectus penna [2.110]: *cycnis senescentibus penna exigua dura in pluma frontis innascitur. Sunt qui scribu[n]t ea penna cerebrum oloris ledi s[u]avissime canere; existimant eum tunc moriturum. Audivi ego canentis cycnos in paludibus Scytharum. Incolae ignorabant an ille esset moriturus qui canebat.*

The legendary "swan song," attributable to the ancient Greeks, was a commonplace among the Romans. Cicero noted how swans, sacred to Apollo, sang with exceptional sweetness at the moment of their death (*cygni . . . providentes quid in morte boni sit cum cantu et voluptate moriantur, Tusc.* 1.30.73), and Pliny also acknowledged the tale (*olorum morte narratur flebilis cantus, NH* 10.32). Leto makes reference to the tradition (*existimant*) but ignores the correction by the natural historian himself. Pliny main-

---

147. Vat. lat. 3263, fol. 18v: *mola teruntur et sive in sacris sive in cibis iterum et iterum admoventur;* cf. Pliny, *NH praef.* 11; 18.83–84; 18.112.

tains that the "swan song" is not borne out by observation or experiment (*falso, ut arbitror, aliquot experimentis, NH* 10.32).[148] In fact, Leto has construed Ovid's *penna*, the shaft of a hunter's arrow, as quite literally a fatal feather in the swan's head (see chapter 2). How, then, to uphold Ovid? Perhaps expanding on what the thirteenth-century philosopher Bartolomeo Anglico had remarked, that upon death the swan "sings with a shaft stuck in his brain" (*morte penna infixa cerebro canit*), Leto inserts his own Plinian observation and substantiates his reading of the *Fasti* with what he witnessed on his trip abroad.[149] Moreover, he passed his "scientific" explanation along to his students and to members of the Roman Academy such as Antonio Volsco. Volsco's notes to *Fasti* 2.110–11 appear on fol. 35v; the glosses read "as the swan: a swan who sings most sweetly and sorrowfully at the point of death. pierced: who has things stuck . . . hard feather: with an old feather, which is very hard" (*veluti olor: cingnius* [sic] *qui mortis tenpore dulicissime et miserabiliter canit. traiectus: qui habet infixa . . . penna dura: senili quae durior est*). Volsco has repeated the notion that mature swans die from a lethal feather, effecting a last, beautiful song. And Paolo Marsi, in his *Fasti* comment at *dura penna* (2.110), writes about the swan's melodious dying note:

> This is because swans when they are old have a kind of hard little feather on their forehead, as though they had been pierced at birth; Pomponio noticed this in the far confines of Germany and so did I in Ionia. Indeed, the older swans have that pierced brow, others don't. Therefore Ovid does not say *dura penna* without reason; I am only amazed that others have not observed this.

> *Quia in senecta pennam quandam habent duriusculam frontem* [sic] *natam velut traiectam, quod observavit Pomponius in extrema Germania et ego in Ionia. Seniores enim cycni illam traiectam habent, ceteri non. Poeta igitur non sine ratione hoc dixit, sed miror ab aliis non fuisse observatum.*

Marsi wishes to prove Ovid correct; after all, the *auctor* did not say what he did "without reason" (*sine ratione*). Marsi refers to Leto's trip to Germany, which interestingly enough occurred just before Marsi's *editio princeps* went to press. Marsi himself had gone to Ionia—the coastal Aegean region of central Turkey—in the entourage of the *condottiere* Nicolò Canal

---

148. Zabughin (1910–12), vol. 2 (1910), 148–49; Frazer, vol. 2, 307; Arnott (1977).
149. Stocchi (2003, 185).

in 1469.¹⁵⁰ Leto's experience was legitimization for Marsi's own encounters, as well as the gold standard for comparing text and *realia*. Leto's news might have made it to the ears of Antonio Costanzi as well, and the thesis of the lethal feather and the swan song remained active into the middle of the next century in the work of Vincenzo Cartari, *Le imagini de i dei de gli antichi*.¹⁵¹

Elsewhere in his commentary on the *Fasti*, Marsi reveals that he employed his powers of observation while abroad but that he, too, in the end applied his experience to substantiate traditional authority. At *F.* 1.76 Marsi debates the nature of the aromatic *spica Cilissa* (see chapter 3).¹⁵² Marsi claims Ovid's reference must be to a plant with a flowering top, "Cilician *bristle* (*spica*), and from this we must understand nard, of which Pliny says 'all kinds have a pleasing scent'" (*spica Cilissa, et de nardo intelligit, de quo Plinius "odoris gratia omnibus maior"* [*NH* 12.44]). As Pliny talks about many species of nard, personal experience comes to Marsi's aid. Marsi again refers to his empirical observations while on the coast of Turkey in 1469. "Even if you do not read in Pliny about the nard of Cilicia," Marsi explains,

> that does not matter. For truly, Pliny does not say that nard does not grow in Cilicia, but he praises especially Syrian nard and next after it the Gallic and the Cretan [kind]. Furthermore, remember that Syria borders on Cilicia, so that what grows in Syria can also sprout in that part of Cilicia which borders on Syria. Moreover, I picked spikenard on the coast of Cilicia with my very own hands, and I showed it to my audience when I lectured on this line.

> *Etsi Cilissum nardum non legas apud Plinium, non refert. Non enim inquit Plinius non nasci in Cilicia nardum, sed in primis laudat Syriacum, proxime Gallicum et Creticum* [*NH* 12.45]. *Adde quod Syria iuncta est Ciliciae, ut*

---

150. Marsi joined the entourage of Canal in order to record Canal's deeds as Captain General against the Turks. Canal was unsuccessful in defending the island of Negropont, the ancient Euboea (June 15, 1470). See della Torre (1903, 170–91); Ventura (1974, 666).

151. Costanzi's *Fasti* comment at 2.110 is as follows: *dum imminente morte cantum flebilem facit penna eius* **cerebrum laedi**, *Magnus Albertus et Isidorus litteris mandaverint, quamvis Aristoteles et Plinius ea de re nihil scripserint* (emphasis mine). Albertus Magnus (*De Animalibus* 8.72) and Isidore of Seville (*Ethym.* 12.7.18–19) mention only the legend that the swan sings sweetly at the point of death, and nothing more. Stocchi (2003, 186, fn. 22). For preliminary comparisons between Leto's and Marsi's remarks on the swan song, see Bracke (1989, 298), and Bianchi (1981, 80).

152. This passage has also been remarked upon in Grafton and Jardine (1986, 84–85).

quod in Syria nascitur possit in ea parte Ciliciae nasci, quae Syriae iuncta est. Ego autem in ora Ciliciae spicam meis manibus legi et auditoribus meis ostendi, cum haec legerem.

Marsi betrays his empirical spirit: that he examined nature in the places he visited, and even brought plant specimens back to Rome, is significant to note. In this regard Marsi may be said to resemble the late-sixteenth-century naturalist Ulisse Aldovrandi (1522–1605), who collected and pasted in his notebooks dried plants from his travels, while at the same time recording pertinent passages from classical botanical authors.[153] But of course Marsi roamed the Turkish shore with a certain expectation, based upon his reading of Ovid; in investigating nature, he saw what he wanted to see.

Marsi notes that this discussion came about

> while I was lecturing on this passage and father Sabinus, who then was alive, and others were railing against me, because I wished the spikenard to be understood, while they were of the opinion that the most highly-praised saffron from Cilicia was meant. Nor did they notice the error in which they were engaged.[154]

> *cum legerem hunc locum et pater Sabinus, qui tunc vivebat, et alii in me invehebantur, quoniam de spica nardi voluerim intelligi, cum ipsi de croco ex Cilicia laudatissimo provenienti intelligendum esse censerent. Nec advertebant quo in errore versarentur.*

The issue consumed Marsi, who wished to be proven correct. He continued the debate in the *Emendatio locorum* appended to his *Fasti* commentary, when he was in Venice supervising the printing of his first edition. Marsi's new corroborative evidence was the recently begun translation of Dioscorides by the Venetian Ermolao Barbaro. Marsi applauds Barbaro, a "most erudite young man, upon whom all praise of letters has been heaped" (*eruditissimus iuvenis et omni litterarum laude cumulatissimus Hermolaus Barbarus*). From Barbaro, Marsi's opponents "will positively find that nard

---

153. Findlen (1994, 64–65).
154. It is unclear who Marsi means when he refers to *pater Sabinus*; Pomponio Leto died in 1498. Another *Sabinus* could be Angelo Sabino, active as a scholar ca. 1468–76; we do not know when he died, however. He was a professor at the *Studium Urbis*, and his commentary on Juvenal was published in Rome in 1474. He was engaged in a contentious rivalry with Domizio Calderini. See Sanford (1948, 102–5).

also grows in Cilicia" (*invenient certe et in Cilicia nasci nardum*).[155] Barbaro as a scholar must have been an influential example for Marsi. A great philologist, more interested perhaps in determining the original words of a classical author than their scientific accuracy (as the *Castigationes* on Pliny imply), Barbaro also appealed to direct observation, as demonstrated in his accompanying commentary on Dioscorides.[156]

Marsi's obsession with *spica Cilissa* reveals his own interdisciplinary outlook and a methodological interdependence between text and object. He relied on a variety of research tools, both philological and empirical, and his voyages gave him another source for reflection. One need only read the *Bembice,* twenty poems in two books detailing events and the sites Marsi visited in 1468, to see the challenges that travel presented to the Classics-colored *status quo*. Marsi's reliance on ancient *auctoritas* is evident on the one hand in the poem recording his stopover in Malta, "*Inter navigantes quod ad inclytam urbem et illius portum applicuimus*"; his experience of the island is colored by classical literature. Marsi counsels

> After having come here by an error of our way, hear
> > by what name the island is called, Bembo father.
> 'There is a fertile island Melita close to the barren Cosyra'
> > which lies between the Phoenicians and the Sicilians
> 'whence,' as the ancients said, 'come the little dogs called Melitaean';
> > so be you my witness, Book 6 of Strabo,
> for some deny [this interpretation]: it behooves them to introduce their
> > witness.

> *Huc errore viae postquam devenimus, audi*
> > *insula quo dicta est nomine, Bembe pater.*
> "*Fertilis hec Melyte sterili vicina Cosyrae*" [cf. Ovid, *F.* 3.567]
> > *Sidonios inter Trinacriosque iacens*
> "*unde Meliteos*" *veteres dixere* "*catellos;*"
> > *Strabonis testis sis mihi sexte liber* [6.11.3; cf. Pliny, *NH* 3.152]
> *nanque negant alii: testem his adducere fas est.*[157]

In this poem Marsi makes evident his deference to authority, claiming that

---

155. Leto later came to agree with Marsi about the nature of *spica Cilissa*; in his post-1488 *Fasti* notes, he writes, "nard produces a spike, not a blossom" (*nardus spicam emittit non florem;* Vat. lat. 3263, fol. 2v). By this time Leto may also have read the work of Barbaro, his own former student.
156. Nauert (1979); Riddle (1980, esp. 8, 46–48); Ramminger (1999).
157. Vatican City, BAV, Reg. lat. 1385, fol. 32r.

whoever disagrees with his explanation of Malta's nomenclature should find his *own* classical witness for support. For Marsi, it is fitting and proper to describe the island according to ancient testimony; one need not look beyond the parameters of Greek and Latin literature. In fact, he moves on to the story of the escape of Dido's sister to Malta, borrowed again from the *Fasti*, 3.523–656.

On the other hand, in this poem it is also evident that Marsi compared what he read with what he saw and that he determined that the classical text was a static and incomplete picture of the real world. Marsi's first description of Malta had been in Ovid's words, "there is a fertile island Melita close to the barren Cosyra" (*F.* 3.567); however, in the second half of the poem Marsi relates in part his own personal experience:

Formerly bountiful, now the island remains barren
    and there is no honoring the poor farmer,
because already the fourth season has borne a dry harvest
    and no rain shower has fallen.

Fertilis hec quondam nunc infecunda quiescit,
    agricolae et miseri nullus habetur honos,
quarta quod arentes iam contulit area messes
    et nullus pluviae decidit hymber aque. (fol. 32v)

While simultaneously modeling his words on those of Ovid (cf. *tertia nudandas acceperat area messes, F.* 3.557), Marsi makes an implicit judgment about the discrepancy between Ovid's idyllic view of the island and the current facts of the matter. Certainly in a creative genre such as poetry, and in a travelogue at that, a slight quibble with a classical author would not seem inappropriate. A commentary on the author would be an entirely different case. But when Marsi later taught students the text of the *Fasti* in Rome, he interpolated his observations, clearly not just to explain the text but also to point out the truth in light of his experience. "I myself passed over to that island," Marsi writes in his commentary on Ovid, "and in the year 1468 it was not fertile, on account of the drought. For a whole four years it had been without rain. Still, its soil is fertile when it rains" (*nos ipsi in eam insulam traiecimus, nec eo anno qui fuit Mccclxviii a natali Dominico erat fertilis, propter siccitatem. Quadriennio enim integro aquis pluviis caruerat. Fertile tamen solum habet cum aquatur*).

Yet, in the end, Marsi and so many of the humanists could not completely disengage from the classical learning that they imbibed and the lens of *auctoritas* through which they viewed much of the world. Marsi agrees, for example, with Ovid that Malta's "soil is fertile when it rains." And Antonio Costanzi betrays an even greater fidelity to *auctoritas*. One cannot simply read what one wants into the text or twist an author's words. He offers advice in his explanation of *cetera ne simili caderent labefacta ruina* at *Fasti* 2.59, where Ovid recounts that Augustus had "seen to it that the rest of the temples should not suffer the same collapse and ruin" as the temple of Juno Sospita. In Ovid's time, no temple to Juno Sospita remained. Therefore, Costanzi says, "you will not find a temple to Juno Sospita restored by Augustus anywhere, although I remember when I was young, many disagreed" (*Sospitae Iunonis templum ab Augusto refectum nusquam invenies, quamvis memini me adulescente multos contra sentire*). Attentive to Ovid's very words, Costanzi says the poet "would not be saying 'Sospita *is said* to have been enhanced with new shrines'" (*nec diceret "Sospita delubris dicitur aucta novis," F.* 2.56). Be vigilant, Costanzi tells his students: "we must pay careful attention, so that we do not interpret this line in such a way as to seem to disagree with the poet" (*diligenter itaque animadvertendum est ne ita interpretemur hunc locum* [2.59] *ut a poeta dissentire videamur*).[158]

What we finally witness here is a desire to see Rome whole, either in the mind's eye or in the writings of the Romans themselves. Observing, indeed comparing, ruins or any range of natural phenomena with what could be read in Ovid was a means to supplement classical antiquity. Nothing could completely replace antiquity; nevertheless, as we will see in the next chapter, new life could be breathed into antiquity through its reuse by the moderns.

---

158. Ovid seems to think that a temple to Juno Sospita once existed on the Palatine hill, but there is no evidence that one ever did; for the confused identity of possible coterminous temples and controversial discussion thereof, see Richardson (1992, 217–18) and Coarelli (1996). Leto and Marsi are silent on the matter.

CHAPTER FIVE

Antiquarianism II

CHRISTIAN *FASTI* AND PAPAL CONNECTIONS

ON SUPERSTITION AND MAGIC

As noted before, Paolo Marsi was not immune to the attacks of rivals and nay-sayers. We can be sure that he glossed the rite of the Mute Goddess at *Fasti* 2.571 with a degree of personal interest. For his explanation of the mystifying ritual, he recounts an experience from his trips with Bernardo Bembo in 1468 and Nicolò Canal in 1469. How it precisely happened that the ancient divinity silenced the lips of calumniators, Marsi says,

> the poet Ovid does not reveal. Still, let me interpret his words according to the secret rite itself, which is easy enough for me, since I have witnessed it in many places just as Ovid reported. Furthermore in Euboea there was a certain holy man both Greek by birth and learned in Greek letters; I left ship to go see him at a certain time while I was spending the winter in Chalcis. Now and then, in fact, he wanted me to show him something of our literature. Once I found him with a book whose title was *On Arcane Magic* by a certain Thessalian. Among the other rites I noticed this one written in Greek, which he wanted to try out because there were some slanderers who would not stop harassing him with abusive words. Wonderful to say: he suppressed their verbal attacks. The

same thing happened in my presence also when I was in Seville and later on in Rhodes.[1]

Poeta tamen id non aperit. Nos tamen sua verba cum mysterio interpretemur, quod facillimum est nobis qui vidimus id idem fieri pluribus in locis eoque modo quo a poeta refertur. Praeterea religiosus quidam in Euboea erat qui, ut genere Graecus, ita Graecis litteris eruditus. Ad quem aliquando cum per hiberna in Chalcide essemus e triremi confugiebam. Volebat enim interdum ut aliquid nostrarum litterarum aperirem. Hunc semel repperi librum tenentem cuius inscriptio erat "de arcanis Veneficiis" cuiusdam Thessali. Inter cetera Graece scriptum hoc sacrum adverti, quod ille eo tempore voluit experiri cum essent aliquot maledici, qui eum conviciis lacessere non desinebant. Mirum quidem dictu est; compescuit illorum maledicentiam. Idem accidit et me praesente in Hispali et postea Rhodi.

The influence of Ovid, declaring personal participation in ceremonies ("I myself jumped through the flames placed three in a row" / *certe ego transsilui positas ter in ordine flammas,* he says on the Palilia *F.* 4.727), would have been emblematic for Marsi. In this instance, Marsi's eyewitness experience provides proof for the information in Ovid about the Mute Goddess.

Although Marsi does not delve further into mystic ritual, his comment on the Mute Goddess reveals both a curiosity and an awareness of theurgy, the operation of miracles through supernatural or divine intervention. It may also explain, at least to a degree, his search for the tomb of Pallas with the burning lamp that could never be extinguished. If we continue to think about Western esotericism, we should recall that Marsi was on good terms with Ludovico Lazzarelli, a briefly active member of Pomponio Leto's Academy who was called *doctus* by Marsi.[2] In 1481, Lazzarelli met the

---

1. For the Romans, Thessaly was the proverbial land of witchcraft: see Horace, *C.* 1.27.21; Plaut., *Amph.* 1043; Juvenal 6.610. On the other hand, could Marsi be referring to a version of the astrological *De virtutibus herbarum* by Thessalus of Tralles (1st century AD)? Compare the property of maidenhair, mixed in a potion at 2.6.6: "and if someone drinks from it, he cannot be hurt by criminal misdeeds" (*et si quis ex eo biberit, non potest a facinoribus ledi*); cited in Friedrich (1968, 244). For the text's *fortuna* see Pingree (1976). Marsi's account is quoted by Rodolphus Hospinianus (1547–1626), *De festis Iudaeorum et Ethnicorum, hoc est, de origine, progressu, ceremoniis et ritibus festorum dierum Iudaeorum, Graecorum, Romanorum, Turcarum, et Indianorum libri III* (Tiguri: In Officina V Volphiana, 1611), 66 (*Mutae Deae festum*).

2. *spectamus alumnos / iam Marsum doctos Sulpitiumque viros*; Lazzarelli's autograph *Fasti christianae religionis,* BAV, Vat. lat. 2853, fol. 77v, repeated on fol. 164v. The second reference is to the Academician Sulpizio da Veroli. Marsi is but one member of the Roman Academy who wrote a poem in honor of Lazzarelli and his work; see New Haven, CT, Beinecke Rare Book and Manuscript Library, MS 391, fols. 243r–246r.

prophet Giovanni "Mercurio" da Correggio in Rome. As Correggio's disciple, Lazzarelli converted to Christian hermeticism and completed Marsilio Ficino's translation of the *Corpus Hermeticum*. Lazzarelli's ideas of transformation and regeneration at that time became more overtly Christian.[3]

Perhaps we can attribute the one example of Christian allegory in Marsi's *Fasti* commentary to the influence of Lazzarelli and other humanists like him. Marsi enters a long excursus on the fabled death of Pan at the mention of the Greek god's name at *Fasti* 1.397. He quotes at length the story about the Egyptian sailor Thamus from Plutarch's "On the Obsolescence of Oracles" (*De defectu oraculorum*). During the reign of Tiberius, while sailing to Italy by way of the Ionian islands of Paxi, Thamus was mysteriously called upon to proclaim opposite Palodes, "Great Pan is dead." The moment he did so, great wailing arose from the shore. Marsi prefaces his rendering of Plutarch's story with "although the story is reported by Eusebius, I will take it from a Greek manuscript of the author himself" (*quamvis ab Eusebio referatur, a graeco tamen codice ipsius auctoris accipiemus*). The implication of a Greek manuscript—and of its translation by Ermolao Barbaro—may very well be a red herring, intended to act as corroborative proof for Marsi's own reading.[4] Marsi's retelling of Plutarch follows the author completely, except for one additional phrase shown in italics below. Marsi says that

> Thamus himself was summoned by Tiberius Caesar, and Tiberius placed such confidence in the story that he launched an investigation and inquiry into the identity of Pan, *for he was to be understood as God*. However, the numerous philosophers whom he consulted assumed that he was the son of Mercury and Penelope.

Thamum vero ipsum a Tyberio Caesare accersitum adeoque adhibuisse fidem facto Tyberium ut sciscitaretur et quaereret de Pane, quem nam deum intelligi

---

3. For further literature see Moreschini, Saci, and Troncarelli (2009), Copenhaver (2009), Hanegraaf and Bouthoorn (2005), Crisciani (2000), and Ruderman (1975).

4. Marsi refers to the [Περὶ τῶν Ἐκλελοιπότων Χρηστηρίων] *quem nunc divini ingenii iuvenis, tam graecis quam latinis litteris ornatissimus atque utroque dicendi genere praestantissimus simul et omni studiorum laude cumulatissimus, Hermolaus Barbarus magnificentissimi equitis Zachariae filius, me hortante latinum facit*. No translation has come down to us that I am aware of. There is mention of it in the claim by Ioannes Trithemius, *De scriptoribus ecclesiasticis* (Basileae: Johann Amerbach, 1494), as reported in Stickney (1903, 31), that among Barbaro's unpublished works were Latin translations of Plutarch's *De Iside et Osiride* and *Dialogus quare oracula defecerint*. Barbaro, in his *Corollario*, refers only to the former work, and it appears that this was in fact not a translation but a compilation gleaned from ancient sources; see Dionisotti (1968, 157).

> *oporteret. Coniectasse autem consultos ab eo frequentes philosophos eum esse qui ex Mercurio et Penelope natus esset.*

Marsi has interpolated "he was to be understood as God" (*quem nam deum intelligi oporteret*), and in so doing suggests that the Roman emperors recognized the presence of Christ as if by instinct and that the pagan world prefigures Christianity. He builds upon the authorial wisdom of Plutarch; he furthermore rejects the allegorical interpretation transmitted by Eusebius, that the wailing at Pan's death came from the pantheon of demons expelled forever when Christ defeated the Devil (*haec ille verum Eusebius, haec et similia accidisse refert ad illud Tyberii tempus quo quidem tempore Salvator et Dominus noster cum hominibus conversatus omne daemonum genus ab humana vita depulit*).[5] Marsi interprets the death of Pan as the passion of Christ, for

> other, most holy men of our religion claim that the voice was heard from Paxi on the night which followed Passion Sunday, in the nineteenth year of the reign of Tiberius, indeed when Christ died. By this voice, a kind of miracle that came from the silence of the deserted crags, it was announced that our Lord and God had passed away. For what does Pan signify but "all," and so the Lord of the whole entire world had died.

> *at alii religionis nostrae viri sanctissimi asserunt eam vocem auditam e Paxis ea nocte quae secuta est passionis dominicae diem xix anno Tyberii quo quidem Christus passus est, qua voce miraculo quodam ex solitudine desertorum scopulorum edita nunciabatur illud dominum scilicet et deum nostrum passum. Quid enim pan significat, nisi totum. Sic totius et universae naturae dominus passus erat.*

Marsi's Christian allegory on the death of Pan had such a lasting impact on his readers that it later entered the work of Rabelais and has been identified as the ultimate source of *Pantagruel* 4.28, and it also found its way into the E. K. gloss to Pan in May of Spenser's *The Shepheardes Calendar*.[6]

---

5. Cf. *Praeparatio Evangelica* 5.17.6, ed. K. Mras, *Eusebius Werke* 8:1 (Berlin: Akademie-Verlag, 1954), 254.

6. See Screech (1955, esp. 41–44). Compare the Medicean Florence versions of Pan; an enthroned Pan, representing the "divine power" over everything in heaven and on earth, appears in Luca Signorelli's painting *Court of Pan* (Bober 2000, 234–35).

THE ROMAN ACADEMY AND ANNIVERSARIES

The *Fasti* commentators attempted to unlock the mysteries of the ancients and cultic practice. Ovid's poem was an antiquarian's dream. In Ovid's calendar the humanists could see something of their own feast year and customs and beliefs. The commemorative nature of the calendar allowed for identification and participation, and even imitation.

Ovid claims to have participated in the Palilia, and likewise members of Leto's Roman Academy celebrated it. The Roman Academy's commemoration of the Palilia, the ancient Roman festival dedicated to the divinity of agriculture Pales, believed to coincide with the founding and hence "birthday" of Rome, is well documented. In his funeral oration for Pomponio Leto, delivered on June 10, 1498, Pietro Marsi affirms that his professor had resurrected the Palilia and won for it the Roman Academy's right to crown poets on this day.[7] The celebration, held at Leto's house on the Quirinal, was typically accompanied by several opening speeches, a banquet, and a poetic contest. Not surprisingly, the poems were often *Genethliaca* for the city of Rome. Domizio Palladio composed his *Carmen in Romae Urbis Genethliacon* for the commemorative birthday celebrations of 1484, and in it he too glorifies Leto for having restored the ancient observance (*Hic* [sc. Laetus] *tibi, diva Pales, antiqua volumina volvens / candidior voluit restituatur honos*).[8] A manuscript in the Vatican Library preserves another poem, this one anonymous, but likewise entitled *in urbis Romae natalem celebratum die 21 mensis aprilis 1484*.[9]

Leto had received the privilege to crown poets from the emperor Frederick III while in Germany during the winter of 1482–83.[10] April 1483 is the first year, it has generally been conceded, for which we have documented proof of the Palilia celebrations; this was the first "official" ceremony. Jacopo Volaterrano has left a record of the events of that day:

---

7. *Sed, inquies, animus . . . non contentus, non fessus, ut urbis natalem a se renouatum ac religiose celebratum, poetica laurea honestaret, ac posito ingeniis premio, ardentes animos inflammaret, annuente Xyxto quarto pontifice maximo, ut id de more, ac uetusto iure Codicis, facere liceret, media hyeme, calcatis Germaniae niuibus, et Alpium pruinoso uertice ritu Herculis expugnato, imperatorium diploma emeruit.* Quoted in Dykmans (1988, 83, fn. 76).

8. *Carmen in Romae Urbis Genethliacon*, ll. 43–44, in *Domici Palladii Sorani Epigrammaton libelli. Libellus elegiarum, Genethliacon Urbis Romae, In locutelium* (Paris: Georg Wolf and Thielmann Kerver for Jean Petit, ca. 1499).

9. Vatican City, BAV, Vat. lat. 2836, fols. 322r–324v; in Tournoy-Thoen (1972, 220–23). For other *genethliaca*, and for later revivals of the Palilia celebrations, see Muecke (2007, 114–18).

10. Accame (2008, 68–69).

On the Esquiline at the house of Pomponio, on the Sunday which followed, the birthday of Rome was celebrated by the literary Academy. After the solemn rites, presided over by Demetrio of Lucca, prefect of the Vatican library, Paolo Marsi delivered the oration. They took repast at the church of San Salvatore, where the sodality had prepared a sumptuous banquet for the lettered men and university students. Six bishops were present at the banquet, and very many scholarly and noble youths. The privilege which had been granted to the sodality by the emperor Frederick III was read at table, and many verses were recited, even from memory, by various learned young men.

In Exquiliis prope Pomponii domum, die dominico qui sequutus est, a sodalitate litteraria, celebratum est Romanae Urbis Natale. Sacra solemniter acta, Demetrio Lucensi, bibliothecae pontificiae prefecto operante, Paulus Marsus orationem habuit. Pransum est apud Salvatoris sacellum, ubi sodalitas litteratis viris et studiorum studiosis elegans convivium paraverat; sex antistites convivio interfuere et eruditi ac nobiles adolescentes quamplures; recitatum est ad mensam Federici III Cesaris privilegium sodalitati concessum, et a diversis iuvenibus eruditis versus quamplures etiam memoriter recitati.[11]

We are told that Paolo Marsi delivered the inaugural speech for the 1483 ceremonies. The Roman Academy almost certainly celebrated the birthday of Rome earlier than 1483, as Marsi's commentary attests. In the *editio princeps* from December 24, 1482, his *Genethliacon* already appears at *F.* 4.31, where Ovid explains the genealogy of ancient Rome.[12] Most likely Marsi inserted his poem as the commentary went to press, with the knowledge that Leto was in Germany right then, petitioning for the right to crown poets; Marsi's *Genethliacon* was his own contribution for the festive occasion that would be held but a few months later. That the composition was intended for recitation on some occasion of Rome's birthday, there can be no doubt. In his *dissertatio*, Baptista Guarino boasts about Marsi:

> Wondrous is that man's talent at speaking, and it is all the more worthy of admiration in that his natural disposition was more inclined to poetry than prose orations; there is no more extemporaneous poet alive. His poem has been inserted in the *Fasti* . . .

---

11. *RIS* 23:3, p. 117. The Esquiline and Quirnal hills were still confused at this time; see chapter 4, fn. 45.

12. A transcription of the poem appears in Vienna, Österreichische Nationalbibliothek, ms. 3111, fols. 69v–73v; see Pontari (2008, 744).

> *Mira in homine dicendi facultas atque eo maiore admiratione digna quo natura illa ad carmen multo quam ad pedestrem orationem fuit promptior, nullus nostra tempestate extemporalior poeta. Illius carmen est Fastis insertum . . .*[13]

Moreover, there is internal proof that Marsi's *Genethliacon* existed in some form even before December, 1482, suggesting that indeed, such poetic contests had been going on for a long time. In his commentary Marsi notes that the *Genethliacon* printed at 4.31 is but a shortened version of what he had composed years before:

> The genealogy that has been explained by a various number of writers, I have excerpted from the most accurate historical accounts, both Greek and Latin, and in the last years have reduced into a brief compendium, the *Natalis Romanus*.

> *Generationis series a multis variisque scriptoribus explicata, a nobis ex fidelissimis historiographis tam graecis quam latinis excerpta inque breve compendiolum superioribus annis natali quidem Romano redacta est.*

Rosella Bianchi has discovered that Marsi quotes from his metrical composition in his Lucan commentary. On fol. 5r of an *editio princeps* of the *Pharsalia, Inc.* II.3 at the Vatican Library, Marsi (or a copyist) has written: *in natali diximus "Iam cum fundamina primum / designanda forent . . . ,"* corresponding to the verses of the *Genethliacon* as they can be pieced together from the *Fasti* commentary at 4.812, 816, and 818.[14] Although we do not have a precise date for Marsi's Lucan commentary, he had already presented it to his patron Giorgio Cornaro by the time of his *Fasti* commentary, as he makes clear in the preface.[15] From the references to the *Genethliacon* on fol. 5r and elsewhere in the *Pharsalia,* it appears that its title varied between *Natalis Urbis* and *Natalis Romanus*,[16] suggesting that

---

13. *Opera Marci Antonii Sabellici* (Venetiis: Albertinus de Lisona Vercellensis, 1502), fol. 114r.
14. Bianchi (1981, 76, 94).
15. *Non enim sola Fastorum gloria tete manet sed quae ad institutionem vitae humanae pertinent. Tuo etiam nomini dedicantur officialia ipsa praecepta, tanto a nobis labore et diligentia lucubrata ut prodire ex ipsis verae academiae fontibus videantur. Quin et ingens ipsa Pharsalia et artis rhetoricae praecepta summa cum vigilantia et fide a nobis interpretata tuoque itidem nomini dedicata, fore quidem existimo immortalem tibi gloriam paritura. . . .* Presumably Marsi hoped Cornaro would help publish his commentary on the *Pharsalia,* as well as a commentary on the *Rhetorica ad Herrenium*.
16. Bianchi (1981, 78, fn. 24).

even at the time of the Lucan commentary, the poem was still a work in progress. Commemorations of the Palilia were therefore not a recent invention of Academy members in 1483.

Marsi's obsession with Rome's birthday extended beyond poetic composition, however. He was determined to ascertain the day of Rome's founding, and his mission culminated in his exegesis on the *Fasti*. Marsi instituted April 20 as the date to celebrate Rome's birthday, and in 1483 the celebration did take place on the day for which he had made his case.[17] Marsi wished to prove this date regardless of the difficulty, but also with what appears to have been an ulterior motive, as discussed below. The date of Rome's founding was, in fact, a much debated point in the Roman Academy; at *Fasti* 4.721, Marsi says: "there are some who want the birthday of Rome to fall on April 22" (*sunt tamen qui volunt xxii die Aprilis esse*). Indeed, Antonio Volsco pled for the Palilia falling on the 22nd (*quae celebrantur secundo et vigesimo die Aprilis*),[18] in so doing most likely echoing his mentor Pomponio Leto. In the Maffei manuscript (Ferrara, Biblioteca Comunale Ariostea, II.141), *Palis et natalis Romae* has been written in next to April 22 on the calendar on fol. 4r, and *x kal. Mai Natalis Vrbis Romae* (i.e., April 22) appears in the margin of fol. 71v in red, although a later hand has changed this to *xi kal Mai* (April 21).

Why would there be such uncertainty concerning a Roman date? We should not forget the fluidity of the calendar even in Caesar's time, as well as the regional variants in calendars that Ovid reminds us of (*F.* 3.87–98, 6.59–64).[19] Anniversaries were thus not strictly anniversaries. In 45 BC, Julius Caesar undertook a reform of the calendar; by his decree, on January 1 of that year, the days now followed the cycle of the sun rather than the moon. The lunar calendar of the Republican period was replaced so that the Roman year became more or less aligned with the tropical year, calculated from one spring equinox to the next. Adjustments needed to be made to the Julian calendar over time, however, since dates did gradually fall behind the sun. Yet the immediate problem for Caesar was converting from Republican to Julian time. Commemorative occasions no longer corresponded between the two systems.

Scholars therefore focused their energies on calculating anniversaries. The Romans had always possessed an "anniversary mentality," more so than the Greeks, and were preoccupied with the recurrence of significant

---

17. April 20, 1483, was a Sunday, the Sunday referred to in Volaterrano's account. See Tournoy-Thoen (1972, 212, fn. 1).

18. Rome, Biblioteca Vallicelliana, MS R. 59, fol. 144v.

19. For an excellent discussion see Feeney (2007, 148–53).

days. "Days" were more important than "dates," and if that meant changing a date on the new civil calendar, so be it. This gave Caesar quite a lot of authority over the calendar, the chance to mold it; Cicero jokingly remarked on Caesar's power when he replied to someone's observation that the constellation of the Lyre would be rising the next day: "Yes, by decree." In the *Fasti*, Ovid wrote, "even now the times were in error until this too became one of Caesar's many concerns" (*sed tamen errabant etiam nunc tempora, donec / Caesaris in multis haec quoque cura fuit*, 3.155–56).[20] Of course, Ovid adapted the calendar for his own motives as well.

Considered special as commemorative occasions were "birthdays," not just of individuals, but also of historic battles and events, and of permanent religious monuments. The dedication day of a temple was referred to as its *dies natalis*, for example.[21] Naturally, the anniversary of Rome's founding held particular significance. Ovid, while offering seven competing causes behind the origins and the importance of the Palilia, solidified its association with Rome's founding on April 21. His last interpretation of the agricultural festival explains that Romulus gave orders to his people to transfer to new homes and to set fire to their old houses. The event was commemorated annually from that time on (*Fasti* 4.801–6). In due course, additional occasions were marked and attached to this day. In 45 BC, the same year he reformed the calendar, Caesar (a new Romulus) initiated games on the Palilia and people wore crowns in his honor to celebrate his victory at Munda.[22] Later, in AD 121, Hadrian dedicated the cult and temple of Venus and Rome on the date of the Palilia. Imperial associations accrued.[23] The Italian antiquarian Foggini (1713–83), who is credited with excavating remnants of the marble *Fasti* at Praeneste, comments that under the Christian emperors, April 21 was not in fact suppressed but augmented, and it was used also as the birthday of Constantinople, the "new Rome" (*Nova Roma*).[24]

The founding of Rome continued to be a day held in esteem by Renaissance humanists. The foundations of cities were closely connected with the foundations of buildings, a throwback perhaps to the ancient Roman concept that a temple's inauguration was its *dies natalis*. Astrologers in the

---

20. The anecdote about Cicero is given in Plutarch, *Caes.* 59.3 (Feeney 2007, 196); for Ovid, see ibid., 202–3.

21. Ibid., 148.

22. Ovid omitted this victory, one that ended the civil wars against the republican armies but caused much bloodshed. See Herbert-Brown (1994, 118–19).

23. Price (1996, 816–17); Beard (1987).

24. Petrus Franciscus Fogginius, *Fastorum anni Romani a Verrio Flacco ordinatorum reliquiae ex marmorearum tabularum fragmentis Praeneste nuper effossis collectae et illustratae* (Rome: [s.n.] 1779), 58.

employ of Agostino Chigi went to some trouble to draw up an election chart and to propose April 22, 1506, as the foundation date for Chigi's villa in Rome.[25] Chigi often played host to the Roman Academy, and he would have known the Academician Lorenzo Bonincontri, who authored a *De rebus coelestibus* and *Tractatus electionum*. In Marsi's circle some argued April 22 was the birthday of Rome, as Marsi himself comments at *F.* 4.721; this had become an accepted date again in Chigi's time.[26]

Ovid had invoked April 21 as the Palilia. Paolo Marsi played with this date in order to achieve a particular goal, however, giving a convoluted explanation for the validity of April 20. His methodology, and the reason for what he has trouble proving, can be traced as follows, beginning with roundabout and wordy remarks at *Fasti* 4.721:

> The Palilia will be on the 12th of the calends of May, that is, April 20 . . . if we interpret the poet [Ovid] correctly, we will understand the 20th, [and] if we follow Plutarch,[27] Pliny,[28] and Varro[29] logically, we will do so likewise. Plutarch says [π]ρῶ ενΔεκατῶν κα᾿ΛΗνΔῶν μαίῶν [sic], that is, "on the day before the 11th of the calends of May," and as for those who say "12th," you should reason this way, that one way of speaking is "the 12th of the calends" and another "the day before the 12th," for you include as the first day in the reckoning, the day which you are counting from. Whether Plutarch then says "before the eleventh" or "the twelfth," you will count eleven or twelve from that day of the Calends and understand "the day before." There should be no difference in expression between "on the eleventh of the calends" and "before the eleventh," or similarly "the eleventh." I therefore deduce the Palilia to be on the 20th of April.
>
> *xii calen. Mai. hoc est xx die Aprilis erunt festa Palilia. . . . si recte poetam interpretamur, xx diem tenebimus, idem si Plutarchum, si Plinium, si Varronem sequimur. Plutarchus inquit* [π]ρῶ ενΔεκατῶν κα᾿ΛΗνΔῶν

---

25. See Quinlan-McGrath (1986).
26. It is possible that April 22 was a favored date for the Palilia because then the celebrations would fall closer together with the Pasquinalia on April 25. See D'Onofrio (1990, 49) and A. Reynolds (1987).
27. Cf. *Rom.* 12: Ὅτι μὲν οὖν ἡ κτίσις ἡμέρᾳ γένοιτο τῇ πρὸ ἕνδεκα καλανδῶν Μαΐων, ὁμολογεῖται, καὶ τὴν ἡμέραν ταύτην ἑορτάζουσι Ῥωμαῖοι, γενέθλιον τῆς πατρίδος ὀνομάζοντες.
28. Cf. *NH* 18.247: *hoc est vulgo appellatum sidus Parilicium, quoniam xi. kal. Mai. urbis Romae natalis . . .*
29. *R. R.* 2.1.9: *Romanorum vero populum a pastoribus esse ortum quis non dicit? Quis Faustulum nescit pastorem fuisse nutricium, qui Romulum et Remum educavit? Non ipsos quoque fuisse pastores obtinebit, quod Parilibus potissimum condidere urbem?*

μαίϖν [sic], *hoc est "ante undecimum calendarum Maiarum," et qui dicunt xii calen. ita accipias, ut aliud sit dicere "xii calen.," aliud "ante duodecimum," nam primum numerabis ab ipso die calendarum. Cum vero dicet "ante undecimum" sive "duodecimum" numerabis xi aut xii ab ipso die calendarum et tenebis postea diem antecedentem. Nonne differentia aliqua esse debet in sermone cum ita loquimur "ad xi calendarum" et "ante xi," sic cum "undecimo" dicimus. Qua ratione ex his colligemus xx die Aprilis esse Palilia.*

Plutarch, the only author Marsi quotes, clearly gives a date of April 21; Pliny is in agreement, while Varro sets the foundation of Rome on the day of the Palilia but does not specify the date. Deference to textual authorities does not help if Marsi wants to persuade his audience of an April 20 birthday. Marsi demonstrates that he understands the Roman system of calendric computation: "AD" (*ante diem*) is a standard part of the formula and can be taken for granted in terms of translating the date. He logically concludes that "on" or "before" the eleventh day yields the same date on the calendar. There is a wanton disconnect, however, between this statement and the next: "I therefore deduce the Palilia to be on the 20th of April," he announces, ignoring that the eleventh in the Julian calendar for May is still not equal to April 20 by any reckoning. Why has Marsi misinformed his audience? Does he hope that the student writing down the lecture notes at the time is too busy to notice what he has just said? It helps to return to the beginning of Marsi's exegesis: "the Palilia *will* be (*erunt*) on the 12th of the calends of May," he claims, and this is the heart of the matter. Marsi is insinuating a realignment of the calendar.

He gives his audience further "evidence," asserting, "should these reasons not be convincing, let me add others" (*sed haec nihil valeant, afferantur aliae rationes*). He brings in authoritative witnesses that culminate in empirical observation for support, but he does not specify his sources:

> In the indices of the ancient *Fasti* calendars and in the oldest codices that day is marked as the 20th of April. Nor is this the proof; let us finally put our trust in the marble fragments, where the day has been inscribed thus.

> *In indicibus Fastorum veterum et codicibus vetustissimis xx die Aprilis festum illud notatum est. Nec his creditur; credatur tandem marmoribus, in quibus eodem die idem inscriptum est.*

There is no mention of which manuscripts Marsi looked at, if indeed any, and he alludes to epigraphical evidence that is seemingly non-existent.

Marsi saves his most trusted explanation for last, however, relying on Ovid himself. Marsi declares that he will tally the days in Ovid in consecutive order, and by counting the dates from April 13 to the end of the month, he will demonstrate that the Palilia does fall on the 20th:[30]

> What does Ovid say next? "On the following day make for safe harbors, sailor" [4.625], and this stands for the 14th day of the month. Next he says "When the third light has dawned after Venus's Ides, make a sacrifice, priests, with a *forda* cow" [629–30]. That means the third day from the Ides, that is, the 15th day of the month. Lest anyone hem and haw and laugh as though I talk nonsense, because by this method I am taking you all the way to the end of the month and showing you that it is so and can't be otherwise, [note that] Ovid says next: "Once Cytherea ordered this day to go more quickly, and hurried the heavenly steeds" [cf. 673–74], and here he is still talking about the 15th day of the month, and he appends: "so that as soon as possible on the following day the favorable signs would give the august youth the title of command" [cf. 675–76] and designates the 16th day. Next he says, "But when your fourth Light-bringer looks back on the Ides that have just passed, on this night the Hyades occupy Dōris" [cf. 677–78], and he reveals that this is likewise the 16th day, for counting four days from the 13th will be the 16th. There follows next "when the third light has risen after the Hyades' departure, the Circus will have horses separated in the starting gates" [679–80], and this means on the third day from the Hyades' setting. So that will be the 18th day of the month of April. . . . Then "Night has gone, and Aurora comes up. I am asked for the Parilia" [721], and this stands for the 20th day. Is this enough, or do you wish me to say more? Or have I not calculated correctly? No indeed, if one doesn't calculate the days as I have done, he will upset the whole order.

> *Quid postea? "Luce secutura tutos pete, navita, portus"* [4.625], *et significat xiiii diem mensis. Deinde "Tertia post Veneris cum lux surrexerit Idus, / pontifices, forda sacra litate bove"* [629–30]. *Significat tertio die ab idibus, hoc est xv die mensis. Ne quis tergiversetur et rideat tanquam vana loquamur, quia hac ratione deducam vos usque ad finem mensis constareque faciam*

---

30. "Let us cull from passages in Ovid, and so that we can't be misled, let us start from the Ides. We know that that day is the 13th of April: 'Jupiter takes possession of April's Ides with the *cognomen* Victor.'" (. . . *colligamus ex poetae locis et ne decipi possimus, incipiamus ab Idibus. Certum est illam diem esse tertiam decimam mensis Aprilis "Occupat Aprilis Idus cognomine Victor Iuppiter"* [621–22]).

aliter esse non posse, postea inquit "hanc quondam Cytherea diem properantius ire / iussit et aethereos praecipitavit equos" [cf. 673–74] *et significat etiam de xv die mensis, et subdit: "ut titulum imperii quam primum luce sequenti / Augusto iuveni prospera signa darent"* [cf. 675–76] *et designat sextam decimam diem. Deinde "Sed iam praeteritas ubi quartus Lucifer Idus / respicit: hac Hyades Dorida nocte tenent"* [cf. 677–78], *et ostendit eandem diem xvi, nam a tertio decimo die numerando iiii erunt xvi. Postea prosequitur "Tertia post Hyadas cum lux erit orta remotas / carcere partitos Circus habebit equos"* [679–80], *et significat tertio die ab occasu Hyadum. Sic erit decima octava die mensis Aprilis.* . . . *Postea "Nox abiit, oriturque Aurora. Parilia poscor"* [721] *et significat vicesimam diem. Estne id satis, vultisne me plura dicere? An non bene haec computaverim? Immo nisi quis ita computet, totum ordinem pervertet.*

Marsi succeeds at his task by combining the 16th and the 17th of April into the 16th, thus moving the founding of Rome up one day.[31]

Marsi has dealt plausibly with a passage in Ovid, 4.673–78, that has puzzled modern critics. In his commentary and edition, Bömer initially goes about solving this dating by counting from the Ides of April as Marsi does. In that case *luce secutura* (625) must mean the day after the Ides, that is, the 14th of April, and *Tertia lux* (629) the 15th. *Quartus Lucifer* (677) should accordingly be the 16th; however, this does not correspond with what we know from the Julian calendar, namely, that the setting of the Hyades occurred on the 17th. Ovid had spoken of *luce sequenti* two lines earlier, on 675; should this not be accepted as the 16th, sequentially speaking? Although *luce sequenti* and *quartus Lucifer* ought to refer to the same day simply in terms of the Latin prose, the calendar is returned to the correct alignment only if they are interpreted as the 16th and the 17th respectively. The Cerialia then falls correctly on the 19th, *tertia lux post Hyadas,* and the rest of the month is synchronized.[32]

Marsi accepts Ovid's literal meaning, counting *luce sequenti* (l. 675) and *quartus Lucifer* (l. 677) two times as the 16th. This allows him going forward to arrive at a date of April 20 for the Palilia. Marsi has succeeded in substantiating a date which he had trouble proving earlier on, and his logic here is not out of line. Of course, in the meantime he has misdated certain

---

31. D'Onofrio (1990, 52).
32. Bömer, 2:262–3. Fantham (1998, 219) agrees that *Quartus Lucifer* (l. 677) heralds April 16, but she calls this "poetic dating" to solve the discrepancy between the Republican and Julian calendars caused by Caesar's addition of a day to the month. By combining two days into one, Ovid is able to celebrate the Cerialia on April 19.

events, such as the horse races which took place during the Cerealia on April 19. Moreover, if he continues with his own professed logic of counting the days until the end of the month, he will have only twenty-nine days instead of thirty.

Nonetheless he assures his audience how "easily it will be apparent when the end of the month is reached" (*quod facile cognoscetur, cum ad finem usque prosecuti erimus*). He fudges a date of April 28 for the Robigalia (*F.* 901), and he subsequently misinterprets the sun's thrice rising in the heavens and the ongoing games in celebration of the Floralia (*F.* 943–44) to mean a single date of April 30, three days *from* the Robigalia.[33]

Marsi achieved his goal. But why was he so adamant about changing the date of the Palilia from April 21 to April 20? The clue is partially provided by his subsequent remark:

> Therefore let it be agreed by all and especially by the members of the Academy that the Palilia and birthday of Rome falls on April 20, a day which this literary sodality most solemnly observes, since it is the feast day of the most holy martyrs Victor, Fortunatus, and Genesius, the patrons of our Academy. And therefore this day is celebrated by all of the faithful [members].
>
> *Constet ergo omnibus et nostrae in primis Academiae xx die Aprilis esse Palilia et natalem urbis, quem diem sodalitas nostra litteraria religiosissime colat, propter festum sanctissimorum martyrorum Victoris, Fortunati, et Genesii eiusdem sodalitatis protectorum, quod eodem die a fidelibus cunctis celebratur.*

Once the Roman Academy was reinstated under papal control in 1479, it needed a religious overtone. The selection of the feast day of the three martyrs Victor,[34] Fortunatus, and Genesius, falling conveniently only a day before April 21, is not accidental. The names Victor and Fortunatus, evocative of ancient Roman temples or shrines to Victory and Fortune, suggest the favored destiny of Rome. The name of St. Genesius might have

---

33. *"In medio cursu tempora veris erunt"* [902]: *et demonstrat vigessimum octavum diem mensis. Ultimo loco inquit "Cum Phrygis Assaraci Titonia fratre relicto"* [943] *aut, ut emendati codices habent, "Cum Priami coniunx Titonia fratre relicto / sustulit immenso ter iubar orbe suum," et significat tertio die a medio vere, et ab ipso xxix die. Sic erit trigesimus et ultimus Aprilis dies. Quod si hanc nostram computationem non probabis, vide ne totum ordinem pervertas. Nam nisi hanc serves, recto ordine ad finem usque non procedes.*

34. This is pope Victor I, native of Africa, whose feast day falls on July 28 in the church calendar, although there are attestations to April 20 in some martyrologies. See Monachino (1969), cols. 1281–85.

etymological echoes for the birth, i.e. genesis, of Rome. De Rossi noted also that the combined feast day of these three saints was not a traditional or well-known one; it occurs only in the Martyrologio Usuardi.[35] He highlights the figure of St. Genesius in particular, a mime actor in Rome who converted to Christianity and was martyred during the persecutions under Domitian. The choice of St. Genesius as a patron saint for the Roman Academy would have been quite appropriate, since under Leto the Academy revived the reading and production of ancient Roman drama. In fact, students performed from Plautus and Terence during the Palilia celebrations, and Antonio Volsco's *Fasti* manuscript contains many references to those two dramatists.[36]

It is unclear how many times the Roman Academy celebrated the Palilia on April 20, other than in 1483. The following year, the ceremony took place on April 21. If the date of April 20 did not always remain steadfast, the association with St. Victor certainly did, underscoring the importance of a "day" over a "date." For this, there is evidence in the student miscellany, Ottob. lat. 1982. The feast of St. Victor is cited in combination with the *dies natalis,* found in the calendar on fol. 79r. The same person who annotated the *Fasti* on fols. 71v–73v has marked this April commemoration, and he transcribed the epitaph for Andrea Brenta on fols. 79v–80v as well.[37] Since Brenta died in February 1484, it is logical to assume that the calendrical notation of Rome's birthday on fol. 79r was written in 1483. Although no specific date is mentioned, Victor is represented, the patron saint for whom Marsi argued in his *Fasti* commentary. The names of saints Fortunatus and Genesius seem to have fallen away, probably out of convenience.

In his *Fasti christianae religionis,* a composition emulating Ovid but chronicling the feasts of the liturgical year, Ludovico Lazzarelli explains how the Palilia is still honored in the Christian calendar. In the early 1480s, Lazzarelli was in Rome and had found friends and mentors in Leto's Academy.[38] He gives his explanation of the Palilia in a passage marked as April 22 (*Lux decima at Maias praecedat laeta kalendas*).[39] He recounts the joy at

---

35. De Rossi (1890, 89). See also Lanciani (1892, 360).
36. See Accame (2008, 60–61); Greco (1974); Cruciani (1980); Bober (2000, 238–39).
37. Bracke (1992b, 22–23).
38. Corfiati (2003, 251) believes that Lazzarelli arrived in Rome in 1479 with his then-patron Lorenzo Zane; previous scholars have given a date of 1473. Cf. Arbizzoni (2005, 181–82). For a succinct summary of scholarship on Lazzarelli, see the introduction in Moreschini (2009); for a good overview of Lazzarelli's life and work, see Saci (1999).
39. Lazzarelli began his *Fasti christianae religionis* in 1469 or shortly thereafter. The verses concerning the Palilia were written most likely at the end of 1483 or beginning of 1484. See Fritsen

the observance of Rome's founding, now as then (*Nos ad laetitiam condita Roma vocat, / gaudebant festa veteres hac luce Quirites*). After declaring that the birth of Christian Rome, site of the new Jerusalem, surpasses that of pagan Rome, Lazzarelli describes which saint is now honored, and whose patron he is:

> The same day that restores the [ancient] rites is present for you, Victor,
>   when you, Victor, have the annual tribute for your death.
> On this observed day the Palilia has retreated: now the day
>   which had bestowed its honors on Pales has you, Victor.
> Rome worships you on the Esquiline; the dear society of poets
>   ahead of others assembles at the altars and worships you.
> Grant them the everlasting honor of the laurel leaf!
>   You, Victor, have the rank of both Apollo and Bacchus.

> *Lux eadem tibi, Victor, adest quae sacra resarcit,*
>   *annua cum mortis praemia, Victor, habes.*
> *Hac celebrata die cessere Palilia, nunc te,*
>   *Victor, habet, dederat quae sua liba Pali.*
> *Exquiliis te Roma colit, te convocat aris*
>   *ante alios vatum dulce sodalitium.*
> *Perpetuos illis lauri da frondis honores!*
>   *Et Phoebi et Bacchi tu loca, Victor, habes.*

Now it is St. Victor who awards the laurel crown at the poetry competition, and St. Victor who presides over the accompanying banquet, a clear allusion to the celebration of Rome's birthday that was first sanctioned in 1483. In fact, the sodality was renamed *Societas Literatorum S. Victoris in Esquiliis* after its reform under the authority of the Church.[40]

THE OLD AND NEW ROME

Lazzarelli's *Fasti* invites the question, How religious did the poetry composed by antiquarians in this period become? Did the statutes and privileges, set up in the papacy of Sixtus IV and watched over by his brother, Cardinal Domenico della Rovere, really effect an atmosphere of intellectual

---

(2000a, 117–18, 127). The verses I quote are from Lazzarelli's autograph manuscript, Vatican City, BAV, Vat. lat. 2853, fols. 163v–164r. For an analysis of Lazzarelli's poem and genre, see Miller (2003).

40. With variations in the title; De Rossi (1890, 85) gives this particular example.

stagnation and turn the reinstated Roman Academy into nothing more than a "religious confraternity," as Egmont Lee has suggested?[41] What was the position of Roman humanists who—allowing for differences in individual reactions—were caught between ancient pagan and modern Christian Rome?

The dilemma is not unlike that faced by Ovid, composing his *Fasti* under the emperor Augustus. Lazzarelli has been shown to exhibit "a kind of anxiety of Ovidian influence," negotiating a balance between his classical model, the *Fasti,* and his polemics, the Christian faith.[42] For example, Lazzarelli reminds the triumphant city of its former deception by the pagan gods to whom it offered sacrifice, gods who had been brought in from elsewhere. He lists and describes the transferred deities (Saturn, Hercules, the Trojan Penates) in language that is reminiscent of the *Fasti,* however.[43]

In a primitively drawn miniature in his autograph manuscript, Lazzarelli has depicted his Muse presenting the *Fasti christianae religionis* to Sixtus IV, who is shown in papal tiara.[44] An accompanying verses declares, "I humbly kiss the ground at your holy feet, / Sixtus, and I give to you the work of my excessive toil" (*Ante pedes sacros humilis figo oscula terrae, / Sixte, tibi immodici doque laboris opus*).[45] As Lazzarelli had been stranded in Rome when his employer, Lorenzo Zane, newly elected papal legate to the Turks, journeyed to the East, he now approached the pope for literary patronage. On fol. 2r, above a miniature portraying Lazzarelli speaking to his Muse, the poet writes, "Certainly Sixtus will be able to stop cruel fate and shift the course of the uncivilized menace which has thundered forth" (*Sixtus enim poterit crudelia sistere fata / et mutare feras quae tonuere minas*). Using wordplay (*Sixtus / sistere*), he pleads for a change in his fortunes while he praises the pope's ability to curb the pagan tide. Lazzarelli glorifies his sought-out patron on many occasions throughout the poem, portraying Sixtus IV as the leader of Rome's urban and spiritual renewal, as *alter Augustus* in terms clearly reminiscent of Ovid (*Tu quoque templorum positor reparator et urbis* fol. 201r; cf. *Fasti* 2.63).

---

41. Lee (1978, 204).
42. Miller (2003, 179).
43. *Tu vanis, heu, Roma, deis decepta, litabas / translatos venerans numina vana deos. / Cum Carmente dei venerunt Arcades olim / . . .* (fol. 163v of the autograph manuscript). For Lazzarelli's four examples of transferred divinities, Miller (2003, 182) cites *Fasti* 2.279 and 5.644; 1.233–36; 5.645; and 1.527–28 and 4.77–78 for comparison.
44. Vatican City, BAV, Vat. lat. 2853, fol. 3r.
45. The miniature is reproduced as figure 3a in the appendix of Schröter (1980). On fol. 246v of Lazzarelli's autograph manuscript, a version of the dedication to Sixtus IV (*ante pedes sacros*) appears again.

The theme of Sixtus IV as *alter Augustus* is a well-attested literary conceit, one that Sixtus himself approved of. In his epigram *De urbe Roma a Sixto iterum condita,* Roman Academy member Aurelio Lippo Brandolini writes that before Sixtus, Rome was no longer a city but a cadaver (*non urbs, iam Roma cadaver erat*), but the pope "established a new Rome; he gave back the city its beauty" (. . . *Romam immo condidit ipse novam; / reddidit hic urbi formam* . . . , ll. 28–29).[46] Repeating the famous analogy of Suetonius (*Aug.* 28.3) that Augustus found Rome a city of bricks but left it in marble, Giannantonio Campano writes in an epigram to Pietro Riario: "the Rome of Augustus which through the ages was of brick / the reign of Sixtus has now turned into marble" (*Coctilis Augusti fuerat per saecula Roma: / Nunc Sixti faciunt tempora marmoream,* ll. 1–2).[47] This does not mean that everyone associated with the Academy and Roman humanism in general approved of the pope's renewal of Rome. Evangelista Fausto Maddaleni Capodiferro, for example, criticized the reuse of ancient stone, such as bits of the Colosseum fitted for the building of the Ponte Sisto.[48]

Nonetheless, humanists very frequently flattered Sixtus IV, and they looked to him for literary patronage in the same way that Ovid may have looked to Augustus or Germanicus. Brandolini praised Sixtus IV for his creation of the Vatican Library, which surpassed ancient Rome's Palatine Library, and he compared the Vatican itself to a home of the Muses.[49] Sixtus supported a broad spectrum of learning, even if his own literary interests were limited to theology.[50] To say that antiquarian intellectual pursuits became religious, and the Roman Academy a dull institution when it was reinstated under Sixtus IV, is an overstatement. Instead, the relationship between the humanists and the papacy was symbiotic.

For the nature of the relationship, one might further note Lazzarelli's revisions in his autograph *Fasti* composition. They reveal his constant search for patrons between 1482 and 1484, and they suggest the frustration he would have felt at the pope's death on August 12, 1484. In his working draft Lazzarelli looked not only to Sixtus but also to the Aragonese rulers of Naples (*I, mea Musa, precor, regem pete Parthenopeum, / Ferdinandus is est gloria summa ducum,* fol. 175r; 182r) and the French king Charles VIII (*I*

---

46. Vatican City, BAV, Vat. lat. 5008, fols. 62v–63r; cited in Muecke (2007, 112).

47. Epigram 8.18 in *Opera* (Rome: E. Silber, 1495). The poem appears as VII.30 in de Beer (2013, 195).

48. Muecke (2007, 112–13).

49. Schröter (1980, 215–16). For the founding of the Vatican Library see Ruysschaert (1969; 1973).

50. Lee (1978, 201), cataloging Sixtus's reading list, notes that it did not transcend "in subject matter or approach, the fields of Church history, Canon law, or scholastic philosophy and theology."

mea Gallorum regem pete Musa verendum, / qui tenet a magno nobile nomen avo / Carolus . . . fol. 175r).⁵¹ Among drafts of dedications on fol. 178r, Lazzarelli has scribbled ten lines of verse that begin,

> Sweet sodality, oh most famous band of poets,
> you who have established the fountain of the Muses on the Esquiline,
> take the concluded little books as my pledge,
> accept this work for judgment with an impartial heart.

> *Dulce sodalitium turba o celeberrima vatum,*
> *Castaliam Exquiliis qui statuistis aquam,*
> *suscipite exactos haec pignora nostra libellos,*
> *librandum aequo animo suscipite istud opus.*

This passage should be read in conjunction with a set of verses on the flyleaf: "Sacred throng of allied poets, the reason why Rome is brilliant, I send you these books in the original. There is no need to direct my poem to Clarian Apollo; what the band of poets approves, even Apollo himself approves" (*Sacra sodalitii vatum qua Roma coruscat / Turba, tibi archetypos hos ego mitto libros. / Non opus est Clario mea mittere carmina Phoebo; / Quae chorus iste probat Phoebus et ipse probat*). The sodality of poets to whom Lazzarelli refers is of course the Roman Academy, who not only read his work, but had also suggested a range of dedicatees. A list of the humanists' names appears in the April verses celebrating Rome's birthday, and many of these humanists later congratulated Lazzarelli on his composition. A Yale manuscript of the *Fasti christianae religionis* has thirteen poems appended in Lazzarelli's honor, verses written by Bartolomeo Platina, Sulpizio da Veroli, Paolo Marsi, and Aurelio Brandolini, among others.⁵²

The antiquarians were the real audience for Lazzarelli's *Fasti* imitation; Lazzarelli intended them to be his definitive readership. Of course, as dual recipients of the poem, Leto's circle and the pope did share a common

---

51. Dedications to Ferdinand of Aragon, King of Naples, and his son Alfonso, Duke of Calabria, appear also on fols. 173r and 178r. A deluxe copy of the *Fasti christianae religionis* made for Ferdinand of Aragon and his son is preserved in New Haven, CT, Beinecke Rare Book and Manuscript Library, MS 391, and two manuscripts for Charles VIII are in San Severino Marche, Biblioteca Comunale, MSS 3 (CCV) fasc. 1, and 207 (IV) fasc. 3. See Fritsen (2001).

52. Lazzarelli tells the rulers of Aragon that he submitted his work "to a number of learned men for reading and perusal" (*libros . . . legendos complurimis doctissimis viris proposui*) and that "each and every one added his opinion about the work's dedication" (*addebantque de dicando opere quilibet suam sententiam*); MS 391, fols. 2v–3r. Lazzarelli is referring to the *dulce sodalitium* to whom he had given his draft. The list of Roman Academy members was continually revised by Lazzarelli.

bond in their conviction that the old and the new Rome were part of a continuum. Both groups shared a belief in Rome's inevitable hegemony, its political destiny based upon former greatness. In his *Fasti* commentary (1.582), Marsi had reported with enthusiasm the unearthing of a colossal bronze statue of Hercules during the destruction of a temple near the Ara Maxima. This statue later formed part of Sixtus's collection donated to the Capitol, in a calculated, symbolic display that the curia now dominated the former municipal heart of Rome. Under the auspice of papal authority, Rome's medieval symbol of a lion was being replaced with the wolf and other similar reminders of the city's mythic origins and ancient pedigree. Henceforth the Capitoline was transformed from a communal center into a Christian cosmopolis, or empire.[53]

In the decades following the papacy's return from Avignon to Rome, humanists too began to regard their city as the inheritor of *imperium*.[54] Paolo Marsi himself regarded the Capitol as one of the seven wonders of the world, which he confidently predicted would last until eternity.[55] When Marsi stopped along the coasts of the Adriatic and Mediterranean on his journey to Spain in 1468, he beheld all the sights with distinctly Roman eyes. Addressing the Syracusans in verse, he claimed that he and his employer, Bernardo Bembo, had come "to see in all lands the monuments / of our ancient leaders, monuments of our ancestors" (*veterum monumenta ducum, monumenta parentum / omnibus in terris cernere*) and the citadel "where formerly the Roman fathers prospered" (*quondam Romani quo viguere patres*).[56] It is specifically the bias of Roman *imperial* culture that colored Marsi's outlook on ancient ruins. This bias is evident in his description of the Croatian city Pula, "which formerly was called Pietas Julia" (*que quondam Pietas Julia dicta fuit*). Pula became a stronghold of Caesar between 46 and 45 BC, and after the commander's death and the transition to Octavian's reign, the city came to be called Pietas Julia Pola.[57]

---

53. See Miglio (1982).

54. For the development of this idea in the Renaissance, see especially Stinger (1998). Note chapter 5, "The *Renovatio Imperii* and the *Renovatio Romae*."

55. "The famous seven wonders of the entire world are praised / and recounted by our ancient fathers. / . . . / As greatest is boasted the Capitol of exalted Rome / and its glory will live to the very last day" (*Inclyta laudantur toto miracula septem / orbe per antiquos enumerata patres. / . . . / Maxima iactantur celsae Capitolia Romae / gloria et extremum vivet adusque diem*). In "*Ad illustrem don Herricum de regali palatio Hispalensi*" of the *Bembica peregrina (Bembice)*, Vatican City, BAV, Reg. lat. 1385, fol. 28v. The Capitol had already entered the canon of *mirabilia* in some late antique and medieval sources; the "Romanization" of the seven wonders is a distinct product of imperial tendencies. See Lanowski (1965), cols. 1020–30, and Madonna (1976).

56. In "*Senatui Populoque Syracusio Marsus et Cronicus*," fol. 8r of the *Bembice*.

57. Tamaro (1971, 17); Girardi-Jurkíc (1986, 17).

The Augustan period heralded a phase of grand architectural construction, transforming Pula into a proper imperial city. Marsi enthusiastically reports, "you might see as testimony the arch of parian marble" (*Aspicias arcus pario de marmore testes*), referring to the triumphal arch of the Sergii, erected in honor of three brothers, civil and military functionaries, after the victory at Actium.[58] As is often the case with imposing ruins, however, the monuments were a reminder to Marsi of former Roman greatness. At the end of his poetical description of Pula, he laments,

> When shall it pass that you return to your glory
> progenitor Rome? Would that former honors might be restored
>   and all your former power, illustrious Rome;
> may you extend your embrace to the ruled world again.

> *Quando erit ut redeas ad decus ipsa tuum*
> *Roma parens? Utinam prisci referantur honores*
>   *et quicquid poteras, inclyta Roma, prius;*
> *regnatis iterum pandas tua brachia terris.* (ll. 20–23)[59]

Marsi held Rome to be the rightful heir of *imperium*, of former imperial glory.

Marsi and the humanists in Rome believed not only in the city's cultural *imperium* but also in its linguistic *imperium*, a conviction whose origin and strength can be traced to Lorenzo Valla. From his *Fasti* commentary, we know that Marsi wanted to follow in Valla's footsteps.[60] For Valla, the Latin language was a medium of commerce, a mercantile method of exchange whereby Rome might pass on her values, her cultural and spiritual goods, to other nations.[61] According to Valla in his remarks in the 1440 *Elegantiae*, "there is the Roman Empire, where the Roman language rules" (*Romanum Imperium ibi esse, ubi Romana lingua dominatur*).[62] He elaborated on and extended this claim in his 1455 inaugural lecture at the University of Rome. In the published *Oratio in principio [sui] studii*, the humanist argued,

---

58. Girardi-Jurkić (1986, 17).
59. The lines are in *"Ad Cronicum ubi Polam ap[p]licuimus,"* fol. 6r of the *Bembice*.
60. At F. 2.685, *satis et a Valla iampridem et longe post a Pomponio nostro et alias a nobis disputatum est*.
61. The bibliography on Valla's thought is vast, but on this subject see especially the article by Camporeale (1995).
62. Garin (1952, 596).

> . . . it seems to me that holy religion and true learning coexist, and where there is not the one there cannot be the other, and because our religion is eternal, so Latin letters will be eternal.
>
> . . . *mihi videntur religio sancta et vera litteratura pariter habitare et ubicunque altera non est, illic neque altera esse posse et quia religio nostra eterna, etiam latina litteratura eterna fore.*

The humanist who earlier had attacked the temporal claims of the Church through the Donation of Constantine now held that the Christian empire of Rome and its language, with all the concomitant benefits for civilization, were geographically co-extensive. Valla's new emphasis was that Latin letters and the arts flourished thanks to the authority of the Apostolic See. As to the decline in learning in Asia and Africa in particular, Valla claimed that this happened "because the Latin language was expelled with the *imperium*; consequently all the good arts were in like manner expelled and barbarism took its former hold" (*quia lingua latina cum imperio eiecta est, ideo omnes bone artes pariter eiecte sunt et pristina barbaries rediit in possessionem*).[63]

The idea that Christian Rome had transmitted Latin culture, which was ultimately ousted from Africa, is repeated in Marsi's poem in the *Bembice* dedicated "To Saint Augustine in Africa in the city of Hippona on his feast day and at his temple on August 28, 1468" (*"Oratio ad Divum Augustinum in Aphrica et urbe Hipponae in eius die festo ad eiusdem templum v. kalendis septembribus 1468"*). In his own kind of Christian *Fasti*, and representing his interest in the recurring rites of the Roman calendrical year, Marsi writes:[64]

> At length we moored our bark on the sands of Hippona
>   and the barbarous shore was pressed with Latin imprint.
> You were once bishop and most distinguished father of this clime,
>   and the Barbary Coast bowed to your eloquence.
> . . . .
>   Nothing but the name of Christ was honored,
> religion was spread widely through your speech
>   and your name was illustrious over all the earth.

---

63. Rizzo, 79; text of *Oratio*, 198.
64. Fols. 12r–12v.

> *Hipponae tandem cimbam firmamus arenis*
> *et praemitur Latio barbara arena pede.*
> *Huius eras praeses quondam et pater optimus orae*
> *Barbariesque tuo paruit eloquio.* (ll.13–16)
> ....
> *Excultum Christi nil nisi nomen erat*
> *relligioque tua facta est amplissima lingua*
> *claruit et toto nomen in orbe tuum.* (ll. 22–24)

Marsi plays on the cultural and geographical meaning of *barbaries*.[65] Clearly, in Marsi's opinion the Church Father and model of Christian Latin eloquence St. Augustine had spread Christian religion and classical letters simultaneously in coastal North Africa.

In attempts to reconcile a curriculum of classical, "pagan" authors with the Christian faith, it was in fact the very example of the Church Fathers, who had been trained in Roman rhetoric, that the humanists often employed. Antonio Costanzi, for example, takes the time in the preface of his *Fasti* commentary to defend Ovid against the theologians who

> do not understand that they themselves with a degree of impiety oppose Saints Augustine, Lactantius, and Eusebius, the holiest of men, who borrowed both liturgies and eloquence from our ancestors and so added a certain splendor and beauty to our religion.
>
> *non intelligunt se non sine impietate quadam divo Augustino, Lactantio, Eusebio atque aliis praeterea, viris sanctissimis, adversari, qui a maioribus nostris et cerimonias et dicendi copiam mutuati religioni nostrae splendorem quendam ac pulchritudinem adiecerunt.*

Furthermore, the Augustinian ideal of a new City of God, that earthly restoration of the heavenly realm, would not have been lost on Marsi.[66] Flavio Biondo had already earlier dedicated his antiquarian interests to the service of a renovated papal Rome, declaring in the proemium of the *Roma Triumphans* (1459), addressed to Pius II,

---

65. See the entry in *Firmini Verris Dictionarius. Dictionnaire Latin-Français de Fermin Le Ver*, ed. B. Merrilees and W. Edwards (Turnholt: Brepols, 1994), 41. This lexicon is datable to 1440 and is therefore an accurate reflection of contemporary linguistic usage.

66. For an account of the importance of Augustine in the age of humanism, see Kristeller (1969, esp. 362–64) for the classical ideal that Augustine and other Church Fathers represented. Something of the popularity of *The City of God* in Italy can be gauged by the holdings in the Vatican Library, documented by Buonocore (1996).

And so I tried to see if I could place and submit before the eyes and mind of the men of our age, who are robust in talent and learning, Rome flourishing in just the manner Augustine wished to see it triumph, acting as a mirror, example, image, and lesson of every virtue and correct, blessed, and happy living.[67]

Itaque coepimus tentare si speculum, exemplar, imaginem, doctrinam et omnis virtutis et bene, sancte ac foeliciter vivendi rationis, Urbem Romam florentem ac qualem beatus Aurelius Augustinus triumphantem videre desideravit, nostrorum hominum ingenio et doctrina valentium, oculis et menti subiicere ac proponere poterimus.

Marsi no less visualized the ruins of Rome within the context of a great Christian empire. He equated ancient Rome and its colonies with the Renaissance seat of the papacy and Christian religion, as is evident in his lament for the basilica at Hippo Regius, in whose apse the cathedra of St. Augustine had stood.[68] Wanting to see what was left (*et cupimus templi sacra videre tui*), Marsi apostrophizes:

> Carthage your parent bore you, Hippona received you,
>   on this soil were temples consecrated to you.
> Oh unspeakable crime, oh ignominy of our age!
>   Now they have fallen into ruin, the vegetation and shade of the
>   woods cover them.
> Woe, this nation adverse to such a great parent destroyed them,
>   and the Berber stranger has oppressed your flock.
> A faithless nation is insensible now to a faithful people,
>   and there is no love of Roman religion.

Te peperit Cartago parens, Hippona recepit
    hocque dicata tibi templa fuere solo.
Heu scelus infandum, heu nostri dedecus aevi!
    diruta nunc silvae gramen et umbra tegit,
diruit heu tanto gens haec adversa parenti
    depraessitque tuas barbarus hostis oves.
Perfida gens populo nunc est insensa fideli
    nullus et Ausoniae relligionis amor. (ll. 27–34)

---

67. Quoted and discussed by Tomassini (1985, 19). See also Nuovo (1998) and, more generally, Anselmi (1981).
68. See Perler (1967); furthermore J. Lassus, "Hippo Regius," in Stillwell (1996, 394–96), with bibliography.

In his reaction to the crumbled church in Hippona, Marsi betrays his preconceived notions. He travels with a cultural bias that is both classical and Christian.[69]

PROPAGANDA FOR THE CHURCH

Antonio Costanzi likewise believed in the political supremacy of Rome and the sovereignty of the Church. While Marsi visualized Numidian Africa as a colony of Rome, Costanzi did not have to go as far afield. For Costanzi, the March of Ancona belonged in Rome's orbit. He dedicated his *Fasti* commentary and antiquarian research to the interests of the Church and to the protection of Fano.

Costanzi made three trips to Rome, where first-hand contact with the City surely sealed his opinion of her cultural superiority. His first trip came about as a result of meeting the emperor Frederick III, who stopped in Fano on his way to Rome, where he was to discuss measures against the Turks with the pope. Costanzi gave a welcome oration in Fano on December 17, 1468, which so impressed the emperor that he invited Costanzi to join his entourage. In Rome, the emperor then knighted Costanzi and crowned him poet laureate.[70] At the death of Pope Paul II on July 26, 1471, Costanzi, now a member of the *Consiglio dei Cento,* was sent as Fano's ambassador to the College of Cardinals. It is this second trip to which Costanzi refers in his comment on the Janus temple at *Fasti* 1.245. Costanzi spent several months in curial circles, pressing suits on behalf of Fano's communal independence against the lord of Rimini, Roberto Malatesta, and on September 1 he was joined by two other prominent orators to congratulate the newly elected Sixtus IV and to remind him of papal protection and responsibility toward Fano.[71] Costanzi's final trip to Rome occurred in April 1474, a diplomatic mission to prevent Fano from becoming, like its neighbor Senigallia, a papal vicariate under Sixtus's nephew Giovanni della Rovere.[72]

---

69. Pomponio Leto undoubtedly also influenced Marsi; his published walking tours of Rome (*Excerpta*) betray an interest in Christian as well as classical topography. Moreover, a mix of Christian elements are present in the Varro *De lingua Latina* student lecture notes from 1484–45, Vatican City, BAV, Vat. lat. 3415. See Accame (2008, 174–75) and Accame Lanzilotta (2000, 80).

70. Formichetti (1984, 371).

71. Castaldi (1916, 287–88). Compare the communal records from August 23, 1471, which say about Costanzi *omnes . . . comendaverunt* [sic] *solertiam et diligentiam oratoris predicti* (288, fn. 2), with Costanzi's remark at *Fasti* 1.245, *cum ad urbem me contulissem orator missus a senatu Fanensi ad Sixtum iiii Pontificem Maximum.* Sixtus IV was elected pope on August 23.

72. Ibid., 292.

176 • CHAPTER FIVE

Costanzi's commentary is dedicated to Federico da Montefeltro, not only as literary and artistic patron of the Court of Urbino but also as *condottiere*. Federico normally rendered his military services on short term and to the highest bidder. For example, he fought both on behalf of Florence (1469) and against Florence (1479) in the wars against the papacy. But when it came to the Malatesta family, especially Sigismondo—his peer, neighbor, fellow *condottiere,* and most bitter rival—Federico was a staunch ally of the pope, who promoted him to Captain General of the Church in 1462.[73]

Federico da Montefeltro and Pope Pius II both had their reasons for feuding with Sigismondo Malatesta, and thus they came to a unanimous accord. The contest between Federico and Sigismondo began in 1444 and centered on territory. Sigismondo's holdings included the coastal cities of Fano, Senigallia, and Rimini. Federico wanted access to the Adriatic; Sigismondo challenged Federico's right to rule as Lord of Urbino.[74] The two princes were also rivals when it came to lifestyle. For his part, Pius favored Federico. The latter's personal conduct and his synthesis of Christianity and antiquity fell more in line with the tastes and preference of the pope. Sigismondo had a reputation for violence and perversion, and he leaned too much to paganism.[75]

In the years 1459–63, Pius increasingly stripped Sigismondo of his territories.[76] The antagonism culminated in 1462. In April, Pius actually canonized Sigismondo to Hell and burned him in effigy in Rome.[77] Battles ensued in the summer; Sigismondo occupied Senigallia on August 12, 1462, but was routed by the papal troops of Federico the very next day. The final conflict took place in Fano on September 25, 1463, when Sigismondo capitulated to the army of Federico. A few weeks later Senigallia and other towns fell. Sigismondo was left with the sole holding of Rimini, which was preserved for him by the peace treaty.[78]

Costanzi finds cause to celebrate the successful siege of Fano at *Fasti* 1.691, a verse on keeping the fields free from darnel, a weedy grass that can damage the eyes if eaten. "Darnel (*lolium*)," Costanzi says,

---

73. Pernis and Adams (2003, 35).
74. Ibid., 28.
75. Ibid., 30, 35–41.
76. See Jones (1974, 220–39).
77. Pius drew on slander from a letter by Federico that had circulated sixteen years before. Federico was present at the burnings of straw effigies in Rome, but he believed that the pope had gone too far (Pernis and Adams 2003, 29, 34).
78. Jones (1974, 232, 237).

mixed with grain, will both harm the eyes and induce sleep. The famous scientist and physician Mario dei Bartolelli, and the luster and pride of Fano's nobility Ugolino Palazzi, explained this . . . when the troops of the Supreme Pontiff Pius II were besieging my home Fanum Fortunae, with you [Federico] acting as Captain General. Indeed [the effect] was possible to see in all the crossroads, throughout the streets, in the marketplace, in common places of business, when deep slumber had taken by surprise those sleepers who had eaten bread corrupted by darnel.

mixtum frumento et oculis nocet et somnum inducit, quod cum Pii secundi summi Pontificis copiae, te duce atque imperatore, Fanum Fortunae meam patriam obsiderent, . . . explicarunt . . . Marius Bartholellus philosophus ac medicus illustris et Ugolinus Palatinus Fanensis nobilitatis splendor et decus. Erat enim cernere in omnibus compitis, per strata viarum, in foro rerum venalium, in officinis plebeios homines, ubi eos somnus oppresserat dormientes, cum edissent panem lolio vitiatum.

It would seem that part of Fano's success was due to an experiment involving bread, laced with darnel, proffered to Sigismondo's soldiers.[79]

These events form the background for Costanzi's dedicatory preface. Addressing Federico of Urbino, he writes:

Who indeed is more worthy of the title of these commentaries, which for the most part dwell on Roman affairs? For not to mention that which among the citizens of Fano no stretch of time, no forgetfulness will ever erase, Fanum Fortunae, my native home and a celebrated Roman colony, was restored by you to the dominion of the Supreme Pontiff Pius II.

Quis enim te dignior horum commentariorum titulo, ubi magna ex parte de rebus Romanis agitur? Nam ut taceam id quod apud Fanenses nulla temporis longitudo, nulla unquam delebit oblivio, redactum abs te Fanum Fortunae,

---

79. Pietro Mario Bartolelli was born into a merchant family that dealt in spices. He was a civic humanist with interest in the works of (among others) Petrarch, Poggio Bracciolini, and Leonardo Bruni. He most likely taught as well as practiced medicine. See Uguccioni (2001, 14–16). Mario had an equally learned brother, Giovanni Peruzzo dei Bartolelli, nicknamed *doxa* ("glory"), who was a mathematician, mapmaker, architect, medalist, and mechanical engineer; see ibid., and Battistelli (1998, xviii). Costanzi refers to Giovanni at *F.* 4.422 (*Perutius Doxa Fanensis, vir acri ingenio admirandoque qui omnes totius orbis provincias separatim expinxit*). Giovanni designed a port in Fano in 1478 (*is est quem anno salutis Mccclxxviii senatus Fanensis triumvirum legit portui designando, qui nunc me quaestore magna impensa ad Ar[z]illam flumen extruitur*). Ugolini Palazzi commanded Fano's military again in 1473 (Guarnieri 1961, 124).

patriam meam, non incelebrem coloniam Romanorum, in Pii Secundi summi Pontificis ditionem.

Since they concern Rome, the *Fasti* are appropriate to the history of Fano, which has returned to Roman, that is papal, sway. The proper dedicatee is subsequently Federico, Rome's allied commander and military savior of Fano. The *Fasti* is a mirror of Roman dominance, recurrent and inevitable.

Costanzi expresses an intimately personal political preference. Sigismondo Malatesta had invited Costanzi to teach in Fano early on in his career, but Costanzi rejected the offer for a post in the Dalmatian city of Arbe, which was autonomous.[80] He did not return to Fano until Sigismondo's defeat in 1463, when he was recalled to help negotiate the surrender, according to the author of Costanzi's funeral oration.[81] Costanzi is frequently referred to as *libertatis amator* in this oration. *Libertas* is shorthand for *libertas ecclesiastica,* or Liberty under the Church; in effect, Fano traded one authority for another. At Sigismondo's defeat, Fano, a *signoria* or subject commune, reverted to direct papal lordship. The papal overlord was in many ways comparable to the foreign *signori,* who as outsiders installed a small number of representative officials or troops in the territories under their control.[82] This allowed for a greater degree of communal autonomy than the local ruling families did; usually the pre-existing engines of government were allowed to stay in place. Nevertheless, Fano was still a satellite of Rome, an outlying province of the Papal States, as Costanzi himself makes clear in the *Fasti* preface. He strikes a delicate balance, advocating Fano's relative independence compared to its neighbors while still inside the spheres of the Church.

Within both the text of his commentary and the preface, Costanzi treats the *Fasti* allegorically in order to uphold the political supremacy of the Church. In his remarks at 4.954 he enters into a combined antiquarian and political digression. He describes a local historical landmark, the

---

80. Formichetti (1984, 371). Costanzi's rejection of Sigismondo is better understood in light of Sigismondo's father Pandolfo. In 1405 Fano successfully petitioned Pandolfo Malatesta and then enjoyed relative autonomy. Councilors represented the city and were modestly involved in finances (raising loans, farming taxes), legislation (presenting and hearing petitions), and security (organizing defense, granting troops, sending ambassadors). New councilors were even elected locally instead of appointed. See Jones (1960, 224–26).

81. . . . *volens ac libens et laetus Antonius quam invenerat a civibus partam libertatem excellenti ingenio divinisque consiliis et confirmavit et auxit.* Octavius Cleophilus Fanensis, *Oratio ad senatum Fanensem* in *Antonii Constantii Epigrammatum libellus* [. . .] (Fano: Hieron. Soncino, 1502), fol. 37v.

82. For a clear analysis of the ruling families and forms of government in the Papal States, see Law (1981).

Arch of Fano, which was erected in 9 BC in the reign of Augustus and marked the Via Flaminia at the western entrance into Fano. The frieze on the upper portico of the arch was partially destroyed during the city's siege by Federico of Urbino in 1463. In his 1480 manuscript Costanzi records the inscription that afterwards remained visible (see figure 9): "they were bronze and gilded letters almost a foot long, which were appropriate to the majesty of such a great emperor, and of his achievement" (*erant enim aeneae litterae atque aurate pedali fere altitudine ac tanti imperatoris maiestati atque operis congruentes*),

> IMP. CAESAR. DIVI. F. AVGVSTVS. PONTIFEX. MAXIMVS. COS. XIII.
> TRIBVNICIAE POTESTATIS. XXXII. IMP. XXVI. PATER PATRIAE.
> MVRVM. DEDIT. CVRANTE. L. TVRCIO. SECVNDO. APRONIANI.
> PRAEF. VRB. FIL. ASTERIO. V. C. CORR. FLAM. ET. PICENI.

In the reproduction of the inscription Costanzi follows the tradition of the famous antiquarian Ciriaco d'Ancona, one of his boyhood teachers, who in 1423 recorded the original and undestroyed text of the arch. Years later Lorenzo Astemio compared and combined the *silloge* of Ciriaco and Costanzi so that he could reconstruct the inscription on the arch for his 1505 edition of *Urbium, civitatum, oppidorum quaeque alia id genus sunt*.[83] The exercise in epigraphy attests to Costanzi's antiquarian bent and can be compared to the insertion and use of inscriptions in the *Fasti* commentaries by Leto and Marsi.

The arch had been a longtime symbol of local pride in Fano, reproduced for example on medieval seals of the city, and Costanzi's rendering of its inscription is not without political overtones. Indeed, he imparts a lesson on citizenship with a story about Ciriaco (*F.* 4.954):

> Ciriaco d'Ancona, an illustrious man and a most skillful explorer of antiquity, read the inscription in a large assembly of Fanensian citizens and interpreted it for us boys. While he enthused at greater length, it was just as if the half-buried glory of Fano by his agency came back to life.
>
> *Cyriacus ille Anconites, vir inclytus et vetustarum rerum solertissimus indagator, magno Fanensium civium conventu [titulum] legit nobis pueris atque interpretatus est, cum exultaret maiorem in modum perinde ac eius opera semisepulta Fanensium gloria revivisset.*

---

83. Ciriaco's copied inscription is *CIL* XI. 2,1, n¹6218–6219. See Weiss (1965, 352–54).

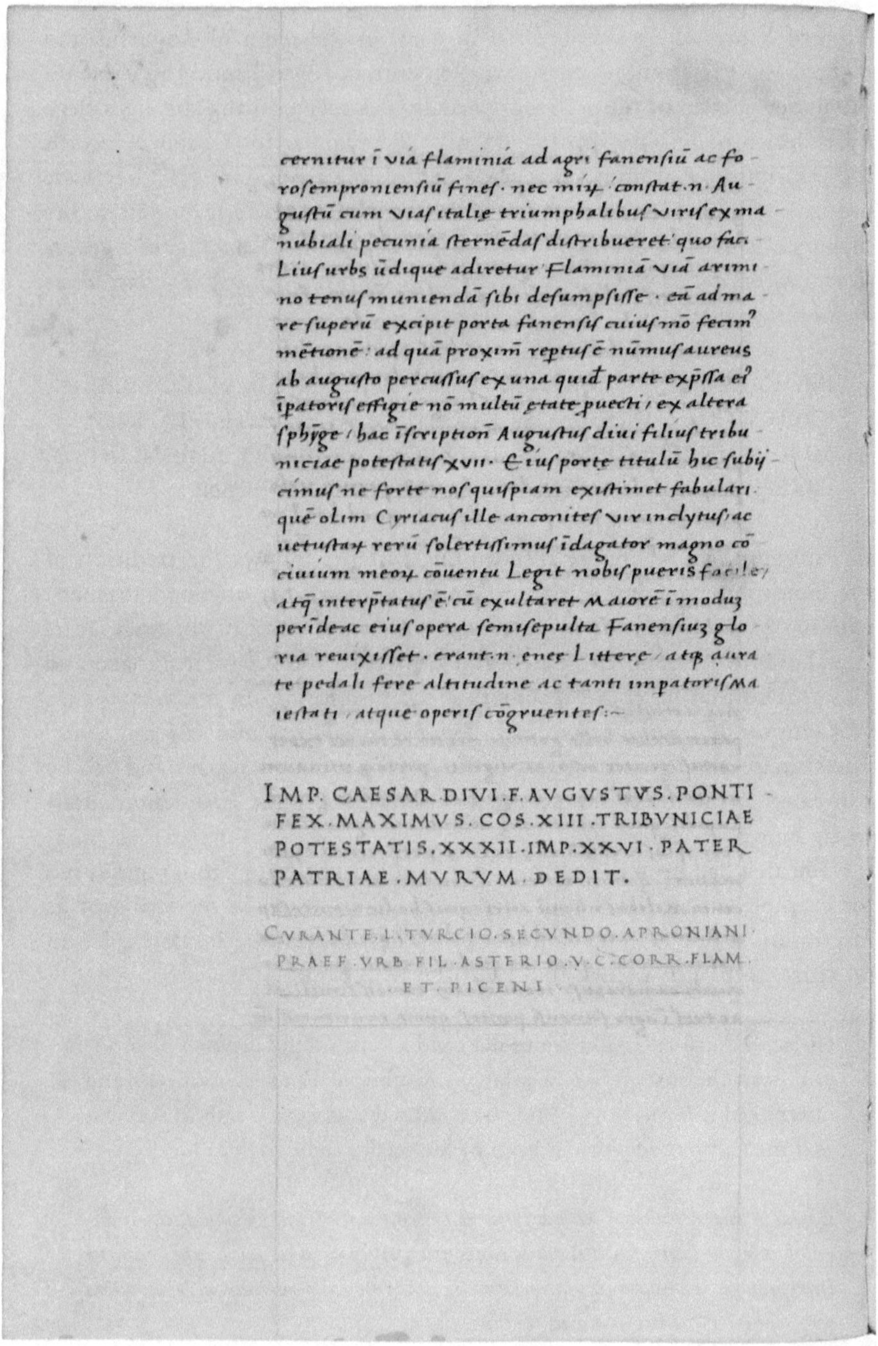

cernitur ī via flaminia ad agri fanensiū ac fo-
rosempronienfiū finef. nec miɤ. conſtat. n. Au-
guſtū cum viaſ italię triumphalibuſ viriſ ex ma-
nubiali pecunia ſternedaſ diſtribueret quo faci-
liuſ urbs ūdique adiretur flaminia via arimino tenuſ muniendā ſibi deſumpſiſſe. eā ad mare ſuperū excipit porta fanenſis cuiuſ m̄o fecim?
metionē: ad quā proxim̄ reptuſē nūmuſ aureus
ab auguſto percuſſuſ ex una quid parte exp̄ſſa eſ
ı̄patoriſ effigie nō multū ętate puecti, ex altera
ſphẏge, hac īſcriptiō Auguſtuſ diui filiuſ tribu-
niciae poteſtatū xvii. Eiuſ porte titulū hic ſubij-
cimuſ ne forte noſ quiſpiam exiſtimet fabulari
quę olim Cyriacuſ ille anconiteſ vir inclytuſ ac
uetuſtaɤ rerū ſolertiſſimuſ īdagator magno cō
ciuium meoɤ. couentu Legit nobiſ pueriſ facile,
atq̃ interp̄tatuſ ē cū exultaret maiorē ī moduȝ
per ideac eiuſ opera ſemiſepulta Fanenſiuȝ gloria reuixiſſet. erant n. eneƷ Littere, atq̃ aurate pedali fere altitudine ac tanti ı̄patoriſ ma-
ieſtati, atque operiſ cōgruenteſ:-

IMP. CAESAR. DIVI. F. AVGVSTVS. PONTI-
FEX. MAXIMVS. COS. XIII. TRIBVNICIAE
POTESTATIS. XXXII. IMP. XXVI. PATER
PATRIAE. MVRVM. DEDIT.

CVRANTE. L. TVRCIO. SECVNDO. APRONIANI
PRAEF. VRB. FIL. ASTERIO. V. C. CORR. FLAM.
ET. PICENI.

FIGURE 9. Antonio Costanzi, autograph manuscript (1480). Vatican City, BAV, MS Urb. lat. 360, fol. 145r. Reproduced with permission of the Biblioteca Apostolica Vaticana.

Ciriaco d'Ancona had climbed a ladder to transcribe the inscription on the Arch of Fano, and afterwards, text in hand, had assembled the citizens of Fano to rally them with civic pride and imperial nostalgia. This act of rousing public allegiance by appealing to a classical monument is not unlike Cola di Rienzo's 1344 discovery of the bronze tablet with Vespasian's *lex de imperio* (whereby the Roman people invested the emperors with power) and his political harangue in St. John the Lateran. Cola di Rienzo wished to make the people sovereign over the Empire, but he also wanted to restore Rome as *caput mundi*.[84] Costanzi, for his part, wished to celebrate that Fano was autonomous, but under the auspices of the Church.

The arch, as mentioned, had been erected at the Via Flaminia in the reign of Augustus. The emperor had begun restoring the ancient Via Flaminia in 27 BC, and had already built a commemorative arch at its very end, in Rimini. It was probably then that Augustus turned his attention to Fano and the construction of its gate, as well as its city walls. Augustus's interest in Fano was not without reason: he had settled a colony of his veterans there between 31 BC (the date of the Battle of Actium) and 27 BC. Consequently, the arch in Fano stood at a symbolic location. It marked the axis of the Via Flaminia, where it ends at the Adriatic coast and turns north towards Pesaro and Rimini. The arch therefore connected Rome with her colonies, not only Fano but also Pesaro and Rimini.[85]

Costanzi was well aware of Fano's history as "a celebrated Roman colony" (*non incelebris colonia Romanorum* in the commentary's preface), and in his view the ancient Roman colony becomes the precursor of the contemporary papal colony. Costanzi demonstrates his knowledge of the Augustan foundation of Fano and understanding of the subsequent political significance of its arch in the passage again at the end of *Fasti* Book 4, where he recounts:

> It is a well-known fact that when Augustus apportioned the roads to be paved in Italy with money from the victors' spoils, that Rome might more easily be accessed from all points, he took on the construction of the Via Flaminia all the way to Rimini. The gate of Fano, which I have just mentioned, takes the Via Flaminia to the Adriatic sea. Near the gate a gold coin struck by Augustus has been found. On one side there is an image of the emperor not much advanced in age, on the other a sphinx with

---

84. Mitchell (1960, 470–71); also Weiss (1988, 40–41).
85. Battistelli and Deli (1983, 39, 45); Luni (2000, 17, 29).

the inscription AUGUSTUS DIVI FILIUS TRIBUNITIAE POTESTATIS XVII.[86]

Constat enim Augustum cum vias Italiae triumphalibus viris ex mannubiali pecunia sternendas distribueret, quo facilius urbs undique adiretur, Flaminiam viam Arimino tenus muniendam sibi desumpsisse. Eam ad mare superum excipit Porta Fanensis cuius modo fecimus mentionem, ad quam proxime repertus est nummus aureus ab Augusto percussus, ex una quidem parte expressa eius Imperatoris effigie non multum aetate provecti, ex altera sphynge hac inscriptione: AUGUSTUS DIVI FILIUS TRIBUNITIAE POTESTATIS XVII.

In this comment Costanzi emphasizes Augustus's strategy of imperial expansion and self-fashioning as ruler and benefactor. This strategy would parallel the policy of the expansionist Church. In light of the dedicatory preface, surely Costanzi, defender of the Church and its secular "colonization" of Italy, has given the explanations he chooses for his *Fasti* commentary some forethought. Perhaps it is no coincidence that Costanzi's digression occurs at the end of Book 4, the culmination of Ovid's honoring Augustan Vesta;[87] the sacred flame of Vesta was always carried to Rome's new colonies.

Further instances of political readings are evident at the end of Book 6 of Costanzi's *Fasti* commentary. At line 770 Costanzi writes that the Carthaginian general Hasdrubal

at that time [207 BC] was killed at the Metaurus river, which flows into the Adriatic at Fano, my native home. In my time the tusk of an elephant, testimony to the victory by the Romans, was discovered in the river's bank.

hoc tempore caesus est ad Metaurum flumen, quod ad Fanum Fortunae, patriam meam, in mare superum cadit, in cuius alveo temporibus nostris dens[88] elephantis repertus est, testis victoriae Romanorum.

The Roman victory happened at the Battle of Metaurus, when Hasdrubal was forced into combat and defeated. Fano is situated along the

---

86. Costanzi has apparently confused a *quinarius* showing Victory with early imperial coins in the East, which showed a portrait of a sphinx (Weiss 1965, 353, fn. 6).

87. For the honoring of Vesta on the Palatine hill, see Fantham (1998, 272–76).

88. *Dens* has dropped from the printed editions of Costanzi's commentary, but it can still be read in the autograph manuscript, Urb. lat. 360.

left bank of the Metaurus river; it is in this valley that the decisive battle took place. Polybius relates that during the battle, six elephants were killed and four were captured.[89] Costanzi displays in his comment an archeological interest in the past. The eighteenth-century historian P. M. Amiani quotes Costanzi and an archival record of the discovery of an elephant tusk in Orciano.[90] Costanzi has gone further, placing the elephant tusk's discovery in the context of Roman dominance and surely hinting at modern implications: the rivalry between Carthage and Rome figured mythically in the feud between Federico and Sigismondo Malatesta, and Costanzi would have known of Federico of Urbino's symbolic association with the eagle and with Roman generals, Scipio Africanus in particular. Costanzi could then take advantage of Sigismondo's identification with the elephant, the Malatesta family's *impresa*. Sigismondos's symbol bore military, triumphant, and imperial overtones.[91] But Sigismondo's enemies could use the symbol in reverse, as the defeat of Hasdrubal and his elephants at the Battle of Metaurus occurred right in Fano's backyard. Indeed, what looks like the rump of an elephant can be seen in the keystone of the Arch of Fano.

The Battle of Metaurus held significance for Fano. The history of Fano and the Roman victory in the second Punic War are interwoven. In 1453 Flavio Biondo compared the words of Livy to a local tradition, and he agreed that Monte Sdrovaldo, *Mons Hasdrubalis,* derived its name from the defeat of Hasdrubal in the Metaurus battlefield nearby, in the area of Fermignano slightly southwest of Fano.[92] Costanzi altered Biondo's location of the battle, however, through a toponym of his own making. He moved the battle site directly to the Fano environs:

> [There is] at Metaurus a hill commemorative of this fight, which through a corruption for Aphricanus, they call Aphrianus. This is [the place] where Hasdrubal wanted his camp when Marcus Livius arrived with all his infantry arrayed ready for battle, as Livy writes. Good heavens! May whoever has considered the shape of this place, judge this historian not from Padua but from Fano.

---

89. Polybius 11.1.12. Cf. Livy 27.49.1.
90. Amiani (1751, 1:13–14). The elephant tusk was moved to the Museo Oliveriano in Pesaro.
91. Pernis and Adams (2003, 81–82, 98–100, 107–14). Sigismondo also adopted much of the symbolic imagery of the Roman general Scipio for himself. There was fluidity and balance between comparisons of the fellow *condottieri* Sigismondo and Federico. For elephantine imagery on the Arch of Fano, see Deli (1988, 36–39).
92. Deli (1992, 7–8).

> ... *apud Metaurum eius pugnae monumentum collis quem depravato vocabulo pro Aphricano Aphrianum appellant. Hic est ubi castra metari Asdrubal voluit, cum M. Livius omnibus peditum copiis ad conferendum proelium instructis advenit, ut T. Livius scribit* [27.48]; *quem historicum, dii boni, quicunque loci eius faciem fuerit contemplatus, non Patavinum existimaverit sed Fanensem.*

Perhaps with Biondo's *mons Hasdrubalis* in mind (in addition to the Livy reference), Costanzi has identified the *collis,* an embankment or dike known locally in Fano as the *ripe di Friano*.[93] Relocating the Roman defeat of Hasdrubal was important enough to the Fano psyche and Costanzi to make the classical author Livy, now in agreement with the battle's location, an honorary citizen of Fano.

Witness as well the etymology of *Fanum Fortunae* (i.e., Fano): scholars have hypothesized a link between the victory over Hasdrubal and the consecration of a *fanum* to the goddess Fortuna in Rome, since both events occurred on the same day, June 24.[94] For Costanzi and so many of his peers and predecessors, a city's origins, its history, could be traced in its name. Hence Fano's very name would suggest that the events of 207 BC were prophetic. They were a harbinger of what would happen in 1463. Fano was fulfilling its destiny.

While the above remains implicit and thus to a certain extent speculative, Roman supremacy is an explicit motif in the final comments of the passage on the Battle of Metaurus. Costanzi mentions in passing Senigallia, which had been one of the strategic encampments of the Roman consular armies, allowing for the surprise confrontation with Hasdrubal. He then launches into a digression. Sixtus IV had recently turned Senigallia into a papal vicariate, and Costanzi glorifies the city's custody under papal sway at *F.* 6.770:

> Indeed the Sena river, where Livy encamped when he joined his forces with Nero, is the one which flows into the Adriatic at Senigallia. It is thirteen miles distant from the Metaurus river. At this time the most illustrious and magnanimous Duke Giovanni della Rovere—nephew of the Supreme Pontiff Sixtus and a prefect of Rome, whom you, eminent Federico, not unworthily adopted into your bloodline, seeing as he has a most noble disposition and uncommon wisdom—is expanding the city,

---

93. Ibid., 11.
94. Battistelli and Deli (1983, 20, 31–36).

spaciously distributed into quarters and sectors, with a new ring of walls. He is restoring the city to its former compass. . . . Most recently we see paved streets, a port, public spaces, and splendid buildings, completed with incredible speed, as well as the most fortified citadel there is, constructed at such great toil and expense that it can rightly be considered impregnable.

Sane fluvius Sena ad quem fuerunt castra Livii, cum Nero se illi adiunxit, is est qui ad Senogalliam urbem mare ingreditur, quod distat a Metauro flumine ad xiii milia passuum. Eam hoc tempore illustrissimus dux atque magnanimus Ioannes Roboreus, Sixti summi Pontificis nepos ac praefectus urbis, quem tu inclyte Federice non immerito tibi generum ascivisti, ut est eminentissimo ingenio ac prudentia singulari, in regiones ac vicos apertissime distributam novo murorum ambitu auget et ad priscam amplitudinem redigit. . . . nos vidimus proxime viarum strata, portum, fora, aedes magnificas incredibili celeritate confectas, item arcem omnium munitissimam ac tanto impendio et industria fabricatam ut iure inexpugnabilis censeatur.

In this paragraph, which still deals with the Battle of Metaurus, Costanzi establishes a direct connection between imperial Roman supremacy in the past and papal Roman supremacy in the Renaissance.

Senigallia had fallen to ecclesiastical troops on October 5, 1463, only two weeks after Fano's capitulation.[95] Fano quickly stabilized as a direct papal dominion; we have seen how its citizens, under the ambassadorship of Costanzi, offered their continuing allegiance to Sixtus IV, eager, no doubt, to keep their communal autonomy. On the other hand, Senigallia was marked by revolt for the ten years following Sigismondo Malatesta's defeat. It overthrew the *signorie* of Antonio and later of Giacomo Piccolomini, nephews of Pius II. Under the Piccolomini the reconstruction of the city, which had been conducted with great zeal by Sigismondo, ground to a halt, and this was a cause of malcontent among the citizens of Senigallia.[96] Papal sovereignty was finally exerted and maintained through the machinations of Federico of Urbino and Sixtus IV. On October 10, 1474, Giovanni della Rovere, Sixtus's nephew, was married to Federico's daughter Giovanna di Montefeltro and assigned the vicariates of Senigallia and Mondavio.[97] With the birth of a son, Francesco Maria, in 1490, a new

---

95. Mancini (1926, 183).
96. Ibid., 184–85, 198.
97. F. Petrucci (1989, 347).

local ruling family established itself.⁹⁸ It is important to note that Fano was left untouched by a change in overlords, however. Costanzi's diplomatic mission to Rome in 1474 was a success: Fano retained its communal independence and did not become a papal vicariate as Senigallia did.

In his praise for Giovanni della Rovere and the benefits he bestows upon Senigallia, Costanzi glosses over papal nepotism. He illustrates how Sixtus IV and his nephew have been able to win the goodwill of the citizens, who had previously been sincerely devoted to the Malatesta. Costanzi would have known that Sigismondo had brought new life to Senigallia, formerly a thirty-six-hut village and a hideout for bandits. Sigismondo first brought change by encouraging immigration,⁹⁹ and then he also began an impressive building program, his intent being to give the city the ancient Roman *forma quadrata* with triangular towers at the corners and a *rocca*.¹⁰⁰ When Antonio Piccolomini was invested with the *signoria* of Senigallia after Sigismondo's defeat, it was precisely the interruption of this building program that distressed the citizens.¹⁰¹ With this knowledge, Costanzi praises the building achievements of Giovanni della Rovere. Receptive to Sigismondo's example, Giovanni della Rovere began restoration and expansion of the *Rocca* in 1480–81.¹⁰²

It is precisely during this period of construction that Costanzi wrote his *Fasti* commentary. Thus Costanzi's commentary had a double function: besides presenting the text of Ovid, it was an antiquarian vehicle of propaganda for the new papal vicariate of Senigallia. In addition, since Giovanni della Rovere's father-in-law, Federico of Urbino, was the dedicatee, politics and literary activity could conveniently converge.

Finally, what seems to characterize the Roman rulers, both classical and ecclesiastical, and link them in Costanzi's commentary, are the roles of founder and builder. Augustus had settled Fano the first time; in 1463 Pius II initiated the phase in history when Fano was a papal province. And while Sigismondo Malatesta was the modern-day founder of Senigallia, Giovanni della Rovere and the papacy he represented were the restorers of the city. For Antonio Costanzi, Christendom's *renovatio imperii* was a natural extension of its *renovatio urbis*.

---

98. Anselmi (1969, 22).
99. See Anselmi and Paci's 1972 edition of Andreano (hereafter Anselmi and Paci), 15.
100. Anselmi (1969, 19).
101. Anselmi and Paci, 20.
102. Formichetti (1984, 348).

AFTERWORD

As characterized by Fritz Graf, the Roman year was as an unrolling process, with each festival depending on the previous one and paving the way for the next.[1] The unfolding narrative of ancient Rome was orchestrated to unravel her history. Ovid depicted Roman culture and identity in the *Fasti*, but he also manipulated the calendar to introduce new civic and religious associations. The ability to manipulate time, both for ecclesiastical and political ends, continued to be an important aspect and function of the calendar in both the Middle Ages and the Renaissance.

Among his antiquarian pursuits, Pomponio Leto discovered and preserved a rustic Roman calendar on stone, called the *Menologium rusticum vallense*, and he lectured on and discussed Ovid's *Fasti*. The calendar—both material object and literary composition—was scrutinized to reveal a picture of "Romanness," and it gave readers a sense of national identity. The antiquarians of Renaissance Rome and their patrons saw themselves as heirs of *imperium*.

Still to be described is the *Venetian* connection with Roman antiquarianism and the city state's interest in Ovid's *Fasti*. Even though Paolo Marsi's commentary can be placed within a Roman milieu, the publication of his work took place in Venice, and this was for several reasons. As pointed

---

1. Graf (1997).

out in studies on the reception of Vergil, Venetian printers produced a disproportionately large number of books during the Renaissance, and they specialized in works that contained supplementary material such as the commentary.[2] Furthermore, Paolo Marsi had a number of personal connections in Venice. In 1468 he undertook a trans-Mediterranean voyage in the entourage of the Venetian ambassador to Spain, Bernardo Bembo. One of the motivations for Marsi's journey was the alleviation of anguish after Leto had been extradited from Venice by order of Pope Paul II. At that point Marsi had been employed as tutor in the Cornaro household, a post that Leto himself had held a few years before. The first edition of Marsi's *Fasti* commentary was printed on December 24, 1482, by the firm of Baptista de Tortis in Venice, at the behest and expense of Giorgio Cornaro, as is made clear in the *Emendatio locorum* or errata-explanations at the end of the volume.

What interest might the noble Venetian Giorgio Cornaro have had in supporting a humanist project that fundamentally had to do with Rome and had its proper context and setting in the circle of Pomponio Leto's Roman Academy? The conviction of Marsi's Venetian patron Bernardo Bembo is enlightening. In his private commonplace book Bembo expressed the sentiment, "the Venetians are called new Romans."[3] Venice had long looked to Constantinople, the original "new Rome," for a model of ancient identity and grandeur. However, in the imperial, expansionist age of Venice a more Western ideal replaced the Byzantine prototype, and especially after Constantinople fell to the Turks, "there was special reason to acclaim Venice as the new 'new Rome.'"[4] The fifteenth-century chronicler Marc' Antonio Sabellico went so far as to suggest that Venice was superior to ancient Rome, finding her more commendable "for sanctity of laws, for equity of justice, and for goodness."[5] Sentiments such as these define what historians have called "the myth of Venice." As summarized by Craig Kallendorf, the Venetians were supposed to cultivate wisdom, courage, temperance, and justice, an ideology underscored by an accommodating humanism of moral severity, pronounced piety, and committed republicanism.[6] The Renaissance historian Marin Sanudo agreed with Sabellico on the conceit of a Venice morally superior to Rome: Venice already surpassed Rome in

---

2. Kallendorf (1999, 12).
3. Ibid., 17; Chambers (1970, 12).
4. Chambers (1970, 18–24). Venice defeated its maritime rival Genoa at the Battle of Chioggia in 1380, beginning a territorial expansion in the Italian mainland.
5. Bouwsma (1968, 90–91).
6. Kallendorf (1999, 14, 23).

its origins, he claimed, because she was not founded by shepherds but by the powerful and nobly born.⁷

Sanudo's declaration implies that it was the patricians who sought a new rhetoric to celebrate the values of their social group and to promote the myth of Venice. It was the "patrician cult of antiquity"⁸ that informed the search for Roman roots. Classical architectural orders were adapted to the Cornaro family palace on the Grand Canal, for example.⁹ And, as was the case with many patrician families, the Cornaro now claimed a distinguished Roman lineage. The inspiration for direct descent from ancient Romans often came from similar-sounding names: Jacopo Antonio Marcello traced his genealogy to his supposed illustrious forefather Marcus Claudius Marcellus; likewise, the Cornaro established as their ancestry the *gens Cornelia*.¹⁰ No wonder, then, that Giorgio Cornaro supported the publication of Paolo Marsi's Roman antiquarian *Fasti* commentary. In deference to his patron, Marsi praises the Cornaro lineage in several of the prefaces to each book of the *Fasti*. For example, as the commentary on March unfolds, Marsi professes, "now the third monument of my toil follows, / oh Giorgio, venerated progeny of the ancient Scipiadic race" (*Tertia nunc nostri subeunt monumenta laboris, / Scipiadum antiqui generis venerata Georgi / progenies . . .*). In addition, at the beginning of Book 6, Marsi proclaims:

O ancient Scipiadic race, o revered offspring and
    everlasting honor to Venetian soil, Giorgio Cornelio,
to you my homage and glory ascend.

O genus antiquum, soboles venerata, Georgi
    Scipiadum et Venetis decus indelebile terris
Corneli, tibi noster honor, tibi gloria surgit. (ll. 1–3, 1482 ed.)

The Cornaro also employed visual rhetoric to substantiate their family tree, ordering paintings to illustrate the triumphs of their supposed ancestor, Publius Cornelius Scipio Nasica.¹¹ Thus it was that the son of Marsi's patron, Francesco Cornaro, commissioned from Andrea Mantegna

---

7. Chambers (1970, 25–26).
8. Ibid., 28. The relation of the powerful families in Renaissance Venice to the cult of antiquity informs Patricia Brown's full study (Brown 1996).
9. Chambers (1970, 126–27); Kallendorf (1999, 17).
10. Brown (1996, 231–32).
11. Chambers (1970, 25).

FIGURE 10. Andrea Mantegna, *The Introduction of the Cult of Cybele at Rome*, 1505–6. Detail. © The National Gallery, London.

in 1505 *The Introduction of the Cult of Cybele at Rome* for his family palace in Venice (see figure 10). The painting was probably intended to hang in Francesco's private chamber, while the *paterfamilias* Giorgio was still alive.[12] If Francesco's own classical training was minimal, then the *Fasti* commentary dedicated to his father's name would easily have supplied him with a ready-made choice of invention; indeed, Mantegna's iconography indicates a degree of collaboration between humanism and art.

The study of classical texts and the rebirth of the visual arts are recognizable hallmarks of the Italian Renaissance. How far humanists and artists interacted can be debated, but more often than not, humanist involvement is present in paintings that employ learned subject matter. The humanists almost always had a hand whenever classical inscriptions and historical *exempla* appear on a canvas—whether the humanist had personal acquaintance with the artist or provided documentation indirectly through a supplied text.[13] Intellectualism accurately describes the painterly style of Andrea Mantegna, for example. His compositions contain an antiquarianism and academic element difficult to find elsewhere, at least to such a degree, among his contemporaries. *The Triumphs of Caesar*, for instance, exhibits an *all'antica* motif, although the term *all'antica* applies to a type of decoration not necessarily meant to be

---

12. Lightbown (1986, 214).
13. Hope and McGrath (1996, 171).

historically accurate. The soldiers' breastplates, for example, are not typical of the Roman army, and with respect to the monuments Mantegna seems to have been little influenced by his trip to Rome in 1488–90.[14] On the other hand, Mantegna's association with the antiquarians Felice Feliciano and Giovanni Marcanova, who owned over five hundred manuscripts with classical inscriptions, is well known, and his employment at the court in Mantua is in large part due to the shared interests of his patron Ludovico Gonzaga, a bibliophile and scholar interested in Vergil.[15] The inventory of Mantegna's books includes the work of Flavio Biondo and, from among classical authors, Cicero, Juvenal, Martial, Ovid, Sallust, Terence, Valerius Maximus, and Vergil.[16]

In *The Introduction of the Cult of Cybele at Rome*, Mantegna has illustrated a specific event in the career of P. Cornelius Scipio Nasica from 204 BC, a story narrated most fully by Livy (29.10, 11, and 14) and Ovid (*Fasti* 4.247–348). The classical accounts largely agree in their outline: amid the losing battles of the second Punic War, the Romans consulted the Sybilline books and the Delphic oracle. These advised fetching the Phrygian Mother Goddess, or Cybele, from Mount Ida and bringing her cult-image and worship to Rome. The most worthy man of Rome was instructed to receive her; the Senate decreed that this honor be given to Scipio Nasica, a youth of promising civic and military valor. When the ship bearing the goddess arrived on Italian soil at Ostia, the goddess gave a first token of her favor by yielding to the waiting and welcoming hands of the Roman matron Claudia Quinta, whose impugned chastity was thereby believed to be vindicated.

Mantegna's painting, now in London's National Gallery, interpretively and imaginatively combines elements from both Livy's and Ovid's accounts. Livy's story that the Senate voted Scipio Nasica the best man in Rome is accompanied by the report that he was the son of "that Gnaeus who had fallen in Spain" (*qui in Hispania ceciderat*, 29.14). The reference to Scipio's heroic forebears can be found on the tombs in the background in Mantegna's canvas. The inscriptions on the tombs identify them as housing the mortal remains of Gnaeus and his brother Scipio the Elder, both of whom died fighting the Carthaginians. The tombs leave no doubt as to the genealogical tenor of the painting and its purpose in upholding the distinguished ancestry of the Cornaro family.[17]

---

14. Ibid., 163–64; A. Martindale (1979, 67–68).
15. A. Martindale (1979, 23–25, 29–30).
16. Signorini (1996, 106, 113–14).
17. Brown (1996, 253).

For the story of Cybele's transfer, Paolo Marsi quotes from Livy at the appropriate passages, but Ovid's text is nonetheless the principal one which he interprets and upon which Mantegna may have similarly based his illustration of events. In particular, it is Ovid's unfolding of the story, the narrative development, that Mantegna privileges. In Livy's account, Scipio Nasica boards the ship at Ostia in order to welcome the goddess, and he hands her over to the waiting Claudia Quinta on shore. From there, a procession of Roman matrons carries the image of Cybele into Rome. The two most dramatic elements of the story occur in Ostia. By contrast, the tales of Scipio Nasica and of Claudia Quinta are not collapsed in the *Fasti,* and the action is spread over two days and in two different locations. The Claudia Quinta episode is the focus of the first day and transpires at Ostia. Claudia Quinta frees the ship that has run aground on the coast and draws it up the Tiber (*F.* 4.291–328). On the following day, rites of purification are held in honor of Cybele outside the City proper, and thereafter the cult-image is carried in through the Capene Gate to be received by Scipio Nasica (4.329–48). It is this sequence of the second day, with its focus on Scipio rather than Claudia, that Mantegna favors in his painting. The still-burning incense is visible on the litter bearing the goddess to the left; the Scipio family tombs framing this scene effectively portray the Capene gate through which the entourage has just passed. The cortege would certainly be a familiar sight for an audience in Renaissance Venice, a city known for its number of churches and religious processions.[18] A young chief priest directs the procession to the central figure of the composition (cf. *praecedit laeto voltu, F.* 4.343), and the inscription underneath the central kneeling figure reads S HOSPES NVMINIS IDAEI C, "by decree of the Senate, host of the Phrygian Deity" or even "Scipio Cornelio, host of the Phrygian Deity."[19]

It has been a matter of debate among art historians whether this kneeling figure is indeed Scipio, or instead Claudia Quinta or even a votary of the Phrygian cult.[20] The young man in profile gesturing with his right hand to the kneeling figure has also been named Scipio. Ovid devotes most of his storytelling skill to the attestation of Claudia Quinta's purity, an argument that might be used in favor of identifying her with Man-

---

18. See Kallendorf (1999, 15) and, more fully, Chambers (1970, 109–22) for the characterization of Venice as a city of religious ritual.

19. K. Christiansen, no. 135 in the exhibition catalogue *Andrea Mantegna* (Martineau and Boorsch 1992, 414–16).

20. Ibid., 415.

tegna's central figure and in keeping with the hypothesis that the *Fasti* is Mantegna's closest literary source. At this point we should return to Paolo Marsi's commentary, which might provide further clues. In the testimonial story of Claudia's innocence, Ovid twice says that Cybele will yield to "chaste hands" (*casta manu, F.* 4.260 and 324). In the first citation, however, Paolo Marsi understands the reference as applying not to Claudia, but to Scipio Nasica. Marsi remarks at 4.260: "chaste hands: the poet refers to the oracle which said that she should be received by the best man" (*respexit poeta ad oraculum, quod fuit ut ab optimo viro exciperetur*; cf. Livy 29.11).[21] Scipio Nasica has been brought to the forefront as the heroic figure in the Ovidian passage.[22]

Scipio is the heroic figure in Mantegna's painting as well. The kneeling, devoted figure with outstretched hands certainly depicts someone of extreme piety. As the focus of Mantegna's painting, Scipio Nasica, young scion of the *gens Cornelia*, was surely intended as a model of both moral and civic virtue for yet another Cornaro, for whose chambers the painting was commissioned. This reading, finally, is upheld by Marsi's *Fasti* commentary. In dedicating his work to Giorgio Cornaro, Marsi underscores its long-lasting value, not only for his patron, but for his patron's son Francesco as well, one year old at the time of the commentary's first publication in 1482:

> . . . if my words, communicated to you listening at home, ever helped you then, may they do so in the future during my absence as well; and may you keep [this book] with you, whereby under my guidance you can both educate and also instill good morals in your already growing offspring. For indeed, it is not just the honor of the *Fasti* that will remain with you, but also the things in it which pertain to the instruction of the civic life.

> . . . *siquando mea vox coram tibi domi proderat audienti, prosit et in posterum quoque absentis, et tecum habeas unde pullulantem iam tibi sobolem queas et nobis ducibus erudire et bonis quoque moribus instituere. Non enim sola Fastorum gloria tete manet sed quae ad institutionem vitae humanae pertinent.*

---

21. Livy 29.11: *Responsum [oraculi] esse ferunt . . . cum Romam deam devexissent, tum curarent ut eam qui vir optimus Romae esset hospitio exciperet.*

22. Of course this could still leave open for debate whether the kneeling figure or gesturing figure in profile represents Scipio. Either way, if one reads Marsi and Mantegna together, Scipio is the "central" figure of the painting.

In *The Introduction of the Cult of Cybele at Rome,* humanism and art have come together to participate in a common goal. Indeed, Andrea Mantegna and Paolo Marsi with their antiquarian leanings shared common interests. The tie that binds artist and intellectual in this case is not just antiquarianism *per se,* however, but the requirements of a patron. In Renaissance Venice rhetorical principles did not come first. Antiquity was not necessarily studied for antiquity's sake; rather, "the Venetian patriciate appropriated humanism" in service to their own ideals.[23]

---

23. Kallendorf (1999, 23), with reference to King (1986, 25, 174).

APPENDIX I

Renaissance Commentaries on Ovid's *Fasti*

PRINTING HISTORY

Paulus Marsus

1482 (Dec. 24), Venetiis (Venice): Baptista de Tortis
    HC 12238; Goff O–170; BMC V 322

1483 (June 5), [Mediolani (Milan)]: Antonius Zarotus for Johannes de Legnano
    HC 12239; Goff o–171

1485 (Aug. 27), Venetiis (Venice): Antonius Battibovis
    HC *12240; Goff o–172; BMC V 404

1489 (Nov. 10), [Mediolani (Milan)]: Uldericus Scinzenzeler for Gabriel Conagi
    HCR 12241 = H 12243 (with error in year date); Goff O-173; BMC VI 763

1492 (Oct. 27), Venetiis (Venice): Troilus Zani, Presbyter
    HC 12242; Goff O–174; BMC VII 1141

Antonius Constantius

1489 (Oct. 23), Romae (Rome): Eucharius Silber
  H *12244; Goff O–175

Composite Editions

1497 (June 12), Venetiis (Venice): Joannes Tacuinus de Tridino
  HC *12247; Goff O–176; BMC V 531

1502 (Oct. 14), Venetiis (Venice): Joannes Tacuinus de Tridino
  Panzer; Schweiger; NUC; BM

1508 (June 4), Venetiis (Venice): Joannes Tacuinus de Tridino
  Panzer; Schweiger; Adams O–456; NUC; BM

1510 (Feb. 17), Mediolani (Milan): Magister Leonardus Pachel
  Panzer; Schweiger; NUC; BN

[1510: Parisiis (Paris)]: Gilles de Gourmont
  BM

1512: Mediolani (Milan): Magister Ludovicus de Bebulco
  Schweiger; NUC; BM

[1512: Parisiis (Paris)]: Poncetus le Preux
  Schweiger

1520 (April 12), Venetiis (Venice): Joannes Tacuinus de Tridino
  Panzer; Schweiger; NUC; BM; BN

1527: Tusculani apud Benacum (Toscolano): Alexander Paganinus
  Panzer and Schweiger (with errors in year date); NUC; BM; BN

Composite, in Volumes of Ovid's Opera Omnia

1550: Basileae (Basel): Joannes Hervagius
   Schweiger; Adams O-439; NUC; BN

1601: Frankofurti (Frankfurt): typis Wechelianis apud Claudium Marnium et haeredes Joannis Aubrii
   Schweiger; NUC; BM; BN

MANUSCRIPT HISTORY

1427: Vatican City, BAV, Vat. lat. 10672, fols. 2r–68v
   Glosses in Ciriaco d'Ancona's hand.

ca. 1450: Vatican City, BAV, Vat. lat 1595, fols. 254r–331v
   Glosses in Pietro Odi di Montopoli's hand.

ca. 1469/1470: Vatican City, BAV, Vat. lat. 3264, fols. 1r–86r
   Glosses in Pomponio Leto's hand.

ca. 1470: Vatican City, BAV, Chig. H. VI. 204, fols. 1r–74v
   Glosses in Antonio Costanzi's hand.

1480: Vatican City, BAV, Urb. lat. 360, fols. 1r–198v
   Glosses in Antonio Costanzi's hand.

post 1480: Rome, Biblioteca Vallicelliana, MS R. 59, fols. 1r–218r
   Commentary of Antonio Volsco.

post 1482: Ghent, Bisschoppelijke Bibliotheek, Cath. 12 (no. 28), fols. 16r–212r
   Copy of Marsi's printed commentary.

ca. 1485: Vatican City, BAV, Ottob. lat. 1982, fols. 71v–73v
   Comments on *Fasti* from the circle of Pomponio Leto.

post 1488: Vatican City, BAV, Vat. lat. 3263, fols. 1r–119v
   Glosses in Pomponio Leto's hand.

ca. 1490: Ferrara, Biblioteca Comunale Ariostea, II.141, fols. 1r–105v
Glosses in Pomponio Leto's hand.

1498: Sélestat, Bibliothèque Humaniste, ms. 50, fols. 102r–195r
Copy of Marsi's printed commentary (not consulted).

Excluded from study
1482: Munich, Bayerische Staatsbibliothek, Clm 754, fols. 11r–132v
Collectanea in enarrationem Fastorum by Angelo Poliziano

APPENDIX II

Comparison of Manuscript Glosses in Vat. lat. 1595, Ottob. lat. 1982, and Vat. lat. 3263

VAT. LAT. 1595
PIETRO ODI DI MONTOPOLI, CA. 1450

fol. 254r: Publii Ovidii Nasonis Fastorum liber primus ad Germanicum.

fol. 258v: Calendis Januariis in insula Jupiter colitur et Aesculapius, Jani quoque festum est et Junonis, quia ut supra (*sc.*1. 55) praecepit "vendicat Ausonias Junonis cura calendis." (1. 292–93)

Cancer occidit iii nonas Januarias, oritur Capricornus. (1.313)

vi idus dies agonalis. (1.317)

fol. 260v: qua causa volucres mactantur. (1.441)

fol. 261r:
columba uritur. (1.452)
anseris iecur Isidi. (1.453–54)
nocti gallus mactatur. (1.455)

Delphin oritur die agonali cosmice. piatur Janus. est sexto idus Januarias v idus media hyems. (1.457–60)

iiii idus colitur Carmentis et Juturna. (1.461–64)

fol. 263r:
Idibus Januariis sacrum in templo Jovis Augusti nominatio. (1.587–90)

Scipio Aphricanus (1.593)
Metellus (1.594)
Marius (1.595)
Sylla (1.595)
Scipio Numantinus (1.596)
Drusus (1.597)
Augustus (1.599)
Mallius [sic] Torquatus (1.601)
Valerius Corvinus (1.602)
Magnus Pompeius (1.603)
Caesar (1.603)
Fabii Maximi (1.605–6)

fol. 263v:
Festus Pompeius: Scorta appellantur meretrices quia ut pelliculae subigantur omnia namque ex pellibus facta scortea appellantur (Fest. pp. 330 and 331 Müll). Quare ego puto scortea hic pelliculas intestinas cum alius textus habeat exta. (1.629)

fol. 264r:
A Capricorno sol transit in Aquarium. xv kalendas Februarias. Lyra non apparet amplius ix kalendas Fe[bruarias]. Pectus autem leonis occidit. viii kalendas Februarias. (1.651–56)

OTTOB. LAT. 1982
ASSOCIATE OF POMPONIO LETO, CA. 1485

fol. 71v:
Ad Tiberium opus dedicatur quod multe rationes probant. (1.3)

Romulus decem menses instituerat a Martio annum recipiens, Numa rex secundus Romanorum duos, Januarium et Februarium, addidit. (1.27–44)

In kalendis omnium mensium Juno semper colitur. (1.55)
In Idibus Juppiter. (1.56)

fol. 72r:
Festum Esculapii qui in insula Tiberina juxta templum Jovis colebatur, cuius festum eodem die fiebat. (1.292–93)

Occidit octipes cancer in nonas Januarii. (1.313)
Oritur lyra nonis. (1.315)

Antiqui farre et sale sacrificabant, mox tus, mirra, coscum, crocum, acceptum est ex Arabia et Cylicia. Lacrimate mirre apellantur quod e cortice sudant. (1.337–42)

fol. 72v:
aves sacrificantur . . . unde aquila Jovi, pavo Junoni, corvus Phoebo, anser Inacho, gal[li] nocti. (1.441–56)
Eodem die oritur Delphin. (1.457–58)
Sequenti die medium hyemis est. (1.459–60)
Tertio idus Januarii festum Carmentis et Juturnae. (1.461–64)

Carmenta mater Evandri vates sagacissima ex Archadia in Latium cum filio exules venerunt, ubi primum in Aventino Rome fundamenta jecere. (1.477–542)

Idibus Januarii festum Jovis quo die provincie multe sub populo Romano venerunt, et Cesar Augustus dictus est. (1.587–90)
Aphrica Scipioni (1.593)
Nysauros (1.593)
Metello Creta (1.594)
Numidia (1.595)
Numantia (1.596)
Messana (1.595)
Germania Druso (1.597)

fol. 73r:
Sol Aquarium intrat relicto Capricorno x kalendas. (1.651–52)
Pars lyre apparebit. xviiii kalendas canicula que in pectore leonis est occidit. (1.653–56)

VAT. LAT. 3263
POMPONIO LETO, POST 1488

fol. 1r:
P. Ovidi Vita
P. Ovidi Nasonis Fastor[um] Lib[er] I

fol. 1v:
Narratio. Nomina mensium.
De dierum distinctione. (1.1–62)

fol. 2v:
Kalendae Ianuariae. (1.63)

fol. 9r:
consecrata templa ii Iovi et Aesculapio in insula Kal. Ian. (1.292–93)
laus astrologorum. (1.295–310)

fol. 9v:
Agonalia ante vi eid. Ian. (1.317)

fol. 10r:
simplicitas veterum in sacrificando. (1.337–38)
de suis et capricede in sacr[ificando]. (1.349–61)

fol. 10v:
caussa [sic] mactati bovis. (1.362)

fol. 12v:
de avibus. (1.441–56)

fol. 13r:
ante v eid. Ian. hoc est luce Agonali. (1.457–58)
ante iiii eid. media hiemps. (1.459–60)
Carmentae sub Capitolio. Iuturnae in Campo Martio. ante iii eid. (1.461–64)

fol. 17v:
xvi kal. sol trans[it] in Aquarium. (1.651–52)
x kal. Lyra occidit Vesperi. (1.653–54)
aedis Concordiae. (1.637)

BIBLIOGRAPHY

PRIMARY LITERATURE

Alexandar of Villa Dei. 1958. *The Ecclesiale of Alexander of Villa Dei*. Ed. L. R. Lind. Lawrence: University of Kansas Press.

Andreano, G. F. 1972. "Cronaca delle cose occorse ne li anni 1450–1486 per la recostruzione de l'Antica Città de Senegallia trascripte per me Jo: Francesco Andreano del mese di ottobre adì 6 e 7 del l'anno 1534, le quale ho copiate a perpetua memoria, essendo state trovate per me in certo libretto vecchio scripto a mano in casa di ser Bastiano Passero." Ed. S. Anselmi and R. Paci. *Racc. Gen. Storia* 4, int. 19: 1–37. Senigallia.

Anonymous. 1869. *Mirabilia Romae: e codicibus Vaticanis emendate*. Ed. G. Parthey. Berlin: Nicolai.

———. 1986. *The Marvels of Rome. Mirabilia Urbis Romae*. Ed. and trans. F. M. Nichols. New York: Italica Press.

Arnulf of Orléans. 1958. *Arnulfi Aurelianensis glosule super Lucanum*. Ed. B. Marti. Rome: American Academy in Rome.

———. 2005. *Arnulfi Aurelianensis glosule Ovidii Fastorum*. Ed. J. Rieker. Florence: SISMEL edizioni del Galluzzo.

Bede. 1943. *De temporum ratione, in Bedae opera de temporibus*. Ed. C. W. Jones. Cambridge, MA: The Mediaeval Academy of America.

———. 1999. *The Reckoning of Time*. Trans. with introduction, notes, and commentary by F. Wallis. Liverpool: Liverpool University Press.

Codice topografico della città di Roma. 1940–53. Ed. R. Valentini and G. Zucchetti. 4 vols. Rome: Tipografia del Senato.

Costanzi, Antonio. 1502. *Antonii Constantii epigrammatum libellus. [. . .] Octavii Fanensis oratio ad Se[natum] Fanen[sem], Antonii laudes continens. Jacobi Constantii epigrammata quaedam. Ejusdem epicedion in Thadaeam matrem.* Fano: Hier. Soncino.

Cyriac of Ancona. 2003. *Later Travels.* Ed. and trans. E. Bodnar, with C. Foss. Cambridge, MA: Harvard University Press.

Filetico, Martino. 2000. *Martini Philetici: In corruptores Latinitatis.* Ed. M. A. Pincelli. Rome: Edizioni di storia e letteratura.

Flavio, Biondo. 2005a. *Italia Illustrata: Text, Translation, and Commentary. Volume I: Northern Italy.* Ed. C. J. Castner. Binghamton, NY: Global Academic Publishers.

———. 2005b. *Italy Illuminated. Volume I: Books I–IV.* Ed. J. A. White. Cambridge, MA: Harvard University Press.

Giovio, Paolo. 1577. *Elogia virorum literis illustrium.* Basel: Petrus Perna.

Leto, Pomponio. 1993. *Lucrezio.* Ed. G. Solaro. Palermo: Sellerio editore.

Ovid. 1841. *P. Ovidii Nasonis Fastorum libri sex.* Ed. R. Merkel. Berlin: G. Reimer.

———. 1928. *P. Ovidi Nasonis Fastorum Libri VI.* Ed. C. Landi. Turin: Paravia.

———. 1929. *Publii Ovidii Nasonis Fastorum Libri Sex; the Fasti of Ovid.* Ed. and trans. Sir James George Frazer. 4 vols. London: Macmillan.

———. 1957–58. *P. Ovidius Naso. Die Fasten.* Ed. F. Bömer. 2 vols. Heidelberg: C. Winter Universitätsverlag.

———. 1988. *Publii Ovidii Nasonis Fastorum Libri Sex.* Ed. E. H. Alton, D. E. W. Wormell, and E. Courtney. 3rd ed. Leipzig: Teubner.

———. 1998. *Ovid,* Fasti *Book IV.* Ed. E. Fantham. Cambridge: Cambridge Univesity Press.

———. 2004. *Ovid,* Fasti *I. A Commentary.* By S. Green. Leiden and Boston: Brill.

———. 2006. *A commentary on Ovid's* Fasti*, Book VI.* By R. Joy Littlewood. Oxford: Oxford University Press.

———. 2011a. *A Commentary on Ovid's* Fasti*, Book 2.* By M. Robinson. Oxford: Oxford University Press.

———. 2011b. *Ovid: Times and Reasons. A New Translation of* Fasti. By A. Wiseman and P. Wiseman. Oxford: Oxford University Press.

Palladio, Domizio. ca. 1499. *Domici Palladii Sorani Epigrammaton libelli. Libellus elegiarum, Genethliacon Urbis Romae, In locutelium.* Paris: Georg Wolf and Thielmann Kerver for Jean Petit.

Platina, Bartolomeo. 1998. *On Right Pleasure and Good Health (De Honesta Voluptate et Valetudine).* Ed. and trans. M. E. Milham. Tempe, AZ: Medieval & Renaissance Texts and Studies.

Poliziano, Angelo. 1971. *Commento Inedito all' Epistola ovidiana di Saffo a Faone.* Ed. E. Lazzeri. Florence: Sansoni.

———. 1991. *Commento inedito di Fasti di Ovidio.* Ed. F. Lo Monaco. Florence: Olschki.

Scalamonti, F. 1996. *Vita Viri Clarissimi et Famosissimi Kyriaci Anconitani.* Ed. and trans. C. Mitchell and E. Bodnar. *Transactions of the American Philosophical Society* n.s. 86.4: i–vii, 1–246.

Valla, Lorenzo. 1994. *Orazione per l'inaugurazione dell'anno accademico 1455–1456*. Ed. S. Rizzo. Rome: Assoc. Roma nel Rinascimento.

William of Orléans. 2003. *Filologie in de dertiende eeuw: de "Bvrsarii svper Ovidios" van Magister Willem van Orléans (fl. 1200 AD): inleiding, editie en commentaar*. Ed. W. Engelbrecht. 2 vols. Olomouc: Univ. Palackého v Olomouci.

SECONDARY LITERATURE

Accame, M. 2007. "I corsi di Pomponio Leto sul *De lingua latina* di Varrone." In *Pomponio Leto e la prima Accademia romana. Atti della giornata di studi, Roma 2 dicembre 2005*, ed. C. Cassiani and M. Chiabò, 1–22. Rome: Assoc. Roma nel Rinascimento.

———. 2008. *Pomponio Leto. Vita e insegnamento*. Tivoli: Edizioni Tored.

———. 2011. "Note scite nei commenti di Pomponio Leto." In *Pomponio Leto tra identità locale e cultura internazionale: atti del convegno internazionale (Teggiano, 3–5 ottobre 2008)*, ed. A. Modigliani, P. Osmond, M. Pade, and J. Ramminger, 39–56. Rome: Assoc. Roma nel Rinascimento.

Accame Lanzillotta, M. 1980. "L'opera di Festo nel 'dictatum' Varroniano di Pomponio Leto (Vat. lat. 3415)." *Giornale italiano di Filologia* 32: 265–99.

———. 1990. "Il commento varroniano di Pomponio Leto." *Miscellanea greca e romana* 15: 309–45.

———. 1993. "'Dictata' nella scuola di Pomponio Leto." *Studi medievali* 3a, s. 34: 315–23.

———. 2000. "L'insegnamento di Pomponio Leto nello *Studium Urbis*." In *Storia della Facoltà di Lettere e Filosofia de "La Sapienza,"* ed. L. Capo and M. R. Di Simone, 71–91. Rome: Viella.

Adam, P. 1973. *L'humanisme à Sélestat: L'école, les humanistes, la bibliothèque*. Sélestat: Impr. Alsatia.

Alton, E. H. 1930. "The Medieval Commentators on Ovid's *Fasti*." *Hermathena* 20: 119–51.

Alton, E. H., and D. E. W. Wormell. 1995. "Ovid in the Mediaeval Schoolroom." *Hermathena* 94 (1960), 21–38; 95 (1961), 67–82; repr. in *Ovid. The Classical Heritage*, ed. W. S. Andersen, 23–36. New York and London: Garland Publishing.

Alton, E. H., D. E. W. Wormell, and E. Courtney. 1977. "A Catalogue of the Manuscripts of Ovid's *Fasti*." *Bulletin of the Institute of Classical Studies* 24: 37–63.

Amiani, P. M. 1751. *Memorie istoriche della città di Fano*. Fano: G. Leonardi.

Amram, D. W. 1909. *The Makers of Hebrew Books in Italy. Being Chapters in the History of the Hebrew Printing Press*. Philadelphia: J. H. Greenstone.

Anselmi, G. M. 1981. "Città e civiltà in Flavio Biondo." In *Umanisti, storici, e traduttori*, 25–47. Bologna: CLUEB.

Anselmi, S. 1969. *Senigallia e i suoi dintorni*. Senigallia: Edizioni 2 G.

Arbizzoni, G. 2005. "Lazzarelli, Ludovico." *DBI* 64: 180–84.

Arnott, W. G. 1977. "Swan Songs." *Greece & Rome* 24 (2): 149–53.

Baehrens, A. 1883. *Poetae Latini minores* 5. Leipzig: Teubner.

Barchiesi, A. 1994. *Il Poeta e Il Principe. Ovidio e il discorso Augusteo.* Rome and Bari: Laterza.

Barkan, L. 1999. *Unearthing the Past. Archaeology and Aesthetics in the Making of Renaissance Culture.* New Haven, CT and London: Yale University Press.

Barsby, J. 1978. *Ovid.* Oxford: Clarendon Press.

Battistelli, F. 1998. "Origini dell'arte tipografica a Fano e vicende della Biblioteca Comunale Federiciana." In *Edizioni del XVI secolo nel fondo Mabellini, Biblioteca Comunale Federiciana di Fano. Catalogo,* ed. M. Ferri, xvii–xxv. [Ancona] Regione Marche: Centro beni culturali.

Battistelli, F., and A. Deli. 1983. *Immagine di Fano Romana.* Fano: Cassa di Risparmio di Fano.

Beard, M. 1987. "A Complex of Times: No More Sheep on Romulus' Birthday." *Proceedings of the Cambridge Philological Society* 213 (n.s. 33): 1–15.

Bedon, Anna. 1991. *Il Palazzo della Sapienza di Roma.* Rome: Assoc. Roma nel Rinascimento.

Bertolotti, A. 1883. "Professori allo studio di Roma nel secolo XV." *Il Bibliofilo* IV: 89–90.

Bianca, C. 2008. "Pomponio Leto e l'invenzione dell'Accademia Romana." In *Les académies dans l'Europe humaniste,* ed. M. Deramaix et al., 25–56. Geneva: Droz.

Bianchi, R. 1981. "Il commento a Lucano e il 'Natalis' di Paolo Marsi." In *Miscellanea Augusto Campana* I, ed. R. Avesani, G. Billanovich et al., 71–100. Padua: Antenore.

Black, R. 2001. *Humanism and Education in Medieval and Renaissance Italy. Tradition and Innovation in Latin Schools from the Twelfth to the Fifteenth Century.* Cambridge: Cambridge University Press.

———. 2007. *Education and Society in Florentine Tuscany. Vol. 1: Teachers, Pupils and Schools, c. 1250–1500.* Leiden and Boston: Brill.

———. 2011. "Ovid in Medieval Italy." In *Ovid in the Middle Ages,* ed. J. Clark, F. Coulson, and K. McKinley, 123–42. Cambrige: Cambridge University Press.

Blanchard, W. S. 1990. "*O miseri philologi:* Codro Urceo's Satire on Professionalism and Its Context." *Journal of Medieval and Renaissance Studies* 20: 91–122.

Blasio, M. G. 1986. "Lo *Studium Urbis* e la produzione romana a stampa: i corsi di retorica, latino e Greco." In *Un pontificato ed una città: Sisto IV (1471–1484). Atti del convegno, Roma, 3–7 Dicembre, 1984,* ed. M. Miglio, 481–501. Vatican City: Scuola vaticana di paleografia, diplomatica e archivistica.

Bober, P. P. 2000. "Appropriation Contexts. Decor, Furor Bacchicus, Convivium." In *Antiquity and Its Interpreters,* ed. A. Payne, A. Kuttner, and R. Smick, 229–43. Cambridge: Cambridge University Press.

Bober, P., and R. Rubinstein. 2010. *Renaissance Artists and Antique Sculpture: A Handbook of Sources.* London: Harvey Miller Publishing. (Orig. pub. 1986.)

Boissier, G. 1884. "Calendrier Romain." *Revue de Philologie* VIII: 55–74.

Bouwsma, W. 1968. *Venice and the Defense of Republican Liberty. Renaissance Values in the Age of the Counter Reformation.* Berkeley and Los Angeles: University of California Press.

Bracke, W. 1989. "The ms. Ottob. lat. 1982: A Contribution to the Biography of Pomponius Laetus?" *Rinascimento* 29: 293–99.

———. 1990. "L'Ottob. lat. 1982, un codice di scuola della fine del '400." *Res publica litterarum* 13: 27–40.

———. 1992a. "Contentiosa disputatio magnopere ingenium exacuit." In *Roma e lo Studium Urbis. Spazio urbano e cultura dal Quattro al Seicento. Atti del convegno, Roma, 7–10 giugno 1989*, ed. P. Cherubini, 156–68. Rome: Ministero per i Beni Culturali e Ambientali, Ufficio Centrale per i Beni Archivistici.

———. 1992b. *Fare la epistola nella Roma del Quattrocento*. Rome: Assoc. Roma nel Rinascimento.

Braun, L. 1981. "Kompositionskunst in Ovids *Fasti*." *ANRW* II.31.4: 2344–85.

Brizzolara, A. M. 1979–80. "La *Roma instaurata* di Flavio Biondo: alle origini del metodo archeologico." *Memorie dell' Accademia delle Scienze dell' Istituto di Bologna, Classe di Scienze morali* 76: 29–74.

Brown, P. 1996. *Venice and Antiquity. The Venetian Sense of the Past*. New Haven, CT and London: Yale University Press.

Buck, A., and O. Herding, eds. 1975. *Der Kommentar in der Renaissance*. Bonn-Bad Godesberg: Deutsche Forschungsgemeinschaft.

Buonocore, M. 1994. *Aetas ovidiana. La fortuna di Ovidio nei codici della Biblioteca Apostolica Vaticana*. Sulmona: Centro Ovidiano di studi e ricerche.

———. 1995. "Un nuovo codice dei *Fasti* di Ovidio: il Vaticano latino 13682." *Aevum* 69: 101–14.

———. 1996. "Il *De civitate Dei* nei manoscritti del Quattrocento e negli incunaboli alla Biblioteca Vaticana. Considerazioni e proposte." *Humanistica Lovaniensia* 45: 176–88.

Butrica, J. L. 2004. "Attis and the 'Palestinian' Goddesses (Ov. *Fast*. 4.236)." *Exemplaria Classica: Revista de Filología Clásica* 8: 59–67.

Campana, A. 1950. "Scritture di umanisti, Antonio Costanzi." *Rinascimento* I: 236–56.

Campanelli, M. 1993. "Una 'praelectio' lucreziana di Pomponio Leto." *Roma nel Rinascimento* 17–24.

———. 1994. "L'*Oratio* e il 'genere' delle orazioni inaugurali dell'anno accademico." In Lorenzo Valla, *Orazione per l'inaugurazione dell'anno accademico 1455–1456*, ed. S. Rizzo, 25–61. Rome: Assoc. Roma nel Rinascimento.

Campanelli, M., and M. A. Pincelli. 2000. "La lettura dei classici nello *Studium Urbis* tra Umanesimo e Rinascimento." In *Storia della Facoltà di Lettere e Filosofia de "La Sapienza,"* ed. L. Capo and M. R. Di Simone, 93–195. Rome: Viella.

Camporeale, S. 1995. "*Institutio oratoria*, lib. 1, cap. 6,3 e le variazioni su tema di Lorenzo Valla: *sermo* e *interpretatio*." *Rhetorica* 13: 285–300.

Castaldi, G. 1916. "Un letterato del Quattrocento (Antonio Costanzi da Fano)." *Rendiconti dell' Accademia nazionale dei Lincei* XXV: 265–340.

Castellani, G. 1929. "Lorenzo Abstemio e la tipografia del Soncino a Fano." *La Bibliofilia* 31: 413–24.

Castiglioni, A. 1953. "The School of Ferrara and the Controversy on Pliny." In *Science, Medicine, and History*, vol. 1, ed. E. A. Underwood, 269–79. London: Oxford University Press.

Castner, C. J. 1998. "Direct Observation and Biondo Flavio's Additions to *Italia Illustrata:* The Case of Oriculum." *Medievalia et Humanistica,* n.s. 25: 93–108.

Chambers, D. S. 1970. *The Imperial Age of Venice 1380–1580.* London: Thames and Hudson.

———. 1976. "*Studium Urbis et gabella studii:* The University of Rome in the Fifteenth Century." In *Cultural Aspects of the Italian Renaissance: Essays in Honour of Paul Oskar Kristeller,* ed. C. H. Clough, 68–110. Manchester: Mancherster University Press.

———. 1995. "The Earlier 'Academies' in Italy." In *Italian Academies of the Sixteenth Century,* ed. D. S. Chambers and F. Quiviger, 1–14. London: Warburg Institute.

Chartier, R. 1994. *The Order of Books. Readers, Authors, and Libraries in Europe between the Fourteenth and Eighteenth Centuries.* Trans. L. Cochrane. Stanford, CA: Stanford University Press.

Clavuot, O. 1990. *Biondos "Italia illustrata." Summa oder Neuschöpfung? Über die Arbeitsmethode eines Humanisten.* Tubingen: Niemeyer.

Coarelli, F. 1996. "Iuno Sospita [Palatium]." *LTUR* 3: 129–30.

Colantoni, L. 1911. "Il poeta improvvisatore della rinascenza Paolo dei Marsi di Pescina." *Rivista Abruzzese di Scienze, Lettere ed Arti* anno 26, fasc. 4 (April): 177–93; (May): 240–46.

Conte, G. B. 1994. *Latin Literature. A History.* Trans. J. Solodow. Baltimore and London: Johns Hopkins University Press.

Copeland, R. 2012. "Gloss and Commentary." In *The Oxford Handbook of Medieval Literature,* ed. R. Hexter and D. Townsend, 171–91. Oxford: Oxford University Press, 2012.

Copenhaver, B. P. 2009. "A Grand End for a Grand Narrative: Lodovico Lazzarelli, Giovanni Mercurio da Correggio and Renaissance Hermetica." *Magic, Ritual, and Witchcraft* 4 (2): 207–23.

Corfiati, C. 2003. "Il cod. Vat. lat. 2853: per una storia dei *Fastorum christianae religionis libri* di Ludovico Lazzarelli." *Roma nel Rinascimento,* 245–76.

Coroleu, A. 1999. "Some Teachers on a Poet: The Uses of Poliziano's Latin Poetry in the Sixteenth-Century Curriculum." In *Poets and Teachers: Latin Didactic Poetry and the Didactic Authority of the Latin Poet from the Renaissance to the Present,* ed. Y. Haskell and P. Hardie, 167–81. Bari: Levante.

Coulson, F. 1987. "The *'Vulgate'* Commentary on Ovid's *Metamorphoses.*" *Mediaevalia* 13: 29–62.

———. 2002. "Addenda et Corrigenda to *Incipitarium Ovidianum.*" *Journal of Medieval Latin* 12: 154–80.

———. 2008. "Failed Chastity and Ovid: Myrrha in the Latin Commentary Tradition from Antiquity to the Renaissance." In *Chastity,* ed. Nancy van Deusen, 7–35. Leiden: Brill.

———. 2009. "Addenda et Corrigenda to *Incipitarium Ovidianum* II." *Journal of Medieval Latin* 19: 88–105.

———. 2011. "Ovid's *Metamorphoses* in the School Tradition of France, 1180–1400. Texts, Manuscript Traditions, Manuscript Settings." In *Ovid in the Middle Ages,* ed. J. Clark, F. Coulson, and K. McKinley, 48–82. Cambrige: Cambridge University Press.

Coulson, F., and B. Roy. 2000. *Incipitarium Ovidianum: A Finding Guide for Texts in Latin Related to the Study of Ovid in the Middle Ages and the Renaissance.* Turnhout: Brepols.

Crisciani, C. 2000. "Hermeticism and Alchemy: The Case of Ludovico Lazzarelli." *Early Science and Medicine* 5 (2): 145–59.

Cruciani, F. 1980. "Il teatro dei Ciceroniani: Tommaso 'Fedra' Inghirami." *Forum Italicum* 14: 356–77.

Curran, B., and A. Grafton. 1995. "A Fifteenth-Century Site Report on the Vatican Obelisk." *Journal of the Warburg and Courtauld Institutes* 58: 234–48.

Danzi, M. 2005. *La biblioteca del Cardinal Pietro Bembo*. Geneva: Droz.

de Beer, S. 2008. "The Roman 'Academy' of Pomponio Leto. From an Informal Humanist Network to the Institution of a Literary Society." In *The Reach of the Republic of Letters. Literary and Learned Societies in Late Medieval and Early Modern Europe*, ed. A. van Dixhoorn and S. Speakman Sutch, 181–218. Leiden and Boston: Brill.

———. 2013. *The Poetics of Patronage. Poetry as Self-Advancement in Giannantonio Campano*. Turnhout: Brepols.

de Caprio, V. 1991. "'Sub Tanta Diruta Mole': Il fascino delle rovine di Roma nel '400 e '500." In *La tradizione e il trauma: idee del Rinascimento romano*, 51–105. Manziana: Vecchiarelli. (Orig. pub. in *Poesia e Poetica delle Rovine di Roma. Momenti e Problemi*, ed. V. de Caprio [Rome: Istituto nazionale di studi romani, 1987], 23–51.)

Degrassi, A. 1963. *Inscriptiones Italiae* 13.2. Rome: Istituto Poligrafico dello Stato.

Deli, A. 1988. "Schede su Fano romana." *Nuovi studi fanesi* 3: 21–56.

———. 1992. "Battaglia del Metauro, Porta e Porto di *Fanum, Balineum* di L. Rufellio in autori tra '400 e '700." *Nuovi studi fanesi* 7: 7–46.

D'Elia, A. 2009. *A Sudden Terror: The Plot to Murder the Pope in Renaissance Rome*. Cambridge, MA: Harvard University Press.

della Torre, A. 1899. "Un carme latino sopra la persecuzione di papa Paolo II contro l'accademica Pomponiana." *Rivista cristiana*, new ser.: 59–66.

———. 1903. *Paolo Marso da Pescina. Contributo alla Storia dell' Accademia Pomponiana*. Rocca S. Casciano: Licinio Cappelli.

Dempsey, C. 1992. *The Portrayal of Love. Botticelli's "Primavera" and Humanist Culture at the Time of Lorenzo the Magnificent*. Princeton, NJ: Princeton University Press.

de Nichilo, M. 1975. *I poemi astrologi di Giovanni Pontano. Storia del testo*. Bari: Dedalo libri.

Derolez, A. 1979. *The Library of Raphael de Marcatellis. Abbot of St. Bavon's, Ghent 1437–1508*. Ghent: Story-Scientia.

———. 2002. "A Survey of the Mercatel Library on the Basis of the Early Catalogues and the Surviving Manuscripts." In *ALS ICH CAN: Liber Amicorum in Memory of Professor Dr. Maurits Smeyers*, ed. B. Cardon, J. Van der Stock et al., vol. 2, 545–63. Leuven: Peeters.

de Rossi, G. B. 1882. "Note di topografia romana raccolte dalla bocca di Pomponio Leto e testo pomponiano della *Notitia Regionum Urbis Romae*." *Studi e documenti di storia e diritto* 3: 49–87.

———. 1890. "L'Accademia di Pomponio Leto e le sue memorie scritte sulle pareti delle catacombe Romane." *Bullettino di Archeologia cristiana di Roma* V (I): 81–94.

Desjardins, J. 1986. *Les Cent Elégies: Hecatelegium, Florence, 1489, avec quatre élégies inédites de Pacifico Massimi*. Grenoble: Ellug.

de Spirito, G. 1993. "Apollo (et Clatra?), Templum." *LTUR* 1: 58.

———. 1996. "Mons Apollinis et Clatrae." *LTUR* 3: 281.

di Bernardo, F. 1969. *Giannantonio Campano: un vescovo umanista alla corte Pontificia, 1429–1477*. Rome: Università gregoriana.

Dionisotti, C. 1968. "Calderini, Poliziano, e altri." *Italia medioevale e umanistica* 11: 151–79.

Donati, G. 2000. *Pietro Odo da Montopoli e la Biblioteca di Niccolo V, con osservazioni sul 'De orthographia' di Tortelli*. Rome: Assoc. Roma nel Rinascimento.

D'Onofrio, C. 1989. *Visitiamo Roma nel Quattrocento. La città degli Umanisti*. Rome: Romana Società Editrice.

———. 1990. *Un popolo di statue racconta. Storie fatti leggende della città di Roma antica medievale moderna*. Rome: Romana Società Editrice.

Dunston, A. J. 1967. "A Student's Notes of Lectures by Giulio Pomponio Leto." *Antichthon* 1: 86–94.

———. 1973. "Pope Paul II and the Humanists." *The Journal of Religious History* 7: 287–306.

Dykmans, M., S.J. 1987. "La vita Pomponiana de Virgile." *Humanistica Lovaniensia* 36: 85–111.

———. 1988. *L'humanisme de Pierre Marso*. Vatican City: Biblioteca Apostolica Vaticana.

Eatough, G., ed. 1998. *Selections from Peter Martyr*. Turnhout: Brepols.

Engelbrecht, W. 2008. "Fulco, Arnulf, and William: Twelfth-century Views on Ovid in Orléans." *Journal of Medieval Latin* 18: 52–73.

Falzone, P. 2009. "Maturanzio (Mataratius), Francesco." *DBI* 72: 338–41.

Fanelli, V. 1968. "Biondo, Gaspare." *DBI* 10: 559–60.

———. 1979. *Ricerche su Angelo Colocci e sulla Roma cinquecentesca*. Vatican City: Biblioteca Apostolica Vaticana.

Fantham, E. 1985. "Ovid, Germanicus, and the Composition of the *Fasti*." In *Papers of the Liverpool Latin Seminar*, vol. 5, ed. Francis Cairns, 243–81.

———. 1995a. "Recent Readings of Ovid's *Fasti*." *Classical Philology* 90: 367–78.

———. 1995b. "Rewriting and Rereading the *Fasti:* Augustus, Ovid, and Recent Scholarship." *Antichthon* 29: 42–59.

———. 1996. *Roman Literary Culture: From Cicero to Apuleius*. Baltimore and London: Johns Hopkins University Press.

———. 2002. "Ovid's *Fasti*: Politics, History, and Religion." In *Brill's Companion to Ovid*, ed. B. W. Boyd, 197–233. Leiden and Boston: Brill.

Farenga, P. 1994. "Il sistema delle dediche nella prima editoria romana del quattrocento." In *Il Libro a Corte*, ed. A. Quondam, 57–87. Rome: Bulzoni.

———, ed. 2005. *Editori ed edizioni a Roma nel Rinascimento*. Rome: Assoc. Roma nel Rinascimento.

Feeney, D. 1992. "*Si licet et fas est:* Ovid's *Fasti* and the Problem of Free Speech under the Principate." In *Roman Poetry and Propaganda in the Age of Augustus*, ed. A. Powell, 1–25. London: Bristol Classical Press.

———. 1998. *Literature and Religion at Rome. Cultures, Contexts, and Beliefs*. Cambridge: Cambridge University Press.

———. 2007. *Caesar's Calendar. Ancient Time and the Beginnings of History*. Berkeley and Los Angeles: University of California Press.

Findlen, P. 1994. *Possessing Nature. Museums, Collecting, and Scientific Culture in Early Modern Italy*. Berkeley and Los Angeles: University of California Press.

Formichetti, G. 1984. "Costanzi (Costanzo), Antonio." *DBI* 30: 370–74.

Friedrich, H. F. 1968. *Thessalos von Tralles*. Misenheim am Glan: Hain.

Fritsen, A. 2000a. "Ludovico Lazzarelli's *Fasti christianae religionis:* Recipient and Context of an Ovidian Poem." In *Myricae. Essays on Neo-Latin Literature in Memory of Jozef IJsewijn*, ed. D. Sacré and G. Tournoy, 115–32. Leuven: Leuven University Press.

———. 2000b. "Testing *Auctoritas:* The Travels of Paolo Marsi, 1468–69." *International Journal of the Classical Tradition* 6 (3): 356–82.

———. 2001. "Readership and Patronage: The Manuscript History of Ludovico Lazzarelli's *Fasti christianae religionis*." In *Old Books, New Learning. Essays on Medieval and Renaissance Books at Yale,* ed. R. Babcock and L. Patterson, 93–104. New Haven, CT: Beinecke Rare Book and Manuscript Library.

Fubini, R. 1968. "Biondo, Flavio." *DBI* 10: 536–59.

Gaisser, J. H. 1993. *Catullus and his Renaissance Readers*. Oxford: Clarendon Press.

———. 2005. "Filippo Beroaldo on Apuleius: Bringing Antiquity to Life." In *On Renaissance Commentaries*, ed. M. Pade, 87–109. Hildesheim: Georg Olms.

Galinsky, K. 1996. *Augustan Culture. An Interpretive Introduction*. Princeton, NJ: Princeton University Press.

Garin, E., ed. 1952. *Prosatori latini del Quattrocento*. Milan: R. Ricciardi.

Gee, E. 2000. *Ovid, Aratus and Augustus. Astronomy in Ovid's* Fasti. Cambridge: Cambridge University Press.

Gerulaitis, L. V. 1976. *Printing and Publishing in Fifteenth Century Venice*. Chicago: American Library Association.

Ghisalberti, F. 1932. "Arnolfo d'Orléans, un cultore di Ovidio nel S.XII." *Memorie del Reale Istituto Lombardo di Scienze e Lettere* 24: 157–234.

———. 1946. "Mediaeval Biographies of Ovid." *Journal of the Warburg and Courtauld Institutes* 9: 10–59.

Gibson, R. K., and C. S. Kraus, eds. 2002. *The Classical Commentary. Histories, Practices, Theory*. Leiden and Boston: Brill.

Girardi-Jurkíc, V. 1986. *Pula*. Pula: Itarska Naklada.

Goodhart Gordan, P. 1991. *Two Renaissance Book Hunters: The Letters of Poggius Bracciolini to Nicolaus de Niccolis*. New York: Columbia University Press.

Graf, A. 1892. *Roma nella memoria e nelle immaginazioni del Medio Evo* vol. 1. Turin: Loescher, 1882.

Graf, F. 1997. *Der Lauf des rollenden Jahres. Zeit und Kalender in Rom*. Stuttgart and Leipzig: Teubner.

Grafton, A. 1977. "On the Scholarship of Politian and its Context." *Journal of the Warburg and Courtauld Institutes* 40: 150–88.

———. 1983–93. *Joseph Scaliger. A Study in the History of Classical Scholarship*, 2 vols. Oxford: Oxford University Press.

———. 1990. *Forgers and Critics. Creativity and Duplicity in Western Scholarship*. Princeton, NJ: Princeton University Press.

———. 1993. "The Ancient City Restored: Archaeology, Ecclesiastical History, and Egyptology." In *Rome Reborn. The Vatican Library and Renaissance Culture*, ed. A. Grafton, 87–123. Washington: Library of Congress; New Haven and London: Yale Univesity Press; Vatican City: Biblioteca Apostolica Vaticana.

———. 1995. "Tradition and Technique in Historical Chronology." In *Ancient History and the Antiquarian: Essays in Memory of Arnaldo Momigliano*, ed. M. H. Crawford and C. R. Ligota, 15–31. London: Warburg Institute.

———. 2000. *Leon Battista Alberti. Master Builder of the Italian Renaissance*. Cambridge, MA: Harvard University Press.

Grafton, A., and L. Jardine. 1986. *From Humanism to the Humanities.* Cambridge, MA: Harvard University Press.

Greco, A. 1974. "Roma e la commedia del Rinascimento." *Studi romani* 22: 25–35.

Green, C. 2002. "Varro's Three Theologies and Their Influence on the *Fasti*." In *Ovid's Fasti: Historical Readings at Its Bimillennium*, ed. G. Herbert-Brown, 71–99. Oxford: Oxford University Press.

Greene, T. 1982. "Petrarch and the Humanist Hermeneutic." in *The Light in Troy. Imitation and Discovery in Renaissance Poetry*, 81–103. New Haven, CT and London: Yale University Press.

Grendler, P. F. 1989. *Schooling in Renaissance Italy. Literacy and Learning, 1300–1600*. Baltimore and London: Johns Hopkins University Press.

Guarnieri, G. M. 1961. *Annali di Senigallia*. Ancona: Tip. S.I.T.A.

Günther, H. 1981. "Porticus Pompeji." *Zeitschrift für Kunstgeschichte* 44 (4): 358–98.

Gura, D. 2010. "From the *Orléanais* to Pistoia: the Survival of the *Catena* Commentary." *Manuscripta* 54 (2): 171–88.

Gwynne, P. 1995. "A Renaissance Image of Jupiter Stator." *Journal of the Warburg and Courtauld Institutes* 58: 249–52.

Hackens, T. 1960–61. "Mons Apollinis et Clatrae: note de topographie romaine." *Atti della pontificia Accademia romana di archeologia. Rendiconti* 33: 185–96.

Hanegraaf, W. J., and R. M. Bouthoorn. 2005. *Ludovico Lazzarelli (1447–1500). The Hermetic Writings and Related Documents*. Tempe, AZ: Arizona Center for Medieval and Renaissance Studies.

Hankins, J. 1991. "The Myth of the Platonic Academy of Florence." *Renaissance Quarterly* 44: 429–75.

Hansen, M. F. 1996. "Representing the Past: The Concept and Study of Antique Architecture in 15th-century Italy." *Analecta Romana Istituti Danici* 23: 83–116.

Harbert, B. 1975. "Matthew of Vendôme." *Medium Aevum* 44 (3): 225–37.

Havens, E. 2001. *Commonplace Books: A History of Manuscripts and Printed Books from Antiquity to the Twentieth Century*. New Haven, CT: Beinecke Rare Book and Manuscript Library.

Hay, D. 1959. "Flavio Biondo and the Middle Ages." In *Proceedings of the British Academy* 45 [1959]: 97–128. (Reprinted in *Renaissance Essays*, 1988, 35–66 [London: Hambledon Press].)

Herbert-Brown, G. 1994. *Ovid and the* Fasti. *An Historical Study*. Oxford: Clarendon Press.

———. 2002. "Ovid and the Stellar Calendar." In *Ovid's* Fasti: *Historical Readings at its Bimillennium*, ed. G. Herbert-Brown, 101–28. Oxford: Oxford University Press.

———, ed. 2002. *Ovid's* Fasti: *Historical Readings at its Bimillennium*. Oxford: Oxford University Press.

———. 2009. "*Fasti:* the Poet, the Prince, and the Plebs." In *A Companion to Ovid*, ed. P. Knox, 120–39. Chichester and Malden, MA: Wiley-Blackwell.

Hexter, R. 1986. *Ovid and Medieval Schooling. Studies in Medieval School Commentaries on Ovid's* Ars Amatoria, Epistulae ex Ponto, *and* Epistolae Heroidum. Munich: Arbeo-Gesellschaft.

———. 2007. "Ovid and the Medieval Exilic Imaginary." in *Writing Exile: The Discourse of Displacement in Greco-Roman Antiquity and Beyond*, ed. J. F. Gaertner, 209–36. Leiden and Boston: Brill.

Hinds, S. 1987. *The Metamorphosis of Persephone: Ovid and the Self-conscious Muse*. Cambridge: Cambridge University Press.

———. 1992. "*Arma* in Ovid's *Fasti*. Part 1: Genre and Mannerism." *Arethusa* 25: 81–112.

Holland, L. A. 1961. *Janus and the Bridge*. Rome: American Academy in Rome.

Holzberg, N. 2002. *Ovid. The Poet and his Work*. Trans. G. M. Goshgarian. Ithaca, NY and London: Cornell University Press.

Hope, C., and E. McGrath. 1996. "Artists and Humanists." In *The Cambridge Companion to Renaissance Humanism*, ed. J. Kraye, 161–88. Cambridge: Cambridge University Press.

Hoven, R. 1979. "Programmes d'ecoles latines dans les Pays-Bas et la principaute de Liège aux XVIe siècle." In *Acta Conventus Neo-Latini Amstelodamensis: Proceedings of the second International Congress of Neo-Latin Studies, Amsterdam, 19–24 August 1973*, ed. P. Tuynman, G. C. Kuiper, and E. Kessler, 546–59. Munich: W. Fink.

Hülsen, C. 1927. *Le Chiese di Roma nel Medio Evo*. Florence: Olschki.

Jacks, P. 1993. *The Antiquarian and the Myth of Antiquity. The Origins of Rome in Renaissance Thought*. Cambridge: Cambridge University Press.

Johnson, W. R. 1978. "The Desolation of the *Fasti*." *Classical Journal* 73: 7–17.

Jones, P. J. 1960. "The End of Malatesta Rule in Rimini." In *Italian Renaissance Studies. A Tribute to Cecilia M. Ady*, ed. E. F. Jacob, 217–55. London: Faber and Faber.

———. 1974. *The Malatesta of Rimini and the Papal State. A Political History*. Cambridge: Cambridge University Press.

Kallendorf, C. 1999. *Virgil and the Myth of Venice. Books and Readers in the Italian Renaissance.* Oxford: Oxford University Press.

———, ed. and trans. 2002. *Humanist Educational Treatises.* Cambridge, MA: Harvard University Press.

Keseling, F. 1908. *De mythographi Vaticani secundi fontibus.* Published Latin dissertation. Halis Saxonum: Typis Wischani et Burkhardti.

King, M. 1986. *Venetian Humanism in an Age of Patrician Dominance.* Princeton, NJ: Princeton University Press.

Kinney, D. 1990. "Mirabilia Urbis Romae." In *The Classics in the Middle Ages. Papers of the 20th Annual Conference of the Center for Medieval and Early Renaissance Studies,* ed. A. S. Bernardo and S. Levin, 207–21. Binghamton, NY: Center for Medieval and Early Renaissance Studies.

Kristeller, P. O. 1969. "Augustine and the early Renaissance." In *Studies in Renaissance Thought and Letters,* ed. P. O. Kristeller, 355–72. Rome: Edizioni di storia e letteratura.

———, comp. 1963–1992. *Iter Italicum. A finding list of uncatalogued or incompletely catalogued humanistic manuscripts of the Renaissance in Italian and other libraries* (vol. 1–6). London: The Warburg Institute; Leiden: E. J. Brill.

———. 1992. "The Scholar and His Public." In *Medieval Aspects of Renaissance Learning,* trans. and ed. E. Mahoney, 3–25. New York: Columbia University Press. (Orig. pub. 1974.)

La Malfa, C. 2003. "Reassessing the Renaissance of the Palestrina Nile Mosaic." *Journal of the Warburg and Courtauld Institutes* 66: 267–72.

Lanciani, R. 1892. *Pagan and Christian Rome.* Boston and New York: Houghton Mifflin.

Lanowski, J. 1965. "Weltwunder." *RE Supplementband* 10.

Laureys, M. 2003. "Per una storia dell'invettiva umanistica." *Studi umanistici piceni* 23: 9–30.

———. 2006. "Das alte und das neue Rom in Andrea Fulvios *Antiquaria urbis.*" In *Das alte Rom und die neue Zeit—La Roma antica e la prima età moderna. Varianten des Rom-Mythos zwischen Petrarca und dem Barock—Varietà del culto di Roma tra Petrarca e il barocco,* ed. M. Disselkamp, P. Ihring, and W. Wolfzettel, 201–20. Tubingen: Narr.

Law, J. 1981. *The Lords of Renaissance Italy: The Signori, 1250–1500.* London: Historical Association.

Le Bonniec, H. 1989. *Études ovidiennes: introduction aux* Fastes *d'Ovide.* Frankfurt am Main: P. Lang.

Lee, E. 1978. *Sixtus IV and Men of Letters.* Rome: Edizioni di storia e letteratura.

———. 1984. "Humanists and the *Studium Urbis,* 1473–1484." In *Umanesimo a Roma nel Quattrocento,* ed. P. Brezzi and M. de Panizza Lorch, 127–46. Rome: Istituto di studi romani; New York: Barnard College / Columbia University.

Lieberg, G. 1969. "Seefahrt und Werk. Untersuchungen zu einer Metapher der Antiken, besonders der Lateinischen Literatur." *Giornale Italiano di Filologia* 21: 209–40.

Lightbown, R. 1986. *Mantegna. With a Complete Catalogue of the Paintings, Drawings and Prints.* Oxford: Phaidon.

Lo Monaco, F. 1992a. "Alcune osservazioni sui commenti umanistici ai classici nel secondo Quattrocento." In *Il Commento ai testi: atti del seminario di Ascona, 2–9 ottobre 1989*, ed. O. Besomi and C. Caruso, 103–54. Basel [etc.]: Birkhäuser, 1992.

———. 1992b. "Dal commento medievale al commento umanistico: il caso dei *Fasti* di Ovidio." In *Studi italiani di filologia classica* 85= 3a. ser., 10: 848–60.

Lovito, G. 2005. *Pomponio Leto politico e civile: l'umanesimo italiano tra storia e diritto*. Salerno: Laveglia.

Lowe, K. 1994. "The Political Crime of Conspiracy in Fifteenth- and Sixteenth-century Rome." In *Crime, Society, and the Law in Renaissance Italy*, ed. T. Dean and K. Lowe, 184–203. Cambridge: Cambrige University Press.

Luisi, A., and N. F. Berrino. 2008. *Carmen et error: nel bimillenario dell'esilio di Ovidio*. Bari: Edipuglia.

Lumbroso, G. 1890. "Gli accademici alle catacombe." *Archivio della società romana di storia patria* 12: 221–39.

Lunelli, A. 1987. "Leto, Giulio Pomponio." In *Enciclopedia Virgiliana* vol. 3, 192–95. Rome: Istituto della Enciclopedia italiana.

Luni, M. 2000. *Studi su Fanum Fortunae*. Urbino: Quattro Venti.

Maas, M. 1992. *John Lydus and the Roman Past. Antiquarianism and Politics in the Age of Justinian*. London and New York: Routledge.

Maddalo, S. 1991. "I manoscritti Mazzatosta." In *Cultura umanistica a Viterbo per il V centinario della stampa a Viterbo (1488–1988)*, ed. T. Sampieri and G. Lombardi, 47–75. Viterbo: Assoc. Roma nel Rinascimento.

Madonna, M. L. 1976. "'Septem mundi miracula' come templi della virtù. Pirro Ligorio e l'interpretazione cinquecentesca delle meraviglie del mondo." *Psicon* 3: 24–63.

Magister, S. 1998. "Pomponio Leto collezionista di antiquità. Note sulle tradizione manoscritta di una raccolta epigrafica nella Roma del tardo Quattrocento." *Xenia Antiqua* 7: 167–96.

———. 2003. "Pomponio Leto collezionista di Antichità: Addenda." In *Antiquaria a Roma. Intorno a Pomponio Leto e Paolo II*, ed. M. Miglio, P. Farenga et al., 51–121. Rome: Assoc. Roma nel Rinascimento.

Maillard, J.-F., J. Kecskeméti, and M. Portalier. 1995. *L'Europe des Humanistes (XIVe–XVII Siècles)*. Turnhout: Brepols.

Malpangotto, M. 2008. *Regiomontano e il rinnovamento del sapere matematico e astronomico nel Quattrocento*. Bari: Cacucci.

Mancini, L. 1926. "Sinigaglia dai Malatesti ai Rovereschi, 1463–1474." *R. Deputazione di storia patria per le Marche, Ancona. Atti e Memorie*, 4th ser., 3: 183–217.

Marcozzi, L. 2010. "Petrarch e Boccaccio lettori dei *Fasti*." In *Vates operose dierum: studi sui Fasti di Ovidio*, ed. G. La Bua, 169–95. Pisa: ETS.

Marsh, D. 2003. *Francesco Petrarca*. Invectives. Cambridge, MA: Harvard University Press.

Martelli, F. 2013. *Ovid's Revisions: The Editor as Author*. Cambridge: Cambridge University Press.

Marti, B. 1955. "Hugh Primas and Arnulf of Orléans." *Speculum* 30 (2): 233–38.

Martindale, A. 1979. *The Triumphs of Caesar by Andrea Mantegna in the Collection of Her Majesty the Queen at Hampton Court.* London: Harvey Miller.

Martindale, C. 1993. *Redeeming the Text. Latin poetry and the hermeneutics of reception.* Cambridge: Cambridge University Press.

Martineau, J., and S. Boorsch. 1992. *Andrea Mantegna.* London: Royal Academy of Arts; New York: The Metropolitan Museum of Art.

Martinelli, L. Cesarini. 1978. "In margine al commento di Angelo Poliziano alle *Selve* di Statio," *Interpres* 1: 96–145.

Martini, M. 1969. *Domitius Palladius Soranus poeta. Contributo alla storia dell'Umanesimo.* Frosinone: Editrice tip. Casamari.

———. 1979. "Domizio Palladio Sorano, un discepolo di Pomponio Leto." In *L'Umanesimo in Ciociaria e Domizio Palladio Sorano. Atti del Seminario di Studi—Sora, 8–9 dic. 1978,* 81–119. Sora: Centro di studi sorani Vincenzo Patriarca.

———. 1988. "Tre Umanisti Ciociari (sec. XV–XVIII) D. Palladio, B. Cacciante e U. Carrara." In *Eruditi e letterati del Lazio. Lunario romano* 18, ed. R. Lefevre, 235–50. Rome: Palombi.

Masotti, P. M. 1982. "L'Accademia romana e la congiura del 1468." *Italia medioevale e umanstica* 25: 189–204.

———. 1984. "Codici scritti dagli Accademici Romani nel carcere di Castel S. Angelo (1468–1469)." In *Vestigia. Studi in onore di Giuseppe Billanovich,* vol. 2, ed. R. Avesani et al., 451–59. Rome: Edizioni di storia e letteratura.

———. 1987. "Callimaco, L'Accademia romana e la congiura del 1468." In *Callimaco Esperiente poeta e politico del '400. Convegno Internazionale di Studi, San Gimignano, 18–20 ott. 1985,* ed. G. C. Garfagnini, 169–79. Florence: Olschki.

Mazzocco, A. 1975. "Petrarca, Poggio, and Biondo: Humanism's Foremost Interpreters of Roman Ruins." In *Francis Petrarch, Six Centuries Later,* ed. A. Scaglione, 353–63. Chapel Hill: Dept. of Romance Languages, University of North Carolina.

———. 1985. "Biondo Flavio and the Antiquarian Tradition." In *Acta Conventus Neo-Latini Bononiensis,* ed. R. J. Schoeck, 124–36. Binghamton, NY: Center for Medieval and Early Renaissance Studies.

———. 1987. "Linee di Sviluppo dell'antiquaria del Rinascimento." In *Poesia e Poetica delle Rovine di Roma. Momenti e Problemi,* ed. V. de Caprio, 55–71. Rome: Istituto nazionale di studi romani.

———. 2011. "Biondo e Leto: protagonisti dell'antiquaria quattrocentesca." In *Pomponio Leto tra identità locale e cultura internazionale: atti del convegno internazionale (Teggiano, 3–5 ottobre 2008),* ed. A. Modigliani, P. Osmond, M. Pade, and J. Ramminger, 165–78. Rome: Assoc. Roma nel Rinascimento.

McKeown, J. C. 1984. "*Fabula proposito nulla tegenda meo.* Ovid's *Fasti* and Augustan Politics." In *Poetry and Politics in the Age of Augustus,* ed. T. Woodman and D. West, 169–87. Cambridge: Cambridge University Press.

Mercati, G. 1937. "Paolo Pompilio e la scoperta del cadavere intatto sull' Appia nel 1485." *Opere minori* IV, 268–86. Vatican City: Biblioteca Apostolica Vaticana.

Meserve, M. 2006. "News from Negroponte: Politics, Popular Opinion, and Information Exchange in the First Decade of the Italian Press." *Renaissance Quarterly* 59: 440–80.

Michaelis, A. 1891. "Storia della collezione Capitolina di antichità fino all'inaugurazione del Museo (1734)." *Römische Mitteilungen* 6: 3–66.

Miglio, M. 1976. "Capranica, Giovan Battista." *DBI* 19: 154–57.

———. 1982. "Il leone e la lupa. Dal simbolo al pasticcio alla francese." *Studi romani* 30: 177–86.

Millar, F. 1993. "Ovid and the *Domus Augusta:* Rome Seen from Tomoi." *Journal of Roman Studies* 83: 1–17.

Miller, J. 1991. *Ovid's Elegiac Festivals: Studies in the* Fasti. Frankfurt am Main: Verlag Peter Lang.

———. 2002. "*The* Fasti: *Style, Structure, and Time.*" In *Brill's Companion to Ovid,* ed. B. W. Boyd, 167–96. Leiden and Boston: Brill.

———. 2003. "Ovid's *Fasti* and the Neo-Latin Christian Calendar Poem." *International Journal of the Classical Tradition* 10 (2): 173–86.

Minnis, A. J. 1984. *Medieval Theory of Authorship: Scholastic Literary Attitudes in the Later Middle Age.* London: Scolar Press.

Mitchell, C. 1960. "Archeology and Romance in Renaissance Italy." In *Italian Renaissance Studies. A Tribute to Cecilia M. Ady,* ed. E. F. Jacob, 455–83. London: Faber and Faber.

Modigliani, A. 2005. "Printing in Rome in the XVth Century. Economics and the Circulation of Books." In *Editori ed edizioni a Roma nel Rinascimento,* ed. P. Farenga, 65–76. Rome: Assoc. Roma nel Rinascimento.

Momigliano, A. 1950. "Ancient History and the Antiquarian." *Journal of the Warburg and Courtauld Institutes* 13: 285–315.

Monachino, V. 1969. "Vittore I, papa, santo." In *Bibliotheca Sanctorum,* vol. 12, ed. J. Vizzini et al., col. 1281–85. Rome: Istituto Giovanni XXIII.

Monfasani, J. 1988. "Calfurnio's Identification of Pseudepigrapha of Ognibene, Fenestella, and Trebizond, and His Attack on Renaissance Commentaries." *Renaissance Quarterly* 41: 32–43. (Reprinted in *Language and Learning in Renaissance Italy. Selected Articles.* [Aldershot: Variorum, 1994].)

Moreschini, C., M. P. Saci, and F. Troncarelli, eds. 2009. *Ludovico Lazzarelli. Opere Ermetiche.* Pisa: F. Serra.

Morin, D. G. 1923. "Les distiques de Pomponio Leto sur les stations liturgiques du Carême." *Revue Bénédictine* 35: 20–23.

Moss, A. 1996. *Printed Commonplace-Books and the Structure of Renaissance Thought.* Oxford: Clarendon Press.

Most, G. W., ed. 1999. *Commentaries—Kommentare.* Göttingen: Vandenhoeck und Ruprecht.

Muecke, F. 2003. "Humanists in the Roman Forum." *Papers of the British School at Rome* 71: 207–33.

———. 2007. "Poetry on Rome from the Ambience of Pomponio Leto: Topography, History, Encomium." *L'Ellisse* 2: 101–26.

Nauert, C. 1979. "Humanists, Scientists, and Pliny: Changing Approaches to a Classical Author." *American Historical Review* 84: 72–85.

Neuhausen, K. 1996. "Die vergessene 'göttliche Kunst der Totenerweckung': Cyriacus von Ancona als Begründer der Erforschung der Antike in der Frührenaissance." In *Antiquarische Gelehrsamkeit und bildende Kunst: die Gegenwart der Antike in der Renaissance,* ed. K. Corsepius, 51–68. Cologne: König.

Newlands, C. 1995. *Playing with Time.* Ithaca, NY and London: Cornell University Press.

———. 2002. "*Mandati memores:* Political and Poetic Authority in the *Fasti.*" In *The Cambridge Companion to Ovid,* ed. P. Hardie, 200–216. Cambridge: Cambridge Univesity Press.

Nuovo, I. 1988. "'*De civitate Dei—Roma Triumphans*': teologia della storia e storiografia umanistica." In *L'umanesimo di Sant' Agostino,* ed. M. Fabris, 573–87. Bari: Levante.

Osmond, P. 2011. "Testimonianze di ricerche antiquarie tra i fogli di Sallustio." In *Pomponio Leto tra identità locale e cultura internazionale: atti del convegno internazionale (Teggiano, 3–5 ottobre 2008),* ed. A. Modigliani, P. Osmond, M. Pade, and J. Ramminger, 179–98. Rome: Assoc. Roma nel Rinascimento.

Osmond, P., and R. Ulery. 2003. "Sallustius." *CTC* 8: 237–40.

Paci, G., and S. Sconocchia, eds. 1998. *Ciriaco d'Ancona e la cultura antiquaria dell'umanesimo: Atti del convegno internazionale di studio: Ancona, 6–9 febbraio 1992.* Reggio Emilia: Diabasis.

Pade, M., ed. 2005a. *On Renaissance Commentaries.* Hildesheim: Georg Olms.

———. 2005b. "Niccolò Perotti's *Cornu Copiae:* Commentary on Martial and Encyclopedia." In *On Renaissance Commentaries,* ed. M. Pade, 49–63. Hildesheim: Georg Olms.

———. 2011. "Pomponio Leto e la lettura di Marziale nel Quattrocento." In *Pomponio Leto tra identità locale e cultura internazionale: atti del convegno internazionale (Teggiano, 3–5 ottobre 2008),* ed. A. Modigliani, P. Osmond, M. Pade, and J. Ramminger, 95–113. Rome: Assoc. Roma nel Rinascimento.

Palermino, R. 1980. "The Roman Academy, the Catacombs, and the Conspiracy of 1468." *Archivium Historiae Pontificae* 17: 117–55.

Pasco-Pranger, M. 2006. *Founding the Year. Ovid's* Fasti *and the Poetics of the Roman Calendar.* Leiden and Boston: Brill.

Peeters, Félix. 1939. *Les "Fastes" d'Ovide. Histoire du texte.* Brussels: Falk.

Pellegrin, E., et al., eds. 1975–. *Manuscrits classiques latins de la Bibliothèque Vaticane.* Paris: Centre National de la Recherche Scientifique.

Pépin, J. 1956. "La 'théologie tripartite' de Varron." *Rev. Ét. Aug.* 2: 265–94.

Perler, O. 1967. "Hippo Regius." In *New Catholic Encyclopedia,* vol. 6, 1137–38. New York: McGraw-Hill.

Pernis, M. G., and L. S. Adams. 2003. *Federico da Montefeltro and Sigismondo Malatesta. The Eagle and the Elephant.* New York: Peter Lang. (Orig. pub. 1996.)

Peruzzi, M. 2004. *Cultura Potere Immagine. La Biblioteca di Federico di Montefeltro.* Urbino: Accademia Raffaello.

Petrucci, F. 1989. "Della Rovere, Giovanni." *DBI* 37: 347–50.

Petrucci, N. 1994. "Pomponio Leto e la rinascita dell'epitaffio antico." In *Eutopia. Atti del convegno internazionale 'vox lapidum.' Dalla riscoperta delle iscrizioni antiche all'invenzione di un nuovo stile scrittorio*, 19–44. Rome: Quasar.

Pettegree, A. 2010. *The Book in the Renaissance*. New Haven, CT and London: Yale University Press.

Piacenti, P. 2007. "Note storico-paleografiche in margine all' Accademia Romana." In *Pomponio Leto e la prima Accademia Roman*, ed. C. Cassiani and M. Chiabò, 87–141. Rome: Assoc. Roma nel Rinascimento. (Orig. pub. in *Le Chiavi della Memoria. Miscellanea in occasione del I Centenario della scuda Vaticana di Paleografia Diplomatica e Archivistica* [Vatican City: Scuola vaticana di paleografia, diplomatica e archivistica, 1984], 491–549.)

Pingree, D. 1976. "Thessalus Astrologus." *CTC* 3: 83–86.

Platner, S. B., and T. Ashby. 1926. *A Topographical Dictionary of Ancient Rome*. Oxford: Oxford University Press.

Pontari, P. 2008. "Marsi, Paolo." *DBI* 70: 741–44.

———. 2009. "Mazzatosta, Fabio." *DBI* 72: 543–45.

Porte, D. 1982. "Les *Fastes* d'Ovide et leur imitation dans les calendriers du XIIe siècle." In *Colloque Présence d'Ovide*, ed. R. Chevalier, 195–217. Paris: Les Belles Lettres.

———. 1993. "Les trois mythologies des 'Fastes.'" In *Mythos in mythenloser Gesellschaft*, ed. F. Graf, 142–57. Stuttgart: Teubner.

Preller, L. 1881. *Römische mythologie*, 3rd ed. Berlin: Weidmann.

Presicce, C. P. 2000. "I grandi bronzi di Sisto IV dal Laterano in Campidoglio." In *Sisto IV. Le Arti a Roma nel Primo Rinascimento. Atti del Convegno Internazionale di Studi*, ed. F. Benzi, 189–200. Rome: Assoc. culturale Shakespeare and Co. 2.

Prete, Sesto. 1972. "Versi editi et inediti dell' umanista Fanese Antonio Costanzi," supplemento al *Notiziario di informazione sui problemi cittadini—Fano 5*.

———. 1978. "Antonio Costanzi and his Epigrams." In *Studies in Latin Poets of the Quattrocento*, 103–18. Lawrence: University of Kansas Press.

———. 1991. "Osservazioni sul commento ai *Fasti* di Ovidio dell'umanista Antonio Costanzi." In *Cultura poesia ideologia nell'opera di Ovidio*, ed. I. Gallo and L. Nicastri, 213–20. Naples: Edizioni scientifiche italiane.

———. 1993. "Antonio Costanzi: la sua vita, le sue opera." In *Umanesimo fanese nel '400. Atti del convegno di Studi nel V. Centenario della morte di Antonio Costanzi—Fano 21 giugno 1991*, 45–67. Fano: Comune di Fano; Sassoferrato: Istituto internazionale studi piceni.

Price, S. R. F. 1996. "The Place of Religion: Rome in the Early Empire." In *The Cambridge Ancient History, Vol. 10: The Augustan Empire, 43 BC–AD 69*, ed. A. K. Bowman, E. Champlin, and A. Lintott, 2nd ed., 812–47. Cambridge: Cambridge University Press.

Putnam, M., and J. Hankins. 2004. *Short Epics*. Cambridge, MA: Harvard University Press.

Quinlan-McGrath, M. 1986. "A Proposal for the Foundation Date of the Villa Farnesina." *Journal of the Warburg and Courtauld Institutes* 49: 245–50.

Ramminger, J. 1999. "Zur Entstehungsgeschichte des *Dioskurides* von Ermolao Barbaro (1453–1493)." *Neulateinisches Jahrbuch* 1: 189–204.

———. 2005. "Barbaro's Supplement to Dioscorides." In *On Renaissance Commentaries*, ed. M. Pade, 65–85. Hildesheim: Georg Olms.

Rao, E. 1988–90. "The Humanistic Invective as Literary Genre." In *Selected Proceedings of the Pennsylvania Foreign Language Conference*, ed. G. Martín, 261–67. Pittsburgh: Duquesne University Department of Modern Languages Publications.

Rawson, E. 1972. "Cicero the Historian and Cicero the Antiquarian." *Journal of Roman Studies* 62: 33–45. (Reprinted in *Roman Culture and Society: Collected Papers* [Oxford: Clarendon Press, 1991], 58–79.)

———. 1985. *Intellectual Life in the Late Roman Republic*. London: Duckworth.

Reeds, K. 1976. "Renaissance Humanism and Botany." *Annals of Science* 33: 519–42.

Regoliosi, M. 2005. "'Libri' ed 'esperienza': Alberti e le 'litterae.'" In *Leon Battista Alberti: La biblioteca di un umanista*, ed. R. Cardini, L. Bertolini, and M. Regoliosi, 95–99. Florence: Mandragora.

Reynolds, A. 1985. "Cardinal Oliviero Carafa and the Early Cinquecento Tradition of the Feast of Pasquino." *Humanistica Lovaniensia* 34A: 178–208.

———. 1987. "The Classical Continuum in Roman Humanism: The Festival of Pasquino, the *Robigalia*, and Satire." *Bibliothèque d' Humanisme et Renaissance* 49: 289–307.

Reynolds, L. D., ed. 1983. *Texts and Transmission. A Survey of the Latin Classics*. Oxford: Clarendon Press.

Richardson, B. 1999. *Printing, Writers, and Readers in Renaissance Italy*. Cambridge: Cambridge University Press.

———. 2009. *Manuscript Culture in Renaissance Italy*. Cambridge: Cambridge University Press.

Richardson, L. 1992. *A New Topographical Dictionary of Ancient Rome*. Baltimore: Johns Hopkins University Press.

Riddle, J. 1980. "Dioscorides." *CTC* 4: 1–143.

Riedl, R. 1989. *Mars Ultor in Ovids Fasten*. Amsterdam: B. R. Grüner.

Robathan, D. 1970. "Flavio Biondo's *Roma instaurata*." *Mediaevalia et Humanistica* 1: 203–16.

Rose, A. 2001. *Filippo Beroaldo der Ältere und sein Beitrag zur Properz-Überlieferung*. Munich and Leipzig: Saur.

Rosen, E. 1975. "Regiomontanus, Johannes." *Dictionary of Scientific Biography* 11: 348–52. New York: Scribner.

Ruderman, D. B. 1975. "Giovanni Mercurio da Correggio's Appearance in Italy as Seen through the Eyes of an Italian Jew." *Renaissance Quarterly* 28 (3): 309–22.

Rüpke, J. 1994. "Ovids Kalenderkommentar: zur Gattung der libri fastorum." *Antike und Abendland* 40: 125–36.

———. 1995. *Kalender und Öffentlichkeit: Die Geschichte der Repräsentation und religiösen Qualifikation von Zeit in Rom*. Berlin: de Gruyter.

Ruysschaert, J. 1958. "Recherche des deux bibliothèques romaines Maffei des XVe et XVIe siècles." *La Bibliofilia* 60: 306–55.

———. 1969. "Sixte IV, Fondateur de la Bibliothèque Vaticane (15 juin 1475)." *Archivium Historiae Pontificiae* 7: 513–24.

———. 1973. "La fondation de la Bibliothèque Vaticane en 1475 et les témoignages contemporains." In *Studi offerti a Roberto Ridolfi, direttore de "La Bibliofilia,"* ed. B. Biagiarelli and D. Rhodes, 413–20. Florence: Olschki.

Saci, M. P. 1999. *Ludovico Lazzarelli. Da Elicona a Sion.* Rome: Bulzoni.

Salzman, M. 1991. *On Roman Time: The Codex-Calendar of 354 and the Rhythms of Urban Life in Late Antiquity.* Berkeley and Los Angeles: University of California Press.

Sanford, E. 1948. "Renaissance Commentaries on Juvenal." *Transactions and Proceedings of the American Philological Association* 79: 92–112.

Santini, C. 1995. "Ermoldo Nigello e la duplice redazione dei *Fasti.*" In *Aetates Ovidianae. Lettori di Ovidio dall'Antichità al Rinascimento,* ed. I. Gallo and L. Nicastri, 153–68. Naples: Edizioni scientifiche italiane.

Scapecchi, P. 2005. "Pomponio Leto e la tipografia fra Roma e Venezia." In *Editori ed edizioni a Roma nel Rinascimento,* 119–26. Rome: Assoc. Roma nel Rinascimento.

———. 2007. "Scrivere a mano, leggere a stampa." In *Pomponio Leto e la prima Accademia Romana (Atti della giornata di studi, Roma 2 dicembre 2005),* ed. C. Cassiani and M. Chiabò, 41–46. Rome: Assoc. Roma nel Rinascimento.

Scheid, J. 1992. "Myth, Cult, and Reality in Ovid's *Fasti.*" *Proceedings of the Cambridge Philological Society* 38: 118–31.

Schmidt, P. G. 1964. *Supplemente lateinischer Prosa in der Neuzeit. Rekonstruktionen zu lateinischen Autoren von der Renaissance bis zur Aufklärung.* Göttingen: Vandenhoeck & Ruprecht.

———. 2008. "The Commentator Knows Better than the Author." *Journal of Medieval Latin* 18: 117–29.

Schröter, E. 1980. "Der Vatikan als Hügel Apollons unter der Musen: Kunst und Panegyrik von Nikolaus V. bis Julius II." *Römische Quartalschrift* 75: 208–40.

Screech, M. A. 1955. "The Death of Pan and the Death of Heroes in the Fourth Book of Rabelais." *Bibliothèque d'Humanisme et Renaissance* 17: 36–55.

Seznec, J. 1972. *The Survival of the Pagan Gods: Mythological Tradition in Renaissance Humanism and Art.* Trans. B. Sessions. Princeton, NJ: Princeton University Press.

Shofield, R. 1980. "Giovanni da Tolentino goes to Rome: A Description of the Antiquities of Rome in 1490." *Journal of the Warburg and Courtauld Institutes* 43: 246–56.

Signorini, R. 1996. "New Findings about Andrea Mantegna: His Son Ludovico's Post-Mortem Inventory (1510)." *Journal of the Warburg and Courtauld Institute* 59: 103–18.

Smith, C. 1992. *Architecture in the Culture of Early Humanism. Ethics, Aesthetics, and Eloquence 1400–1470.* Oxford: Oxford University Press.

Soldati, B. 1903. "Gl'inni sacri d'un astrologo del' 400." *Miscellanea di studi in onore di A. Graf,* 405–29. Bergamo: Instituto italiano d'arti grafiche.

Speyer, W. 1971. *Die literarische Fälschung im heidnischen und christlichen Altertum. Ein Versuch ihrer Deutung.* Munich: Beck.

Spitz, L. 1957. *Conrad Celtis. The German Arch-Humanist.* Cambridge, MA: Harvard University Press.

Steinmann, M. 1988. "Von der Übernahme fremder Schriften im 15. Jahrhundert." In *Renaissance- und Humanistenhandschriften,* ed. J. Autenrieth and U. Eigler, 51–62. Munich: Oldenbourg.

Stickney, T. 1903. *De Hermolai Barbari vita atque ingenio Dissertatio.* Paris: Société nouvelle de librairie.

Stillwell, R., ed. 1976. *The Princeton Encyclopedia of Classical Sites.* Princeton, NJ: Princeton University Press.

Stinger, C. 1994. "Roman Humanist Images of Rome." In *Roma Capitale (1447–1527),* ed. S. Gensini, 15–38. Pisa: Pacini.

———. 1998. *The Renaissance in Rome.* Bloomington and Indianapolis: Indiana University Press. (Orig. pub. 1985.)

Stocchi, M. P. 2003. "Sull'utilità dei commenti umanistici ai classici." In *Intorno al testo. Tipologie del corredo esegetico e soluzioni editoriali. Atti del Convegno di Urbino, 1–3 ottobre 2001,* 173–93. Rome: Salerno.

Syme, R. 1978. *History in Ovid.* Oxford: Clarendon Press.

Tamaro, B. F. 1971. *Pola.* Padua: Liviana.

Tateo, F. 1995. "Sulla polemica fra Poliziano e Leoniceno." *Euphrosyne,* n.s. 23: 369–78.

Thomas, R. 2001. *Virgil and the Augustan Reception.* Cambridge: Cambridge University Press.

Thomson, D. F. S. 2011. "Propertius, Sextus." *CTC* 9: 153–246.

Thorndike, L. 1934. "The Attack on Pliny." In *History of Magic and Experimental Science,* vol. 4: 593–610. New York: Columbia University Press.

Tocci, L. M. 1986. "La formazione della biblioteca di Federico da Montefeltro: codici contemporanei e libri a stampa." In *Federico di Montefeltro: Lo stato, le arti, la cultura.* Vol. 3: *La Cultura,* ed. G. C. Baiardi, G. Chittolini, and P. Floriani, 9–18. Rome: Bulzoni.

Tommasini, M. 1985. "Per una lettura della *Roma Triumphans* di Biondo Flavio." In *Tra Romagna ed Emilia nell'Umanesimo: Biondo e Cornazzano,* ed. G. M. Anselmi, 9–80. Bologna: CLUEB.

Tournoy-Thoen, G. 1972. "La laurea poetica del 1484 all'Accademia romana." *Bulletin de l'Institut Historique Belge de Rome* 42: 211–35.

———. 1982. *Publi Fausti Andrelini. Amores sive Livia. Met een bio-bibliografie van de auteur.* Brussels: Paleis der Academiën.

Trappes-Lomax, J. 2006. "Ovid *Tristia* 2.549: How many books of *Fasti* did Ovid write?" *Classical Quarterly* 56 (2): 631–33.

Traube, L. 1911. *Vorlesungen und Abhandlungen. 2: Einleitung in die lateinische Philologie des Mittelalters.* Munich: Beck.

Trümpy, H. 1979. *Die Fasti des Baptista Mantuanus von 1516 als Volkskundliche Quelle.* Nieuwkoop: B. de Graaf.

Uguccioni, M. 2001. "La *Disceptatio convivalis prima* di Poggio Bracciolini nella testimonianza di Pietro Mario Bartolelli." *Nuovi studi Fanesi* 15: 7–33.

Ulery, R. 2005. "Sallust's *Bellum Catilinae* in the Edition of Venice 1500: The Medieval Commentary and the Renaissance Reader." In *On Renaissance Commentaries*, ed. M. Pade, 7–28. Hildesheim: Georg Olms.

Ullman, B. L. 1955. "The Dedication Copy of Pomponio Leto's Edition of Sallust and the 'Vita' of Sallust." *Studies in the Italian Renaissance*, 365–72. Rome: Edizioni di Storia e letteratura.

Ussani, V. 1904. "Le annotazioni di Pomponio Leto a Lucano." *Rendiconti della Reale Accademia dei Lincei, Scienze Morali*, Ser. Quinta, XIII: 366–85.

Ventura, A. 1974. "Canal, Nicolò." *DBI* 17: 662–68.

Viarre, S. 1966. *La survie d'Ovide dans la littérature scientifique des XIIe et XIIIe siècles*. Poitiers: Centre d'études supérieures de civilisation médiévale.

Vircillofranklin, C. 2002. "'*Pro communi doctorum virorum comodo*': The Vatican Library and Its Service to Scholarship." *Proceedings of the American Philosophical Society* 146 (4): 363–84.

Vogel, S. 2000. "Der Leser und sein Stellvertreter—Sentenzsammlungen in Bibl. Des 15 Jahrhunderts." In *Lesen und Schreiben in Europa 1500–1900: vergleichende Perspektiven*, ed. A. Messerli and R. Chartier, 483–501. Basel: Schwabe.

Volk, K. 1997. "'*Cum carmine crescit et annus*': Ovid's *Fasti* and the Poetics of Simultaneity." *Transactions of the American Philological Association* 127: 287–313.

Wallace-Hadrill, A. 1987. "Time for Augustus: Ovid, Augustus, and the *Fasti*." In *Homo Viator: Classical Essays for John Bramble*, ed. M. Whitby, P. Hardie, and M. Whitby, 221–30. Bristol: Bristol Classical Press.

———. 1997. "*Mutatio morum:* The Idea of a Cultural Revolution." In *The Roman Cultural Revolution*, ed. T. Habinek and A. Schiesaro, 2–22. Cambridge: Cambridge University Press.

Weiss, R. 1961. "Andrelini, Publio Fausto." *DBI* 3: 138–41.

———. 1963. "Biondo Flavio archeologo." *Studi romagnoli* 14: 335–41.

———. 1964. "Petrarch the Antiquarian." In *Classical, Medieval, and Renaissance Studies in Honor of B. L. Ullman*, vol. 2, ed. C. Henderson, 199–209. Rome: Edizioni di storia e letteratura.

———. 1965. "L'Arco di Augusto a Fano nel Rinascimento." *Italia medioevale e umanistica* 8: 351–58.

———. 1988. *The Renaissance Discovery of Classical Antiquity*. 2nd ed. London: Blackwell.

White, Paul. 2013. *Jodocus Badius Ascensius: Commentary, Commerce and Print in the Renaissance*. Oxford: Oxford University Press / British Academy.

Wilkinson, L. P. 1955. *Ovid Recalled*. Cambridge: Cambridge University Press.

Wind, E. 1968. *Pagan Mysteries in the Renaissance,* new and enlarged ed. London: Faber.

Wiseman, T. P. 2004. "Where Was the Nova Via?" *Papers of the British School at Rome* 72: 167–83.

Wormell, D. E. W. 1979. "Ovid and the *Fasti*." *Hermathena* 127: 39–50.

Wouters, A. 1988. *Codex Cremifanensis 305. Studie van een onbenut middeleeuws Ovidius-handschrift*. Unpublished Master's dissertation, Katholieke Universiteit Leuven.

Wren, K. W. 2006. "Poetry and 'Spirited' Ancient Sculpture in Renaissance Rome: Pomponio Leto's Academy to the Sixteenth-Century Sculpture Garden." In *Aeolian Winds and the Spirit of Renaissance Architecture*, ed. B. Kenda, 103–24. London and New York: Routledge.

Yates, F. 1983. "The Italian Academies." In *Renaissance and Reform: The Italian Contribution. Collected Essays*, vol. 2: 6–29. London and Boston: Routledge and Kegan Paul.

Zabughin, V. 1906. "L'insegnamento universitario di Pomponio Leto." *Rivista d'Italia* IX (II): 215–44.

———. 1909/1910–12. *Giulio Pomponio Leto. Saggio Critico*. 2 vols. Rome: La Vita Letteraria; Grottaferrata: Tipografia Italo-Orientale S. Nilo.

Zanker, P. 1988. *The Power of Images in the Age of Augustus*. Trans. H. A. Shapiro. Ann Arbor: University of Michigan Press.

GENERAL INDEX

aetiologies, in the *Fasti*, 11

Alberti, Leon Battista: antiquarianism of, 117, 121–23; as archaeologist, 127; on empirical observation, 123; epigraphical interests of, 121; as pilgrim, 123–24

Alexander Villedieu, 9, 21

allegory, Christian, 153–54. *See also* Christianization

Almadiano, Battista, 53–54, 61–62

Alton, E. H., 72

Ancona, Trajan's arch in, 120

anniversaries, as important in ancient Rome, 158–59. *See also* calendar; Palilia

antiquarianism, 64, 95, 101–86 *passim*; in Arnulf of Orléans, 18; and art, 190; Cicero on, 6–7; and engineering, 123; ideological aspects of, 189; and Roman *imperium*, 187; and travel, 120–21; Varro as founder of, 105. *See also* commentators; Roman Academy; Rome

Ara Maxima, 132, 170

Ara Pacis Augustae, 4

archaeology: as central to Roman humanism, 102; and excavation, 131; and texts, 101–2

Arnulf of Orléans, 9, 10–11, 12, 13–15, 16, 17, 18–21, 22, 24

Ars *amatoria*, 1, 11

ars dictaminis, 21. *See also* education

Astemio, Lorenzo, 94

astrology: antiquarians' use of, 159–60; Augustus' use of, 4

astronomy: and chronology, 16; commentators on, 40, 73; in the *Fasti*, 46–47, 67; Marsi on, 34–35; poetry about, 9; under Augustus, 4. *See also* calendar; Germanicus; Manilius

Asylum, 125–26

Augustine, Saint, 19, 172–74

Augustus: birth of, 24; calendar reforms of, 72–73; death of, 61; and the history of Fano, 181–82, 186; month named after, 24; Ovid's addresses to, 1–2, 4–5, 50–51; as patron, 168; and propaganda, 3; time manipulated by, 3–4, 64; title of, 49

227

authority, of ancient texts, 23, 92, 125–27; commentators' attitudes toward, 117, 126, 130–31, 140–50, 161. *See also* archaeology; observation, empirical

Bade, Josse, 70

Barbaro, Ermolao, 147–48

Barchiesi, A., 3, 28n122

Barsby, J., 2

Bartolelli, Pietro Mario, 177n79

Basilica of Constantine, 116

Baths of Diocletian, 117

Beard, M., 2–3

Bede, 17–18

Bembo, Bernardo, 78, 96, 110, 151, 170, 188

Bembo, Pietro, 101

Bernard of Chartres, 22

Beroaldo, Filippo, 100

Bianca, C., 112

Bianchi, R., 157

Biondo, Flavio, 104–6, 117, 120, 124–25, 128, 173, 183–84; as antiquarian, 128; on Christian Rome, 130; epigraphy used by, 137; etymology used by, 135; *Fasti* used by, 125–26; influence of, 136–37; *Italia Illustrata*, 129; on Pliny, 140; topographical research by, 125–27, 137; trust in authority by, 126, 141

Biondo, Gaspare, 129

Black, R., 43n48

Blanchard, W. S., 77

Blasio, M. G., 112

Botticelli, Andrea, 43

Bömer, F., 163

Bracke, W., 36

Brandolini, Aurelio, 168

Braun, L., 50n68

Cacus, 117

Caesar, Julius, calendar reforms of, 17, 24, 73, 158–59

Calcagnini, Caelio, 73

Calderini, Domizio, 42–43, 75

calendars: ancient, 2, 4–5; appended to the *Fasti*, 8–9; aristocratic, 6; authority of, 64; and commentary, 64; didactic functions of, 6–7, 9; errors in, 16–17; *Fasti* as, 46; and feast years, 155; fluidity of, 158; *horologia* as, 4; Julius Caesar's reform of, 17, 24, 73, 158–59; Marsi's realignment of, 160–64; as narratives, 7, 187; oral and written, 5; Ovid's consultation of, 63; Ovid's manipulation of, 187; and social status, 64–65. *See also* astronomy

Campana, A., 92

Campano, Antonio, imprisonment of, 111

Campano, Giannantonio, 168

Campano, Giovanni Antonio, 114, 138

Canal, Nicolò, 78, 96, 145, 151

Capitoline: added to Rome, 127; museums on, 138; as seat of Christian Rome, 170; transformation of, 170; Vergil's depiction of, 118

Carmenta, 8, 46, 117, 133

Castel Sant'Angelo, 78, 110–11, 115

catacombs, Roman Academy's interest in, 106, 130

Celtes-Protacius, C., 27

Celtis, Conrad, 26

ceremonies: in the *Fasti*, 48–49; Marsi's participation in, 151–52. *See also* Palilia

Chigi, Agostino, 160

Christianization, of Ovid by commentators, 18, 23–24

churches, as landmarks of ancient sites, 130

Circus Maximus, 103

Ciriaco d'Ancona, 42, 117, 119–20, 122, 179–81; as teacher of Costanzi, 121, 124; travel by, 143

Claudia Quinta, 191–93

Cola di Rienzo, 181

Colonna, Giovanni, 117

commentaries: combined with poetry, 97; format of, 22, 65–66; as lecture notes, 65; merging with texts, 22–23; as open-ended, 6, 12; printed versions of, 73–87

commentators: and astronomy, 73; audiences for, 69–70, 72, 100; brevity and verbosity of, 68–72, 98; employment of, 74, 83; as *grammatici*, 74; and history, 49–50; invective by, 83–87; on natural history, 90–92; as polymaths, 34–35, 65–68; printing's effect on, 77; reputation of, 72, 87–94; status of, 83; work habits of, 65–66. *See also* patronage

Concord, Temple of, 56–57, 62

Constantinople, and the Roman past, 7

Conte, G. B., 9n41

Cornaro, Giorgio, as patron, 30, 32–33, 82n65, 85–86, 97, 188–90, 193–94. *See also* patronage

Costanzi, Antonio, xi, xiii, xvi, 25–26, 29, 44, 65, 146, 173; absent from Rome, 87–88; on astronomy, 47–48; attitude toward printing, 77, 93–94; and authority, 150; brevity of, 71–72, 98; career of, 77, 175; and Ciriaco d'Ancona, 121, 124; on the dedication of the *Fasti*, 53–62; education of, 41–42; epigraphical interests of, 179; *Fasti* commentaries by, 53–62, 89–90, 92–93, 175–80, 182–83, 186; on the history of Fano, 177–84; influence of, 29–30; on the Julian calendar, 72–73; on nard, 90–92; and patronage, 64–65; as poet, 95–96, 98–100; precursors of, 117; publication of, 29–30, 94; reputation of, 89; as rival of Marsi, 41, 87–88, 93, 98; and the

Roman Academy, 44–45, 109; on the ruins of Rome, 102–3, 116; self-promotion by, 98, 100; travel to Rome by, 116, 175–76

Cybele, importation to Rome, 190–94

De Rossi, G. B., 165

dedication, of the *Fasti*, 50–62; to Augustus, 50–51; to Germanicus, 51–52, 54; to Tiberius, 51–52. *See also* Augustus; Germanicus; patronage

della Rovere, Giovanni, 44, 175, 184–86

della Torre, A., 33–34, 35

Dioscorides, 91–92, 147–48

education, use of the *Fasti* in, xii–xiii, 10–11, 65

emendation. *See* texts, editing of

emulation. *See* imitation

Engelbrecht, W., 17, 19–20

epigraphy. *See* inscriptions

Epistulae ex Ponto, 10, 55

equinox, date of, 16–17, 47–48. *See also* astronomy; calendars

Ermold Nigellus, 7–8

etymology: Arnulf of Orléans' use of, 20; Biondo's use of, 135; Marsi's use of, 135; pedagogical use of, 15, 20n87; as source for topography, 125, 135; Varro's use of, 105

Eusbeius, 153–54

Evander, 117, 133

Everard of Béthune, 21

exile, of Ovid, 1–3, 25; alleged return from, 23–24; and the dedication of the *Fasti*, 53, 55; poetry written during, 3, 7–8, 59. *See also Epistulae ex Ponto; Tristia*

Fano: Arch of, 179–81; history of, 177–78, 182–84; siege of, 177–79; as Roman colony, 177–78. *See also* Costanzi

Fantham, E., 163n32

Farnese, Alessandro, 128–29

fasti, examples of, 4–5

Fasti (Ovid), *passim;* aetiologies in, 11; as antiquarian handbook, 102–4; dedication of, 50–62; didactic functions of, xii–xiii, 10–11, 65; as enigmatic, 67; as guide to Roman culture, 48–49, 65; as guide to Roman topography, 12–13, 103–5; incompleteness of, 3, 28; religious quality of, 67; reputation of, 2, 43; title of, 14

Fasti Antiates Maiores, 63

Fasti Praenestini, 4–5, 63–64, 139–40

Federico da Montefeltro, Duke of Urbino, 41, 88–89, 98–99, 176–79, 183–86. *See also* patronage

Feeney, D., 3n10

Festus, Sextus Pompeius, 6

Filetico, Martino, 84–85

Florence, as center of learning, 43

Foggini, Pietro, 159

Forum Boarium, 125, 127, 136, 141; Marsi on, 132–33

Francesco from Pesaro, 25

Frederick III, Emperor, 98–99, 155, 175. *See also* patronage

Frontinus, *De aquis urbis Romae,* 119, 125

Fulco of Orléans, 10, 20–21

Gaisser, J., xvin8

Gambitelli, Zagarello, 89–90

Genesius, Saint, 164–65

Genethliaca, for Rome: of Domizio Palladio, 109, 155; of Paolo Marsi, 96, 155–57. *See also* Palilia

Geoffrey of Vinsauf, 10

Germanicus: confused with Tiberius, 54–59; as dedicatee of the *Fasti,* 8, 24, 39, 50–52, 54; as patron of Ovid, 11, 55, 57–61, 168; as poet, 9, 60

Giovanni del Virgilio, 24

Graf, F., 187

Grafton, A., 47–48

Guarino, Battista, 65–67, 72–73, 80n58, 95–96, 156–57

Guarino da Verona, 42, 55

Gwynne, P., 139n136

Hankins, J., 112

Hasdrubal, 182–84

Heinsius, Nicolaus, 27

Henry of Settimello, 8

Herbert-Brown, G., 2n8, 23n103

Hercules: bronze statue of, 132–33, 170; Temple of, 6

hermeticism, 153

Heroides: as school text, 10; Volsco's work on, 38–39

Hilary of Orléans, 10

Hinds, S., 2

Horace, *Ars Poetica,* 98

horologium Augusti, 4

Hugh Primas, 10, 21

humanism: and archaeology, 102; and art, 190–91; and religion, 166–75. *See also* antiquarianism; commentators; Roman Academy

Hülsen, C., 105

imitations: of Ovid, 26–28, 82, 97, 169–70; of Vergil, 28

inscriptions: antiquarians' use of, 118–19, 121–23, 134, 137, 161, 179, 181; fake, 138–39. *See also* observation, empirical

intercalation, 17, 34, 72–73. *See also* Caesar, Julius; calendars

Janiculum: added to Rome, 126–27; cult of Janus on, 135, 137

Janus: Ovid addressed by, 95; Quadrifons, 136–37; temple of, 4, 18, 105, 134–35, 137

Jerome, Saint, 24

John Lydus, 7

Johnson, W. R., 2

Juno Sospita, temple of, 150

Juturna, 46

Kalends, etymology of, 15

Kallendorf, C., 188, 194n23

Lactantius, 23

lacus Iuturnae, 141–43

Lake Nemi, ships of, 127

Latin, as language of *imperium*, 171–72

Lazzarelli, Ludovico, 152–53, 165–69

lectures, transcription of, 79–80. *See also* printing

Lee, E., 34, 167

Leto, Pomponio, xiii, xv, 30, 32–33, 35, 39–40, 43–46, 74–76, 78, 83, 88, 102, 110, 112, 117, 129, 158, 165; antiquarian methods of, 106–7, 128; and the calendar, 187; career of, 75–76; crowning of poets by, 155–56; epigraphical interests of, 137–40; extradition and imprisonment of, 78, 110, 114–15, 188; and the *Fasti*, 36–37, 52, 59, 114; on Frontinus, 119; as head of the Roman Academy, 107; invective by, 83–84; on Juturna, 141–43; lectures by, 80; manuscripts of, 46–47; and the Palilia, 155; on plagiarism, 79, 81; precursors of, 117–18; on Roman topography, 105–6; on Sallust, 115; on swans, 39–40, 144–45; travel by, 143–46

literature, as source for the past, 121. *See also* authority

Littlewood, R. J., 3n11, 23n103

liturgical year, as rival to the *Fasti*, 21–22. *See also* calendar

Livy, 126, 136–37, 139, 183–84, 190–92

Lo Monaco, F., 36, 77

Loschi, Antonio, 117–18

Louis the Pious, 7–8

Lovato Lovati, 8

ludi saeculares, 4

Lyre, rising and setting of, 16, 47, 159

Macrobius, calendar of, 6–7, 9, 11, 16, 48, 64

Maecenas, 50

Maffei, Agostino, 114–15

Maffei, Raffaele, 112

magic, 151–54

Malatesta, Sigismondo, 176, 168, 183, 186

Manilius, 9

Mantegna, Andrea, 189–94

Mantuanus, Baptista, 26

Manuzio, Aldo, 26

Marsi, Paolo: on astronomy, 34–35, 47–48; authorities cited by, 130–31, 141; as authority, 80–81; *Bembice*, 114–15, 148–49, 172–73; career of, 31, 74–76; on the Capitoline, 170; on Christian Rome, 172–73; on Cybele, 192; on the date of the Palilia, 160–64; on the death of Pan, 153–54; on the dedication of the *Fasti,* 50–51, 53, 59n82, 62; emendations by, 82–83; empirical observation by, 143, 146–47; encyclopedic knowledge of, 66–67; epigraphy used by, 134; etymology used by, 135; on the Forum Boarium, 132–33; as friend of Volsco, 40; *Genethliacon* of, 96, 156–57; influence of, 29–30; influenced by Biondo, 136; influenced by legend, 134; influenced by Valla, 75; invective used by, 83–86; lectures of, 69–70, 79–80; Lucan commentary of, 157; and the Palilia, 155–57, 160–64; patronage of, 189–90, 193–94; as poet, 96–97; printing welcomed by, 78; publication of, 29–31; reputation of, 80–82; as rival of Costanzi, 41, 87–88, 93, 98; Rome as home of, 33–36, 44–45; and Roman topography, 115–16, 133; self-promotion by, 30–31, 97, 100; on swans, 145; travel by, 43, 145–46, 148–49, 151–52, 170, 174–75, 188; in Venice, 31, 33, 75, 187–88; verbosity of, 68–71

Masurius Sabinus, 5

Matthew of Vendôme, 10, 21

Maturanzio, Francesco, 38

May of Spenser, 154

Mazzatosta, Fabio, 114

Merula, Bartolomeo, 29–30, 77–78

meta Romuli, 124

Metamorphoses, 1, 10; Arnulf of Orléans' commentary on, 22; Lactantius' citation of, 23; manuscripts of, xv; popularity of, 12

Miller, J., 23n103, 105n15, 167n42

Mirabilia urbis Romae, 12–13, 104, 119, 124–25, 129–30

miracles, 152

Morisot, Claude, 27

Most, G. W., 64n4

Mount Soracte, 128, 140

myrrh, 48–49

natural history: commentators on, 90–92; *Fasti* as source for, 13–14; and myth, 49

Neckam, Alexander, 10, 14, 49

Negropont, siege of, 78, 96

Newlands, C., 3, 28n122

Nigellus, Ermold, 50

Nisus (*Comentarii Fastorum*), 5

Nobilior, M. Fulvius, 6

observation, empirical: antiquarians' practice of, 128–40; and literary evidence, 123, 140; by Paolo Marsi, 146–47; by Pomponio Leto, 143–44

Odi, Pietro, 45, 46, 48, 49–50; on the dedication of the *Fasti,* 52

Orléans, as center of classical study, 10, 16, 21

Orsi, Roberto, 87

Ottavio, Francesco, 42

Ovid, works of. See *Ars amatoria; Epistulae ex Ponto; Fasti; Heroides; Metamorphoses; Remedia amoris; Tristia*

Palazzo dei Conservatori, 132–33. *See also* Capitoline

Palilia: date of, 158–66; Ovid on, 155, 159, 162; Roman Academy's revival of, xvi, 84, 106–7, 109, 128, 155–58, 169

Palladio, Domizio, 44, 109, 155

Pallas, tomb of, 133–34

Pan, death of, 153–54

Pantheon, 101

Parentalia, 133

Pasco-Pranger, M., 2, 23n103

Pasquinalia, 113n46

patronage: of Costanzi, 41, 176; and the humanists, 50–51, 167–69; of Ovid, 57–61, 167–68; of Marsi, 193–94; papal, 110, 172. *See also* Augustus; Cornaro, Giorgio; Federico da Montefeltro; Germanicus; Maffei, Agostino; Paul II; Pius II; Sixtus IV

Paul II, 78, 110, 188

Pedanius Dioscorides, 92

Perotti, Niccolò, 67–68, 77

Petrarch: and Augustan Rome, 117–18; invective by, 85; on the monuments of Rome, 103–4, 117–18; trust in literary sources by, 117

pilgrimages, to Rome, 13, 104, 123–24. *See also* travel

Pius II, 176–77, 186

plagiarism, 78–80. *See also* printing and publishing

Platina, Bartolomeo, 88, 111–12

Pliny the Elder, as authority, 49, 140, 146–47. *See also* authority; natural history

Plutarch, 153–54

poetry: by commentators, 22, 166, 169–70; contests in, 157. *See also* imitation

Poggio Bracciolini, 117–19

Polenton, Sicco, 24–25

Poliziano, Angelo: as poet and commentator, 100; and Rome, 43; study of Ovid by, 42–44

Pompilio, Paolo, 113

Porta Carmentalis, 136–37

Porta Ostiense, 118

Porta San Paolo, 129–30

Porte, D., 9

Praeneste mosaic, 140

printing: and academic reputation, 77–78, 87–94; and commentaries, 73–94; Costanzi's attitude toward, 93–94; as detrimental to Latin scholarship, 77; economics of, 93, 97; plagiarism facilitated by, 78–79; as source of error, 77, 86; in Venice, 26, 29–31, 75, 97, 187–88

Propertius, Volsco on, 38–39, 41

Pula, 170–71

Pyramid of Cestius, 118–19

Quirinal, as site of Leto's house, 74, 88, 106, 137, 155; confused with Esquiline, 156

Rabelais, 154

Regiomontanus, Johannes, 35

religion, in the *Fasti*, 67

Remedia amoris, 10

Remus, tomb of, 119

reputations, of commentators, 72, 77–81, 83, 87–94. *See also* commentators; Costanzi; Marsi

restoration: of the *Fasti*, 26–28; of Rome, 102–3, 166–68

Rhenanus, Beatus, xv

Robinson, M., 2

Roma Instaurata (Biondo), 105–6, 124–25, 129–30

Roman Academy, xi, xiii, xv–xvi, 33, 36, 38, 43–45; and anniversaries, 155–65; and antiquarianism, 106–16; distinguished from *sodalitas*, 112–13; dramatic performances by, 165; editorial choices of, 112; history of, 108–110; influences on, 128–29; invective in, 83–84; naming of, 112–13; paleo-Christian interests of, 130; and the Palilia, xvi, 84, 106–7, 109, 128, 155–58, 164–65, 169; poetry by, 169–70; reinstatement of, 110, 64–65; religious associations of, 164–67; and the Studium Urbis, 112–13; suppression of, 78, 110–112. *See also* Leto, Pomponio; Marsi, Paolo

Rome: as center of learning, 88; and Constantinople, 7; destiny of, 170–71; foundation of, 188–89; as heir of ancient *imperium*, 170–71, 184, 187; Marsi's presence in, 33–36, 87–88; as model for Venice, 188; as new Jerusalem, 166; Ovid as guide to, 103–4; Ovid's alleged return to, 23–24; printing in, 88; renewal of, 102–3, 134, 166–68; ruins of, 102, 118–19, 174; as seat of Christian empire, 172–74; walking tours of, 129, 138; as wilderness, 118. *See also* Palilia; pilgrimages; topography

Rucellai, Bernardo, 106

Rüpke, J., 5, 6

Sabellico, Marc' Antonio, 188

Sallust, Leto's commentary on, 106–7, 115

San Giorgio in Velabro, 136–37, 141–43

Santa Maria Nova, 131

Santini, C., 50n69

Santo Stefano Rotondo, 129

Sanudo, M., 188–89

Scalamonti, Francesco, 119, 121

Scipio Nasica, P. Cornelius, 191–93

Scylla, 12

Senigallia, 184–86

Septizonium, 117

Sixtus IV, 88, 115, 132, 166–68, 170, 175, 184–86

spica, identification of, 13, 90–92, 146–47

Stephen of Tournai, 20

Studium Urbis, 74–75, 88, 112

supplements: to the *Aeneid*, 28; to the *Fasti*, 26–28

swans, debates concerning, 39–40, 144–45

Syme, Ronald, 2

texts, editing of, 19, 42, 82–84, 102, 140. *See also* authority

Theater of Pompey, 124

Theodulf, 10

Thomas, R., 28

Tiberius: as dedicatee of the *Fasti*, 39, 51–52; confused with Germanicus, 54–59

time: Augustus' manipulation of, 3–4, 64; reckoning of, 17–18. *See also* calendar

topography, Roman: antiquarians' interest in, xi; Biondo on, 126; and Christian churches, 129; *Fasti* as source for, 12–13, 103–5; mistakes in, 131, 137–39; toponyms as evidence for, 124–25. *See also Mirabilia urbis Romae; Roma Instaurata;* Rome

Traube, L., 7

travel: and antiquarianism, 120–21, 140–50; and authority of texts, 140–50; by Ciriaco d'Ancona, 143–44; by Leto, 143–44; by Marsi, 145–46, 148–49, 151–52, 170, 174–75, 188. *See also* pilgrimages

Tristia, 10, 55. *See also* Epistulae ex Ponto; exile

Urbino, as center of learning, 88–89, 93–94

Urceo, Codro, 68, 77, 78–79

Valla, Lorenzo, 45, 68, 75, 171–72

Varro, M. Terentius: as antiquarian, 105;

De lingua Latina, xiii; as source for Ovid, 105

vates: commentators as, 95; definition of, 60, 95; Germanicus as, 60; Ovid as, 22, 95

Vatican Library, foundation of, 88, 115, 168

Vatican Obelisk, 102

Vegio, Maffeo, 28

Veneto, Francesco, 25

Venice: foundation of, 188–89; Marsi's visit to, 31–33, 75, 78; as new Rome, 188; printing in, 26, 29–31, 75, 97, 187–88

Venus and Cupid, Temple of, 104

Venus and Rome, Temple of, 131

Vergil: as source for Petrarch, 103; supplements to, 28

Verino, Michele, 43

Verrius Flaccus, 4–6, 63–64; *De verborum significatu,* 6, 64

Via Flaminia, 179–81

Via Nova, 130–31

Via Sacra, 130–31

Vincent of Beauvais, 13, 49

Vives, J. L., 68

Volaterrano, Jacopo, 155–56

Volsco, Antonio, xiii, 31–32, 38–41, 83–84, 129, 158, 165; on the dedication of the *Fasti,* 52, 58–59; as friend of Marsi, 41; on the *Heroides,* 38–39; invective by, 84; on Propertius, 41; on swans, 145

Wallace-Hadrill, A., 3n10

William of Orléans, 10–15, 16–20, 47–48

Wiseman, A., 2n2

Wiseman, P., 2n2

Wromell, D. E. W., 2

zodiac, 16. *See also* astrology; astronomy

INDEX LOCORUM

Callistratus
  Digest
    50.4.14, **70**
Cicero
  Academica
    1.9, **7**
  De finibus
    5.2–6, **6**
  Tusculan Disputations
    1.30.73, **144**
Horace
  Satires
    1.9.1, **131**
    1.73, **20**
Homer
  Iliad
    2.489, **xi**
Livy
  Ab urbe condita
    2.49.8, **136**
    29.10–14, **191–93**

Ovid
  Ars amatoria
    1.331–32, **12**
  Epistulae ex Ponto
    2.1, **55–56**
    2.8, **56**
    4.6, **60–61**
    4.8, **59–61**
    4.9, **60–61**
  Fasti
    1.3–4, **52, 81–82**
    1.7–8, **xv**
    1.19–20, **60**
    1.25, **60**
    1.55, **15**
    1.76, **13, 90–92, 146**
    1.101–2, **22, 95**
    1.121, **18**
    1.176, **18**
    1.213, **19**
    1.245–46, **111, 115, 134–35, 175**

1.258, **137**
1.285–86, **58–59**
1.289–92, **63**
1.316, **42**
1.337–42, **48**
1.340, **48**
1.358, **18**
1.397, **153**
1.419, **13**
1.521, **133**
1.582, **132, 170**
1.589–93, **49, 61**
1.645–49, **56–58**
1.654, **16**
1.669, **18**
1.691, **176–77**
1.693, **144**
1.708–9, **115–16, 141**
2.9, **xvi**
2.11, **105**
2.44, **20**
2.56–59, **150**
2.63, **167**
2.75–76, **16**
2.79, **118, 144**
2.109–111, **39–40, 145**
2.119, **xi**
2.119–148, **139**
2.183, **72**
2.201, **136–37**
2.263–64, **13–14**
2.326, **20**
2.389, **31**
2.391–92, **103**
2.571, 84–85, **151–52**
2.601, **130**
2.685, **75**
2.852, **74**
2.863–64, **81–82**

3.1, **98**
3.87–98, **158**
3.122–26, **70**
3.155–56, **72–73, 159**
3.161–66, **17–18, 34**
3.177, **22, 95**
3.406, **35**
3.431, **105**
3.522, **129**
3.523–656, **149**
3.567, **148**
3.707–8, **121**
3.772, **19**
3.809–10, **47**
3.824, **82**
3.829, **19**
3.836–37, **103**
3.849–52, **16–17, 47, 73**
4.11, **85**
4.31, **96, 156–57**
4.82, **57–58**
4.109, **96**
4.223, **139**
4.236, **83**
4.247–348, **191–93**
4.265–66, **139**
4.280, **96**
4.345, **129**
4.409, **144**
4.499–500, **12**
4.625–721, **162–63**
4.721, **158, 160–61**
4.727, **152**
4.748, **98**
4.801–6, **159**
4.812–18, **157**
4.954, 42, **178–81**
5.195–222, **43**
5.294, **138**

5.725, **18**
6.59–64, **158**
6.176, **99**
6.267–68, **11, 20**
6.395–96, **130–31**
6.479, **131**
6.711, **40**
6.770, **184–85**
6.812, **6, 22**
Metamorphoses
    8.6–151, **12**
    14.1–74, **12**
    15.876, **22**
Remedia amoris
    737–38, **12**
Tristia
    2.207, **1**
    2.549, **3, 28**

Pliny
    Natural History
        10.32, **144–45**
        12.44–45, **90, 146–47**
        31.27, **140**
Varro
    De Lingua Latina
        5.71, **141**
Vergil
    Aeneid
        1.68, **84**
        1.263, **84**
        8.348, **118**
    Georgics
        2.43, **xi**

INDEX MANUSCRIPTORUM / INDEX OF MANUSCRIPTS

Brussels, Bibliothèque Royale, 5369–73, **8**

Ferrara, Biblioteca Comunale Ariostea, II.141, **36, 59, 114–15, 158**

Ghent, Bisschoppelijke Bibliotheek, Cath. 12 (no. 28), **30n3**

Kremünster, Stiftsbibliothek, 305, **9**

Naples, Bilioteca Nazionale, IV F 8, **36n21**

Paris, BnF, nouv. acq. lat. 1523, **8–9**

Rome, Biblioteca Angelica, MS 1348, **143**

Rome, Biblioteca Vallicelliana, MS R. 59, **39, 40n30, 52**

Vatican City, BAV, Chig. H. VI. 204, **41, 53**

Vatican City, BAV, Ottob. lat. 1982, **36, 45–50, 52, 57, 62, 109, 165**

Vatican City, BAV, Reg. lat. 1385, **148n157**

Vatican City, BAV, Reg. lat. 1709, **8**

Vatican City, BAV, Reg. lat. 1826, **25n110**

Vatican City, BAV, Urb. lat. 360, **41, 92,** *180*

Vatican City, BAV, Vat. lat. 1595, **36n20, 45–50, 52**

Vatican City, BAV, Vat. lat. 3262, **26n115,** *134*

Vatican City, BAV, Vat. lat. 3263, **36, 39–40, 45–50, 53, 135, 138–39, 144–45**

Vatican City, BAV, Vat. lat. 3264, **36, 37,** *39, 52, 113–14, 135*

Vatican City, BAV, MS Vat. lat. 10672, **52,** *122*

Venice, Biblioteca nazionale Marciana, Marc. lat. XII.15 (4008), **24n105**

TEXT AND CONTEXT
Frank Coulson, Series Editor

Text and Context is devoted to the study of manuscripts and manuscript culture from late antiquity to the Renaissance. Works published in the series encompass all aspects of manuscript production, including the material culture of the codex, editions of new texts, manuscript catalogs, as well as more theoretical studies. The series covers vernacular as well as Latin manuscripts, and studies that deal with the interaction of Latin and the vernacular are particularly welcome.

Antiquarian Voices: The Roman Academy and the Commentary Tradition on Ovid's Fasti
    ANGELA FRITSEN

The Community of St. Cuthbert in the Late Tenth Century: The Chester-le-Street Additions to Durham Cathedral Library A.IV.19
    KAREN LOUISE JOLLY

Collections in Context: The Organization of Knowledge and Community in Europe
    EDITED BY KAREN FRESCO AND ANNE D. HEDEMAN

Classroom Commentaries: Teaching the Poetria nova *across Medieval and Renaissance Europe*
    MARJORIE CURRY WOODS

Renaissance Postscripts: Responding to Ovid's Heroides *in Sixteenth-Century France*
    PAUL WHITE

www.ingramcontent.com/pod-product-compliance
Lightning Source LLC
Chambersburg PA
CBHW021139230426
43667CB00005B/185